Monographs of the Center for Southeast Asian Studies,
Kyoto University
English Series no. 9

SOUTHEAST ASIA:
NATURE, SOCIETY AND DEVELOPMENT

Monographs of the Center for Southeast Asian Studies, Kyoto University

English Series

1. Takashi SATO, *Field Crops in Thailand*, 1966
2. Tadayo WATABE, *Glutinous Rice in Northern Thailand*, 1967
3. Kiyoshi TAKIMOTO (ed.), *Geology and Mineral Resources in Thailand and Malaya*, 1969
4. Keizaburo KAWAGUCHI & Kazutake KYUMA, *Lowland Rice Soils in Thailand*, 1969
5. Keizaburo KAWAGUCHI & Kazutake KYUMA, *Lowland Rice Soils in Malaya*, 1969
6. Kiyoshige MAEDA, *Alor Janggus: A Chinese Community in Malaya*, 1967
7. Shinichi ICHIMURA (ed.), *The Economic Development of East and Southeast Asia*, 1975
8. Masashi NISHIHARA, *The Japanese and Sukarno's Indonesia*, 1976
9. Shinichi ICHIMURA (ed.), *Southeast Asia: Nature, Society and Development*, 1977

Japanese Series:

1. Joji TANASE, *Primitive Form of the Idea of the Other World*, 1966
2. Toru YANO, *Modern Political History of Thailand and Burma*, 1968
3. Takeshi MOTOOKA, *Agricultural Development of Southeast Asia*, 1968
4. Yoshihiro & Reiko TSUBOUCHI, *Divorce*, 1970
5. Shigeru IIJIMA, *Social and Cultural Change of Karens*, 1971
6. H. STORZ (trans. by H. NOGAMI), *Burma: Land, History and Economy*, 1974
7. Shinichi ICHIMURA (ed.), *Southeast Asia: Nature, Society and Economy*, 1974
8. Yoneo ISHII (ed.), *Thailand: A Rice-Growing Society*, 1975
9. Yoneo ISHII, *Political Sociology of Theravada Buddhism*, 1975
10. Shinichi ICHIMURA (ed.), *The Economic Development of East and Southeast Asia*, 1975
11. Takeshi MOTOOKA, *Rice in Indonesia*, 1975
12. KUCHIBA, TSUBOUCHI & MAEDA, *The Structure and Change of Malayan Villages*, 1976
13. Masashi NISHIHARA (ed.), *Political Corruption in Southeast Asia*, 1976
14. A. ECKSTEIN (trans. by S. ICHIMURA, *et al.*), *Economic Trends in Communist China* (forthcoming)

Southeast Asia: Nature, Society and Development

Contributions to Southeast Asian Studies

edited by

SHINICHI ICHIMURA

Monographs of the Center for Southeast Asian Studies Kyoto University

THE UNIVERSITY PRESS OF HAWAII
Honolulu

Main entry under title:

Southeast Asia: Nature, Society and Development

(Monographs of the Center for Southeast Asia Studies,
Kyoto University)
   Includes bibliographical references and index.
   1. Asia, Southeastern—Addresses, essays, lectures.
I. Ichimura, Shin'ichi, 1925–   II. Series: Kyōto
Daigaku. Tōnan Ajia Kenkyū Sentā. Monographs of the
Center for Southeast Asia Studies, Kyoto University.

DS503.4.S68   959   77-777

ISBN 0-8248-0543-7
ISBN 0-8248-0554-2 pbk.

Filmset in Hong Kong by Asco Trade Typesetting Ltd.
Printed in Hong Kong by South China Photo-Process Printing Co. Ltd.

Contents

v

Preface

This is a collection of articles on Southeast Asia originally published, mostly in Japanese, in *South East Asian Studies* (*SEAS*), the quarterly journal of the Center for Southeast Asian Studies, Kyoto University. The articles are selected primarily to demonstrate to the English-speaking world the lines of research pursued at Kyoto University, and to stimulate the interest of foreign scholars in the activities of the Center.

The Center for Southeast Asian Studies at Kyoto University is a research institute officially established in 1965 after several years of unofficial existence, and now has twenty-four permanent researchers and four visiting scholars from abroad. It plays a central role in promoting area research on Southeast Asia at Kyoto University. More than one hundred scholars at other faculties and research institutes of Kyoto University also contribute to Southeast Asian studies as affiliate members of the Center, through participation in the Center's various research projects. The research results are made available both in Japanese and English in *SEAS*, Japanese and English monographs, reprint series and discussion papers. Information on these publications is provided in CSEAS, 1977, the latest bulletin of the Center. The quarterly journal is available on subscription through the Japanese Society for Asian Studies (c/o Kinki Hatsumei Center Building, 14 Kawara-machi, Yoshida, Sakyo-ku, Kyoto 606), and the bulletin and publications listed therein are obtainable from the Center.

From its inception the Center has aimed at promoting multi-disciplinary area research on Southeast Asia, and has included physical sciences as an integral part of area research because it recognizes the substantial influence of environmental and ecological factors on the social and economic life of Southeast Asian people. The Center began its research activities with three comprehensive country research projects, and also sent a number of individual scholars on field trips to Southeast Asia. The comprehensive approach has resulted in the following publications: Yoneo Ishii (ed), *Thailand—A Rice-Growing Society* (in Japanese), Sobun-sha, Tokyo, 1975; M. Kuchiba, Y. Tsubouchi & N. Maeda, *Studies on Malay Rural Communities* (in Japanese), Sobun-sha, Tokyo, 1975; Thee Kian-Wee & S. Ichimura, *The Regional Economic Survey of South Sumatra Province*, LIPI, Jakarta, 1975; and Y. Kaneko & J. Luthan, *The Structure of the Indonesian Economy in 1969*,

LEKNAS, Jakarta, 1973. English translations of the works in Japanese will be available shortly.

The Center has also emphasized comparative studies of Southeast Asian countries. Some such projects have been completed and the results published in various forms: S. Ichimura (ed), *The Economic Development of East and Southeast Asia*, University Press of Hawaii, Honolulu, 1975; discussion papers and articles in *SEAS* related to the project "Impact of Industrialization on Rural Communities near Capitals"; many articles in *SEAS* 12 related to the "Man and Nature in Southeast Asia" project; and articles in *SEAS* related to the project "Evaluation of Productivity of Delta Areas in Southeast Asia."

Southeast Asian studies are also undertaken at many other institutions in Japan. For a general survey of these studies, reference may be made to Akira Nagazumi, "Southeast Asian Studies in Japan," *Archipel* 9, CEDRASEMI, Paris, 1975, and Yoneo Ishii, *Contemporary Southeast Asia (A): Sociology and Anthropology*, The Center for East Asian Cultural Studies, Tokyo, 1976. The latter survey is to be followed by similar surveys for history and Politics & Economics by S. Ikuta and T. Tomosugi.

I hope that this translation of Japanese contributions to Southeast Asian studies will be favorably received by English-speaking readers, and plan in future to publish further translations of important articles hitherto inaccessible to overseas scholars.

I wish to express my gratitude to Mr. Peter Hawkes and Mrs. Stephanie Hawkes for their assistance with the English of these specialized articles and to my colleagues, Professor Koichi Mizuno and Mr. Yasuyuki Mitani for the preparation of the Index.

Kyoto, Japan   Shinichi Ichimura
March 9, 1977   Director

Acknowledgments

"Interdisciplinary Research and Area Studies," by Shinichi Ichimura, was previously published in slightly different form in *Journal of Southeast Asian Studies*, volume 6, no. 2 (September, 1975), pp. 112–120.

"Thai Pattern of Social Organization: Notes on a Comparative Study," by Koichi Mizuno, was previously published in slightly different form in *Journal of Southeast Asian Studies*, volume 6, no. 2 (September, 1975), pp. 127–134.

"Islam and Divorce among Malay Peasants," by Yoshihiro Tsubouchi, was previously published as "Mare noson ni okeru Isuramu to rikon," in *Tonan Ajia Kenkyu* [Southeast Asian Studies], volume 13, no. 1 (June, 1975), pp. 3–18, and translated into English by Peter and Stephanie Hawkes.

"Authority and Leadership among the Orang Hulu," by Narifumi Maeda, was previously published as "Jakun Community no shakai chitsujo," in *Tonan Ajia Kenkyu* [Southeast Asian Studies], volume 7, no. 3 (December, 1969), pp. 342–362.

"A Note on Buddhistic Millenarian Revolts in Northeastern Siam," by Yoneo Ishii, was previously published in slightly different form in *Journal of Southeast Asian Studies*, volume 6, no. 2 (September, 1975), pp. 121–126.

"Descriptive and Comparative Studies of the Khamet Phonology," by Yasuyuki Mitani, was previously published as "Kametogo onsotaikei no kijutsu to hikaku gengogakuteki kosatsu," in *Tonan Ajia Kenkyu* [Southeast Asian Studies], volume 3, no. 3 (December, 1965), pp. 22–51.

"The Glutinous Rice Zone in Thailand—Patterns of Change in Cultivated Rice," by Tadayo Watabe, was previously published as "Thai ni okeru [mochi ine saibai ken] no seiritsu," in *Tonan Ajia no shizen, shakai, keizai* edited by Shinichi Ichimura, (Kyoto: Center for Southeast Asian Studies, 1974), pp. 205–225, and was translated into English by Peter and Stephanie Hawkes.

"Physiography of Rice Land in the Chao Phraya Basin," by Yoshikazu Takaya, was previously published in slightly different form in *Tonan Ajia Kenkyu* [Southeast Asian Studies], volume 9, no. 3 (December, 1971), pp. 375–397.

"Environmental Determinants Affecting the Potential Dissemination of High Yielding Varieties of Rice—A Case Study of the Chao Phraya

Basin," by Hayao Fukui, was previously published in slightly different form in *Tonan Ajia Kenkyu* [Southeast Asian Studies], volume 9, no. 3 (December, 1971), pp. 348–374.

"Agro-Hydrologic Regions of the Chao Phraya Delta," by Yoshihiro Kaida, is a revised version of "A Subdivision of the Chao Phraya Delta in Thailand based on Hydrographical Conditions," in *Tonan Ajia Kenkyu* [Southeast Asian Studies], volume 11, no. 3 (December, 1973), pp. 403–413.

"An Approach to the Capability Classification of Paddy Soils," by Kazutake Kyuma and Keizaburo Kawaguchi, was previously published in slightly different form in *Proceedings of the Second ASEAN Soil Conference*, volume 1 (Bogor: Soil Research Institute, 1973), pp. 283–294.

"The Political Elite Cycle in Thailand in the pre-1973 Period," by Toru Yano, was previously published in slightly different form as "The Political Elite Cycle in Thailand," in *The Developing Economies*, volume 12, no. 4 (December, 1974), pp. 311–327.

"The Dispute between Sukarno and Hatta in the early 1930's," by Kenji Tsuchiya, was previously published as "Sukarno to Hatta no ronso," in *Tonan Ajia Kenkyu* [Southeast Asian Studies], volume 9, no. 1 (June, 1971) pp. 61–88, and translated into English by Peter Hawkes.

"A Study of Philippine Manufacturing Corporations," by Kunio Yoshihara, was previously published in slightly different form in *The Developing Economies*, volume 9, no. 3 (September, 1971), pp. 268–289.

"The Conditions governing Agricultural Development in Southeast Asia," by Takeshi Motooka, was previously published in slightly different form in *The Developing Economies*, volume 5, no. 3 (September, 1967), pp. 425–445.

"Economic Analysis of the Rice Premium Policy of Thailand," by Hiroshi Tsujii, was previously published as "Thaikoku raisu puremiamu seisaku no jisshoteki keizai bunseki," in *Tonan Ajia Kenkyu* [Southeast Asian Studies], volume 13, no. 3 (December, 1975), pp. 358–384, and translated into English by Peter and Stephanie Hawkes.

"On the Two-Gap Analysis of Foreign Aid," by Mitsuo Ezaki, was previously published in slightly different form in *Journal of Southeast Asian Studies*, volume 6, no. 2 (September, 1975), pp. 151–163.

"The Impact of the 'Oil Crisis' on Southeast Asia," by Yasukichi Yasuba, will be published as "Tonan Ajia ni okeru sekiyu kiki," in *Tonan Ajia Kenkyu* [Southeast Asian Studies], volume 14, no. 4 (March, 1977).

Introduction

Interdisciplinary Research and Area Studies

SHINICHI ICHIMURA

METHODOLOGICAL AND INSTITUTIONAL PROBLEMS OF INTERDISCIPLINARY RESEARCH IN AREA STUDIES

Although there are many problems in development research that can be adequately analyzed along the lines of traditional single disciplinary research, these studies frequently reach the boundaries of each discipline and require some way of combining with the knowledge of neighboring sciences to further the analysis. This combination of knowledge may be encyclopedic only in the sense that the various inquiries, into the same or related problems by various disciplines, are attempted simultaneously, and their conclusions are arranged in parallel or cumulative fashion to facilitate a synthetical understanding of the different aspects of the development process. Such research may be called *multidisciplinary*. *Interdisciplinary* research, however, implies more interactive co-operation of several disciplines for the purpose of obtaining a broader or deeper understanding of common problems. It sometimes means a new inquiry into the *zwischengebiet* (in-between area), a development of new conceptions or a reintegration of different information in various disciplines. In actual development research, however, the distinction between multidisciplinary and interdisciplinary research work is not necessarily very clear-cut. Normally, the most appropriate way of dealing with a complex of problems in developing countries is a com-bination of these two types of research efforts. Hereafter, *interdisciplinary* research will be used in the sense of this combination.

The basic reasons for the need of interdisciplinary research on developing countries are: (1) insufficient specialized knowledge of primitive societies, (2) the compartmentalization of sciences and (3) inadequate conceptual frameworks of modern sciences in the West for

1

the study of problems in developing countries. A few concrete examples may explain the argument more clearly. The first case is a simpleminded application of modern economic analysis to development problems in Asia. Many blunders committed by famous economists in presenting a too optimistic prognosis for the future of South and Southeast Asian economies are, in most cases, due to the separation of demography from an economic analysis of development and the neglect of the sociopolitical process of nation-building connected with economic development in these new states. The second example is a study of the spread of a "high-yielding variety" of rice in Southeast Asia. The Green Revolution is usually studied by agronomists and agricultural economists. But unless the study is supplemented by the related research work of agricultural engineers on the environmental conditions, anthropologists on the accompanying social process, and political scientists on its political implications, the general significance of the Green Revolution can never be adequately understood. As a result, overly optimistic policy suggestions and judgments have produced misleading agricultural policies.

For these reasons there are definite advantages, at least at the present stage of our scientific inquiries, in organizing research institutions as multidisciplinary rather than as monodisciplinary bodies. Since, however, there are a variety of ways of organizing multidisciplinary research institutions, and past experiences in academic circles are almost exclusively monodisciplinary, very careful consideration must be given to the institutional problems of such new organizations. There would seem to be two important considerations, administrative and methodological. Although our experience in interdisciplinary research is still very limited, this article reviews postwar experiences in managerial and research experimentation of interdisciplinary institutions and thereby suggests better institutional and methodological ways of promoting area studies, and a new methodology for other scientific fields.

FIVE TYPES OF NEW INSTITUTIONS AND THEIR ADMINISTRATION

The new institutional arrangements established for interdisciplinary research may be classified as follows:

(*a*) governmental or semigovernmental research institute;
(*b*) university research institute;
(*c*) private or business research institute;
(*d*) intramural research program;
(*e*) research project.

The first three are ways of organizing new research institutions for interdisciplinary research, and the last two are ways of supporting interdisciplinary research in established institutions. Hence the last two are not necessarily inconsistent with the first three institutions.

(*a*) Many governmental ministries have research sections or some research institutes attached. Their research work is usually limited to the activities assigned to the ministries, so that they have no reason to be interdisciplinary. Since, however, policy problems are properly solved only by synthesizing various approaches, the need for interdisciplinary research for important government decisions is clear. The difficulty of recruiting specialists and of establishing good contacts with academic circles often necessitates the establishment of semigovernmental research institutes. Two examples are RAND corporation in the U.S. and the Institute of Developing Economies in Japan, which are interdisciplinary research institutes.

(*b*) Many universities in Europe, the U.S., and Japan have established independent research institutes apart from the departments or colleges, mainly to carry out research not directly connected with education. Some of them may be considered interdisciplinary. The Institute of World Economy and International Relations in Moscow, the South Asia Institute of Heidelberg University, the Institute for Advanced Studies at Princeton, and the Center for Southeast Asian Studies of Kyoto University are some of the interdisciplinary research institutes established as academic institutions.

(*c*) Governmental or university institutes do not necessarily meet the practical demand for quick answers to the questions of private businesses. Consequently, private institutes and consulting companies are sometimes established as interdisciplinary institutions. The Stanford Institution in the U.S., the Nomura Research Institute, and the Mitsubishi Research Institute in Japan are of this type. There seem to be two ways of administering a private institute. One is to run it as a consulting company. It must have its own staff and information system to carry out research. The other is to make it an organizer of interdisciplinary research projects. It needs only the minimum number of core presonnel, a fair number of assisting staff and secretaries, and good contacts with universities and government agencies as well as with private businesses. In either case, this type of institute is much more liberal than the first two types in the salary scale of individual specialists and allocation of research funds or choice of research projects. The director's leadership role can be more easily performed in these institutes than in the governmental and university institutes.

(*d*) Intramural research programs have been the typical way of organizing interdisciplinary research activities in area studies of

American universities. Recruiting scholars from various departments, such programs as the Southeast Asia Program at Cornell University organize interdisciplinary research activities as well as graduate education. The same method has been adopted by some Australian and Japanese universities. The serious shortcoming of this method is that the scholars recruited for area research programs cannot get full credit in their own department for their work. For the departments are naturally discipline-oriented, and area studies are often subsidiary to professional training. Besides, the possibility of the program being dissolved makes the scholars' commitment to the research temporary and superficial. For these reasons it has always been very difficult to recruit outstanding scholars in area studies or development research. Joint appointments cannot fully overcome the difficulty. This method is inappropriate particularly for attracting young scholars to new research fields, which require an adventurous spirit and long-term fieldwork. Despite these difficulties, this is a very effective way of experimenting in new research fields. The final decision on institutional arrangements can be made at the later stage.

(*e*) Giving grants to interdisciplinary research projects is an obvious way of promoting this type of research and has been adopted by many foundations, university grant committees, and government agencies. Flexibility in allocating research funds is an advantage of this method, but short-term support and the uncertainty which accompanies it are the inherent disadvantages.

So how should the advantages and disadvantages of these five types of organizations for interdisciplinary research be evaluated?

ADMINISTRATIVE EFFICIENCY AND THE REWARD SYSTEM FOR SCHOLARS

The criteria for evaluating these institutions must be established from two points of view. The first is whether they are administered efficiently, and the second is whether their organization system can attract high-quality scholars and accomplish outstanding scholarly research projects. Regarding the first aspect of administrative efficiency, there are at least three points to consider: (*a*) allocation of funds for research and personnel expenses, or financial administration, (*b*) recruitment of capable research workers and their further training, or personnel administration, (*c*) choice of appropriate research problems and successful execution of research work, or research administration.

The second point is concerned with substance, the first with form. Ragner Frisch once said that good research institutes are the ones with good research workers. In this sense, the most important question in

TABLE 1

ADMINISTRATIVE EFFICIENCY AND AN EVALUATION OF THE REWARD
SYSTEM OF FIVE TYPES OF ORGANIZATIONS

	Gov. Inst.	Univ. Inst.	Bus. Inst.	Intr. Prog.	Proj.
i. financial ad.	B	C	A	B	B+
ii. personnel ad.	B	B	A	A	A
iii. research ad.	C	B	B	A	A
1. salaries	B−	B	A		
2. extra income	B	A	B−		
3. research exp.	B	A−	B+	A	B
4. free time	B	A	C	B	B
5. promotion	C	B	B+	C	C
6. prestige	B	A	C	C	C
7. stability	B	A	B−		
8. freedom	C+	A	C	A	A+
9. recognition	C	B−	B	A	A
10. honor	B	A	C	B+	B

The symbols, A, B, and C stand for good, fair and poor. + and − signs are used in the
same way as in school records.

evaluating research institutes is which institution attracts more outstanding scholars. This question is deeply interconnected with the
research administration just mentioned, because outstanding scholars
are very much concerned with the question of whether, and in what
way, good research is promoted and bad research discouraged, and in
what way new, essential inquiries are stimulated. It is difficult to list
exhaustively all the incentives that attract capable scholars to institutions or research programs and projects. But it must be particularly
emphasized that pecuniary remuneration plays only a small part as an
incentive in the reward system for research institutes.

The following list of factors is offered as a frame of reference for
analysis of the reward systems of interdisciplinary research institutions:

(1) official salaries
(2) opportunities to earn extra income
(3) research expenses guaranteed or easily obtainable
(4) free time beyond obligatory work
(5) chances of promotion in salary and position
(6) social prestige accompanying the position
(7) stability of position
(8) freedom or flexibility in selecting research subjects

(9) fair and prompt recognition of research achievements and
(10) accessibility to social honor

Many of these incentives are mutually related and depend not only on the reward system of one institution but also on the social environment in which the institution is placed. Hence, it is impossible to make any general statement, by comparing the five types of organizations with the three points of administrative efficiency and the ten criteria mentioned earlier as a frame of reference. Nevertheless, it may be of interest to offer some personal observations based on my experiences in Japan and discussions with many directors of interdisciplinary research institutes all over the world.[1]

This table does not require much explanation. Caution in interpretation is desirable, however, because there are many varieties of each type of institution and different ways of judging each criterion. Much depends on the actual administration of each organization, which is determined not only by its institutional arrangements but also by its history, personnel, and environmental conditions. Of particular importance is the appointment of the director or the program leader and key senior scholars who can truly guide the interdisciplinary research work. The table gives a general indication of the effects of the institutional framework on each criterion.

University institutes seem to be the poorest in financial administration. The reason is that, in leading Japanese governmental universities, the budgets are always determined annually according to the number of personnel in each institute or department, and significant amounts are not allocated to interdepartmental research groups. Private business institutes seem to have the largest degree of freedom in allocating funds under the leadership of responsible directors.

If they have a group of specialists, private business institutes seem to have the best personnel administration. They also have freedom in

1. In the autumn of 1970, I had the opportunity of visiting most of the interdisciplinary research institutes in the U.S. and Europe, including Czechoslovakia, Poland, and the USSR. Most of them specialized in area studies. Nevertheless, the views expressed here are primarily based on my personal experiences and observations as the director of an interdisciplinary research institute at Kyoto University, Japan. Hence, the opinions of this article may be biased in favor of university institutes. A friend of mine in a responsible position in a governmental institute holds that university professors are usually very poor administrators. Since, however, the necessary number of capable administrators needed is very small, it should be posible to find exceptionally capable administrators with a sufficient knowledge of the scholarly world. Hence, the opinions of my friend must be considered against the advantages of university research institutes whose directors are elected from university professors.

temporarily recruiting suitable specialists from other research organization. It is another question, however, whether they can recruit
appropriate experts for interdisciplinary research work.

In research administration there does not seem to be any significant
difference between the three institutions, but government institutions
are more strictly restricted by inappropriate regulations. Since such
regulations do not restrict intramural research programs and research
projects, the last two types of arrangements seem to enjoy a high degree
of freedom of these three administrative aspects. The only difficulty in
this case is that the crucial figure who utilizes this freedom, the director
or program leader, often cannot be persuaded to stay for a considerable period of time.

Pecuniary remuneration as an incentive must be considered not
only in terms of an official salary but also in terms of opportunities to
earn extra income. As a whole, university institutes seem to have the
best arrangement, because professors are given maximum freedom to
earn extra income. Often extra income, rather than official salaries, is
allocated according to the ability of research workers and thereby
increases the efficiency of research. This holds true, however, only for the
fields which are in demand or are socially recognized. But it is unlikely
that private business institutes would have research workers in impractical fields, so that even there, university institutes seem to have a
comparative advantage. Interdisciplinary research in its ideal form
usually includes some research workers whose research results are not
in demand by profit-making institutions.

The difference in research expenses does not seem to be very great
but the free time provided to each researcher differs markedly from one
type of organization to another, as the table shows. Promotion according
to the performance of individual researchers seems to be made more
fairly and promptly in private institutions than in governmental
institutes, where the seniority system prevails. University institutes are
placed between these two.

Social prestige and stability of position is still very high for university
professors, though there are many exceptions, and this advantage holds
only for reputable universities. Recognition of research achievements
comes from two sources. One is from within the institution; the other
is from academic and intellectual circles. The latter source is very
directly connected with accessibility to social prestige. Fewer opportunities to gain recognition in publications, to associate with the well-
established scholarly world, to make personal contact with outstanding
scholars by attending national and international conferences or to join
in international research teams make private business institutes and

government institutes less attractive to prestigious scholars, though the situation is changing rapidly in this respect.

The more psychological satisfaction derived from achievement in research itself, the less important become pecuniary and other material incentives in determining the placement of scholars in these institutions. Concerning the forms of interdisciplinary research institutes to be established, the great advantage of old, prestigious and large universities cannot be denied, because there are many specialists ready to cooperate with each other in interdisciplinary research, and any research results are most readily recognized in academic circles. For these reasons the interdisciplinary institutes located within or affiliated with the best universities are very attractive for young capable scholars who are about to embark on an academic career and know that area studies or interdisciplinary research is not yet firmly established in the academic world.

Admittedly, this same environment makes many university professors self-centered or leads them to self-satisfaction, making many universities mere ivory towers. Thus they often deviate unduly from practical, significant, or policy-oriented research. For this reason it is highly desirable, on the one hand, to devise a certain reward system for recognizing practical or policy-oriented research and, on the other hand, to open the way for interchange of personnel between the three types of organizations. Intramural research programs and research projects must be used to supplement research work at these three institutions.

METHODOLOGICAL PROBLEMS OF INTERDISCIPLINARY RESEARCH AND THEIR SOLUTION

One definite advantage of establishing an independent research institute designed for interdisciplinary research rather than having an intramural research program within a university is that many kinds of scholars in different fields can have close contact with each other and thereby constantly learn, formally and informally, different ways of thinking, research methods, and established knowledge in neighboring sciences. The advantage is particularly great when discussions take place on questions of common interests from the point of view of different disciplines. Such discussions would never be possible unless many researchers worked together in the same institute, talked with one another, and felt responsible for the research results of the institute as a whole. The importance of friendly but careful informal discussions can hardly be exaggerated. The kind of information and preliminary discussions obtained from informal talks among colleagues cannot be obtained so easily by reading published documents, which are often too partial and formalized. In such fields as area studies, where many problems still remain unsettled or even unformulated, the raw materials of information, experiences or even casual observations in fieldwork and, of course, the front knowledge of related sciences are essential to discovering topics for research.

Such discussions with colleagues in the same or related fields make it easier to evaluate the relative importance of topics and examine the possibility of formulating research problems. Experience shows that the most successful interdisciplinary research carried out is if some specific problem is formulated as a central theme, which is of common interest to scholars in different disciplines. This way of identifying problems and coordinating efforts in formulating the problem is really the key to the success of interdisciplinary research. This is one of the advantages of independent interdisciplinary institutes.

Inconsistency of speech and action is particularly noticeable in interdisciplinary research. The deed-to-talk ratio must be very low indeed. The above-mentioned advantage shows at least one way of overcoming the methodological difficulty of interdisciplinary research, which can most easily be realized at independent research institutes but can be applied to other institutes with some adaptations. Together with the two additional advantages of independent institutes, which will be discussed later, this advantage is summarized below:

(1) easier selection and formulation of research problems common to multiple disciplines

(2) closer collaboration between senior and junior research workers and

(3) ready cooperation with matching research programs in other institutions at home and abroad.

If these points are successfully implemented, the most difficult problems of interdisciplinary research will be solved, especially with regard to area studies or development research.

Two concrete research studies are worth citing here as successful examples of interdisciplinary research. The first is T. Watabe's "The Glutinous Rice Zone in Thailand" (chapter 6 herein); the second is H. Fukui's "Environmental Determinants Affecting the Potential Dissemination of High-Yielding Varieties of Rice," (chapter 8 herein).

Watabe, professor of agronomy at Kyoto University, succeeded in clarifying the historical changes which brought about the spread of glutinous rice varieties in Thailand, by distinguishing the various kinds of rice chaff contained in primitive bricks discovered in old temple buildings at different places in Thailand. The discovery of such bricks was accidental. One of his colleagues, Takaya, associate professor of geomorphology at Kyoto University, casually talked about this discovery while both of them were doing fieldwork in northern Thailand. Subsequent working seminars with agronomists, Thai historians, rice taxonomists, and geographers suggested a more careful sampling of bricks, and as a result, his unique, pioneering piece of work was produced, shedding light on an undocumented part of Thai history.

Fukui's article resulted from a joint project by a group of scholars participating in a joint seminar at the Center for Southeast Asian Studies, Kyoto University. The discussion started informally, at lunch, and cast serious doubt on popular optimism about the spread of the IRRI variety of rice in the Chao Phraya basin in Thailand. A presentation of this cautious view to an international conference on the Green Revolution sparked a series of working seminars attended by quite a variety of scientists who had common interests in the Green Revolution in Southeast Asia. They included geographers, agronomists, soil scientists, irrigation engineers, economists, and agricultural economists. After a very careful exchange of views and a joint effort to analyze the same problem from various points of view in these workshops, this unusual interdisciplinary paper was successfully written, and has proved correct in warning against too much optimism on the Green Revolution in Southeast Asia. These two examples show how interdisciplinary research can be successfully carried out.

The importance of collaboration between senior scholars with sufficient experience in area studies and junior postdoctoral researchers is not adequately recognized by many scholars and administrators of research institutes and grant-giving foundations. Junior scholars or graduate students are often sent to remote villages or bustling urban areas without any effective research guidance in area studies. Without appropriate advice at crucial moments, junior researchers often waste time and energy and end up with few research results. The essential problem here is how to guide the research of junior scholars in the field. This may be achieved if there is close collaboration between senior and junior researchers before the latter departs for his fieldwork. The former should always be accessible either at the local centers or at the home center.

Another reason for the importance of senior and junior cooperation is sometimes overlooked. It is the longer period required to train capable interdisciplinary-oriented specialists for area studies. First, there are additional language requirements. It is not exceptional for successful fieldwork to require the mastery of two foreign languages. Secondly, they must familiarize themselves with people and societies that are radically different from their own. To economize on the time required for such training, constant association with senior scholars with long years of experience, and frequent association with visitors from the native countries are very desirable. This is convenient if junior scholars are affiliated with multidisciplinary research centers where such opportunities are amply provided.

In order to carry out interdisciplinary research in area studies, the research workers must always be ready to contact researchers in related institutes or universities at home and abroad. It goes without saying that the best way of executing area studies is to work together with native scholars in the same or related fields. This arrangement can be facilitated if they are able to respond to the demands for research programs designed by native scholars on their own initiative. Since different kinds of problems are likely to be proposed, and they are likely to be made by a limited number of leading scholars in developing countries, response to such demands is easier if there are only a few multidisciplinary contact points in developed countries. This aspect is increasingly important to ensure the relevance of fieldwork carried out by junior researchers, and to avoid the charge of intellectual or political neocolonialism. This type of international cooperation is also extremely effective for the training of junior scholars in developing countries as well as in developed countries. Young Ph. D.'s who have returned to developing countries usually need more training and research experience in order to analyze the problems of their native countries. International cooperation offers an excellent opportunity for their further education and the promotion of interdisciplinary research in area studies for development research.

Thus an ideal interdisciplinary research institute needs a core group of multidisciplinary workers and a large number of affiliated researchers in many fields. It must be administered in a manner that guarantees maximum degree of contact in formal seminars and on informal occasions. These three points are essential.

THE SIZE OF AN INTERDISCIPLINARY INSTITUTE AND ITS ADMINISTRATION

All the considerations presented seem to imply that the size of such an institute must be fairly large. The larger the size, the more difficult is the task of administration. The leadership of the director is especially important for administering an interdisciplinary institute, because the difficult problem of coordinating different disciplines in scholarly research is often ultimately solved by the director's judgment. Most experienced directors seem to hold the view that the number of senior scholars should not exceed about twenty. The primary reason for limiting the size of the institute is the enormous burden on the director. The ideal director must combine a wide and balanced knowledge of different disciplines with excellent managerial skills. It is very difficult to find such a director. If one is found, he cannot remain efficient for very long unless he is given sufficient time to keep learning while assuming the role of director. This certainly is not very easy, because scientific knowledge depreciates quickly and the duties of a director require an almost unlimited amount of time. One way of overcoming this difficulty would be to have plural deputy directors who can alternate directorships every two or three years, so that any one of them can continue his scholarly activity while doing administrative work.

Needless to say, twenty senior scholars are not enough to carry out a variety of interdisciplinary researches. Hence, the institute must have a large number of affiliated researchers within and outside the university or the institute. This means that it must organize intramural research programs and/or research projects to supplement the research activities of its own staffs. This arrangement can be made most ideally if an interdisciplinary research institute is established as part of a large university with many departments and disciplines. If there are scholars of many disciplines on the same campus, opportunities for informal association are many. Thus, one conclusion of this article is that institutes outside large universities will have more difficulties working in an interdisciplinary form and will thus tend to be more or less monodisciplinary.[2]

2. For further insights *see*: Deutsch, Karl W., John Platt, and Dieter Senghaas, "Conditions Favoring Major Advances in Social Sciences," *Science* (February 1971); Rieger H. C., "Some Problems of Interdisciplinary Research", *Inter-Discipline* (January 1966); Wood, B., "Area Studies," in *Encyclopedia of Social Sciences*.

1

Thai Pattern of Social Organization: Notes on a Comparative Study

KOICHI MIZUNO

INTRODUCTION

In 1950 Embree characterized Thai society as loosely structured in contrast with a Japanese-like, closely woven social system.[1] Since then his article has served as a general guide for Thai studies. As data has accumulated, however, there have been reconsiderations of the application of his concept "loose structure" to Thailand. For example, his analysis has been described as impressionistic: while it is phrased in structural terms, the evidence he adduces is in terms of individual behavior rather than social structure. This failure to distinguish the dimensions of culture, society, and personality makes the notion of structure, to say the least, fuzzy. Moreover, the concept of looseness becomes ambiguous in comparative perspective, since one feels confusion about which cultural aspect should form the basis for a general characterization of loose structure in social or personality terms.[2] It seems clear that the confusion and consequent criticisms which have arisen over Embree's usage of his term "loose structure" have derived from his failure to establish a proven framework of comparison. Struck by the marked contrast with Japanese society, Embree immediately proceeded to look for data to substantiate what had been initially little more than a metaphorical device. I suspect that what Embree really had hoped to analyze was neither social structure nor institutionalized behavior but patterns of social organization. The term, social

1. John F. Embree, "Thailand—A Loosely Structured Social System," *American Anthropologist* 52 (1950): 181–193.
2. Hans-Dieter Evers, ed., *Loosely Structured Social Systems, Thailand in Comparative Perspective*, Cultural Report Series No. 17 (New Haven: Yale University, Southeast Asian Studies, 1969), pp. 16–17, 23–24, 43, 59, 79–82, 109–111.

organization,[3] I use here refers to the morphological, structural, and cultural arrangements of a social group which are imperative for human life; by pattern, is meant their characteristic features, logically found in common throughout basic social groups of a society or community.

This article represents an attempt to delineate the Thai pattern of social organization as it is found in the traditional rural community of *muban* Don Daeng in Northeast Thailand. It is based on data from my field work in this village, the major results of which have already been reported in a series of discussion papers.[4] The approach there was mainly structural. Here, I will try to summarize the same data in an organizational approach to the social system.

GROUP MORPHOLOGY

The village, Don Daeng, is located 20 kilometers by road south of the town of Khon Kaen. It consists of 132 households in a dense nuclear settlement. Villagers, while ethnically Thai-Lao, undoubtedly regard themselves as Thai citizens and have much in common with other lowland Thai peasant communities in growing rice (though of the glutinous type) and observing the Buddhist Trinity. As is common elsewhere in the country, the village contains very few social groups. Basically each villager is a member of the domestic group, of his own personal kindred, and of the Don Daeng community, which is to a large extent symbolized by the *wat* Phothibanlang.

The most salient feature is that the village is a bilateral society in which only the domestic group and personal kindred are prevalent: there is an absence of descent groups of any kind. By definition kindred is an ego-oriented bilaterally reckoned kin group; in any society kindreds necessarily overlap one another endlessly since they do not have any fixed ancestral points of reference.[5] In Don Daeng, kindred extends to

3. For the concept of social organization, see for example: Walter Goldschmit, *Man's Way, A Preface to the Understanding of Human Society* (New York: Holt, Rinehart and Winston, 1959), pp. 61–62.

4. The field research was carried out during 1964–1966, and the comprehensive report is *Social System of Don Daeng Village, A Community Study in Northeast Thailand*, Discussion Paper Nos. 12–22 (Kyoto: Center for Southeast Asian Studies, Kyoto University, 1971). Other articles in English are: "Multi-household Compounds in Northeast Thailand," *Asian Survey* 8, no. 10, Institute of International Studies, University of California (1968); 842–852; "Japanese Scholarship on Southeast Asian Villages—A Socio-Anthropological View," *Foreign Values and Southeast Asian Scholarship*, edited by Joseph Fischer, Research Monograph No. 11 (University of California, Center for South and Southeast Asian Studies, 1973), pp. 211–236.

5. George P. Murdock, "Cognatic Forms of Social Organization", in *Social Structure in Southeast Asia*, edited by George P. Murdock, (Chicago, Ill.: Quadrangle Books, 1960), p. 4.

the second cousin and in practice includes all immediate family members. Strictly speaking kindred is not a social group, but rather a category from which necessary members are recruited as occasions arise at various stages in life, and for house building, harvest, and transplanting. In other words each villager has a set of dyadic relations through kinship which extends radially from himself.

In the village the family usually takes the form of a domestic unit sharing a common house, kitchen, and household economy. Such units may be nuclear families (68 percent), stem families (27 percent), or other variants (5 percent). The nuclear family, however, is not based on Western ideas of individualism, nor is the stem family organized on the lineal ideas traditionally found in the Japanese family. The villagers' notion of family can be understood as a shallow, radial extension of the kinship core (an analytical unit consisting of parents and unmarried children), being neither confined to the core itself with the ideology of nuclear family, nor extended lineally to either ascending or descending couples. Circles of such radial extension overlap one another and do not allow segmentation of the village through kinship.[6]

There exist multihousehold compounds in this village which the households of one or more daughters (in a few cases, of sons) cultivate jointly with the household of the parents, who own the rice fields. The association is temporal, since it appears only as a phase in the family cycle and does not continue beyond one generation. Unlike the Japanese *dozoku* kin group which is organized around descent among *ie*[7] and functions in the politico-jural realm, the Thai multi-household compound functions exclusively in the domestic realm.

In Don Daeng there are 19 multihousehold compounds, and these involve 45 of the 132 households of the village. The parental households involved are of rather longer standing than other households in the village, but it is unlikely that they form a privileged group or enjoy special rights in the utilization of water, public land, forest, or unarable fields. These means of agricultural production are not communally owned by the village itself, and all households have equal rights and are independent of each other economically. Unlike the traditional Japanese village, Don Daeng has never functioned as a unit of production. It exists as a community merely in the sense that the village occupies a vaguely defined area; villagers' needs are to a large extent

6. Near the entrance of the village, there was a small shrine called *puta*. The term means "grandfather," but the shrine appears to be treated as the home of guardian spirits of the land and village, rather than of an ancestral spirit.
7. The traditional Japanese family, which can be understood as an extreme emphasis on a lineal extension of kinship core.

satisfied within it, and they have developed a common feeling through various experiences of administrative, social, and religious activities.

INTERNAL STRUCTURE

Whatever the morphological pattern may be, as long as villagers live together in groups it is imperative for them to develop appropriate role systems within whatever kind of social group they form. In fact there exist locally books of instruction and guidance, which advise people about their roles within the domestic group,[8] and these are recited by elderly persons on appropriate occasions.

Parents are supposed to perform the following five roles: to train the children to make a livelihood, to teach them to refrain from doing evil, to instruct them in proper behavior, to find spouses for them, and to bequeath property to them. The children are expected to reciprocate by fulfilling five duties: to help their parents as much as possible, to become such persons as the parents can bequeath property without misgivings, not to disgrace the parents, to take care of the parents in their later days, and to render religious service after their death. Between husband and wife there are five rules of conduct. The wife should serve her husband well by refraining from uttering harsh words and abusing him, she should not commit adultery, she should attend carefully to the household affairs by preparing food and taking care of valuables and the hearth, she should manage the property her husband acquires, and finally she should respect her elders and her husband's relatives by following their instructions. The husband is expected in turn: not to belittle his wife, not to speak ill of her, not to commit adultery, to entrust his wife with his property and to give her personal ornaments lest she should feel humiliated. The instruction books also include advice about the ideal role of the son-in-law. As long as he loves his wife he must love his parents-in-law and their house and farm, their land and buffaloes. A good son-in-law is expected to exert himself in making a living and not to frustrate his family; he should not be idle, arrogant, or delinquent in his duties to his family.

To be sure, roles are assigned to each individual family member. They are, however, stated simply in terms of sex, age, and generation. Respectfulness to the male, elder, or parents, is a positive feature which characterizes the internal structure of the Don Daeng family. Yet this

---

8.   For example: Com Buntabed, *Maha Anisong 108 Kan* [The Great Merits 108 volumes] (Bangkok: Liangchieng Press 1959), pp. 559–566; Buncan Buacan, *Phua Son Mia* [Husband's teachings to his wife] (Khon Kaen: Khlangnanawithja n.d.), pp. 15–18; Phrakhru Anujodthamphan, *Photaw Son Lugkhoei* [A father's instructions to his son-in-law] (Khon Kaen: Shlangnanawithja 1957), pp. 5–7.

feature does not involve much authority. Authority within the domestic group is restricted to a minimum, and the members seem to enjoy relative equality.[9] The father is regarded as head of his household's family, and the children are taught to respect their parents. But the rules of conduct merely show what is proper and what is not: they are in no sense prescriptive. The children select spouses of their own choice. They decide on their own initative whether they will help in the farming or not. Their duties are not unilaterally imposed in the role expectation between parents and children. The husband represents his household to the outside, but in almost all cases he consults with his wife in deciding important household affairs. Generally women are treated well, and there are no institutionalized situations under which they are frustrated in their own family. Among siblings there is little difference in rights and duties.

This minimal authority applies equally to the village as a community, since the constituent households have equal status with respect to their rights and duties. Social stratification of the village correlates largely with the relative age of household head, size of farmland, and stage of family cycle.[10] The villagers' socioeconomic statuses are continuous and do not form fixed strata with differentiated roles allotted to constituent members. Village leaders tend to be of higher socioeconomic status, but authority is not vested in any particular categories. Leaders' influence depends largely on their culturally bound personal prestige and spreads through the ramifying dyadic relations of bilateral kinship networks in which status and role are structured only by sex, age, and generation. The village headman is the only person who has authority because of his administrative office. In fact, he exercises the power to call the village meeting, and with the help of other village leaders carries out several kinds of village activities.[11] Yet his authority is not great. This is indicated in his way of organizing the labor force for communal activities. The only way he can do this is to urge their cooperation at village meetings and wait for spontaneous response from those attending. He can neither coerce villagers nor take any action against those who do not participate in communal work. Sanctions are always diffuse and no formal action is taken unless the offence is criminal.

These structural features of village life anticipate another interesting

9. This feature is in striking contrast to the Japanese authoritarian family.
10. A full analysis will be found in my report: "Social Stratification," in *Social System of Don Daeng Village*, chapter 5, Discussion Paper No. 16 (Kyoto: Center for Southeast Asian Studies, Kyoto University, 1971), pp. 112–133.
11. The village activities are described in my report: "Government," (*Social System of Don Daeng Village*, chapter 6, pp. 143–165.

pattern with respect to the relation between the individual and the group. In Don Daeng, members of farm households engage in miscellaneous nonagricultural activities, and individual members are allowed to keep their earnings. Members are neither bound to a norm which prescribes them to hand it all over to the household head, nor is the father's authority powerful enough to absorb it on behalf of the household. Members are permitted freedom from the group in using what they have earned. In practice, however, they tend to give some of the earnings to the parents and so help to supplement farm income to keep up the household economy. This shows that while individual members are relatively free from the group, they do not fail to observe their commitment to it by a sense of sympathy to other individual members. Similar situations can be observed in the case of Don Daeng as a community.

This pattern of members' commitment to a group may be called dyadism. By this term I do not mean dyadic contract,[12] rather I use it to imply a pattern of group solidarity in which individuals are bound together primarily by the importance attached to sympathy toward dyadically related people rather than by being obliged by authority. The pattern differs both from the Japanese-like collectivism, in which, traditionally speaking, the group tended to absorb all the energy of the individuals and demanded their self-sacrifice on behalf of itself, and from Western individualism, in which constituent members, as a right, have equal standing in the group to which they belong.

CULTURAL ARRANGEMENTS

The third aspect of social organization is its cultural arrangements, which largely refer to values and ideology shared by group members. One of the recurrent themes expressed in local proverbs is the value placed on reciprocity among those who are familiar with each other.[13] Beyond such circles the social relation involves a sense of general mistrust and suspicion. Thus one is admonished "not to eat at someone else's house without thinking about it"; "not to rely on water from villages

---

12. For the concept of dyadic contract, see for example: George M. Foster, "The Dyadic Contract in Tzintzunzan, Patron-Client Relationship," *American Anthropologist* 65 (1963):1280–1281.

13. Local sayings and proverbs are collected in a Thai text: Prichayan, *Phasid Isan Lae Nanaphasid* [Proverbs of the Northeast and various others] (Bangkok: Wathanaphnid Press, 1956), pp. 57–69. Some analysis of the proverbs of the text has been carried out in my report: "Themes and Proverbs," (*Social System of Don Daeng Village*, chapter 8, Discussion Paper No. 19, (Kyoto: Center for Southeast Asian Studies, Kyoto University, 1971), pp. 214–236.

the other side of the river"; or "not to believe what others say, however nice it may sound", since "otherwise it will bring you trouble." Neighbors, relatives, and fellow villagers are those whom one should respect, love, and rely on the most. A proverb says: "speak to your relatives, or relations between you will disappear." Among those familiar with each other there prevail such themes as "mutual help," "sharing," "not to be selfish," and "not to be greedy." The fact that they are expressed in local sayings suggests that villagers recognize the value of interdependence and reciprocity in their group life.

These values are, however, subject to limitation by the counter-theme that the individual is socioeconomically independent. "It is just like a dim light in the distance to think about elder siblings, and it is useless to think of younger siblings; ultimately one will not find anyone except oneself to rely on." This theme of self-reliance is accompanied with the villagers' dislike for interfering with others, dominating other people, or being controlled by other people. In fact, since "one works for one's bread" without depending on others, "one should not interfere with other people." At the same time one should not force other people to do anything they will do by themselves. A proverb says: "When cattle will not eat grass, do not force them and break their horns; when pigs will not eat bran, do not hit them." (You can take a horse to water but you cannot make him drink.) Similarly, another saying expresses a dislike for being coerced by other persons: "Do not let others pinch your fingers and cut your hands."

Assuming that status and role are not structured on the basis of authority, that social groups lack a strict norm and coercive force, and that cultural premises advocate a sense of independence, it is important to inquire into the forces that bring the people together to form functioning groups in Don Daeng. From the foregoing discussion, it seems that the villagers' conformity partly depends on a sense of respect toward the male, relatives, and elders; a dyadic sympathy for other individual members; and on the value placed on interdependence and reciprocity. Yet there are still other cultural forces which help to produce conformity among villagers and thus maintain the social order of functioning groups. They are submission to the prestige of village leaders, a world view which gives sanction to the legitimacy of leadership, and other cultural premises about social relationships.

The villagers' image of leadership generally subsumes those figures who are relatively wealthy, honest and moral, well-educated in the local sense, devout in Buddhism and unselfish, and who are gentle and considerate in manner, generous and benevolent to followers, and persuasive. A person who has these culturally bound personal qualities is looked up to as *phuyai* and is distinguished from *chainoi*, the reverse character. From these qualities leaders derive the prestige which is the basis of their following. Leaders' self-estimation shows, in fact, that while most think themselves quite average in knowledge and ideas, and ability to read and write, all are confident in rating themselves among the most devout, moral, and unselfish.[14] Legitimacy of village leadership depends much on their world view, which encourages the personal qualities mentioned above.

Villagers, as devout Buddhists, believe in *karma*, the guiding law of the universe, by which one's action inevitably brings its consequences in this or the other world. Acts in accordance with the teachings of the Lord Buddha deserve to be counted as merit (*bun*), while acts against the teachings are counted as demerit (*bap*). And it is only meritorious actions that have good consequences; vicious actions result only in evil consequences, as expressed by various sayings. With this concept of *karma*, the universe is perceived as a set of hierarchically ordered stations. The hierarchy depends on the balance of merit and demerit, or the merit which has been established in former lives. More meritorious beings occupy higher stations and are assured greater freedom from suffering. This set of hierarchical stations constitutes the universe, centering on Mount Meru and surrounded by seven circular belts of oceans, divided from each other by seven annular mountains.[15] It is likely that a person of higher socioeconomic status is assumed to occupy a higher position in this moral hierarchy. The actions of a person of higher socioeconomic status are regarded as more meritorious. And he is required to show benevolence toward those of lower socioeconomic status. As long as leaders meet this expectation, they are followed by their fellow villagers.

The world view involves other cultural premises which determine the pattern of social relations among villagers. "Do not forget yourself [one's position in the moral hierarchy]" is a recurrent theme expressed in local sayings. For villagers *khwam metta karuna* and *katanyu katawethi* are the greatest virtues which should be observed following the Lord Buddha. *Metta* refers to benevolence with which to bring happiness to other people, while *karuna* indicates the compassion with which to save others from unhappiness. Their school textbook teaches the children that

---

14.   See my report, "Government," pp. 141–142.
15.   References are: Lucien M. Hanks, "Merit and Power in the Thai Social Order," *American Anthropologist* 64 (1962):1247–1261; and Wendel Blanchard et al., *Thailand, Its People, Its Society, Its Culture* (New Haven, Conn.: Human Relations Area File, Press, 1958), p. 91.

these concepts are very important virtues in social life.[16] *Metta karuna* which has been received is felt as *bunkhun* (merciful favor) by the recipient. *Katanyu* means to feel gratitude for this *bunkhun*, and *katawethi* refers to returning it. *Bunkhun* from parents is most important of all, and it is because of gratitude for *bunkhun* that sons are ordained as monks and children support parents in their old age. Failure will be counted as demerit, for as a proverb says "to feel *bunkhun* towards the cat only when it catches the rat eating silk worms, is just like children feeling *bunkhun* towards parents only when they are dependent." Thus "one should not forget oneself" and should be willing to reciprocate the *bunkhun* which one has received. *Topthaen* is the word applied to that action.

Another cultural theme is "to maintain harmonious relations with other people." One should neither speak ill of other people, nor think of oneself only as good. "When you say you are good, you should not overlook that others are much better." Such a person is just like those who "boast of squatting without seeing others sitting more comfortably on tree stumps." Furthermore, the idea of an eye for an eye is not desirable, since it is conceived that any evil act will automatically bring evil to the doer. "If you want others to fall into danger, you will fall into danger; if you want others to die, you will die first." On the contrary, "if you want to be loved by other people, you should love them first," but "if you want to be hated, you may hate them first." Thus one is encouraged to suppress one's feelings so that others will be pleased or will not be angered.

These local saying not only express "harmonious relations," but also suggest a theme of completedness of action. In other words, any action, even though directed at other people, has consequences for the doer. It is doubtful as to how far this premise regulates actual behavior in ordinary village life. Yet it still has some significance in the pattern of social relations. Assuming that a benevolent action is taken on behalf of the doer himself without considering the people to whom the action is directed, there would be no constraining forces driving them to reciprocate the benevolent action. They may be permitted not to reciprocate, as it may be wrong for the benefactor to expect reciprocation beforehand. Reciprocation is not obligatory in the social dimension, although it is culturally valued as desirable. In contrast to Japanese society, the Thai notions of *bunkhun* and *topthaen* emphasize the benevolent action of the superior, rather than the obligation of the inferior.[17]

---

16. Ministry of Education, Thailand, *Baeb Rian Wicha Sangkhomsugsa Samrap Chan Prathom Pi Thi 3* [Civics, text for the third year] (Bangkok, 1959), pp. 57–58.

17. The Japanese equivalent of this concept is *on* and *ongaeshi*.

OVERVIEW

In the foregoing I have summarized the social system of Don Daeng from an organizational point of view. The data used here is limited to a small rural community in the Northeast so that it may be questioned whether the same pattern is applicable to other rural communities of Thailand. Yet its main features, at least, do not seem to contradict reports from other community studies.[18] It can then be assumed that what has been analyzed in this article represents a general pattern of social organization in traditional Thai rural society. It may be further hypothesized that the pattern continues among those who have migrated to the metropolitan area, members of such various associations as factories, enterprises, or political parties, and personnel of the modern bureaucracy, as an informal pattern.

The present analysis does not show any negative evidence which undermines Embree's view. On the contrary, it seems to involve much empirical evidence supporting it. Would it then be acceptable, following Embree, to apply the term loosely structured to the organizational pattern of the Don Daeng social system? I am inclined to say no and would suggest the phrase is misleading and inaccurate in the light of the analysis of this article. Embree's use of the term "structure," calls for the sociological notion of "structure of society," whereas the subject of the present analysis deals with an organizational pattern of the social system which has a broader implication than the structure per se. The term, "loose," easily evokes a specter of "no order," "randomness," or "anomie," none of which are the case in the Don Daeng social system. Moreover, "loose" is too general and abstract a word to summarize the organizational characteristics of the social system. It would be preferable to choose a more concrete and positive term which can suggest a social organizational form; for example, figure-focal entourage vis-à-vis *iemoto* for Japanese, clan for Chinese, caste for Indian, or club for American society.[19] Besides as the term, "loose," often implies a polar concept, it would be disadvantageous to use it as an accurate summary for the cultural pattern of a particular society or community. Where should American or Indonesian society be placed on the scale of a loose-tight continuum?

18. For example, John E. de Young, *Village Life in Modern Thailand* (Berkeley and Los Angeles: University of California Press, 1955); Howard Keva Kaufman, *Bangkhuad, A Community Study in Thailand* (Locust Valley, N.Y.: J. J. Augstin, 1960); Konrad Kingshill, *Ku Daeng, The Red Tomb, A Village Study in Northern Thailand* (Chiengmai: The Prince Royal's College, 1960).

19. See Lucien M. Hanks, "The Corporation and the Entourage: A Comparison of Thai and American Social Organization," *Catalyst*, no. 2 (Summer, 1966): 55–63, and Francis L. K. Hsu, *Clan, Caste, and Club*, (New York: D. Van Nostrand, 1963).

From my point of view there is no value in discussing whether the organizational pattern of the Don Daeng social system should be classified in terms of "loose" or "tight." More fruitful tasks at the present moment are to set up some theoretical framework for a comparative study of social organization, through systematically observing the data so far collected in various societies, without introducing the terms "loose" and "tight." Such work will help to solve the issues involved in comparisons which have been raised by critics.[20] This article has discussed the organizational pattern of the Don Daeng social system in terms of the morphological aspects of basic social groups, internal structure of status and role, stratification and authority, the individual and group, group solidarity, and such cultural arrangements as reciprocity, sense of independence, pattern of conformity, leadership image, and world view which maintain social order. Since the list of these items by no means constitutes a complete inventory for comparison, a theoretical exploration should be further encouraged. It would certainly permit comparison, correlation, and classification of data which would otherwise remain in disarray. Until various societies and cultures have been compared on the basis of a common framework, the terms, "loose" and "tight," are better kept in storage.

---

20. For example: A. Thomas Kirsch, "Loose Structure, Theory or Description?"; and Clark E. Cunningham, "Characterizing a Social System, the Loose-Tight Dichotomy," *Loosely Structured Social Systems, Thailand in Comparative Perspective*, op. cit., pp. 45–46, 109–110.

2

Islam and Divorce among Malay Peasants

YOSHIHIRO TSUBOUCHI

INTRODUCTION

Many studies have confirmed the close relationship between kinship structure and the occurrence of divorce. Following the assertions of Loeb and Gluckman that the pattern of kinship structure relates directly to divorce,[1] theories have tended to seek explanations in group affiliation which define the points of contact of kinship structure and other factors.[2] But this approach confines explanations of human behavior in the family to the bounds of group affiliation. In this article I attempt to show the limitations of intergroup politics in explaining divorce, through an evaluation of the influence of the laws and supporting values of Islam, which were introduced into Malay society and are not directly related to the kinship structure.

The sources used in this article are the results of surveys carried out between 1968 and 1972 in three farming villages in West Malaysia: Padang Lalang in Kedah, Galok in Kelantan and Bukit Pegoh in Melaka.[3]

1. Edwin M. Loeb, *Sumatra, Its History and People* (Vienna: Institutes fur Vorkerkunde der Universitat Wien, 1935); Max Gluckman, "Kinship and Marriage among the Lozi of Northern Rhodesia and the Zulu of Natal," *African Systems of Kinship and Marriage*, ed. A. R. Radcliff-Brown and D. Forde (London: Oxford University Press, 1950).

2. E. R. Leach, "Aspects of Bridewealth and Marriage among the Kachin and Lakher," *Man* 57, no. 59 (1957); Charles Ackerman, "Affiliations: Structural Determinants of Differential Divorce Rates," *American Journal of Sociology* 69, no. 1 (1963).

3. I am grateful to Professor Masuo Kuchiba and Dr. Narifumi Maeda for permission to use their unpublished materials and for helpful comments on this article. The survey in Padang Lalang was carried out by Kuchiba, that in Bukit Pegoh by

Padang Lalang is a paddy farming village located on the coastal plain of Kedah, the granary of West Malaysia, about 7.5 km north of the state capital of Alor Setar. Recently the development of the Muda River irrigation project has made double cropping possible. The settlement is scattered in a ribbon pattern along an irrigation canal and has a population of 897 in 180 households.

Galok in Kelantan is about 30 km from the state capital of Kota Bharu. It is situated on the fluvial terraces of the Kelantan River, and the main occupations are paddy growing, rubber tapping, and tobacco cultivation. The settlement is scattered in a ribbon pattern along a road, and the population is 680 in 147 households.

Bukit Pegoh in Melaka is about 13 km from Melaka town and is situated on a narrow coastal strip near the sea. The main sources of income for its population are paddy farming, rubber tapping, and migratory work. The houses are located on an islandlike rise in the paddy fields and the population is 481 in 89 households.

The kinship structure of these three villages can be thought to be basically the same, and yet a remarkable difference in the occurrence of divorce is observed.

KINSHIP STRUCTURE, LAW AND VALUES

2.1. In principle the kinship system of Malay peasants recognizes the equal significance of the male and female sides of the family. Although the father's name is attached to the child's name, that is, a patrilineal Arabian-type law has been adopted in the naming system, in practice the ego is at the center of a bilateral kinship system. Because no family names exist, the number of generations is limited by the family's powers of recollection. No kin group that can succeed to an inheritance or honor an ancestoral shrine is formed.

At the time of marriage the husband makes a payment to the wife, but this is an arrangement between individuals, and the kin as a group does not participate in the procurement or division of this money. The average marriage payment on first marriage is: 540 Malaysian dollars in Padang Lalang (for marriages from 1959 to 1968);[4] 360 Malaysian dollars in Bukit Pegoh (from 1956 to 1971);[5] and 230 Malaysian dollars in Galok (1961 to 1970). These sums approximate to 20–30 percent of

---

Maeda and that in Galok by myself. For statistical data in each village, I drew on Masuo Kuchiba, Yoshihiro Tsubouchi, and Narifumi Maeda, eds., *Studies of Malay Villages* (Tokyo: Sobunsha, 1975). (in Japanese).

4. At the time, the exchange rate was $1 U.S. = $2.4–3.0 Malaysian.
5. Calculated from Tables 3–6 in Narifumi Maeda, "Marriage with Near-Kin in a Malay Village, Melaka," *Southeast Asian Studies* 10, no. 4 (1973) (in Japanese).

the villager's average annual income, but one can hardly say these people request large marriage payments. For a woman marrying for the second time the marriage payment is much smaller; for example, in Galok it is about half that for the first marriage.

Marriage between cousins is not given particular priority, but in Bukit Pegoh 18.1 percent of all marriages were between first cousins. In Padang Lalang the percentage was 9.1, and in Galok, 3.4. In Bukit Pegoh and Padang Lalang marriages between second cousins were strikingly few in comparison with those between first cousins, while in Galok there were approximately the same number. The overall rate of marriage between kin was 42.5 percent in Bukit Pegoh, 20.6 percent in Padang Lalang, and 15.1 percent in Galok.

There are no rules concerning community endogamy in the three villages; the endogamy rate was 47.6 percent in Bukit Pegoh, 22.0 percent in Padang Lalang, and 25.4 percent in Galok. Bukit Pegoh has clear boundaries, but both Padang Lalang and Galok are ribbon settlements with ill-defined boundaries. There are also no special rules on marital residence in the three villages; the compound of the husband's side, of the wife's side, or a new compound may be chosen. In Padang Lalang and Galok the tendency is to chose the side richer in farming land, that is, paddy fields and rubber plantations; slightly more newly-married couples live in the husband's compound than in the wife's compound. In Bukit Pegoh, where dependence on farming land is small and most income is derived from nonfarm sources such as migratory work, the converse is true.

Property is held individually, and the property of one household is the sum of the couple's and other family members' property. Property acquired jointly by the couple is divided equally in the case of divorce.

Inheritance can be governed by either Islamic or customary law (*adat*). If Islamic law is applied, males gain in the ratio of 2 to 1, while if customary law is followed both sexes receive an equal share. There is a tendency for comparatively prosperous people to chose Islamic law, but it is not always strictly applied and the continuing tendency to equal division between male and female shows that the principle of fair division is common.[6]

The nuclear family pattern of a household centered on one husband and wife is widespread, but there is no ideology that households should

6.   For details on inheritance see Masuo Kuchiba, Yoshihiro Tsubouchi, and Narifumi Maeda, "A Paddy Farming Village in the Northwestern Part of Malaya—The Fragmentation of Landholding," *Southeast Asian Studies* 3, no. 1 (1965) (in Japanese); Yoshihiro Tsubouchi, "Land and Residence among Malay Peasants on the East Coast of Malaya," *Southeast Asian Studies* 10, no. 1 (1972) (in Japanese).

be organized on a nuclear family basis. Group affiliation in the Malay family is lower than in the Japanese family; rather there is an awareness of the accumulation of a network of related people.[7] The household is established around the couple and may include near relations from this network, although all members of the household do not necessarily expect to stay permanently. In certain situations aged parents will be taken into the children's home, or grandchildren will go to live with grandparents, and this is regarded as natural.

Thus this kinship system, with its flexible family structure, provides the basis for a new family life if a couple's relationship should collapse, and such a situation presents few problems. Since there is no fixed family grouping in which people should live, it is easy for one partner to leave if tension arises over dissatisfaction with the family residence.

2.2. Islam is an important foreign element which sets behavioral criteria for the Malays. Under Islamic laws covering marriage, divorce, and inheritance, the following four types of divorce are permitted.

(a) *Talak* or repudiation, is a unilateral declaration of divorce by the husband, who should inform a religious judge (*kathi*) or his representative of the fact within a fixed time. Then follows a prescribed period of waiting (*idah*) during which the husband may revoke the *talak*. This procedure is called *rojok*, and is allowed twice. The third *talak* against a wife may not be revoked; only if she is divorced after a recognized marriage to another person is she allowed to remarry her first husband. The prescribed period of waiting for an older woman is three months ten days, and for a younger woman until the cessation of the third menstrual period, or if she is pregnant, until delivery.

(b) *Pasah* is divorce granted by a religious judge in cases where the whereabouts of one spouse is unknown.

(c) *Tebus talak* means the wife purchases *talak*, and this is used in cases where the wife wants a divorce.

(d) *Ta'alik* is divorce which can be requested by the wife if the husband contravenes special conditions agreed to in the marriage contract.

There are some differences in Islamic law between states in Malaysia, but these procedures are basically similar in the three states considered here.

2.3. Islamic law is extremely adaptable in its application. Here I will give some examples concerned with marriage and divorce.

7. Narifumi Maeda used the term "family circle" for the Malay concept of the family in "Family Circle, Community and Nation in Malaysia," *Current Anthropology* 16, no. 1 (1975). The same use of the term is found in Yoshihiro Tsubouchi and Narifumi Maeda, "Coresidence of Alternative Generations among Malay Peasants," *Southeast Asian Studies* 12, no. 4 (1975) (in Japanese).

Example 1. It is the husband's duty to make a marriage payment on the occasion of marriage. However, the sum is not specified by Islamic authorities but is left to the discretion of the society.

Example 2. Under Islamic law a man is permitted to have up to four wives. But under one of the laws of Islam it is possible for a man to have many more sexual partners by keeping slaves, and under another it is possible to have many wives over a period of time by frequent divorce. Conversely polygamy can be forbidden by wide interpretation of the law that all wives must be treated as equals, since equality, in the strict sense of the word, is impossible.

Example 3. *Talak*, the husband's exclusive right to divorce, does not need the wife's consent and can be carried out freely. In addition, the husband will almost automatically consent to the wife's will, meaning that divorce can take place very easily if either partner wishes it. On the other hand *Hadith* (tradition) holds that God finds divorce the most offensive of all acts tolerated by Him, and this opinion may be emphasized as a deterrent.

Thus diametrically opposed interpretations of Islamic law are possible, although it is important that any interpretation be fully upheld by the religion. Which interpretation of Islamic law is adopted by a society is probably determined by that society's traditions before Islamization and by the extent of its contact with other religions and cultures.

2.4. As stated, the kinship structure of Malay society readily allows divorce. This is supported by the fact that in the society of the Jakun proto-Malays, whose kinship structure is almost identical to that of the Malays but who have not been influenced by Islam, divorce is quite common, though not as common as in Malay society.[8] Thus when Islamic law was accepted by such a society it is likely that divorce became even easier. One reason is that divorce can be justified as an individual's action in God's name under Islamic law.[9] Conversely,

8. On the Jakun, see Narifumi Maeda, "The Aborigines in Malaya," *Southeast Asian Studies* 3, no. 2 (1965) (in Japanese); idem, "Among the Orang Hulu (Jakun) of Ulu Endau, Johor," *Southeast Asian Studies* 3, no. 5 (1966) (in Japanese); idem, "A Jakun Kinship Terminology," *Southeast Asian Studies* 4, no. 5 (1967a) (in Japanese); idem, "Familial Forms of the Jakun (Orang Hulu) in Malaya," *Southeast Asian Studies* 5, no. 3 (1967b) (in Japanese); idem, "Marriage and Divorce among the Jakun (Orang Hulu) of Malaya," *Southeast Asian Studies* 6, no. 4 (1969) (in Japanese).

9. The opinion of Tadahiko Hara that Muslim society is individualistic is clear in this sort of situation in his "Occupations and Value-System in a Moslem Village in Chittagong, East Pakistan," *Southeast Asian Studies* 7, no. 1 (1969) (in Japanese). The theory that, as relations between God and the individual are the most important, Muslim society functions on the principle of individualism is also found in Justus M. Van der Kroef, *Indonesia in the Modern World* (Bandung: Mass Baru,

contact with Christian society, or with the traditional thinking of Christianity that divorce should be avoided, has led to emphasis of similar thinking in the Islam tradition among the Malays. This thinking has probably spread through the initiatives of the intellectual and the religious elites rather than developing from the populace, but in this case, too, divorce is restrained in the name of religion.

Of the three villages under investigation the traditional type of divorce in accordance with Islamic law is found in Galok. In place of a *kathi*, the *imam* of the village handles the notice of divorce in an impartial, businesslike manner. A person issuing a declaration of *talak* must pay a 12-dollar registration fee to the religious office, and 40 percent of this is retained by the *imam*. This sum exceeds the daily wage of a laborer and is income which the *imam* cannot ignore.

The Malays of Melaka, because of the location of their state, have frequent contact with Europeans and Chinese; and one must bear in mind that the influence from these cultures is considerable. In about 1960 a state religious department, the *Jabatan Ugama Islam*, was set up, the number of religious judges was reduced and the system of religious administration was unified. This office is instrumental in discouraging divorce; the religious judges and their representatives, the *imams*, try to persuade people who come to register a divorce to give up the idea.[10] In addition a religious teacher who was famous in the area and was living in Bukit Pegoh also stressed the undesirability of divorce.

Kedah falls somewhere between Kelantan and Melaka, tending toward the traditionalism of Kedah. In this state, however, the leaders of the religious administration urge the people in public lectures to reflect on the fact that there are too many divorces.

DIVORCE—THE DATA

3.1. Table 1 shows the marriage and divorce statistics of the three states. Judging from the ratio of the numbers of divorces to marriages, the divorce trend is highest in Kelantan, then in Kedah, and lowest in Melaka. But as I was unable to obtain past data I could not judge whether these differences are traditional. If one accepts that the divorce trend was not lower in the past than at present, one can infer that the trend in the early 1930s was lower in Melaka than in the other two

---

1954). The same opinion is found in B. Ter Haar, *Adat Law in Indonesia*, translated from the Dutch by the Institute of Pacific Relations (New Haven, Conn: Human Relations Area Files, 1948). But he also states that Islam, like Christianity, strongly censures divorce, which seems an overemphasis of one interpretation of Islam.

10.   Dr. Narifumi Maeda to Yoshihiro Tsubouchi.

TABLE 1
CHANGES IN MARRIAGES AND DIVORCES IN THE THREE STATES
OF WEST MALAYSIA

Year	KELANTAN			KEDAH			MELAKA		
	Marriages	Divorces	Rojok	Marriages	Divorces	Rojok	Marriages	Divorces	Rojok
1930							1,358	653	97
1931							1,118	548	70
1932							1,233	537	69
1933							1,369	551	66
1934							1,640	526	66
1935							1,549	519	57
1936							1,466	545	74
1937							1,771	595	53
1938							1,576	461	46
1939							1,452	514	57
1940							1,690	629	64
1941							2,063	587	75
1942							1,892	629	75
1943							3,066	940	101
1944							3,223	1,344	166
1945							2,793	1,699	216
1946							1,936	993	87
1947							1,859	759	75
1948	12,488	11,625	683	7,724	5,032	884	1,767	711	52
1949	13,256	11,384	1,007	7,222	4,645	1,116	1,924	670	66
1950	12,326	11,163	768	8,945	5,170	1,117	2,159	729	78
1951	13,131	10,247	923	9,621	4,977	1,323	2,693	805	100
1952	11,391	9,298	805	7,266	4,801	1,061	2,235	633	77
1953	11,092	8,777	657	6,778	4,285		1,943	648	70
1954	10,003	7,549	681	5,789	3,968	1,087	1,871	604	60
1955	11,639	7,660	702	5,814	3,634	984	1,945	632	54
1956	13,830	7,846	749	4,836	3,173	737	2,099	625	69
1957	7,611	4,747	467	6,940	3,924	982	1,939	560	66
1958	10,723	8,530	644				1,969	536	60
1959	10,054	6,856	738				1,977	582	56
1960	9,810	6,363	668				2,003	564	61
1961	7,176	5,068	514				1,865	544	50
1962	8,399	5,463	517				1,441	213	18
1963	7,987	5,278	1,447				1,687	315	9
1964	8,264	5,270	584	5,105	2,589	671	1,633	263	26
1965	8,275	5,052	519				1,773	260	18
1966	8,177	4,395	810				1,672	170	13
1967	6,933	4,489	458				1,813	225	11
1968	7,703	4,423	419				1,772	225	12
1969	8,668	4,518	546				1,860	204	13

Table 1 (Cont.)

1970	8,136	4,352	583	1,908	240	6
1971				2,025	210	4

Source: The original figures were collected by the religious offices in each state. This table is compiled from the works of Shirle Gordon "Marriage/Divorce in the Eleven States of Malaya and Singapore," *Intisari* 2, no. 2 (n. d.); Djamour, *Malay Kinship and Marriage in Singapore*; Teruyo Umeda, "Women in Malaya—A Report of Fieldwork in Kedah," *Southeast Asian Studies* 3, no. 5 (1966) (in Japanese); Narifumi Maeda, "The Changing Peasant World in a Melaka Village—Islam and Democracy in the Malay Tradition," (Ph. D. diss., University of Chicago, 1974); Tsubouchi, "Marriage and Divorce among Malay Peasants in Kelantan, Malaysia" *Southeast Asian Studies* 10, no. 3 (1972).

states. From 1931–1935 the divorce rate was 38.8 per 100 marriages in Melaka. And in the five years from 1951–1955 the rate per 100 marriages was 76.0 in Kelantan, 61.4 in Kedah, and 31.1 in Melaka.

As mentioned earlier the divorce rate in Melaka has been relatively low since early times. But from 1962 it showed a phenomenal decrease, and in 1966–1970 was only 11.8 per 100 marriages.[11] In contrast to Melaka, divorce traditionally has been common in Kelantan. Recently there has been a gradual decline in the divorce rate, though without the sharp drop seen in Melaka, and in 1966–1970 the divorce rate was 56.0 per 100 marriages. Nevertheless this is higher than the divorce rate in Melaka in the early 1930s. In Kedah it is not possible to ascertain trends clearly because of lack of data, but in 1964 the divorce rate per 100 marriages was 50.7, which suggests a gradual decline in recent years.

The divorce statistics also indicate the following differences. The percentage of *rojok* to divorce is highest in Kedah, and is relatively low in Kelantan and Melaka. In the period 1951–1955 the figures were 25.6 percent in Kedah,[12] 10.9 percent in Melaka, and 8.7 percent in Kelantan. This suggests that, in Kelantan, divorce tends to be carried through once the declaration has been made, while in Kedah the possibility of reconsideration and cancellation of the divorce is quite high. The figures for Melaka also suggest that divorce follows mature consideration by the couple. The differences may reflect that, in Kedah, consideration is given after the initial notification of divorce, and in Melaka, before; the former may be a phenomenon of an early stage in the decrease in divorce, the latter one of a late stage.

11. These figures are quite low, but they are higher than the figures for the same period in Japan. From 1966–1970 the percentage of divorce to all marriages in Japan was 9.0 percent.
12. Data for 1953 is lacking.

3.2. Marked differences were found in the incidence of divorce in the three villages. The percentage of divorces to marriages ever celebrated was 40.6 in Galok (Kelantan), 16.1 in Padang Lalang (Kedah), and 10.2 in Bukit Pegoh (Melaka). And as some residents were divorced more than once, one should also consider the percentages of ever-divorced people to ever-married people: 37.7 in Galok, 17.7 in Padang Lalang, and 7.2 in Bukit Pegoh.[13]

In Bukit Pegoh there were only thirteen reported cases of divorce among residents, so for more detailed comparisons I shall consider Galok and Padang Lalang, where there were many cases of divorce. Table 2 shows the percentage of ever-divorced to ever-married people on an age and sex basis. It is noticeable that in Padang Lalang data were often not available for women, but, assuming that women divorcees do not greatly outnumber men, and with one exception in a younger age group with few divorces, the percentage of ever-divorced to ever-married people is higher in Galok than in Padang Lalang. Table 3 shows the number of people ever-married by the number of divorces experienced. The number of people in Galok who have been divorced more than once is striking. Tables 4 and 5 show the number of divorces based on the duration of marriage and the number of children respectively. Because of the many uncertain cases in Padang Lalang it is difficult to make accurate comparisons, but from general trends the following seem true. The percentage of divorces occurring within the first year of marriage was higher in Galok at 28.4 and 24.8 for men and women respectively, compared with 13.1 and 12.5 in Padang Lalang. The percentage of divorces with children was 42.0 for men and 40.2 for women in Galok, and somewhat higher at 47.4 percent for men and 75.0 percent for women in Padang Lalang.[14] From this comparison one can say perhaps that a decrease in the incidence of divorce entails a decrease in the number of habitual divorcees and in the number of early divorces.

3.3. Here I will consider how marriage between relatives relates to the divorce trend in the three villages. In Bukit Pegoh divorce occurred in 5.6 percent of marriages between relatives, and this was low in comparison with 13.7 percent in marriages between nonrelatives. In Padang Lalang the rates of divorce were 7.3 percent in marriages between relatives, and 19.9 percent in marriages between nonrelatives, which,

13.　Cases of *rojok* are not treated as divorce.
14.　The gap in the figures for men and women in Padang Lalang can be attributed to a tendency for the women to omit divorces with no children when they are asked about divorce. It seems highly probable that many divorces with no children are included in the "not clear" category in Table 2.

TABLE 2
Number and Percentage of Ever-Divorced People, By Sex and Age-Group

Galok (Kelantan)

Age group	MALE			FEMALE		
	Ever married	Ever divorced	percent	Ever married	Ever divorced	percent
10–19	—			11	1	9.1
20–29	31	3	9.7	40	8	20.0
30–39	33	9	27.3	34	13	38.2
40–49	30	14	46.7	38	19	50.0
50–59	22	15	68.2	23	12	52.2
60–	16	10	62.5	19	8	42.1
Total	132	51	38.6	165	61	37.0

Padang Lalang (Kedah)

Age group	MALE				FEMALE			
	Ever married	Ever di-vorced	Not clear	percent	Ever married	Ever di-vorced	Not clear	percent
10–19					5		1	
20–29	29	3		10.3	57	10	4	17.5
30–39	58	7	1	12.1	61	7	3	11.5
40–49	37	8		21.6	31	6	2	19.4
50–59	23	5		21.7	32	6	7	18.8
60–	26	10	1	38.5	31	7	10	22.6
Total	173	33	2	19.1	217	36	27	16.6

although higher than in Bukit Pegoh, show a similar frequency relationship between the two types of marriage. In contrast, in Galok there was little difference between the two types, the divorce rate in marriages between relatives being 40.7 percent, and in marriages between non-relatives, 40.1 percent.

For marriages between first cousins the divorce rate is 0 in Bukit Pegoh, 1.9 percent in Padang Lalang, and 66.7 percent in Galok. The villagers, in each of the villages, mentioned that in cousin marriages the couple should find it easy to get on well, but should divorce follow then the relationship between the parents, who are siblings, might deteriorate. In Bukit Pegoh and Padang Lalang it appears that problems seldom

TABLE 3
DIVORCED PEOPLE BY NUMBER OF DIVORCES EVER EXPERIENCED

No. of divorces* ever experienced	GALOK (KELANTAN)		PADANG LALANG (KEDAH)	
	Male	Female	Male	Female
0	80	103	138	154
1	29	31	23	33
2	9	12	7	2
3	6	12	3	1
4	3	4		
5	1	2		
6	3			
Not clear	1	1	2	27
Total	132	165	173	217

*Excluding two cases of divorce through *pasah* in Galok. The figures for Padang Lalang are from Kuchiba's unpublished data.

TABLE 4
NUMBER OF DIVORCES BY DURATION OF MARRIAGE

DURATION	MALE		FEMALE	
	Galok	Padang Lalang	Galok	Padang Lalang
Less than 1 year	27	5	29	2
About 1 year	23	7	18	4
2	14	7	19	5
3	10	5	14	1
4	8		4	1
5	3	3	8	
6	1	1	8	
7	2		4	2
8	1	2	1	
9	0		3	1
10+	6	8	9	
Total	95	38	117	16

N.B. The cases which were not clear (5 for men in Galok, 11 for men in Padang Lalang and 23 for women in the latter) are not included in this table.

TABLE 5
DIVORCES BY NUMBER OF CHILDREN

No. of Children	MALE		FEMALE	
	Galok	Padang Lalang	Galok	Padang Lalang
0	58	20	70	4
1	28	12	33	11
2	8	2	9	1
3	4	3	4	
4	1	1	0	
5+	1		1	
Total	100	38	117	16

N.B. Unclear cases (11 for men and 23 for women in Padang Lalang) are not included in this table.

arise between couples who are first cousins, or that if they should arise means of reconciliation are often effective. In Galok this sort of solution seems not to work. Here there is a tendency to avoid marriage between first cousins for fear of divorce. In other words, as previously stated, the percentage of first-cousin marriages is much lower than in the other two villages; instead there are more marriages between more distant relatives, such as second cousins.

Data for the three villages on community endogamy were insufficient to throw any light on divorce. The data for Galok alone show that the divorce rate in intracommunity marriages was 28.6 percent and in extracommunity marriages 44.6 percent, indicating a trend for fewer divorces in intracommunity marriages.

DISCUSSION

4.1. Although the three villages have basically the same kinship structure, there are differences in the incidence of marriage and divorce between kin, including cousins. However, the fact that marriage with relatives is common cannot completely explain infrequency of divorce. As pointed out, the divorce rate between kin, together with that between nonrelatives is highest in Galok, lowest in Bukit Pegoh, and about in the middle in Padang Lalang. The evident lack of restraint on divorce between kin in Galok suggests that kin marriage and restraint are not essentially related. Marriages between first cousins in Bukit Pegoh and Padang Lalang involved strong restraint on divorce, but first cousin marriages accounted for only 18.1 percent and 9.7 percent, respectively, of all marriages in these villages. Thus marriage between cousins offers

TABLE 6
MARRIAGE AND DIVORCE AMONG MOSLEMS IN SINGAPORE

YEAR	MARRIAGES	DIVORCES	DIVORCES PER 100 MARRIAGES	YEAR	MARRIAGES	DIVORCES	DIVORCES PER 100 MARRIAGES
1921	2,055	1,133	55.1	1950	2,506	1,501	59.9
1922	2,073	1,239	59.8	1951	2,699	1,526	56.6
1923	2,113	1,205	57.0	1952	2,658	1,474	55.5
1924	3,089	1,285	41.6	1953	2,445	1,417	58.0
1925	2,616	1,311	50.1	1954	2,457	1,357	55.2
1926	2,633	1,335	50.7	1955	2,472	1,247	50.4
1927	2,554	1,466	57.4	1956	2,414	1,074	44.5
1928	2,556	1,421	55.6	1957	2,303	1,201	52.1
1929	2,469	1,428	57.8	1958	2,332	1,149	49.3
1930	2,307	1,366	52.9	1959	2,116	577	27.3
1931	2,177	1,264	58.1	1960	1,814	574	31.6
1932	2,084	1,277	61.3	1961	1,560	401	25.7
1933	2,006	1,260	62.8	1962	1,483	447	30.1
1934	2,163	1,132	52.3	1963	1,690	430	25.4
1935	2,070	1,159	56.0	1964	1,698	324	19.1
1936	2,039	1,182	58.0	1965	1,928	366	19.0
1937	2,320	1,208	52.1	1966	1,911	301	15.8
1938	2,065	1,241	60.1	1967	1,894	374	19.7
1939	2,014	1,145	56.9	1968	1,971	200	10.1
1940	2,213	1,249	56.4	1969	1,972	244	12.4
1941	2,440	1,267	51.9	1970	2,272	219	9.6
1942	2,949	1,139	38.6	1971	2,471	241	9.8

				1972	no data
					2,662
1943	3,582	1,705	47.6		
1944	2,907	2,165	74.5		
1945	2,982	2,046	68.6		
1946	3,095	1,734	56.0		
1947	2,784	1,588	57.0		
1948	2,605	1,545	59.3		
1949	2,516	1,401	55.7		

Sources: 1921–1964 Djamour (1959), p. 117 and Djamour (1966) p. 129, p. 183; 1965–1968 *Singapore Year Book 1968*, p. 80; 1969–1970 *Singapore 1971*, p. 262; and 1971–1972 *Singapore 1972*, p. 63, p. 265.

only a partial explanation of the low number of divorces in these two villages. According to Maeda, in Bukit Meta, a village adjacent to Bukit Pegoh, marriages between first cousins totaled 8.1 percent of all marriages, and those between kin (including first cousins) totaled 22.5 percent. These percentages are lower than in Bukit Pegoh and about the same as in Padang Lalang. In Bukit Meta divorce on the basis of all marriages was 7.5 percent and on the basis of ever-married people was 5.5 percent, lower than in Bukit Pegoh.[15] This also suggests that restraints on divorce between cousins and kin should not be over-emphasized.

The idea that community endogamy restrains divorce would be supported by findings that divorce is less frequent in intracommunity marriages than in extracommunity marriages in a particular community, but from this one cannot say that a low rate of community endogamy is always linked with a high divorce rate, or that a high rate of community endogamy is linked with a low divorce rate. This is clear from the fact that although the rate of community endogamy in Padang Lalang is lower than in Galok the divorce rate is also lower.

The differences in divorce rate in the three villages ultimately cannot be explained by differences in social structure or kinship structure; the effect of modernization of Muslim society must also be considered.

4.2. Comparison of the three villages, at any one time, and observation of the changes in the number of marriages and divorces by state (Table 1), indicate that while traditional Muslim society accepted the tolerance of divorce inherent in the kinship structure of the Malay people, the modern interpretation of Islam that discourages divorce is now taking effect.

Galok in Kelantan is thought to be representative of traditional Malay Muslim society, but can all of Kelantan be considered an area of traditional Muslim society? The investigations of the Firths in a fishing village on the coast of this state, and of Downs in a paddy-cultivating village in the district of Pasir Puteh indicate that divorce is common in those regions. The percentage of people who had married more than once was 82.6 percent for men and 80.0 percent for women in the fishing village (Firth) and 63 percent in the paddy-cultivating village (Downs).[16] These values include cases where the previous spouse

15. See Maeda, "Marriage with Near-Kin in a Malay Village, Melaka," pp. 493, 499.
16. Rosemary Firth, *Housekeeping among Malay Peasants*, 2d ed. (London: The Athlone Press, 1966), p. 28; Richard Downs, "A Kelantanese Village in Malaya," in *Contemporary Change in Traditional Societies*, vol. 2, "Asian Rural Societies," (Urbana, Ill.: University of Illinois Press, 1967), p. 144.

TABLE 7
MARRIAGES AND DIVORCES AMONG MOSLEMS IN INDONESIA
(IN THOUSANDS)

YEAR	MARRIAGES	DIVORCES	ROJOK	DIVORCES PER 100 MARRIAGES	ROJOK PER 100 DIVORCES
1950	1,276	629	43	49.3	6.8
1951	1,443	815	61	56.5	7.5
1952	1,310	783	59	59.8	7.5
1953	1,417	723	76	51.0	10.5
1954	1,383	735	56	53.1	7.6
1955	1,313	760	62	57.9	8.2
1956	1,086	584	42	53.8	7.2
1957	1,148	598	40	52.1	6.7
1958	1,242	672	49	54.1	7.3
1959	1,320	697	56	52.8	8.0
1960	1,254	654	55	52.2	8.4
1961	1,162	606	48	52.2	7.9
1962	1,036	593	45	57.2	7.6
1963	1,321	670	56	50.7	8.4
1964	1,130	613	46	54.2	7.5
1965	1,178	578	48	49.1	8.3
1966	1,097	513	37	46.8	7.2
1967	804	325	20	40.4	6.2
1968	1,042	468	24	44.9	5.1
1969	1,099	411	24	37.4	5.8
1970	854	298	11	34.9	3.7
1971	867	276	9	31.8	3.3
1972	989	303	10	30.6	3.3
1973	768	238	8	31.0	3.4
1974	785	217	8	27.6	3.7

Sources: *The Statistical Pocketbook of Indonesia*, each year from 1953–1963 and the 1970–1971, 1972–1973 and 1974–1975 editions.

had died so do not show only divorce, but are nevertheless higher than the corresponding values of 38.6 percent for men and 41.2 percent for women in Galok. These investigations took place in 1940 and 1958, respectively, in settlements quite far from a town. Even if the death rate were high, the traditional divorce trend was probably higher than in present-day Galok.

Conversely in the village of Kubang Benban in the same district as Galok, but adjacent to the town where the district office is situated, an investigation at about the same time as that in Galok showed the proportion of people who had been divorced to be fairly low at 26.8 percent

TABLE 8
MARRIAGE AND DIVORCE AMONG MOSLEMS IN INDONESIA

REGION	YEAR	MARRIAGES	DIVORCES	ROJOK	DIVORCE PER 100 MARRIAGES	ROJOK PER 100 DIVORCES
West Java	1953	355,170	217,237	17,763	61.2	8.2
	1964	245,081	152,029	13,047	62.0	8.6
	1970	223,457	81,423	2,893	36.4	3.6
	1972	255,229	83,099	2,909	32.6	3.5
	1974	209,900	68,353	2,881	32.6	4.2
East Java	1953	451,898	243,163	37,613	53.8	15.5
	1964	244,944	149,109	9,384	60.9	6.3
	1970	265,859	107,533	4,084	40.4	3.8
	1972	299,749	110,322	3,177	36.8	2.9
	1974	233,339	74,757	2,597	32.0	3.5
Central Java	1953	376,490	187,834	11,433	49.9	6.1
	1964	238,661	137,826	7,383	57.7	5.4
	1970	209,203	77,320	2,539	37.0	3.3
	1972	234,762	77,704	2,223	33.1	2.9
	1974	183,716	51,894	1,584	28.2	3.1
D. K. I. Jakarta	1953	28,623	11,706	1,194	40.9	10.2
	1964	32,434	12,981	1,397	40.0	10.8
	1970	26,340	4,971	259	18.9	5.2
	1972	27,239	3,833	173	14.1	4.5
	1974	20,603	2,485	112	12.1	4.5

	1953	30,933	11,796	460	38.1	3.9
	1964	4,426	3,225	63	72.9	2.0
D. I. Yogyakarta	1970	19,862	5,284	146	26.6	2.8
	1972	22,278	4,664	112	20.9	2.4
	1974	20,198	3,350	82	16.6	2.4

Sources: 1953 Djamour (1959), p. 135; 1964 Nugroho, *Indonesia, Facts and Figures* (Jakarta: Terbitan Pertjobaan, 1967), p. 175; 1970 *Statistical Pocketbook of Indonesia 1970 and 1971*, p. 43; 1972 *Statistical Pocketbook of Indonesia 1972 and 1973*, p. 70; 1974 *Statistical Pocketbook of Indonesia 1974 and 1975*, p. 54.

for men and 19.4 percent for women.[17] This shows that even in Kelantan gradual change is underway and that there is striking regional differentiation.

4.3. Change is not only taking place in Malaysia. Followers of Islam in Singapore (mainly Malays) and in Indonesia in recent years have registered a decrease in the number of divorces. Changes in numbers of marriages and divorces between Moslems in Singapore are shown in Table 6. The decrease in divorce in Singapore, even more than in Melaka, has been promoted institutionally, backed by the law reform of 1957 (effective from December, 1958) and the concomitant establishment of a matrimonial court.[18] The law was strengthened in 1966 to further restrict divorce. In comparison, the role of local Muslim leaders in Singapore has not been as great as in Melaka; although divorce is condemned as offending the will of God, in practice it is controlled by using the law.

In Indonesia, too, there have developed various movements to restrict divorce.[19] As Table 7 shows, a decrease in the number of divorces appeared from about 1965. Changes in numbers of marriages and divorces in Java by region (Table 8) show a remarkable decline in divorce in the cultural centres of Java, including the cities of Jakarta and Yogyakarta.

CONCLUSION

Divorce takes place in accordance with the values a society ascribes to the ties between husband and wife. These values can develop from the kinship structure peculiar to the society but may also enter independently from outside. The works of Gluckman (1950), Leach (1957), Fallers (1957), Ackerman (1963) and other anthropologists do not go beyond consideration of the relationship between group affiliation and the phenomenon of divorce.[20] In a society where values have come from

17. Yoshihiro Tsubouchi, "Two Villages in Kelantan—Peasants' Life in a Remote Village and One Near a Town," *Southeast Asian Studies* 2, no. 4 (1974) (in Japanese), p. 492.

18. On the matrimonial court in Singapore, see Judith Djamour, *The Muslim Matrimonial Court in Singapore* (London: The Athlone Press, 1966). On divorce in Singapore before this change, see Judith Djamour, *Malay Kinship and Marriage in Singapore* (London: The Athlone Press, 1959).

19. Compare, Clifford Geertz, *The Religion of Java* (Illinois: The Free Press of Glencoe, 1960), pp. 250f; S. Takdir Adisjahbana, *Indonesia: Social and Cultural Revolution* (London: Oxford University Press, 1966), p. 115; Justus M. Van der Kroef, *Indonesia in the Modern World* (Bandung: Masa Baru, 1954). Bruce Grant, *Indonesia* (Melbourne: Melbourne University Press, 1964), pp. 129ff.

20. Gluckman, "Kinship and Marriage among the Lozi of Northern Rhodesia and

outside, theories of structure and group affiliation can only explain relative differences within a settlement or region.

The kinship structure of the Malays freely permits divorce. And at the time when Islam entered the society this characteristic of the kinship structure must have been reflected directly in the phenomenon of divorce, which undoubtedly was quite common. Against this background Islam has served both to stimulate divorce and, contrarily, to limit it. In the former case, the interpretation of Islamic law which justifies divorce as an individual's action in God's name further facilitated divorce. In the latter case, the restraint on divorce should be explained by the response of Islam to a wave of modernization rather than by the simple idea that the elements of restraint are inherent in Islam. In this apparent contradiction one can see the adaptability of Islam, although this may well be a general feature of world religions that have survived a long period of man's history. However, in comparison with Catholicism, for example, one can probably say of family phenomena that Islam skillfully handles a great variety of situations. Here I have tried to substantiate this feature of Islam through its position vis-à-vis the phenomenon of divorce.

the Zulu of Natal"; Leach, "Aspects of Bridewealth and Marriage among the Kachin and Lakher"; Lloyd Fallers, "Some Determinants of Marriage Stability in Busoga: A Reformulation of Gluckman's Hypothesis," *Africa* 27, no. 2 (1957); Ackerman, "Affiliation: Structural Determinants of Differential Divorce Rates."

3

Authority and Leadership among the Orang Hulu

NARIFUMI MAEDA

INTRODUCTION

The purpose of this article is to provide an ethnographic description of leadership structure among the Orang Hulu, or Jakun, in the Malay Peninsula and to consider hamlet cohesiveness in comparison with the Malays. Fieldwork was conducted in 1965 through 1966 in Orang Hulu hamlets along the Endau River, which forms a section of the border between Pahang and Johor. Because this article constitutes a part of my ethnography of the Orang Hulu, information on such particulars as family, marriage, divorce, kinship, and economy has been omitted here.

IN THE HOUSEHOLD

Sa-kelamin, a family or household, is the basic unit among the Orang Hulu. Generally a single family, consisting of the conjugal couple and unmarried children, occupies a house. The wife and husband are equal; and neither seems to exercise authority over the other in a formal manner. There are several cases of marriage where the husband is younger than the wife or where a man marries, for the first time, a woman who has been married before. Even though the conjugal couple is an important unit of social activity, as seen from the word designating family, the mechanism uniting the spouses does not work strongly. For example, in resolving conflicts each spouse works with his or her consanguineal relatives; individual property is clearly separate; divorce and remarriage are simple processes and common practice.

The division of labor between the sexes is clear. In the house a wife is said to be "skipper" *nakhoda*[1] and is responsible for household

1. J. R. Logan, "The Orang Binua of Johore," *Journal of the Indian Archipelago and Eastern Asia* 1 (1847):273; Walter W. Skeat and Charles O. Blagden, *Pagan Races of the Malay Peninsula* (London: MacMillan & Co., 1906), p. 513.

matters, in which the husband rarely interferes. When a man has to move because of his work, his wife is expected to follow him, but this does not necessarily indicate her submissiveness to his will; rather, the motivation seems to be that of economic advantage. If the husband's job does not bring in enough money, the wife may decide not to go with him and even divorce him.

The spouses call each other by their personal names, and after the birth of a child by a teknonym. This contrasts with Malay couples who address each other in sibling terms, that is, except when using personal names, a husband calls his wife *adek* (or younger sibling) and she calls him *abang* (or elder brother). The affairs of the couple are strictly the business of the husband and wife, and nobody else is supposed to interfere. However, if a husband uses physical violence on his wife, the headman may fine him (in one case the fine was reportedly thirty-two Malaysian dollars). Either the husband or the wife may initiate a divorce, which differs from the Muslim practice of the Malays. There is no formal difference in the status of the first wife and the second.

Very young children are left to do what they want and are hardly ever scolded or beaten. Weaning a child may be postponed until it is five or six years old, if there are no younger siblings. Even an eight- or nine-year-old boy with younger siblings may sometimes ask for the mother's breast. Mothers may also feed their own, or adopted, children with canned milk. Some children develop the habit of sucking the teat of a feeding-bottle. Feeding is not regulated but is done whenever the baby cries. Parents rarely become angry with their children and, moreover, do everything possible to soothe an ill-tempered, fretful baby. A boy around the age of ten years may sometimes look after a baby, but usually only the father and elder brother play with the child. Like the Malays, the Jakun use a swing (*buai*), comprising a cradle of a cloth (*sarong*) which is folded and hung from beams, to soothe a crying baby or put him to sleep. While playing with a baby, adults often toy with the genitals, or hold the baby up to their face; but children over five or six years of age are taught to be ashamed of exposing themselves. Excretion is not strictly regulated during childhood. When a child grows older, however, he is taught by older friends to go to the riverside, into a field, or behind a bush for this function. The mother, who has more contact with the child, takes a greater part in disciplining him than the father, who tends to spoil him.

A boy (10 years old) who had quarreled with another was severely scolded by his mother because he did not consider the harmony of the hamlet. His father did not say anything although he was present.

A mother cut short the hair of her adopted daughter (12 years old) saying that she did not do her assigned work properly.

As the child grows older, though, the father takes on a fearsome aspect. This is especially true for boys who must learn to work in the jungle from their father. The father will often threaten them with the use of physical force—a threat which, incidentally, is seldom carried out. The mother continues to scold her children even when they are grown. On being rebuked, the child often accuses others or pretends ignorance of his wrongdoing in order to escape blame. If an adult treats a child unjustly, the child avoids him and becomes *rojok* (sulky).

A correspondence between the terms for siblings and their birth-order has not been discerned, as it has with the Malay and the Temiar.[2] Siblings are distinguished by relative age, the terms used being *bah* and *adek*, which mean older and younger sibling, respectively. Elder siblings prefer kinship terms to personal names in addressing their younger siblings. The younger address their elders either by personal names or by kinship terms, with no marked preference.

The eldest brother or the husband of the eldest sister is usually expected to look after the younger siblings when their father dies. This is reflected in several households which include a couple and one partner's unmarried siblings. The person who acts as father does not exercise any primogenital authority over the others in the household. He does not control them but only protects them. Further, the young are not explicitly disciplined to obey their elders. It is the older sibling whom everyone expects to take care of the younger. Even in daily life an elder sibling is always generous to a younger one and never forces the latter to give up anything he has.

THE RELATIVES

The sibling-tie is reflected in the sibling-in-law (*ipar*) relationships with the wider range of relatives. An individual has the authority to speak about and interfere in the affairs of his sibling's children. These relationships, directly derived from nuclear-family relationships, do not apply within the natal family but among the newly emerged families, which contain members of the original natal family.

There is no larger independent kinship group than the household. In crises, consanguineal and affinal kin may unite temporarily (occasional kin group). Since this gathering is centered on the concerned "ego," the range of the core kindred, or kindred in general, is not

---

2.   Geoffrey Benjamin, "Temiar Personal Names," *Bijdragen tot de Taal-, Land- en Volkenkunde* 24 (1968): 99–134, Table 2.

definite and will change if the "ego" is different. In such a gathering, no specific relative exercises leadership through formalized authority over the rest. It is said, however, that the opinion of the uncle is influential in matters concerning his niece or nephew.

Gerontocracy is not observed among relatives. The elders' opinion may be referred to for information on past customs, but it does not have any decisive power. Also, a relative with frequent contacts outside the hamlet will be regarded as a leading figure in the circle of his relatives. Although the subordinate-superordinate relation is not clearly formulated in the kinship system, there is some degree of obedience and reserve between *mentuha* (spouse's parent) and *menantu* (child's spouse) or between *ipar* (siblings-in-law). In these relationships, a "power semantic" pronoun is used, *aji* instead of the ordinary *hi*.[3]

INTEGRATION AND CONFLICT IN THE HAMLET

The Hamlet as a Territorial Group

A hamlet is a territorial group or a unit local-group composed of a related core-kin group, and other nonkin. No wider political organization is found. The population of a hamlet varies from fifty to a hundred and fifty. Several household units may live in a place separate from the original hamlet. Generally this group is the embryo of a new hamlet. As newcomers increase, it will gradually establish itself as a hamlet. Alternatively, it may be absorbed into another hamlet or just disappear if the original members leave. Even in its germination period, a hamlet has a recognized leader, usually of the central group of near kin.[4] The size of a hamlet is more or less a reflection of the size of the group that a leader can "take care of" or help.[5] If the size of a hamlet exceeds a certain limit, there is a high possibility of a conflict which may endanger the continuation of the hamlet.

As members of a hamlet are free to stay or leave as they wish, the attractiveness of the leader seems important in maintaining the hamlet at a certain size. Formally, an individual may leave one hamlet for

3. Roger Brown and Albert Gilman, "The Pronouns of Power and Solidarity," in Joshua A. Fishman, ed., *Readings in the Sociology of Language* (The Hague: Mouton, 1968), p. 254.

4. In the course of this research there was no case of disappearance or emergence of a hamlet; but this does not mean that the hamlets were stable. I have described an instance of instability elsewhere in Narifumi Maeda, "Economic Activity Among The Orang Hulu," Discussion Paper No. 23, (Center For Southeast Asian Studies, Kyoto University, 1971).

5. Minoru Kida, *Nippon Buraku* [Japanese villages] (Tokyo: Iwanami, 1967).

another without objection if he is dissatisfied with his headman, if his life is hard, if he is attracted by the reputedly good conditions in another hamlet, or for any other reason. But this freedom is, in fact, only verbal. Practically, the individual bent upon leaving will have to resist the persuasive efforts of the hamlet's headman and other inhabitants to get him to stay; after his departure, he will have to endure the accusation of being a fugitive. Moreover as a newcomer to another hamlet, he cannot expect to be treated as a full member of the community. His personal lack of involvement in the newly adopted community will be heightened by the fact that he will not have his own swidden plot until the next burning. If he moved without trouble, he is still entitled to harvest his cultivation at the former hamlet, or he may temporarily use part of a relative's or the headman's swidden at the new hamlet. A household which does not rely on swidden agriculture can change its residence with much less trouble. In every case of residence change, by far the most important factor is that at least one near relative should live in the new place of residence.

As seen earlier, the freedom of individuals to associate with the hamlet of their choice means that the headman does not have any authority or right to keep a reluctant member in his hamlet; this does not, however, mean that there are no restrictions on an individual's changing residence. At the same time there is no formal means to banish a member. Rumors, gossip, and other such "nuisance tactics" may be used to make remaining in the hamlet difficult for an undesirable. But whatever the case, the goal of the headman is the continued existence of the hamlet.

Batin, Headman

The headman of a hamlet is called a *batin*. The *batin* has control only his hamlet. His role as leader of the hamlet is to settle disputes among individuals of the hamlet, to set dates for important occasions in the hamlet, and to officiate at these affairs. Also, he is expected to act as the hamlet's agent or representative in the outside world. Thus he: (1) deals with other hamlets, (2) negotiates with Malay or Chinese strangers, (3) is the government's representative in the hamlet, (4) transmits the residents' will to the government. According to Syed Husin,[6] the traditional Malay *penghulu* (village headman) had three roles: (1) representative of the *sultan*, (2) representative of the government, (3) leader and spokesman of his *anak buah* (villagers). The *batin's*

---

6. Syed Husin Ali, "Patterns of Rural Leadership in Malaya," *Journal of the Malayan Branch of the Royal Asiatic Society* 41 (1968): 128–129.

role is quite similar to that of *penghulu* as mediator between the upper governmental agencies and the local populace; but the method of appointment, social status, and size of the administration of these two 'administrators' are, of course, different.

The *batin*'s most important function within the hamlet is to settle conflicts, which may range from daily trivialities to criminal cases of homicide. J. R. Logan, who traveled up the Endau River, reports on the *adat* law of Orang Hulu as follows:

> Offences against property or person are, from the mildness of the people, of very rare occurrence. Crimes of all kinds may be expiated by the payment of fines, which are invariably imposed, not in coins, of which very few reach their hands, but in coarse Chinese plates or saucers (*pingan*). Adultery is punishable by a fine of from 10 to 20 pingan according to circumstances; theft the same; murder, which however seems to be almost unknown, 60 pingan. One-half of the fine goes to the Batin and the other half to the injured person. If the offender fail to deliver the pingan he becomes the slave of the latter. Complaints are enquired into by the Batin, who assembles a number of the elders and consults with them. The Batin is considered to be responsible for any property that is stolen. But he cannot convict the thief without confession or direct evidence of the theft. No regular tax is paid to the Batins. But presents are frequently made to them.[7]

The aborigines of Malaya have been characterized as "timid" rather than "peaceful" by the nineteenth-century intellectual Munshi Abdullah bin Kadir,[8] as well as by the contemporary anthropologist Robert Dentan in his book *The Semai: A Nonviolent People of Malaya*.[9] In this respect, the Orang Hulu do not usually take an aggressive attitude toward outsiders, as Logan has correctly reported. However, I personally heard a story that a *batin* of the Anak Endau had been slain, and his position usurped by his younger brother. The Orang Hulu know that present-day criminal cases are handled by Malaysian law.

The *hadat* (*adat*, in Malay), customary law, consists of 'historically transmitted sayings', which categorize normative behavior to which the people are expected to conform. Those who deviate from the *hadat* are expected to be punished in one way or another. On the occurrence of a serious event, the persons concerned gather together at the *batin*'s house, or at an assembly hall if there is one, and discuss the matter

7. Logan, "The Orang Benua of Johore," p. 274.
8. Abdullah bin Kadir, *The Story of the Voyage of Abdullah Munshi*, trans. Arthur E. Coope (Singapore, 1949).
9. (New York: Holt, Rinehart & Winston, 1968).

thoroughly in order that the *batin* can settle it according to the *hadat*. Nowadays, the *batin* penalizes the accused in cash rather than in kind. The *hukum* (Juridical decision) of the *batin* may differ from hamlet to hamlet, and if the litigants are from different hamlets, they will informally inquire beforehand about the *hukum* of the hamlet involved. However, there seem to be no physically coercive authorities or agents to exercise whatever punishment may be decided upon. Formerly, as reported by Logan, those who did not pay the fine had to serve as an *ulor* (slave). Now the ultimate sanctions of the law are unfavorable social opinion, *malu* (shame), and supernatural retribution. In Endau the ultimate sanction is not respect toward one's ancestors, as it is with the Ambon.[10]

One source of the *batin's* authority may be recognition by the government, but the authority of the government does not always personally affect the Orang Hulu. Even the police, unless they actually exercise force, are considered powerless in some critical situations. In one case, a *batin* threatened a young defendant of another hamlet who would not appear in spite of his summons by saying that he would ask the police to arrest him (although he was only accused of twice sending love-letters to a girl in the *batin's* hamlet). The defendant heard of the *batin's* anger and of the alleged police arrest, but did not show up. After some delay and persuasion from his one of his *wali* (guardians), he finally came.

The Orang Hulu proudly declare that they never take another person's belongings without consent, unlike the Malays who, they say, shamelessly steal the property of the Orang Hulu. Any theft in the Orang Hulu community is soon revealed, because the group is small enough for everyone's activities to be known in detail. In spite of the Orang Hulu's statement, theft hardly seems rare, and I was warned in one hamlet to beware of a lightfingered person. During my stay in the hamlet, the news spread that a young man from there had been apprehended for theft from a Chinese shop in the town of Keluang. This did not cause any problem within the hamlet when that person returned, because it happened outside the hamlet; there was no victim nor any positive proof of the accusation in the hamlet.

I have already dealt with the customary laws on adultery or fornication, incest, marriage, divorce or inheritance in another paper.[11] In brief, the role of *batin* in these cases is to mediate and confirm the

---

10. Frank L. Cooley, *Ambonese Adat: A General Description* (New Haven, Conn.: Yale University, Southeast Asia Studies, 1962).

11. Maeda, "Marriage and Divorce among the Jakun (Orang Hulu) of Malaya." *Tonan Ajia Kenkyu* [Southeast Asian Studies] vol. 6, no. 4 (Kyoto University, 1969): 740–757.

marriage contract, approve divorce, supervise the division of property, and so on. The customary fees and fines are transmitted through him.

Sanctions against those who deviate from custom consist of fines which the *batin* decides following the *hadat*. Here he is required to be very cautious so as to deliver a decision acceptable to both the plaintiff and the defendant; otherwise, one party may protest the judgment, or the decision may not be carried out. To decide a case satisfactorily, the *batin* needs to use tact, as well as various stratagems and artifices, to maneuver the elders into agreement and to avoid dissent.

The general pattern of the litigational process may be outlined as follows: Prior to any formal action, informal debate takes place among the hamlet members. Sympathizers of both parties will gather to argue and discuss the issue. The *batin* visits the homes of the people involved to hear their opinions and may informally express his own view for the two parties' consideration. The litigants and other interested hamlet members then repair to the *batin*'s home, where they exchange views and attempt a settlement. This continues for as long as it is considered necessary or possible. Then the *batin* will open a formal hearing (*buka kes*), summoning the persons concerned and their relatives. This tribunal in fact, may be demanded by the plaintiff, in which case the *batin* must decide upon its necessity and date. At the tribunal, the relatives of the concerned parties usually speak for them. When the public hearing is over, the *batin* delivers his decision, which is regarded as the final judgment on the matter. The judgment cannot be changed within the hamlet, which the *batin* controls. If the decision is unsatisfactory to one of the parties, they may leave that hamlet, or attempt to marshal enough public opinion to force the *batin* to retire.

Other important roles of the *batin* include setting the date for and supervising such various important hamlet activities as choosing a new swidden plot, deciding when to begin clearing it, when to start the harvest, and when to "clean" the hamlet.

There is no cooperative land clearing or labor exchange system. Instead, the labor unit in agriculture is the household. However, when they clear new land or harvest crops, all members of the hamlet participate in the activities at the beginning, partly for magical reasons. The Muslim Malays ask a magico-functionary, *pawang*, to purify places for new clearings or housebuilding and to protect the village from disaster and disease, as well as to offer prayers for productivity. The *pawang*-ship is regarded as a speciality.[12] Distinguished from other hamlet

12.   Husin, "Patterns of Rural Leadership in Malaya," p. 110; Richard Downs, "A Kelantanese Village of Malaya," in J. H. Steward, ed., *Contemporary Change in*

members, the *pawang* among the Orang Hulu is said to be a magician with special power to appease the *jin bumi*, or Earth Spirit.[13] The difference between him and the *bomoh*, curer, is not one of quality but of degree. Generally, the *batin* is expected to be a *pawang*. Originally, the roles of the *batin* mentioned earlier were mostly those of the *pawang*. The *pawang* is a mediator between this world and the supernatural one; in this world the *batin* is supreme so the final say is in the *batin*'s hands. This fact becomes important when a *batin* does not act as *pawang*, or when there are several *pawang* in a hamlet. Actually, all *batin* in the hamlets studied are *pawang*.

Purification of the hamlet (*bela kampong*), which is reported in Singapore and among the Endau Malays,[14] is held by the *batin* once a year to protect the hamlet from devils and to keep the people in health and prosperity. That day, which is called *hari besar batin* (the *batin*'s big day), must be celebrated with a feast provided by the *batin*. Unlike the Ambonese, the Orang Hulu do not actually sweep the village.[15] All the members of the hamlet must return for this feast from wherever they are working so the *batin* and his *anak buah* can see the unity of the hamlet. Most of the expenses for the feast will be met by the *batin*, who also decides the proper date for it.

The *batin* is the sole political functionary.[16] It is said that formerly there were the hierarchical ranks of *setia*, *jekerah* or *jerukerah*, above the *batin*, and *pemangkoh*, below him.[17] The Besisi, as reported by Skeat, kept a hierarchy of positions, namely, *batin*, *jinang*, *jukrah*, *penghulu*, *panglima*. The Bermun, according to Logan, were much more stratified, and the Mintira [=Temuan] had, in hierarchical order, positions of *batin*, *jinang*, *jukra* (*jorokra*), *panglima* and *ulubalang*.[18] In the present Proto-Malay resettlement near the town of Rompin, the title *jurukera* is used to designate a person who knows a lot about marriage customs,

     Traditional Societies vol. 2, (Urbana: University of Illinois Press, 1967): 169; W. W. Skeat, *Malay Magic* (London: MacMillan & Co., 1900); R. J. A. Wilkinson, *A Malay-English Dictionary*, (London: Macmillan & Co., 1959).

13. Reported by Logan as *poyang* in "The Orang Binua of Johore," p. 275.

14. I. H. N. Evans, *Studies in Religion, Folk-lore, and Custom in British North Borneo and the Malay Peninsula* (London, 1923), pp. 279–280; Judith Djamour, *Malay Kinship and Marriage in Singapore* (London: The Athlone Press, 1959).

15. *See* Cooley, *Ambonese Adat: A General Description*, pp. 60–62.

16. Exceptionally, a new *batin* at Peta appointed his relative as a deputy under the title of *wakil*.

17. For example, fines for *pakai tuju* (marriage in collusion) differed according to status: *setia*, M$25; *jekerah*, M$16; *tuha* (elders), M$8; *periman* (commoner) M$6.

18. Logan, "The Orang Binua of Johore," p. 275.

etc. The people on the upper Rompin River do not know any title other than *batin*. The Semelai, a Senoi group living in the western part of the Tasek Bela, have similar titles that are granted to each of the settlement heads without any connotation of hierarchy. Such titles, according to a Malay officer, are an arbitrary adoption of the Malay style. The hierarchical titles reported by Skeat and Logan originated in Malay, except for *batin* and *jekerah*. I doubt that the Endau Orang Hulu originally had their own refined hierarchical system.

The legends of the Orang Hulu say that they are descendants of Raja Benua, a younger sister of the Sultan of Johor, who renounced the world and lived in the jungle, adopting a boy and later marrying him. She ruled the Orang Hulu, living at Temehel on the upper Madek River. Her tomb is believed to be on the bank of the Meliam River. Her offspring (*chuchu, chechet, uneng,* and *piot*) dispersed throughout the area. Some of them settled along the Mentelong, a branch of the Endau, where her fourth-generation descendants are said to have lived until recently. (This is based on the information of a *batin* in Jorak; the legends of Raja Benua are found in Hervey and in Miklucho-Maclay.)[19] Hervey states that a queen of Johor, having been obliged by her enemies to flee into the interior, remained there and married a Jakun chief. Their offspring assumed the title of Raja "Beniak." Miklucho-Maclay also mentioned Raja Benua people who were not Mohammedans (though Malays) and whose settlement he had found at Tanjong Genting on the Kahang River. The *batin*-ship seems to have been inherited by the agnate of the *batin*, that is, the descendants of *suku Benua* or *suku saka* [*sakat?*] *batin*, along the Endau. Some claim that if someone other than this *suku saka* assumes the position of *batin* he will fail in his administration.[20] However in the instances studied, only one in four succeeded to his father's position.

The appointment of a new *batin* is discussed after the death or retirement of the incumbent. In considering a successor, the important issue is whether everybody will obey him. Other concomitant conditions are minor. Among the Land Dayak, wrote Geddes,[21] there are three conditions for *tua kampong* (village headman): (1) kinship relations to previous chiefs, (2) age—several years of marriage, but not too old,

19. D. F. A. Hervey, "The Endau and Its Tributaries," *Journal of the Royal Asiatic Society, Straits Branch* 8 (1881): 12. N. von Miklucho-Maclay, "Ethnological Excursion in the Malay Peninsula," *Journal of the Royal Asiatic Society, Straits Branch* 2 (1878): 219–220.

20. An informant explained the death of the former *batin* of Peta by the fact that he was not a *suku saka batin*.

21. W. R. Geddes, *The Land Dayaks of Sarawak* (London: H.M.S.O., 1954).

and (3) wealth, preferably accumulated personally. Conditions (1) and (2) also apply in the Orang Hulu. Concerning condition (3), the Orang Hulu do not believe that good luck necessarily accompanies riches, but to be considered richer than others is important. Besides these three conditions, the *batin* should be an efficient medicine man, a political tactician, and a good speaker. Skeat reported that *batin* had insignia,[22] but I did not find any symbols peculiar to *batin*-ship. In some hamlets a gong is hung outside the *batin*'s house or at the end of the hamlet in order to inform people of danger. This gong (*sentawa*), while magically important, cannot be considered an emblem of the *batin*.

Batin are considered persons who do not express biased opinions and who are reasonable. If a *batin* does wrong, it is thought that he will die. Indeed, people hesitate to become *batin* because the role is felt to be quite difficult. As the *batin*'s authority relies mainly on verbal persuasion, he needs to be reasonable and intelligent enough to have insight into people's minds and to convince elders, who sometimes express contrary opinions behind his back. The more eloquent and charismatic he is, the more he is relied upon. As *primus inter pares*, he has the right to collect and distribute appropriately all fines, and to take some portion of them. He is in a good position to accumulate wealth, since not only fines but most gifts from inside and outside the hamlet go through him. He is proud of being a *batin*, a difficult office which takes ultimate responsibility for *hadat*.[23]

The *batin* can resign of his own volition or be forced to resign (*jatoh*, to fall down) by the complaints of the people. Conversely a clever *batin* may use resignation as a weapon of persuasion. *Batin* who have resigned are called *batin tuha* which means 'elder *batin* who do not have any power'.

In brief, succession to *batin*-ship is "generational" rather than "periodic," restricted to males, and open to those who have the required qualities. Succession usually takes place on the death of the incumbent, but retirement also often happens owing to disagreement within a hamlet; there is no rotation of office and no recognized provision for retirement.[24]

Conflicts within a Hamlet

Since *batin* act as spokesmen in external affairs, outsiders are easily

22. Skeat and Blagden, *Pagan Races of the Malay Peninsula*, p. 95.
23. Edmund Leach, "The Law as a Condition of Freedom." in D. Bidney, ed., *The Concept of Freedom in Anthropology* (The Hague: Mouton, 1963), p. 86.
24. Raymond Firth, *Essays on Social Oranizations and Values* (London: University of London, 1964).

led to regard him as a powerful ruler in the hamlet who can do anything he wants. But, as is clear from the previous section, his primary activities are those of arbitrating conflicts and trying to maintain village unity.

A latent conflict will be observed in the talk, exaggerated and distorted, of people when they are visiting one another (*juros*). Gossip, which is spread mainly by women, is important as a means of expressing personal opinions or complaints and as a means of rallying personal support. It seems to function as an informal mechanism to reduce tensions. If a specific piece of gossip continues or is spoken intentionally in the hearing of the opponents, tension becomes quite high.

As seen in relatives' speculations on marriage and divorce, economics is of vital concern and often a source of conflict. The man who accumulates wealth and uses it to entertain generously can gain prestige and power. Those who appear to hoard their wealth are envied. A good collector and recipient should at the same time be a good distributor, particularly if he is a *batin*. From this point of view, the manager of a small store is getting unfair gain without "labor" and also without redistributing it to his fellows. A retailer in Jorak, for instance, is regarded as a cheat, and is the object of animosity because he takes money from people in the community in the same way as retailers in town, although his profit is actually very minimal. He is an old Chinese who has lived in the jungle as an ordinary Orang Hulu for more than 'twenty' years. The management of the store is handled by his wife who is Orang Hulu. The envy and hostility, in this case, are more or less directed at his wife, particularly by her opponent, an ally of the *batin*'s wife. In time, the hamlet has divided into two groups, camouflaging the real conflict with the issue of the unfair gain of the store. From one side came rumors that the storekeeper's wife practiced black magic and was of loose morals; from the other, it was spread about that the ally of the *batin*'s wife was extravagant, among other things. The *batin* did not apparently side with either party. This issue ended with the shopkeeper's removal to another area.

There is a distinction between those Orang Hulu who have contact with the outside world and those who do not. The former mix with Chinese and Malays and generally speak Malay fluently, although they do not easily convert to Islam. An extreme example of this is a man in Kahang, who lives as much in the Malay style as he possibly can. On the one hand, persons with good outside contacts and news are looked to for counsel; on the other, they may become the objects of hostility and jealousy. Another apparent distinction between these two groups is their pattern of residence in a hamlet. The more extrovert group lives in *ayer* ('water', that is along the river); the more introvert dwells in *darat* or *dalam* ('interior', clearings away from the bank). This pattern is especially clear in Jorak and has attitudinal implications, because in one sense, this division within a hamlet may be said to show a split between those who prefer association with the outside and those who do not. At the moment there are no hostile relations between these two groups but the possibility of a division is ever-present. Most of today's hamlets are situated on riverbanks, but it is said that the Orang Hulu were formerly so timid that they settled in the interior, four or five miles from the bank.

CONFLICTS AND INTEGRITY AMONG HAMLETS

The Orang Hulu along the Endau River regard themselves as belonging to one society, distinguishing themselves from the Orang Hulu of the other rivers. But actually there is no unity between hamlets except that they speak a similar dialect and are in frequent contact with each other.

The *batin* of Denai once remarked, "All hamlets are of one stock, but their minds differ from each other. That is the reason why we do not make one nation." In other words, in spite of a common territorial consciousness, the hamlets are rivals. The rivalry of the hamlets is reflected in the rivalry among *batin*. Most *batin* will readily tell his *anak buah* or outsiders how other *batin* do wrong or how other hamlets are worse, for example, one is unable to control his fellow men, another is occupied only with his own interests, and another is of loose morals, still another will do anything for money. They also say another hamlet's houses are built in a disorderly fashion; the place is dirty; there are too many mosquitos; the women disreputable, etc. The conflicts between hamlets do not really consist in antagonistic personal relations between the inhabitants; rather they result from the maneuvers of the *batin* to retain control. The residents, of course, support such actions to justify their residence under the *batin*.

Presently, there is no council composed of all the *batin*; nor is any formal ranking of the *batin* observable. The hamlet seems to be the minimal and maximal governmental unit for Orang Hulu. As *batin* do not have any authority over other hamlets, incidents involving more than two hamlets must be discussed and dealt with between *batin*. The people appear to rank *batin* informally with regard to their ability to deal with the outside world, the size of their hamlets, or their knowledge of *hadat*. A *batin* who is highly regarded influences other *batin* through his eloquent discourse and tactics. Batin Jamil of Jorak is said to rank first, Batin Ali second, and Batin Yusop third. Batin Tian of Peta is not ranked since he is newly appointed. Jamil's hamlet 'branched-out' of Yusop's father's hamlet while the elder man was still alive and *batin*. His behavior and talk are consistent and rational, and he is courageous (*berani*) enough to ask the government for what the Orang Hulu want and demand that it fulfills its promises to them. At the same time, his reputation as a magician is such that gossips of other hamlets say that he practices black magic. The foster father of *batin* Jamil, Jering, who is also the real grandfather of Yusop, is said to have ruled seven rivers—the Lengo, the Kemapan, the Kenchen, the Pemango, the Lalu, and the Kemedah. Jamil always emphasizes this fact to outsiders, especially government officers, hinting that he is entitled to become Great Batin over all the Endau. When Jamil says "father," he means Jering. The relation between Jamil and Yusop is assumed to be that of uncle and nephew. Yusop, ignoring this foster relation, treats Jamil as *abang* (elder brother), that is, as one elder than him in the same generation, following actual genealogy.

In the nineteenth century, the situation seems to have been different:

> The highest in rank and in nominal authority is the Batin Onastia, the descendent of the ancient Raja Binua. On the Indau [Endau] below the junction of the Simrong and Anak Indau resides the Batin Hamba Raja. The Linggo, a branch of the Indau, is under the Batin Stia Raja who is also the great executive officer; his relation to the Batin Onastia having some resemblance to that between the Malayan Temungong and Sultan of Johore. The Sungi Sly [Selai] is subject to the Batin Singa Dewa. The Simrong [Semberong] in the vicinity of Tanjong Bonko is under the Batin Stia Bati, higher up near Gagau to the Batin Jokra, and still nearer its source to Batin Dewa Kosuna and the Batin Bantara. All these, except the two last, are within the Pahang [Johor] boundary. .... Each Batin has absolute authority within his own jurisdiction, but he refers difficult or unusual cases to a council composed of all the Batins, excepting the Onastia; and matters in which all the Binua [Orang Hulu] are concerned appertain to the same council. Their deliberations are said to be sometimes very prolonged, particularly in affairs of novelty when their knowledge of the old *hadat* does not afford them any precedents.[25]

Misspellings, or incorrect identification, of the names of places and rivers apart, it is not clear whether the titles mentioned were hereditary or just assumed Malay-style titles. We do not know anything about Batin Onastia [Skeat explains it as *Anak Setia, ona + stia* (?)] whose location Logan does not mention and which later travelers to the

25. Logan, "The Orang Bunua of Johore," pp. 273–274.

Endau did not mention. It is also strange that Batin Onastia was excluded from the council of *batin*. At any rate, it is clear that six or seven *batin* established their hamlets along the Endau and Semberong rivers, and that there was some hierarchical relation among them. It is also possible to conjecture that the heads of 'branch' hamlets assumed such titles as the Semelai did. A connection is suggested here with the legend of the foster father of *batin* Jorak who ruled seven rivers.

In any case, it is not necessary to ascertain a rigid and formal subordination and superordination; informal influence through counsel, or warning, among *batin* is clear in present as well as former times. In spite of mutual internal antagonism, there is a strong feeling of group identity among the Orang Hulu as a group separate from the outside world. This identification is reinforced by their consciousness of being an exploited group as well as by kinship and territorial ties.

SUBORDINATE RELATIONS WITH THE OUTSIDE WORLD

For the Orang Hulu the outside world is the whole non-Orang Hulu population of the known universe. Contacts between the Orang Hulu and other ethnic groups are not new; in the nineteenth century they were brought into contact with Malay peddlers, Malay officers, Western travelers and explorers, and a few Chinese settlers. In the twentieth century, more speculators came into the jungles.

The major historical events for the Orang Hulu are: (1) the Japanese crossing of the Endau and march on Keluang during World War II, (2) the Communist uprising and guerilla war, and (3) the mining activity at the foot of Tanah Abang hill. These events are not very helpful in determining a person's exact age but they are very important in the sense that it was these events which brought the greater part of the Orang Hulu population into contact with the outside world.

Gaamén (government)

In the early part of the nineteenth century, Logan wrote:

> The boundary between Pahang and Johore intersects the country of the Binua; the whole of the Anak Indau, and the lower part of the Simrong being in Pahang, and all the other rivers, including the Made, on which they are found appertaining to Johore. The authority of the Bindahara and the Temungong is little more than nominal, the affairs of the Binua being entirely administered by their own chiefs, each of whom has a definite territorial jurisdiction.[26]

26. Logan, "The Orang Bunua of Johore."

Administratively, the Orang Hulu were subordinate to the Bendahara in Pahang State and to the Temunggong in Johor State but were left alone because of the inaccessibility of their territory. At present the situation is the same in that they belong to the sultan of each state, but in practice the newly established Department of Aboriginal Affairs (*Jabatan Orang Asli*) administers their affairs and protects them. The *batin*, after being selected by the people, gets a certificate and 'pocket money' of forty Malayan dollars per year from the government. Legally, he may be deposed by the state government. Generally, he is endowed with certain limited rights within his hamlet, including the prerogative to exploit jungle reserves within government-designated areas. No duties such as taxes are levied on the Orang Hulu. (See The Aboriginal Peoples Ordinance, 1954, Federation of Malaya Government, Kuala Lumpur.)

A field assistant from the Department of Aboriginal Affairs supervises several aboriginal settlements and conveys messages and orders from the government to the people as well as demands from the people to the government, through the *batin*. The field assistant in charge of the Endau settlements on the Johor side is a Malay who lives in the town of Padang Endau. He goes on a tour of inspection once or twice a month to all of the five hamlets along the river. In addition to this routine he guides his superior during inspection tours, transports government-supplied goods, and transmits necessary information to the hamlets. Usually, he keeps in close touch with every *batin*. Criminal cases such as bodily injury or theft, and critical events such as death, birth, and moving to another site should be reported to the field assistant or to any police officer, although there is a general distrust of police and government. Licences to cut rattan, lumber, etc. in the jungle reserve are obtained through the assistant on behalf of the people.

Sometimes the *batin* may report a matter within the jurisdiction of traditional law, if it becomes too difficult to deal with. The *batin* may use the authority of the government, which is backed by economic power, as an instrument in the hamlet's politics. On the other hand, he may conceal an incident from the field assistant to preserve the hamlet's customs; for example, he might not report an illness when the sufferer is treated by a hamlet medicineman. Generally speaking, hamlet residents are completely under the headman's control in their relations with the outside world, and the government official does not interfere in the *batin*'s customary sphere of influence.

Official contact with the external world, then, is the tenuous relation between the field assistant and the *batin*. The *penghulu* (Malay village head) of Padang Endau does not concern himself with Orang

Hulu affairs. The District Office of Mersing, whose jurisdiction Endau is under, only pays the *batin*'s pocket money.

The attitude of the Orang Hulu toward the governmental officials is not one of humility; indeed, the aborigines ask for what they need as if they had an unquestionable right to do so. Since the Orang Hulu have been much exploited, the only thing they expect from an alien is whatever they can obtain by asking (*minta*), as a sort of revenge for past exploitation. "We never steal, we just request," said a *batin*. Conventionally, one who does not have a thing sometimes has the right to ask for it from someone who does, and it is natural for the latter to give it. However, when this relation of have and have-not involves an Orang Hulu and an outsider, the latter feels the request (*minta*) to be unpleasant. Among the Orang Hulu distinction is drawn between goods which can be asked for without consideration and those which are exchanged for a consideration. Toward non-Orang Hulu persons this distinction does not apply: they ask for purchased goods without consideration. This should be distinguished from the attitude of the Orang Hulu within their moral order.[27] Many of the Orang Hulu neglect the rules of the hamlet when dealing with outsiders.

It seems that the Orang Hulu do not fully recognize the government as their ally, and there is some degree of mutual distrust.

Tauke (Chinese employer)

Logan wrote as follows about trade monopoly in the nineteenth century:

> The Malay local authority—who, in matters of Government, has a nominal power, and whose relation to the Binuas is properly that of maintainer and regulator of the Malayan monopoly of their trade—is denominated To Jinang. The Binuas on the Batu Pahat and its branches are under the Bintara or Manki Pimang-gun of Boko. The jurisdiction of the Malayan Penghulu of Batu Pahat extends to Ginting Batu on the eastern Simrong, but, since the water communication became obstructed, the To Jinang of the Indau has engrossed the trade of the Johore portion of the Simrong.[28]

The title *Jinang* or *Jenang* is unknown among the Malays in Padang Endau and the present *penghulu* never trade with the Orang Hulu. Legally any person who is not an aborigine is required to get permission to enter an aboriginal territory, but there are no strict restrictions on commerce or trade in the area. At present it is not Malays but Chinese middlemen who control the Orang Hulu economically. Although the

27.   Maeda, "Economic Activity among the Orang Hulu."
28.   Logan, "The Orang Bunua of Johore."

Orang Hulu do not imagine they are subordinate to the *tauke*, the latter treat them as their laborers. Feasts or weddings are postponed if the *tauke* is reluctant to make the loan to cover expenses. Moreover, most of the Orang Hulu are forced to work for the dealer because they are constantly in debt to him. In a sense the Chinese is an employer of the Orang Hulu. Other Chinese merchants in Padang Endau just receive them as good customers.

Melayu (Malay)/*Sakai* (subjects)

As Favre noted in 1848, " . . . the Jakuns hate the Malays, and the Malays despise the Jakuns."[29] The two groups do not constitute one community in spite of the similarity of physical and linguistic character-istics. Though I do not have enough data to ascertain why the Orang Hulu never converted, and do not want to convert, to Islam (a fact which distinguishes the Orang Hulu from the Malays), presumably historical and ecological factors play an important role in hindering conversion. If we suppose that the aborigines were living in the interior of the country at the time when Islam entered the Malay Peninsula (around the thirteenth century),[30] it seems probable that they would have come to know Islam later than the coast-dwellers, while those living in inaccessible territory would not have known Islam until quite recently. Differences in way of life and habitation as well as economic exploitation made the aborigines *sakai*, dependants or retainers, of the Malay. So the aborigines are still called *Orang Sakai* by Malays, though officially neutral term *Orang Asli* has been used since the war. The attitude developed that the *sakai* are neither Malay nor Muslim. Thus it became convenient for the Malays to exploit them, treating the inhabitants of the interior as non-Malays.

At present the Orang Hulu consciously defy the Malays in daily life, mocking Malay prayer, and despising them as untrustworthy and blameworthy. On the other hand, the Malay style of life prevails among the younger Orang Hulu in their dress and wedding customs. The model is not Chinese but Malay. A wave of modernization has come with 'Malayization' for the Orang Hulu.

Guru (teacher)

There are primary schools at Labong and Mentelong, but no children from other hamlets attend them. This does not indicate a lack of enthusiasm for education in the other hamlets. On the contrary,

29. P. Favre, "An Account of the Wild Tribes Inhabiting the Malayan Peninsula, Sumatra and a Few Neighboring Islands," *Journal of the Indian Archipelago and Eastern Asia* 2 (1848): 272.
30. Q. Fatimi, *Islam Comes to Malaysia* (Singapore: MSRI, 1963).

the children in these places are very keen to study the alphabet and well know that they can expect better treatment with an education. In spite of this eagerness, parents do not let their children go to other hamlets to study because the children are regarded as an important source of labor. The people themselves explain that the parents are so attached (*sayang*) to their children that they cannot stand separation from them. Instead, they demand that the government builds a school in their own hamlet. It is, however, unpractical for the government to build schools in every hamlet, because of the small populations and the future likelihood of people changing their residence.

During the research period, a new school was built in Jorak and was officially opened in 1966. In 1968 there were twenty-five pupils, all young children. The level of education is equivalent to the first grade of the Malay Primary School. The pupils get uniforms, shoes, textbooks, notebooks, etc. free. Two teachers (*guru, che'gu*) from Padang Endau rotate on a three-month basis. During their period of teaching, the teachers live alone in the teacher's house next to the school. They do not seem to mix with the Orang Hulu in spite of their priviledged position of being allowed to stay in the hamlet and teach children. There are several reasons for this. First, the language problem plays an important part. The teachers' command of the language is quite limited since they never learn the Orang Hulu dialect thoroughly, due to the short duration of the teaching period. Second, they are perhaps not very positive in their attitude toward teaching at such an out-of-the-way place, since they are sent by order of their home school. Third, the Orang Hulu are not very eager for contact with them, so teachers are just left alone.

COMPARISON WITH MUSLIM MALAYS

So far I have made some mention of the differences between the Orang Hulu and the Malays; but, impressionistically speaking, there are more similarities between the present-day Orang Hulu communities and the nineteenth-century Malay village. The formation and division of Malay villages was very simple as in Orang Hulu hamlets,[31] and the characteristics of the *penghulu* (village headman) can be applied to the *batin*.[32] One reason for this is, of course, the similarity of environment. But environment is not the total explanation of the phenomena. Other questions arise: What are the differences in social structure between

31.   J. M. Gullick, *Indigenous Political Systems of Western Malaya* (London: The Athlone Press, 1958), pp. 29, 30, 43.

32.   Gullick, *Indigenous Political Systems of Western Malaya*, p. 34.

the Malays and the Proto-Malays? What fundamental features do they
have in common? I do not yet have the answers to these problems, but
would like to sketch out some explorations of them here.

Both Malays and Proto-Malays have what is called *adat*, or *hadat*
(customary rules, a system of customs). It is not surprising that the
various *adat* differ in detail, as is indicated in such Malay sayings as
lain lubok, lain ikannya (literally, "different pools, different fish"), or
lain desa, lain adat ("different villages, different *adat*"). In Malay society,
however,

> In some spheres of Government, functions previously carried out
> through *adat* have been directly taken over by the modern execu-
> tive. The most important of these is the administration of justice
> and the use of force. Both the control of illegitimate expressions of
> violence, and the use of force in legitimate policy, are the exclusive
> monopoly of the administration. *Adat* is therefore without sanction
> in the last resort.[33]

The present Orang Hulu handle their own *hadat* without intervention
from the government, but cannot resort to physical force to carry out
punishment as the Malays do.

Malays use Islamic Law, *hukum shariah*, as well as *adat*. The con-
tradictions between *adat* and Islamic law are often discussed in Malay
society. It must be emphasized that Islamic law, as well as British law,
has been officially confirmed, *adat* being left outside the modern administration. Still, among ordinary people, *adat* is followed in some spheres
rather than Islamic law. For example, Malays celebrate weddings with
great merriment, which is not sanctioned in Islamic law; inheritance
by *adat* and by Islamic law occur with almost equal frequency in Kedah.
This confusion may originate in the historical fact that Islam penetrated
Malay society gradually from upper to lower classes without changing
it drastically,[34] though the Malays' attachment to *adat* is surely also a
factor here.

To understand the position of *adat* in Malay societies,[35] it is useful
to know the *hadat* and its function in the Orang Hulu community. It
seems that the Orang Hulu have been influenced to some extent by
the Malays, and through them by Islam. It is not easy, however, to
discriminate which aspect of *adat* has been affected by which of the two
influences.

33. M. G. Swift, *Malay Peasant Society in Jelebu* (London: The Athlone Press, 1967),
     pp. 78–79.
34. Fatimi, *Islam Comes to Malaysia.*
35. R. O. Windstedt, *The Malays: A Cultural History* (London: Routledge & Kegan
     Paul, 1961), chapter 6.

The meaning of the word *kampong* must be made clear. *Kampong*, or *kampung*, originally meant a "gathering,"[36] and also designates "a homestead or compound where the people gather" or "a settlement" which is composed of such homesteads. In a Malay dictionary compiled by a Malay, the meaning given is "a place where houses, shops and other buildings are gathered, smaller than *pekan* (town)."[37] This is equivalent to Javanese *desa* which is translated as village. Administratively, in Malaysia, a state is divided into districts (*daerah* or *jajahan*), districts into subdistricts (*mukim*), subdistricts into *kampong*. *Kampong* merge on their borders, and it is very difficult to discern their boundaries, geographically and socially.[38] The *penghulu*, head of the *mukim*, earns a monthly salary from the government and is its representative. The head of a *kampong* (generally *ketua kampong*) gets a nominal salary through the *penghulu*. In Kelantan, according to Downs, the *penghulu* is the formal leader and the *ketua kampong* plays an informal role.[39] This outline indicates that modern villages have undergone a simplification from former times when a more refined system was to be found, varying according to ethnic and local differences.[40] The *batin* is not very different from the *penghulu* in relations with the government and is roughly equivalent to the *ketua kampong* in relations with villagers.

It will be worthwhile taking a look at the size of several *kampong* which have been studied.

location of kampong	No. of households	source
Kampong Padang Lalang, Kedah	133	Kuchiba *et al.*[41]
Kampong Jeram, Kelantan	173	Downs 1967[42]
Kampong Jendram Hilir, Selangor	108	Wilson 1967[43]
Kampong Bagan, Johor: Parit Besar	64	Husin 1964[44]
Parit Bengkok	85	Husin 1964[45]
Kampong Bukit Meta, Melaka	55	Maeda 1974[46]
Kampong Bukit Pegoh, Melaka	80	Maeda 1974[47]

36. Wilkinson, *A Malay-English Dictionary* (1959). See *kampong*.
37. Hj. Schamsuldin bin M. Yunus, *Kamus Melayu* (Kuala Lumpur, 1935).
38. Husin, "Patterns of Rural Leadership in Malaya," p. 104.
39. Downs, "A Kelantanese Village of Malaya," p. 133.
40. Husin, "Patterns of Rural Leadership in Malaya."
41. Masuo Kuchiba, Yoshihiro Tsubouchi and Narifumi Maeda, *Marei Noson no Kenkyu* [Malay rural communities] (Tokyo: Sogensha, 1976).
42. Downs, "A Kelantanese Village of Malaya."
43. P. J. Wilson, *A Malay Village and Malaysia* (New Haven, Conn.: HRAF, 1967).
44. Syed Husin Ali, *Social Stratification in Kampong Bagan* (Singapore: MBRAS, 1964).
45. Husin, *Social Stratification in Kampong Bagan*.
46. Maeda, *The Changing Peasant World in a Melaka Village: Islam and Democracy in the Malay Tradition* (Unpublished dissertion, University of Chicago, 1974).
47. Maeda, *The Changing Peasant World in a Melaka village*.

According to the Kedah Annals, a *mukim* is a gathering of forty people (households).[48] The quantitative aspect of a community consists primarily in the fact that the number of residents determines the quality of leadership. To exercise control over more houses than he can take care of by informal means—about ten to fifteen in a Japanese case[49]— a leader needs formal channels to exercise his influence. In the hamlets in Endau, the *batin* of Jorak (thirty-three households) strives for wider power, making the people believe he is gaining the trust and support of the government. Malay *kampong* (or smaller *parit*, or *solok*) consist of more people and of more people of different descent. This is one reason why it is difficult for a *kampong* to be mobilized as a territorial unit. The *ketua kampong* appears to play the role of balancing powers in the *kampong* but little more than that.[50]

The *pawang* play magico-religious roles which sometimes coincide with those of the *batin* and *bomoh*. Malay *bomoh* and *pawang* are much affected by Hindu and Islamic mysticism and knowledge. Four *bomoh* are found in Jorak, but it is generally difficult to find *bomoh* in the Malay *kampong*. Instead, such Islamic leaders as *imam* or *mualim* (in the villages, called *tok imam*, *tok alim*, *tok guru*, *pak lebai*) play an important part in village politics.

In Malay villages leadership is assumed by teachers or rich entrepreneurs. Among the Orang Hulu, those who become teachers and entrepreneurs are not Orang Hulu, but outsiders and exploiters. Retailers within the hamlets, also, are originally Chinese.

Moreover, the relationships between kinship system, social organization, and economic stratification are different for the two peoples. For example, social organization and economic stratification largely rely on the kinship system among the Orang Hulu, while among the Malays economic stratification itself is relatively important.

So far we have reviewed the *adat*, settlement size, homogeneity and heterogenity of settlement, leadership, and *"ordre des ordres."*[51] At present the difference between the Malays and Orang Hulu is large. This difference has been created mainly by environmental factors and adaptation to these factors, and by the degree of influence of Islamic and Western civilizations. In the sphere of leadership, the quantitative difference of population has been transformed to a qualitative difference:

48. Hikayat Marong Mahawangsa (The Kedah Annals): *Suatu mukim, iaitu kampong orgng-nya empat puloh orang* (cited in Wilkinson, *A Malay-English Dictionary* (1959), under *mukim*).

49. Kida, *Nippon Buraku*, p. 154.

50. Downs, "A Kelantanese Village of Malaya."

51. C. Levi-Strauss, *Anthropologie Structurale* (Paris: Plon, 1968), p. 346.

the difference in leadership structure seems to originate in the size of communities. If this point is accepted, it could be said that the Malays and Orang Hulu have basically the same leadership structure.

4

A Note on Buddhistic Millenarian Revolts in Northeastern Siam

YONEO ISHII

INTRODUCTION

The Royal Autograph Edition of the *Phrarātcha-phongsāwadān* or *Royal Chronicles* gives one of the oldest known accounts of a rebellion led by a magic-man, generically called *phū mī bun* or a "man of merit."[1] In 1699,[2] a Lao named Bun Kwāng who styled himself a *phū mī bun* terrorized the governor of Korat with his reputed magical powers, according to the chronicle, and managed to establish himself as the ruler of a city which had been made a Siamese outpost by King Phra Narai (1656–1688). Despite the superior military strength at his command, the intimidated governor was unable to order the immediate arrest of the *phū mī bun*, and, furthermore, humiliated himself by acceding to the insolent demand of the latter for armed men, elephants, and horses. With these reinforcements Bun Kwāng planned a bold attack on the Siamese capital of Ayutthaya. The chronicle records that over four thousand men, eighty-four elephants, and more than one hundred horses were recruited for the rebel.[3] It was only by a carefully designed strategem that the governor successfully persuaded the rebel to move to the central Siamese town of Saraburi, where Bun Kwāng was trapped, and found himself hopelessly exposed to overwhelming Ayutthayan forces sent by the order of King Petracha (1688–1703), who had been informed of the

---

1. Thailand Fine Arts Department, *Phrarātchaphongsāwadān chabap phrarātchahatthalēkhā*, lem 2, tōn 1 (Bangkok: Odeon Store, 1952), pp. 240–245. An English résumé of this story is given in W. A. R. Wood, *A History of Siam* (Bangkok, 1926), p. 222.
2. The Royal Autograph Edition gives C.S. 1054, year of the monkey, which corresponds to 1692–1693. I follow Wood here.
3. *Phrarātchaphongsāwadān*, p. 242.

revolt. The captured Bun Kwāng and his twenty-eight original followers were finally brought to the capital for execution.

Later in history we read little about the rebellions of *phū mī bun*. Nevertheless, the popular belief that the "man of merit" would someday appear in this world in a miraculous way to establish a utopian rule seems to have survived among the Thai-Lao peasants of the Korat Plateau. Thus, at the beginning of the present century, we see *phū mī bun* insurrections throughout Monthon Udon and Monthon Isan from the end of February to the beginning of March, 1902.[4]

The emergence of *phū mī bun* was heralded by the circulation of palm-leaf manuscripts (*lai thaeng*) of unknown origin which predicted the imminent arrival of a great calamity and urged people to prepare for a promised emancipation from the danger.[5] According to one of the circulating manuscripts, when the sixth lunar month of the year of the ox (1902) arrived, *hin hae*, or concretions in lateritic soil which are common in the region, would turn to gold and silver. Wax gourds and pumpkins would become elephants and horses, while short-horned water buffalo and swine would be transformed into *yakkhas* (ogres) which assault men. After these fearful prognostications, the prophecy went on to say, *thao thammikarāt phū mī bun* or "the king of righteousness" would appear as the master of the world. Those who wished to be spared on doomsday must copy the message of the manuscript so that more people might be informed of the coming of the disaster. Let the impeccable collect *hin hae*, which the descending "king of righteousness" would change into gold and silver. Let the guilty hasten to have their sins purged. Let water buffalo and swine be killed before they become *yakkhas* to devour men. Let spinsters hurry to get married so that the *yakkhas* would not hurt them, and so on.

Amidst the turbulence caused by the circulation of the predictive manuscripts, there appeared, in various localities of the Northeast, so-called *phū wisēt* or "men with supernatural powers" who came forward to perform magical rites of purification in response to the request of panic-stricken peasants. Phrakhrū In of the Ban Nong I Tum monastery in Yasothon was one of these *phū wisēt*. He officiated at the rite of *tat kam wāng wēn* (cutting off retributive *karma*) and urged the villagers to

---

4. Tej Bunnag, "Kabot phū mī bun phāk Īsān R. S. 121" ['Millenarian revolt in Northeastern Thailand, 1902'], *Sangkhomasāt Parithat* [*Social science review*], 5 (1967): 82.
5. The following account is based upon: Toem Wiphakphotchanakit, *Prawatisāt Īsān* [*A history of the Northeast*], lem 2 (Bangkok, Samnakphim Samākhom Sangkhomasāt haeng Prathēt Thai, 1970), p. 559.

collect *hin hae*, in order to see them turned into gold and silver when the predicted saviour should arrive.[6]

These *phū wisēt* often staged various "miracles" in order to convince the credulous people of their respective supernatural claims. For example, a flintlock was fired using common sand instead of gunpowder.[7] Some of their 'miracles' were so astounding that the watchers came to believe that the performer must be the awaited *phū mī bun* himself. Fanatics volunteered to serve them, thus, groups of devotees formed around such supernatural leaders.[8] This was the case with Ong Man under whose magical authority a rebellion broke out in the spring of 1902, involving thousands of Thai-Lao peasants in Monthon Isan.

Ong Man's origin is obscure. He is said to have lived for some time in Savannakhet, where since 1901 he had publicly declared himself to be *Chao Prāsātthōng* or *Phayā Thammikarāt Phū Mī Bun* who had descended from heaven to save mankind from sin.[9] With the support of a village doctor of Muang Trakānphutphon named Luang Wichā, alias Ong Fā Luang, Ong Man managed to attract two hundred followers and attempted to attack Ubonratchathani, where he intended to establish his magical rule, presumably by deposing Prince Sanphasitthiprasong, who was named the High Commissioner of the province by King Chulalongkorn (1868–1910). On his march toward the provincial capital, Ong Man met resistance from the governor of Khemarat, who tried to interrupt the rebel's advance by persuading villagers not to believe what he said. In great fury, Ong Man killed two assistants of the governor and captured the governor himself. In order to show off his magical powers he caused the captured Phra Khemarat to be paraded around on a litter, an exhibition intended also for further recruitment of followers. At Ban Saphuyai, now Amphoe Trakanphutphon, Ong Man was joined by six other *phū wisēt* who were made subleaders of his army, which had grown by that time to as many as one thousand men.[10]

In Ubonratchathani, on the other hand, the High Commissioner, who was informed of the unusual development in his province, ordered the dispatch of a small reconnoitring squad to the troubled site only to have it crushed by the rebel army. This defeat contributed to the reinforcement of Ong Man's forces, which gained an additional fifteen-hundred men. Realizing the seriousness of the situation, Prince Sanpha-

6.   Toem, *Prawatisāt*, pp. 560–561.
7.   Toem, *Prawatisāt*, p. 565.
8.   Damrong Rāchānuphāp, Somdet Kromphrayā, *Nithānbōrānnakhadī* [*Stories of the old days*] 5th impression (Bankok, Samnakphim Khlang Witthayā, 1951), p. 423.
9.   Tej, "Kabot phū mī bun", p. 82.
10. Toem, *Prawatisāt*, pp. 563–566.

sitthiprasong mobilized his modern army to crush the rebel before he reached the provincial capital where the Prince resided. On April 4, 1902, the powerful cannon of the intercepting government forces inflicted three hundred casualties on Ong Man's army, which had barely left Ban Saphuyai. Although four hundred prisoners were taken, Ong Man himself is believed to have escaped from the battlefield and crossed the Mae Khong River to the Laotian bank, where he disappeared.[11]

Although severe punishment was inflicted upon *phū mī bun* claimants who were arrested that year for instigating the widespread insurrection and agitation among the Thai-Lao peasants, the popular belief in the coming of *phū mī bun* and his supernatural government seems not to have died out in 1902. We see again in 1924 another incident of *phū mī bun* in Changwat Loei, where four "men of merit" claimed to have descended from heaven to save mankind. This time, too, the prophecy was one of immediate calamity with *yakkhas* attacking helpless men. The four *phū mī bun* of Ban Nong Bakkaeo were not satisfied with performing the purification rite and distributing various talismanic objects to hundreds and thousands of Thai-Lao who came to see them from neighboring provinces, including Roi-et and Mahasarakham, but dared to challenge the provincial authorities by attacking the district office of Wang Saphung with such arms as an old-fashioned muzzle-loading gun and two flintlocks. Although the weakness of the provincial police forces delayed settlement of the trouble for two months, the rebels were eventually suppressed by the arrival of police reinforcements.[12]

MILLENARISM IN THAI HISTORY

Judging from the three historical cases just described, *phū mī bun* insurrections could be regarded as a Thai-Lao version of Buddhist millenarism which has been observed in different forms in different parts of Theravadist Asia.[13] To make possible a comparison with other types of politico-

11.   Toem, *Prawatisāt*, pp. 568–572.
12.   Toem, *Prawatisāt*, pp. 579–587.
13.   For Sri Lanka: Kitsiri Malalgoda, "Millennialism in Relation to Buddhism," *Comparative Studies in Society and History* 12 (1970):424–441; for Burma: Melford E. Spiro, *Buddhism and Society* (London: George Allen & Unwin, 1971), pp. 171–187; E. Michael Mendelson, "Religion and Authority in Modern Burma," *The World Today* 16, no. 3 (1960):110–118; idem, "The King of the Weaving Mountain," *Journal of the Royal Central Asian Society* 48 (1961):229–237; idem, "A Messianic Buddhist Association in Upper Burma," *Bulletin of the School of Oriental and African Studies* 26 (1961):560–580; and for the Karens in Thai-Burma border areas: Theodore Stern, "*Ariya* and the Golden Book: A Millenarian Buddhist Sect among the Karen," *The Journal of Asian Studies* 27, no. 2 (1968):297–328.

religious movements, I wish to examine briefly some of the general features of *phū mī bun* incidents including the pattern of evolution of the movement, the circumstances under which such explosive action took place, the character of its leadership and recruitment of the followers, and finally, the nature of the ideas involved.[14]

As seen in both 1902 and 1924, if not in 1699 where the necessary details are not available, prophecy of a coming catastrophe is circulated, causing widespread uneasiness and agitation among the populace. Against this background there emerge *phū wisēt*, who come to offer the terrified peasants a supernatural means by which the people are promised not only deliverance from the pressing danger but also the opportunity of great blessings in a new dispensation to be brought about by the descending saviour, *phū mī bun*. *Phū wisēt* are heralds of the advent of a messiah. Belief in the latter is generated in the minds of people by miraculous acts of a certain *phū wisēt* of superlative ability. This process is followed by the public declaration of the *phū mī bun* that he is the awaited saviour. A group of religious devotees forms around the *phū mī bun*. His claim to "messiahship" is justified by repeated performance of "miracles," which contribute to the stability and expansion of his group. Given a sufficient number of followers, the *phū mī bun* attempts to establish his earthly kingdom, resulting inevitably in a military confrontation with the established political order of the day. The armed forces under the *phū mī bun* are usually inferior in equipment but their morale is high because of their adamant belief in magical invincibility. The revolts, however, end with the defeat of the rebels when far superior military forces are mobilized by the authorities.

The uneasiness and agitation which help create the preconditions for the emergence of *phū wisēt* and *phū mī bun* are not unrelated to socioeconomic problems confronting people in the region concerned. In the case of the 1902 rebellions in which more than one hundred *phū mī bun* claimants were arrested within the year,[15] agricultural failure, lack of alternative income sources nearby, and hardship caused by exploitative local officials, had made life in the region intolerable.[16] In addition, since the conclusion of the Franco-Siamese Treaty of 1893, the prestige of the Bangkok government had fallen considerably in the eyes of the Thai-Lao peasants of the Korat Plateau.[17] A situation

14. Sylvia L. Thrupp, ed., *Millennial Dreams in Action* (New York: Schocken Books, 1970), p. 13.

15. Tej, "Kabot phū mī bun", p. 84n.

16. Tej, "Kabot phū mī bun", p. 81.

17. Tej, "Kabot phū mī bun", pp. 79–80.

such as this might well be regarded as potentially dangerous, awaiting only the *phū mī bun*.

Personal details of *phū mī bun* are little known. Available sources suggest, however, that they are, in a way, elite members at village or district level. For example, we see in a list of arrested Ongs (*phū wisēt* or *phū mī bun*) such names as Kamnan Sui, commune head of Ban Sang Ming, Amphoe Kasemsima, Luang Prachum of Muang Amnatcharoen, a former district official of *pratuan* rank, Phrakhru In, a monk with the rank of *phrakhrū*. Ong Bunchan, who was killed in flight, was known as Thao Bunchan, *thao* being a sign of Laotian nobility of some rank.[18] Tej Bunnag suggests that 1902 was a time when the adverse effects of territorial integration of the Northeast into the newly consolidated kingdom of Siam began to be felt among the local privileged class of people, who were thereby deprived of their traditional sources of wealth.[19] In fact, in his report to the central government, the High Commissioner of Monthon Isan wrote that "some of the *phū mī bun* were local officials of minor rank (*khun mun phan thanāi*) who still desired to earn their living in traditional ways."[20]

FEATURES OF BUDDHISTIC MILLENARISM

Let us now examine the nature of the idea behind the *phū mī bun* insurrections, which occurred in the Thai-Lao cultural milieu. Before the rationalistic Thammayut movement was launched by Prince Mongkut in the 1830s, most Thai Buddhists were strongly influenced by popular Buddhist literature such as the *Traiphūm*, *Phra Mālai*, and various versions of the *Jātaka* stories, all of which were presented to the populace in multifaceted ways: paintings, sculptures, recitations, sermons, and other means. Even after the religious reform, which was essentially urban elitist-oriented, these books remained major sources through which people were exposed to Buddhist values.

The *Jātakas* are a collection of accounts of the former lives of the historical Buddha before he finally attained "Enlightenment". The basic intention underlying these popular stories is to show how the Master made strenuous efforts to perform such sacrificial acts of merit as are depicted in *Wētsandōn Chādok* [*Vessantara Jātaka*] in order to achieve the final goal of buddhahood. These have led people to believe that the greatness of the Buddha lies in the abundance of *bun* or 'merit', accumulated by him during his long series of rebirths. The *Traiphūm*

18.   Toem, *Prawatisāt*, pp. 574–579.
19.   Tej, "Kabot phū mī bun", pp. 80–81.
20.   Tej, "Kabot phū mī bun", p. 81.

characterizes the Buddha as a *phū mī bun* or 'one who has merit'.[21]

It is to be noted, in this connection, that the same Buddhist cos-mological treatise mentions, in its list of *phū mī bun*, *Paccekabuddhas*, *Aggasavakas* (great disciples), *Arahantakhīnāsawas* (saints), *Bodhisattvas*, and *Cakravartins* (universal monarchs).[22] The last two are particularly noteworthy.

Apart from the Bodhisattva who eventually became the historical Buddha, Theravada Buddhism teaches about another *bodhisattva*, the future Buddha, that is, Maitreya. The coming of the future Buddha and his glorious reign is also a favorite theme of popular Buddhist literature. For example, in the *Traiphūm*, it is promised that those who listen to (the recitation of) the book attentively and faithfully will meet and pay homage to the Maitreya who is coming and will hear the *dharma* which he preaches.[23] In the *Phra Mālai* too, the Buddhist Messiah is quoted as saying to the visiting Phra Mālai that he shall be invited to descend to be born on earth to save mankind.[24]

The idea of the future king, the wheel-turning universal sovereign who is known in Thai as *cakrapat*, is also "ever kept before the public eye in literature, in sermons and in any other channel of publicity."[25] We read, in the *Traiphūm*, that he who has accomplished meritorious acts in his earlier existences, if born as a king, shall reign over all the universe and shall be known as *cakravartin*.[26] The universal monarch is called 'the king of righteousness' (*dhammiko dhammarāja*).[27]

It is to be remembered, in this connection, that one of our *phū mī bun* called himself *Thao Thammikarāt*, or *Phayā Thammikarāt*, which are Laotian or Thai versions of *dhammikarāja*, the 'king of righteousness'. Sometimes, *phū mī bun* refers to the name of a celebrated historical king such as Chao Prasātthŏng (1630–1656). This does not conflict with the claim to be the ideal monarch, because the Theravādist concept of

21. Ongkānkhā khŏng Khrusaphā, *Traiphūm Phra Ruang khŏng Phrayā Lithai*, [*The Traibhūmikathā of Phrayā Lithai*] (Bangkok: Ongkānkhā Khrusaphā, 1963), p. 93; George Coedès and C. Archaimbault, *Les Trois Mondes* (*Thaibhūmi Brah R'vaṅ*) (Paris: École Française d'Extrême Orient, 1973), p. 85.

22. Loc. cit.

23. *Traiphūm*, p. 326; *Les Trois Mondes*, p. 256.

24. Prince Dhani Nivat, "Phra Malai, royal version, by Chaofa Khung, Prince Royal of Ayudhya," *Journal of Siam Society* 37 no. 2 (1949):71.

25. Prince Dhani Nivat, "The Old Siamese Conception of the Monarchy," *The Siam Society Fiftieth Anniversary Commemorative Publication*, vol. 2, Selected Articles from The Siam Society Journal, 1929–53. (Bangkok: The Siam Society, 1954), p. 172.

26. *Traiphūm*, p. 94; *Les Trois Mondes*, p. 86.

27. Balkrishna G. Gokhale, "Early Buddhist Kingship," *The Journal of Asian Studies* 26 (1967):20.

monarchy holds that those kings who were fortified by the prescribed kingly rules of conduct could justify themselves as the 'King of Righteousness'. Some Thai and Laotian kings even bear the title of Dhammarāja.[28]

On the basis of the brief observations made earlier, I am apt to think that the idea of a future king and saviour to come, which is popular among the Buddhists in the Thai Northeast, has found its expression in the vague concept of *phū mī bun*, the claim of a being who appealed to the suffering Thai-Lao peasants.

Millenarism is "essentially a prepolitical phenomenon." It tends to appear in regions where relevant political institutions are lacking or undeveloped, or inaccessible, so that the distressed could find no institutionalized way of expressing their grievance and pressing their claim. Thus the phenomenon is observed among peasants in feudal societies, among peasants in isolated and backward areas in modern societies, among marginal and politically passive elements in the working class, among recent immigrants and among malintegrated and politically inarticulate minority groups.[29] The Thai-Lao peasants in the poverty-stricken Northeast may be counted as one of the groups susceptible to millenarism. They have long been neglected by the central government in Bangkok. The Thai-Lao of the Korat Plateau are culturally closer to the Lao than to the Siamese people of Central Thailand, but politically have been severed from their Lao kinsmen by the establishment of the national boundary along the Mae Khong River and the subsequent efforts of the central government to integrate them into the modern Siamese nation. This is one of the perennial causes of instability in the Northeast.[30] It is surprising to read, however, that as late as 1959 a minor incident in the *phū mī bun* style took place in Korat which cost several lives including that of a Thai district officer. Even more extraordinary, its leader claimed to be a reincarnation of the revered and much more recent monarch, Chulalongkorn (1868–1910).[31]

28. For example, Boromakōt or Mahā Thammarāchā (Dharmaraja) of the Ayutthayan dynasty (1733–1758) and Thammikarāt (Dhammikaraja) of Lang Xang (1596–1622).

29. Yonia Talmon, "Pursuit of the Millennium: the Relation between Religious and Social Change," *The European Journal of Sociology* 3 (1962) : 138.

30. For the position of the Northeast in Thailand, see Charles F. Keyes, *Isan: Regionalism in Northeastern Thailand*, Southeast Asia Program Data Paper No. 65 (Ithaca: Cornell University, 1967).

31. Thai Noi, *Nāyokratthamontrī khon thū 11 kap 3 phūnam patiwat.* [The 11th prime minister and three leaders of the coup d'état,] (Bangkok: Prae Pittaya, 1964), pp. 546–549. The leader of the revolt is here referred to as *phī bun*, the word *phī*

Thus the long-lived belief in *phū mī bun*, the magical saviour, seems still to linger on among some sectors of the Thai-Lao populace of the region.

---

meaning 'the possessed'. The first instance of the use of this derogatory term for *phū mī bun* by the Siamese authorities is, according to Tej Bunnag (op., cit., p. 78n.), in a telegraphic dispatch sent to the central government by the High Commissioner of Monthon Isan dated 12 April 1902.

5

Descriptive and Comparative Studies of the Khamet Phonology

YASUYUKI MITANI

INTRODUCTION

During my fieldwork on Lawa in northern Thailand, 1964–1965, I had the opportunity of studying two other languages spoken by people who are called "Lua," the Northern Thai equivalent for "Lawa," both in Chiangrai province.[1]

One is spoken in at least two villages in Chiangrai province, that is, Ban Huaisan about twenty-five kilometers southwest of Chiangrai and Ban Thako about forty-five kilometers further southwest on the way to Chiangmai, though the latter villagers now almost all speak Northern Thai rather than their own language. The villagers, in their language, call themselves, "Bisu" (Huaisan /bìsù/, Thako /bìsú/). Apparently the Bisu language is not related to Lawa at all, but is a Burmese-Lolo language. It is especially close to "Kha" languages such as Phunoi (Kha Phai Phu Noi) of Phongsali, also known as "Kha Paille" of Upper Nam U, and "Kha Khong" of Laichau; and according to Nishida, it is also close to Pyen (Pyin) of Kengtung. Compare the examples below.[2]

---

1. For Lawa, see my articles in *Southeast Asian Studies* 4, no. 2 (1966): 40–62, and 10, no. 2 (1972): 131–168.
2. TK., HS., Wr. Bur. indicate Thako Bisu, Huaisan Bisu and Written Burmese respectively. Phunoi is cited from H. Roux, "Quelques minorités éthniques du Nord-Indochine," *France-Asie* 92, no. 3, pp. 131–419, "Kha Paille" and "Kha Khong" are taken from P. Lefèvre-Pontalis, "Notes sur quelques populations du nord de l'Indochinie, II" *Journal Asiatique* 9, no. 18 (1896): 129–154, 291–303. Incidentally, Kha Phai in the Nan Province of Thailand is Mon-Khmer; see Kraisri Nimmanahaeminda, "The Mrabri Language," *Journal of the Siam Society* 51, Part 2, Appendix I (1963).

	TK.	HS.	Phu Noi	Kha Paille	Kha Khong	Wr. Bur.
"house"	júm	júm		youm	(pam)	'im
"fire"	bì	bìthɔ̀	bì	bi	bi	mi²
"moon"	ʔùhla	ʔùhla	ùlà	oulla	pela	hla³
"fish"	lɔ̀ŋté	lɔ̀ŋtè	nôtè	yongtè	longtè	(ŋa²)
"buffalo"	jɔ̀	pɔ̀ŋhna	yô	yo	panna	(kywai²)
"water"	láŋ	láŋ	lǎng	lang	lâng	(rei)

The other language, which is the main subject of this article, is spoken at Ban Pangchok, a small village with about thirty households, some five kilometers north of the town of Wiang Papao, Chiangrai province. The villagers are known to some Thai people in this area as "Lua," and the language was once reported to be the Wiang Papao dialect of Lawa.³ It is certainly Mon-Khmer and is closely related to Lawa. However, the villagers call themselves in their language /Rəmèet/,⁴ which is apparently a variant of "Lamet," the name of an ethnic group in northeastern Laos.⁵ The details of Lamet in Laos are not known, but by comparison with some previously published short word-lists of Lamet it is not difficult to see that this language is a dialect of Lamet rather than Lawa. See the following examples.⁶

	WPP.	NT.	Kraisi.	BL.	UP
"pig"	lìik	lik	lìik	lɔic	leic
"hand"	tiiʔ	ti	tiʔ	taiʔ	teʔ
"stone"	Rəʔaaŋ	raagne	khaʔaaŋ	(səmɒuʔ)	(səmoʔ)
"snake"	phuǹ	phigne	phiŋ	(səʔɜɯŋ)	(səʔoiǹ)
"head"	ǹtɔ̀h	ndor	dɔh	(kaiǹ)	(kaiǹ)

Therefore, I would prefer to call this language the Wiang Papao dialect of Lamet (or Khamet).

It may not be long before the Wiang Papao dialect of Khamet ceases to be spoken. Even at the time I visited the village, young villagers used Northern Thai as their first language though they appeared to understand old people who spoke Khamet. However, its importance for linguistic purposes is obvious. So far our knowledge of Mon-Khmer

---

3. Sanidh Rangsit, "Beitrag zur Kenntnis der Lawasprachen von Nord-Siam (Mit Vokabularien)," *Anthropos* 37–40 (1942–1945): 688–710.
4. There is another word /lùaʔ/, but this is a Thai borrowing. The corresponding form for Lawa /ləvɯaʔ, rəvɯaʔ/ should be */Rəwà(a)ʔ/.
5. Also known as Khamet, Kha Met, Kha Lamet, etc. In Thailand they are usually called /khàa mêet/ or /khamêet/.
6. WPP. is Wiang Papao; NT. is Nam Tha Lamet from Lefèvre-Pontalis, "Notes"; Kr. is Khamet in Kraisri, "The Mrabri Language." BL. and UP. are Bo Luang and Umphai dialects of Lawa cited from my notes.

languages in the northern area is very limited, and new knowledge of any single dialect of the area will certainly contribute to Mon-Khmer linguistics in general.

In this article, I will describe the main phonological features of this Wiang Papao Lamet and discuss some phonological correspondences between this and certain other related languages, showing how they are related.

MAIN PHONOLOGICAL FEATURES

2.1 Syllable Structure

In describing the syllable structure of Khamet, it is proper, just as in many Mon-Khmer languages, to distinguish classes of major syllables and minor syllables.[7] A major syllable, of which there are many, is one which can stand before a terminal juncture and can be stressed. A minor syllable is one which cannot stand before a terminal juncture and cannot take stress. The two also differ in composition and show the following structure:

$$\text{Major syllable: C(C)V(V)(C)/T}$$
$$\text{Minor syllable: CV(C)/T}$$

Here, C stands for a consonant, V for a vowel, T for a tone, and ( ) describes optional elements. Major syllables, in general, require the presence of one of the optional elements of the sequence (V)(C), although when unstressed the form C(C)V/T also occurs. I shall discuss this point later.

2.2 Tones

Only two tones occur in major syllables in Khamet: (1) high /(unmarked)/ and (2) low /ˋ/. In the languages of this family, lexical tones are not as common as contrasts of quasi-tonal registers.[8] But in Khamet both appear at the same time phonetically; namely, vowels in low-tone syllables are usually pronounced as breathy, e.g., "fish" kaaʔ [ka:ʔ$_{55}$] and "banana" kàak [kà:k$_{31}$], but breathiness does not seem to be compulsory, and the real distinctive feature is obviously a tonal contrast.

The phonetic pitch pattern of the tones are as follows:

(1) high tone / ⎺ /. The basic pattern is a high level [$_{55}$] [$_{\widehat{55}}$], as in "recall" cɯɯ [tɕɯ:$_{55}$], "dog" sɔʔ [sɔʔ$_{\widehat{55}}$]. In a nonfinal position, when another syllable follows, the pattern is slightly lower [$_{44}$] [$_{\widehat{44}}$] as in "milk" ʔom-pùuʔ [ʔom$_{44}$-], "wild dog" sɔ(ʔ)-ʀiʔ [sɔ(ʔ)$_{\widehat{44}}$-].

7. E. J. A. Henderson, "The Main Features of Cambodian Pronunciation," *Bulletin of the School of Oriental and African Studies* 14 (1952): 149–174.

8. Henderson, "The Main Features of Cambodian Pronunciation."

(2) low tone / `/. The basic pattern is falling [₃₁] [꜔], as in "name" cùɯ [tɕɯ :₃₁], "look for" sɔʔ [sɔʔ꜔]. In a nonfinal position, it is low falling or low level [₂₁₋₁₁] [꜕], as in "charcoal" ŋɔl-pèɛl [ŋɔl₂₁- ~ ŋɔl₁₁-], "to send" tì(ʔ)-tɤɤl [ti(ʔ)꜕-].

2.3 Initial Consonants and Clusters

The initials C-, CC- in major syllables comprise the following eighteen consonants and fourteen clusters:

p	t	c	k		ʔ						
b	d					pl	—	—	kl	—	—
m	n	ň	ŋ			pʀ	tʀ	—	kʀ	hʀ	mʀ
	l			ʀ		—	—	—	kw	—	—
w		j				pj	—	—	kj	—	—
f	s				h	ph	th	ch	kh	—	—

In addition there is a rare three-unit cluster /khw/.[9]

2.3.1 *Voiceless stops* /p, t, c, k, ʔ/

The phones corresponding to these phonemes are usually voiceless unaspirated stops and a voiceless unaspirated affricate [p, t, tɕ, k, ʔ]; e.g., "short" pɔt [pɔt꜓], "cloth" tɔŋ [tɔŋ₅₅], "to see" cɔ̀ɔm [tɕɔ̀ːm₃₁], "neck" kɔɔʔ [kɔːʔ₅₅], "three" ʔɔɔj [ʔɔːi̯₅₅].

In the consonant clusters /pl, pj, kl, kw, kj/, they have the same phones; e.g., "fruit" pleʔ [pleʔ꜓], "kill" pjam [pjam₅₅], "wash" klàaŋ [klaːŋ₃₁], "more than" kwaa [kwaː₅₅], "shut one's eyes" kjap [kjap꜓]. But when the preceding minor syllable ends in a nasal, the voiced and voiceless stops are in free variation; e.g., "heaven" tɔ̀mpliiŋ [-pliːŋ₅₅ ~ -bliːŋ₅₅].

In combination with /ʀ/, the stops are either unaspirated or slightly aspirated; /k/ in this case is an uvular stop [q⁽ʼ⁾], except for /kʀ/ which is followed by a front vowel; so "rain" pʀìiʔ [p⁽ʼ⁾ʀiːʔ₃₁], "knife" tʀàaj [t⁽ʼ⁾ʀaːi̯₃₁], "teacher" kʀùu [q⁽ʼ⁾ʀuː₃₁], "bear" kʀiis [k⁽ʼ⁾ʀiːs₅₅].

Aspirated stops and the aspirated affricate [pʼ, tʼ, tɕʼ, kʼ] are considered here to be clusters /ph, th, ch, kh/; e.g., "heart" pheem [pʼeːm₅₅], "to fry" thɔ̀ɔt [tʼɔːt₃₁], "trousers" chul [tɕʼul₅₅], "tree" khe [kʼeʔ꜓].

2.3.2 *Voiced stops* /b, d/

These are plain voiced stops and not prenasalized or implosive. Examples: "cloud" bot [bot꜓], "bell (small)" deŋ [deŋ₅₅].

9. But /kw/ and /khw/ occur only in Thai loanwords.

2.3.3 *Nasals* /m, n, ň, ŋ/

The corresponding phones are [m, n, ɲ, ŋ]. The cluster /mʀ/ is [mʔʀ], which appears in one item "horse" in my notes. Examples: "nail" miim [mi:m₅₅], "blood" naam [na:m₅₅], "house" ňàaʔ [ɲa:ʔ₃₁], "expensive" ŋɔɔs [ŋɔ:s₈₁], "horse" mʀàŋ [mʔ ʀaŋ₃₁].

2.3.4 *Liquids* /l, ʀ/

/l/ is always a lateral [l] including cases where it is the second element of a cluster, as in "leaf" laaʔ [la:ʔ₅₅], "leech" pliiŋ [pli:ŋ₅₅].

/ʀ/ is generally an uvular sound, but there are several variants. As a single initial consonant, it can be a voiced uvular fricative [ʁ], or trill [ʀ], or trill accompanied by onglide stop [ᑫʀ] [ᴳʀ], all in free variation. But when the preceding minor syllable ends in /-ŋ/, it can only be a flap [ɾ]. Examples: "to do, make" ʀʏʏʔ [ʁʏ:ʔ₅₅ ~ ᑫʀʏ:ʔ₅₅ ~ ...], "knee" pòŋʀòoŋ [-ɾo:ŋ₃₁].

In clusters /pʀ, tʀ, kʀ/, voiceless [χ] and [ʀ̥] are also observed as well as voiced fricative [ʁ] and trill [ʀ] as free variants. Examples: "squirrel" pʀɔɔk [pᐟʀɔ:k₅₅ ~ pᐟχɔ:k₅₅ ~ ...], "buffalo" tʀaak [tᐟʀa:k₅₅ ~ tᐟχa:k₅₅ ~ ...], "goods" kʀùa [qᐟʀu:a̯₅₅ ~ qᐟχu:a̯₅₅ ~ ...].[10]

Voiceless [χ] and [χʀ] without a preceding stop is considered as a cluster /hʀ/ here. Examples: "to love" hʀàk [χ(ʀ)ak₂̂₁], "mountain spirit" hʀooj [χ(ʀ)o:i̯₅₅].

2.3.5 *Semivowels* /w, j/

These are nonfricative semivowels [w, j], as in "hat" wɔɔm [wɔ:m₃₁], "ear" jook [jo:k₅₅].

2.3.6 *Fricatives* /f, s, h/

Except for /h/ in clusters which has been already described, the phones of these phonemes are voiceless fricatives [f, s, h]. But /f/ is found only in Thai borrowings. Examples: "elephant" kòsaaŋ [-sa:ŋ₅₅], "walk" hɯl [hɯl₅₅], "cotton" faaj [fa:i̯₅₅] (<Thai).

The distribution of tones with the above initial consonants includes no systematic restrictions except that voiced /b, d/ combine only with the high tone. However, the low tone combined with /ʔ, h; ph, th, ch, kh; h/ is rare and occurs only in words borrowed from Thai, such as "mother" ʔùuj (compare, Northern Thai ʔũj "grandparents"), and "sickle" khìaw (<NT. khiaw).

---

10.   The contrast between /ʀ/ [ᑫʀ] and /kʀ/ [qʀ] is sometimes unclear, and there could be some mistakes in my notes. In minor syllables, the contrast of /ʀ/ and /kʀ/ is neutralized; compare 2.7.2.

2.4 Vowels

Vowel phonemes which stand in the V(V) position of major syllables constitute a quite symmetric 3 × 3 vowel system, and all those nine vowels can form geminate clusters; the clusters with different vowels are /ia, ɰa, ua/.

i	ɰ	u	ii	ɰɰ	uu			
e	ɤ	o	ee	ɤɤ	oo			
ɛ	a	ɔ	ɛɛ	aa	ɔɔ	ia	ɰa	ua

2.4.1 *High vowels* /i, ɰ, u/

These are respectively high front unrounded [i], high back unrounded [ɰ], and high back rounded [u] or [ʊ]. However, /ɰ/ has a conditioned variant which is slightly rounded [ʉ] before a final /-c, -ň/. Examples: "small" pìk [pik$_{\widehat{21}}$], "to meet" pùɰp [pɰp$_{\widehat{21}}$], "wish" suʔ [suʔ$_{\widehat{55}}$ ~ sʊʔ$_{\widehat{55}}$].

The geminate clusters /ii, ɰɰ, uu/ are long vowels [i:] [ɰ:] [u:] phonetically. Examples: "pig" lìik [li:k$_{31}$], "bat (animal): bɰɰŋ [bɰ:ŋ$_{55}$], "extinguish" suul [su:l$_{55}$].

2.4.2 *Mid vowels* /e, ɤ, o/

/ɤ/ is a mid back unrounded vowel [ɤ], but /e/ and /o/ are slightly lower mid vowels, front unrounded [ẹ] and back rounded [ọ]; e.g., "rise" ʀèh [ʀẹh$_{\widehat{21}}$], "dumb" sɤ̀ʔ [sɤʔ$_{\widehat{21}}$], and "blind" pòl [pọl$_{31}$].

The clusters /ee, ɤɤ, oo/ are [e:] [ɤ:] [o:] respectively. Examples: "landleech" pleem [plẹ:m$_{55}$], "to play: mɤɤl [mɤ:l$_{31}$], "evening" kə̀lpòol [-pọ:l$_{31}$].

2.4.3 *Low vowels* /ɛ, a, ɔ/

Tongue-height is not phonetically symmetrical; for /ɛ/ it is a mid-low front unrounded vowel [ɛ], for /a/ it is a low central unrounded vowel [a], and for /ɔ/ it is a lower mid-low back rounded vowel [ɔ̞] or [ɒ]; so "to spit" pèk [pèk$_{\widehat{21}}$], "wide" wàh [wah$_{\widehat{21}}$], and "beautiful" lɔ̀k [lɔ̞k$_{\widehat{21}}$ ~ lɒk$_{\widehat{21}}$].

Geminate clusters /ɛɛ, aa, ɔɔ/ are corresponding long vowels [ɛ:], [a:], [ɔ̞:] ~ [ɒ:] respectively. Examples: "flea" tɛɛp [tɛ:p$_{55}$], "monkey" waaʔ [wa:ʔ$_{55}$], "six" tɔɔl [tɔ̞:l$_{55}$ ~ tɒ:l$_{55}$].

2.4.4 *Diphthongs* /ia, ɰa, ua/

In syllables where diphthongs are final (-VV #), the vowels are [i:ạ] [ɰ:ạ] [u:ạ], and in syllables with a final consonant (-VVC) they

are shorter [ia] [ɯa] [ua][11]. Examples: "young (child)" pia [pi:a̰₅₅],
"to show" piaʔ [piaʔ₅₅], "saw (n.)" lɯ̀a [lɯ:a̰₃₁], "soft" mɯ̀aj
[mɯai̯₅₁], "goods" kʀùa [qʀu:a̰₃₁], "Lua tribe" lùaʔ [luaʔ₃₁].

2.5 Final Consonants

Final consonants are a subclass of the consonant phonemes. There are
fourteen as follows:

-p	-t	-c	-k	-ʔ
-m	-n	-ň	-ŋ	
	-l			
-w		-j		
	-s			-h

2.5.1 *Stops and nasals*

Stops /p, t, c, k/ and nasals /m, n, ň, ŋ/ in syllable-final position
are unreleased stops [p̚] [t̚] [ⁱtɕ] [k̚] and nasals [m] [n] [ⁱɲ] [ŋ].
Palatals /-c, -ň/ follow a clear glide [i̯]. Examples: "cooked rice"
ʔuup [ʔu:p₅₅], "sleep" ʔiit [ʔi:t̚₅₅], "be lost" làac [la:ⁱtɕ̚₃₁], "go"
wàk [wak₅₁], "suitable" mɔʔ [mɔʔ₅₅], "thunder" kəlnùm [-num₃₁],
"lead (n.)" cùɯn [tɕɯ:n₃₁], "yellow bee" taaň [ta:ⁱɲ₅₅], "boat"
cəlɔɔŋ [-lɔ:ŋ₃₁].

2.5.2 *Liquid /l/*

This was always lateral [l] in the pronounciation of the main
informant, but another informant always pronounced it as a flap
[ɾ].[12] Examples: "two" ʔaal [ʔa:l₅₅~ʔa:ɾ₅₅], "seven" pul [pul₅₅~
puɾ₅₅].

2.5.3 *Semivowels /w, j/*

These are nonsyllabic vowels [u̯] [i̯]; /w/ can be as open as [o̯],
but /j/ never becomes [e̯]. Examples: "to envy" khɔɔj [kʰɔ:i̯₅₅] "padi-
field" kənàaw [-na:u̯₃₁].

2.5.4 *Fricatives /s, h/*

They are voiceless fricatives [s] [h]. Examples: "matches"
kap-tʀòs[-tʀos₅₁], "face" ʀəmpòh [-poh₅₁].

There are several systematic restrictions on the distribution of
final consonants and vowels:

11.   In addition there is one word with a long [i:a] before a consonant, "deer"
    [ki:ak₅₅], which is tentatively considered to be /kjiak/; compare Khamu /tjaak/.
12.   This /-l/ originates from *-l and *-r, but [l] and [ɾ] are free variants in Khamet
    and do not contrast; e.g., "two" ʔaal < *-r, "silver" kəmùul < *-l.

(a) A single vowel is always accompanied by a final consonant; namely, a syllabic structure such as —V # does not exist.

(b) Vowel clusters VV and /-h/ do not combine;[13] but /-ʔ/ combines with both V and VV as in "bag" pəljàaʔ: "girl" kɔ(ɔ)n-pəljàʔ, "man (male)" ʀə̀mèʔ: "husband" ʀə̀mèɛʔ.

(c) The finals /-c, -ň, -j/ and the vowels /i(i), e(e), ɛ(ɛ), ia/ do not usually combine. There is an exceptional combination /-ɛc/ in a single item "to end" /hɛc/, but this has a free variant /hɛk/. This restriction does not exclude the possibility of /uc, uň/, but since /uc, ɯc/, /uň, ɯň/ are 'neutralized' to [ɯⁱtɕ] [ɯⁱɲ] which are taken as /ɯc, ɯň/ in this study, the combinations /uc, uň/ do not exist in my analysis.

(d) Similarly /-w/ and /ɯ, u, ɤ, o, ɔ/ do not combine.

2.6 Weakened Major Syllables

When two syllables S_1 and S_2 combine in this order, there are three possibilities: (1) S_1 and S_2 both have stress, (2) S_1 has half-stress and S_2 has stress, and (3) S_1 has no stress but S_2 has stress. Seemingly different junctures are also involved here, so that I would describe (1) as /$S_1 S_2$/ (2) as /S_1-S_2/ and (3) as /S_1S_2/ as if stress patterns were determined by word juncture (space), internal juncture (hyphen) and the absence of juncture phoneme. However, (1), (2), and (3) actually form a continuum; (1) with (2) and (2) with (3) are often found consecutively in free variation. Examples: "be deaf" /jook luut/ ~ /jook-luut/, "look" /naŋ-sɯɯ/ ~ /naŋsɯɯ/.

It should be obvious by now that minor syllables can stand only in the S_1 position of pattern (3), and that major syllables usually stand in the S_1 and S_2 positions of (1) and (2) and S_2 of (3). But there are some major syllables that can also stand in the position of S_1 of (3) as exemplified by the syllable /naŋ-/ in "book." Such major syllables are restricted to a single vowel, namely, a structure such as C(C)VC/T, and such unstressed major syllables are often, though not always, a free variant of C(C)VVC/T type syllables, as in "when" /ňàmʔeen/ ~ /ňàam-ʔeen/. Therefore, I would like to call the unstressed major syllable in this particular position a 'weakened major syllable'.

The structure C(C)V/T could also belong to the class of weakened major syllables, though it is an exceptional structure as a major syllable. A syllable of this type usually belongs to the class of minor syllables, but it is considered to be a weakened major syllable when it has a C(C)VV(C) type alternant and/or its constituent phonemes are other than those of minor syllables. Examples: "plough" /khɔbok/ ~ /khɔɔ-

---

13.　From a and b, [-Vh] could be /-V/, or [-V:] could be /-VVh/.

bok/, "boy" /kɔnum/ ∼ /kɔ(ɔ)n-num/, "kidney" /bàkὲεw/ ∼ /bàa-kὲεw/, "cigaret" /mùlìi/ ∼ /mùu-lìi/.

2.7. Minor Syllables

There are fewer minor syllables than major syllables and their structure, CV(C)/T, is simpler.

2.7.1 *Tones*

Most minor syllables take only the low tone / ˋ/ [n̂]. So the functional load of the phoneme / ˋ/ is quite small here.[14] But there are rare cases where a minor syllable takes the high tone / / [44̂], so one cannot say there is no tonal contrast in minor syllables. Examples: "string" pəlsiʔ [pəl n̂-], "what" sənmɔ̀h [sən n̂-], but "why" sənʔeen [sən 44̂-].

2.7.2 *Initial consonants*

Of the eighteen consonant phonemes described, only the following seven can stand in the initial position of minor syllables, namely, /p, t, c, k; l, ʀ; s/. The phones are, in general, the same as in major syllables, but for /ʀ/ one finds [q⁽ˤ⁾ʀ] as a free variant.[15] Examples: "lizard" pəltaaŋ [pəl n̂-], "to talk" tə̀lʔuu [tə̀l n̂-] "green" cə̀ŋàal [tɕə n̂-], "gold" kə̀lcɔ̀ɔʔ [kəl n̂-], "gong" lə̀pàaŋ [lə n̂-], "chisel" ʀə̀mtòon [ʀəm n̂- ∼ ˤ ʀəm n̂- ∼ ...], "day" sə̀ŋìiʔ [sə n̂-].

2.7.3 *Vowels*

In minor syllables there are no phonemic contrasts of vowels. But since there are such words as "cave" tham [tʼam₅₅] and "right (side)" tə̀ham [tə n̂ham₅₅], it is necessary to recognize the presence of a vowel phoneme in minor syllables. The vowel is taken as /ə/ here, although alternative solutions are possible. The phones which belong to /ə/ are in general a mid central vowel [ə] or a very weakened [ɔ], but other variants are freely interchangeable depending on environment: (a) [a] when the vowel of a following major syllable is /a/, (b) [ʊ] ∼ [o] when the same is /o/ or /u/, and (c) a slightly centralized [e] when the same is /e/. Examples: "tongue" pə̀ltaak [pəl n̂- ∼ pal n̂-], "sweat" pə̀lʔul [pəl n̂- ∼ pʊl n̂-], "feel well' pə̀lŋèeʔ [pəl n̂- ∼ pel n̂-].

---

14. The tonal contrast in major syllables originates from the original voiced/voiceless contrast of initial consonants, as explained later, but in minor syllables this original contrast of initials is not preserved; e.g. "bomboo shoot" tə̀pàŋ <*d-, "bone" cə̀ŋʔaaŋ <*c-.

15. Therefore one could say that /ʀ/ and /kʀ/ are 'neutralized' in minor syllables.

2.7.4 *Final consonants*

Final consonants in minor syllables are /l; m, n, ŋ/. Nasals are in many words homorganic to the initial consonant of the following major syllable, but not always. Examples: "to rain" sə̀lɛ̀ɛʔ [sə n̑-], "beans" sə̀lpàaj [səl n̑-], "to awake" lə̀mkὲk [ləm- n̑], "drum" sə̀ntuŋ [sən n̑-], "forehead" ʀə̀ŋmɔ̀ɔŋ [ʀəŋ n̑-].

The initial and final phonemes of minor syllables have certain distributional restrictions: they cannot be homorganic, namely, pəm-, tən-, kəŋ-, ləl- etc., do not exist.

2.7.5 /N- /

This is a special phoneme that can constitute a minor syllable CVC- by itself. In other words, it does not belong to the class of C or to V but to the class of CVC. Corresponding phones are syllabic nasals homorganic to the initial consonant of the following major syllable, as in "blossom" ǹklɔh [ŋ n̑-], "word" ǹlɔ̀ɔʔ [l̩ n̑-], "not to have" /Nkooj/ [ŋ n̯-], "it is not" /Nmɔ̀h/ [m̩ n̯-].

2.8. Syllable Combinations

From the point of view of phonotactics, the following four structures seem to belong to the same class, and can take one stress, and stand before the terminal juncture: (1) major syllable (e.g., "child" kɔɔn), (2) minor syllable + major syllable (e.g., "morning" kə̀lsaʔ), (3) minor syllable + minor syllable + major syllable (e.g., "daytime" kə̀lsə̀ŋìiʔ), (4) weakened major syllable + major syllable (e.g., "boy" kɔ̣num).

However, here is the following constraint on the combination of minor syllables and major syllables: the initials of both syllables cannot be homorganic nasals or stops, so such combinations as pə̀(C)-p-, tə̀(C)-t-, etc. do not exist; nor do such combinations as sə̀(C)-s-, lə̀(C)-l-, ʀə̀(C)-ʀ-.[16]

Finally, words, other than compounds which have larger structure, have one of those four structures. And complex words take one of the last three structures.

PRELIMINARY COMPARISON

Khamet (Lamet) was classified by Shorto in his Northern Mon-Khmer group, which comprises Palaung, Riang, Wa, Lawa, Khamu (Khmu), and so on.[17] In this section, I would like to examine what phonological

---

16. Exceptions to this are cases where the minor syllable is a grammatical particle, as in "will smoke" /sə̀suup/ (= {sə̀- + suup}).

17. H. L. Shorto *et al.*, *Bibliographies of Mon-Khmer and Tai Linguistics*, 1963.

correspondences can be found between Khamet, Lawa, and Khamu and what proto-phonemes can be reconstructed for them. However, as the comparisons of Lawa dialects and Khamu dialects are not yet completed, only the initial consonants, which are relatively easy, will be discussed here.[18]

3.1. Stops

The correspondence between Khamet, Khamu, and Lawa initial stops does not provide much of a problem, and one can reconstruct as proto-phonemes the following nine: *p-, *b-, *t-, *d-, *c-(?), *j-, *k-, *g-, *ʔ-. In general, voiceless stops are reconstructed when a Khamet syllable has high tone, and voiced stops are reconstructed when the Khamet tone is low.

3.1.1 *p-

The initial p- of Khamet in high tone syllables corresponds in Khamu to MS. p-, Th. p- (<*p-) and in Lawa to BL. p-, UP. p- (<*p-).[19] There is no problem in reconstructing *p- as the proto-phoneme of this correspondence. Rarely does it correspond to prenasalized voiced mb- in Lawa, but I consider Lawa prenasalized voiced stops to be derived from Proto-Lawa *N- plus either voiceless or voiced initial stops, where *N- is either a syllabic nasal or a nasal final of a minor syllable (*N-, *rəm-, *rən-, etc.), and the decision whether the stops were voiced or voiceless can be made by considering its correspondence to Khamet and Khamu. Thus mb- <*N-p- in this particular case.

	Kmt.	MS.	Th.	BL.	UP.
"shoot"	puuň	piň	piň, piŋ	pɜɯŋ	poiň
"take off"	puuc		puuc	pauk	pɔic
"barking deer"	poos	puaç		pauh	paus
"break(branch)"	ṅpɯk	(pak)	(pak)	pɜup	mbɤk
"ladder"	təmpɔɔŋ	—	—	pɔŋ	mboŋ etc.

The exceptional case is the word "to wash" in which Lawa rather corresponds to *b-.

"to wash"	puh	puh	puh	poh	phoh

18. At the time of translation I felt that quite a few changes were necessary in these reconstructions, but most have been kept as in the original, with some deletions.

19. Kmt. is Khamet, MS. is the Muang Sai dialect of Khamu, Th. is Theng, or the Nghe-an dialect of Khamu, and BL. and UP. are the Bo Luang and Umphai dialects of Lawa. The Theng forms are cited from H. Maspéro, "Matériaux pour l'étude de la langue T'èng" *Bulletin de l' École Française d' Extrême-Orient* 47, (1955): 457–507. The other dialects are from my notes.

3.1.2 *b-

The initial p̀- in Khamet in low tone syllables corresponds in Khamu to MS. p̀-,[20] Th. b- (<*b-) and in Lawa to BL. p-, UP. ph- (<*b-). There is no problem in reconstructing *b- for this correspondence.

	Kmt.	MS.	Th.	BL.	UP.
"evening"	kə̀lpòol	pùar		məpu	mɯa-phu
"be able"	pèen	pùan	bɯan	pɯn	phɯn
"bamboo-shoot"	tə̀pàŋ		tbàŋ	poŋ	phoŋ
"ride"	pàk	pàk	bak	pok	phok
"bright"	pàh		bah	pɯah	phɯah	etc.

3.1.3 *t-

Parallel to *p-, the proto-phoneme *t- can be reconstructed for the following correspondences: Kmt. t-; MS. t-, Th. t- (<*t-); BL. t-, UP. t-, nd- (<*(-)t-).

	Kmt.	MS.	Th.	BL.	UP.
"hand"	tiiʔ	tiʔ	tii	taiʔ	teʔ
"earth"	kə̀tɛʔ	pteʔ	pteeh	taiʔ	teʔ
"mushroom"	tiis	tiiç		taih	tas
"crab"	kə̀taam	ktaam		tam	tam
"tongue"	pə̀ltaak	ntɤɤk	hntaak	tak	ndak	etc.

3.1.4 *d-

Parallel to *b-, *d- can be reconstructed for the following correspondences: Kmt. t̀-; MS. t̀-, Th. d- (<*d-); BL. t-, nd-, UP. th-, nd- (<*(-)d-).

	Kmt.	MS.	Th.	BL.	UP.
"ripe"	ǹtùm		hnduum	tum	thum
"poor"	tùk	tùk	—	tuk	thuk[21]
"take"	tìʔ	tèʔ	deeʔ	—	—
"low"	tèɛm	—	—	ndiam	thiam
"near"	ǹtèʔ	—	—	sǝndaiʔ	sǝndiʔ

The word "to run" is exceptional in that the Lawa forms correspond to *t-.

"run"	tèl	tàr	dar	tɒ	tɔ

20. MS. /`/ represents the second register, namely, breathy vowels. It is very difficult to distinguish the two registers in this language and there might be mistakes in my notes.
21. Could be borrowed from Thai (NT. tũk <*duk).

3.1.5 *c-(?)

The correspondence of Khamet c- in high tone syllables is not clear. In Example (i), it corresponds to c- in Khamu and s- in Lawa,[22] but in (ii) Khamet s- corresponds to the same consonants in Khamu and in Lawa.

		Kmt.	MS.	Th.	BL.	UP.
(i)	"bitter"	caŋ	caŋ	caŋ	sɒŋ	sɔŋ
(ii)	"pain"	suʔ	cuʔ	cuʔ	sɒuʔ	soʔ
	"wish"	suʔ	cuʔ	cuʔ	—	—
	"elephant"	kəsaaŋ	scaaŋ	skjaaŋ	saŋ	saŋ

3.1.6 *ǰ-

Parallel to *b- and *d-, *ǰ- can be reconstructed for: Kmt. c̀-; MS. c̀-, Th. ǰ-, j- (<*ǰ-); BL. c-, UP. ch- (<*ǰ-).

	Kmt.	MS.	Th.	BL.	UP.
"foot"	cèeŋ	cǜaŋ	jɯaŋ	cuaŋ	chuaŋ
"heavy"	kɔ̀cên	—	—	cian	chian, chɯan
"to sew"	cìŋ	—	—	cɯŋ	chiň
"go down"	cǜul	cǜur	ju(u)r	—	—

3.1.7 *k-

Parallel to *p- and *t-, there is no difficulty in reconstructing *k- for: Kmt. k-; MS. k-, Th. k- (<*k-); BL. k-, ŋg-, UP. k- (<*(-)k-).

	Kmt.	MS.	Th.	BL.	UP.
"fish"	kaaʔ	kaʔ	kaa	kaʔ	kaʔ
"child"	kɔɔn	kɔɔn	kɔɔn	kuan	kuan
"cold"	kɛt	kat	—	koat	kɔt
"female"	kɯn	cmkɯn	(cm)kɯn	kɜɯŋ	kɤn
"chin, jaw"	kaap	kaap	kaap	ŋgap	kap	etc.

3.1.8 *g-

As in the case of *b-, *d-, *ǰ-, the phoneme *g- can be reconstructed for: Kmt. k̀-; MS. k̀-, Th. g- (<*g-); BL. k-, UP. kh- (<*g-). But it is difficult to find good examples of Khamu *g- corresponding to Khamet k̀-.[23]

---

22. Kmt. caŋ might be borrowed from Khamu. If so, *c- could be assigned for the correspondence: Kmt. s-; MS. c-, Th. c- (<*c-); BL. s-, UP. s- (<*s-). In general Khamet forms which are very similar and sometimes identical to Khamu might possibly be borrowed from that language.

23. Velars became palatals before front vowels in UP. Th. trgɔt could be a mistake for trget.

	Kmt.	MS.	Th.	BL.	UP.
"think"	kùt	trkèt	trgɔt(?)	kɯt	chit(<kh)
"rat"	ǹkàaŋ	—	—	kɯaŋ	khɯaŋ
"give"	kàh	—	—	kɯah	khɯah
"cock's comb"	tòlkòoj	—	—	?əkui	rəkhui	etc.

3.1.9 *?-

There is no problem in reconstructing *?- as the proto-phoneme for ?-, which corresponds in all dialects.

	Kmt.	MS.	Th.	BL.	UP.
"water"	?oom	?om	?om	ləʔaum	rəʔaum
"chicken"	?ɛɛl	hʔiar	hʔiar	?ɛ	?ɛ
"bone"	còŋʔaaŋ	cʔaaŋ	(c)ʔaaŋ	səʔaŋ	səʔaŋ
"cooked rice"	?uup	—	—	?aup	?aup
"I"	?ɔɔʔ	?oʔ	?oo	?aiʔ	?auʔ	etc.

3.2 Nasals

3.2.1 *m-, *n-, *ň-, *ŋ-

The Khamet m̀ in low tone syllables usually corresponds to MS. m̀, Th. m- (<*m-); BL. m-, UP. m- (<*m-), and there is no problem in reconstructing *m- for this correspondence. Also *n-, *ň-, *ŋ- can be reconstructed in a similar manner.

	Kmt.	MS.	Th.	BL.	UP.
*m-					
"silver"	kòmùul	kmùul	kmuul	maɯ	mau
"you"	mìiʔ	mèe(?)	mee	maiʔ	miʔ
"one"	mòo	mòoj	mooj	—	—
"man"	Ròmèʔ	—	—	?əmaiʔ	rəmiʔ	etc.
*n-					
"urine"	nùm	nùum	nuum	naum	naum
"year"	nùɯm	nùɯm	nɯm	nᶻum	neum
"to aim"	pònèɛ			nɛ	nɛ	etc.
*ň-					
"laugh"	kòňàas	—	—	ňɯah	ňɯas
"candle"	ňòol	ňòor		—	—	etc.
*ŋ-					
"green"	còŋàal	cŋàar	—	səŋa	səŋa
"sun, day"	sòŋìiʔ	smŋìʔ	sŋii	səŋaiʔ	səňiʔ(<-ŋiʔ)
"fire"	ŋàl	—	—	ŋɒ	ŋɔ
"far"	sòŋàaj	—	—	səŋia	səŋai	etc.

3.2.2 *hm-, *hn-, *hŋ-

The initial m- in high tone syllables in Khamet corresponds to MS. m-, Th. hm- (<*hm-), BL. hm-, UP. hm- (<*hm-), for which *hm- can be reconstructed as the proto-phoneme. Also *hn-, *hŋ- can be reconstructed in a similar manner, but there is no case where *hň- can be reconstructed.

	Kmt.	MS.	Th.	BL.	UP.
*hm-					
"ask"	maaň	maaň	maaň(?)	hmaiň	hmaiň
"nail"	miim	—	—	hmaiň	hmaim
*hn-					
"blood"	naam	—	—	hnam	hnam[24]
(?)"large"	nam	nam	hnam	—	—
	"very"				
*hŋ-					
"yawn"	ŋaap		hŋaap	hŋap	hŋap
"paddy"	ŋɔɔʔ	ŋɔʔ	hŋɔɔ	hŋɒʔ	hŋɔʔ

3.2.3 *ʔm-, *ʔŋ-

Sometimes Kmt, m-, ŋ- correspond in Lawa to BL. ʔm-, UP. ʔm- (<*ʔm-) and BL. ʔŋ-, UP. ʔŋ- (<*ʔŋ-). I tentatively reconstruct *ʔm-, *ʔŋ- as the proto-phonemes of these correspondences. In Khamu, they coorespond to (-)m- and ŋ-.

	Kmt.	MS.	Th.	BL.	UP.
*ʔm-					
"ant"	rəmùuc	muuc	hmuuc	ʔmaɯk	ʔmɔic
"ax"	mùj	—	(krmiil)	ʔmau	ʔmɔi
"dry ricefield"	màal	—	—	ʔma	ʔma
*ʔŋ-					
"itch"	ŋàaʔ	ŋàʔ		-ʔŋaʔ	-ʔŋaʔ
"eye"	ŋàaj	—	—	ʔŋea	ʔŋai

Khamet b- immediately after -m also corresponds to Lawa ʔm-. Tentatively *ʔm- is assigned for this correspondence too, on the assumption that *-mʔm- > -mb- in Khamet.

	Kmt.	MS.	Th.	BL.	UP.
"spittle"	(ʔom-)bɛl	—	—	ʔmɛ	ʔmɛ
"sneeze"	tàmbəs			ʔmɔih	ʔmɔs
"cough"	rəmbook			ʔmoak	ʔmauk
"new"	tàmbah	(meʔ)	(hmee)	—	—

In addition to the preceding, there are the following irregular correspondences:

	Kmt.	MS.	Th.	BL.	UP.
"star"	rəmɯň	srmèň	slmeŋ	səʔbəɯŋ	səʔmoiň <*ʔm(?)

---

24. Compare MS. màam, Th. maam <*maam.

| "mouth" | mòom | — | — | ʔəmbɒm rəmbom < (?) |
| "to be, remain" | ŋòot | (jàt) | (jat) | ʔaɯk   ʔaut   < *ʔŋ(?) |

3.3 Semivowels

3.3.1 *j-, *w-

The proto-phoneme *j- is assigned to the correspondence Kmt. j̀-; MS. j-, Th. j- (<*j-); BL. j-, UP. j- (<*j-), and *w- to the correspondence Kmt. ẁ-; MS. w-, Th. v-, w- (<*w-); BL. v-, UP. v- (<*v-).

	Kmt.	MS.	Th.	BL.	UP.
*j-					
"weep"	jàam	jàam	jaam	jɯam	jɯam
"shut one's eyes"	kjap		(kn)jap	jiap	jiap
"die"	jàm	—	—	jum	jum
*w-					
"wide"	wàh	lwàh		vɯah	vɯah
"left (side)"	(tə̀-)wèʔ	-wèʔ	vee	(kə-)veʔ	-veʔ
"hat"	wɔ̀ɔm	—	—	vom	vom etc.

3.3.2 *hj-, *hw-, *ʔj-

The proto-phonemes *hj-, *hw-, *ʔj- can be reconstructed for the correspondences in the following examples:

	Kmt.	MS.	Th.	BL.	UP.
*hj-					
"ear"	jook	—	—	suak	suak[25]
*hw-					
"monkey"	waaʔ	waʔ	hwaa	fɯaʔ	fɯaʔ
*ʔj-					
"village"	jèeŋ	—	—	ʔjuaŋ	ʔjuaŋ

3.4 Liquids

3.4.1 *r-, *l-

There is no problem in reconstructing *r- as the proto-phoneme of the correspondence: Kmt. ʀ̀-; MS. r̀-, Th. r- (<*r-); BL. r-, UP. r- (<*r-); and *l- for Kmt. l̀-; Ms. l̀-, Th. l- (<*l-); BL. l-, UP. l- (<*l-).

	Kmt.	MS.	Th.	BL.	UP.
*r-					
"root"	ʀɛ̀ɛs	rìaç	hria(?)	rɛh	rɛs
"fly (n)"	-ʀɔ̀ɔj	rɔ̀ɔj	rɔɔj	roi	rua
"frog"	ʀòk	ròk	rok	roak	rauk etc.
*l-					
"word"	ǹlɔ̀ɔʔ	rlɔ̀ʔ	ʔrlɔɔ	—	—

25. Compare La'oop Lawa /hjuak/ (according to Schlatter).

"pig"	lĭik	—	—	lɜic	leic	
"black"	làŋ	—	—	lɒŋ	lɔŋ	etc.

3.4.2 *hr-, *hl-

There is no difficulty in reconstructing *hl- for the correspondence:
Kmt. l-; MS. l-, Th. hl- (<*hl-); BL. hl-, UP. hl- (<*hl-).

	Kmt.	MS.	Th.	BL.	UP.	
"leaf"	laaʔ	laʔ	hlaa	hlaʔ	hlaʔ	
"fear"	laat	—	—	hlat	hlat	
"high"	leeŋ	—	—	hloaŋ	hlauŋ	etc.

However, despite the existence of Kmt. ʀ- (high tone), it seems that the
Khamet reflex of *hr- is hʀ-, which corresponds in Khamu to MS. r-,
hr-, Th. hr- (<*hr-) and in Lawa to BL. hl-, UP. hr- (<*hr-).

	Kmt.	MS.	Th.	BL.	UP.
"thin"	hʀiil	—	—	hlɜi	hre
"mountain spirit"	hʀooj	hrooj	hrooj	—	—

3.4.3 *ʔr-, *ʔl-

I tentatively reconstruct *ʔr- for the correspondence: Kmt. ʀ̀;
MS. (-)r̀, Th. (-)r- (<*(-)r-); BL. ʔd-, UP. ʔr- (<*ʔr-); and *ʔl-
for the correspondence: Kmt. l-, l̀; MS. (-)l̀, Th. (-)l- (<*(-)l-);
BL. ʔd-, UP. ʔl- (<*ʔl-).

		Kmt.	MS.	Th.	BL.	UP.
*ʔr-						
	"horn"	ʀùŋ	n(t)rùŋ	cndrɯŋ	ʔdɜɯŋ	ʔrʏŋ
*ʔl-						
	"boat"	cɔlɔɔŋ	clɔɔŋ	clooŋ	—	ʔloŋ
	"long"	leeŋ	—	—	ʔdaŋ, ʔdɯŋ	ʔlaŋ

3.5 Fricatives

3.5.1 *s-, *h-

For the correspondence of s- in all dialects, it is clear that the
proto-phoneme is *s-. Also *h- is reconstructed for the correspondence:
Kmt. h-; BL. h-, UP. h- (<*h-) in a similar manner, although Khamu
words with h- corresponding to Khamet h- cannot be found.[26]

		Kmt.	MS.	Th.	BL.	UP.
*s-						
	"louse"	siʔ	seʔ	see	sɜiʔ	seʔ
	"dog"	sɔʔ	sɔʔ	sɔɔ(ʔ)	sɒʔ	sɔʔ

---

26.   There is of course Proto-Khamu *h-; e.g. "die" MS. haan, Th. haan <*haan.

"bird"	siim	siim	siim	saiň	saim	
"night"	-sɛɛm	psɯam	psɯam	-saum	-saum	etc.

*h-

"walk"	hɯl	—	—	həu	heu
"bathe"	huum	—	—	haum	haum
(?)"bee"	tɔ̀lhaaj	—	—	hɛ	hɛ

3.6 Clusters

In addition to the preceding consonants, the following consonant clusters can be reconstructed: *pr-, *pl-, *ph-; *tr-, *dr-; *kr-, *kh-; *sl-. Of these, the Khamu forms corresponding to *ph-, *kh- are not found, as was the case with *h-.

3.6.1 *pr-, *pl-, *ph-

The cluster *pr- can be assigned for the correspondence Kmt. pʀ-: MS. pr-, Th. pr- (< *pr-); BL. phr-, UP. pr- (< *pr-); *pl- for the correspondence of pl- in all dialects; and *ph- for the correspondence of Khamet and Lawa ph-.

	Kmt.	MS.	Th.	BL.	UP.
*pr-					
"old"	pʀiim	priim	—	phraiň	praim
"hail"	pʀɛɛl			phrɛ	prɛ
*pl-					
"fruit"	pleʔ-	pleʔ	pleeʔ	plɜiʔ-	pleʔ-
"landleech"	pleem	plɯam		plaum	plaum
*ph-					
"heart"	pheem	—	—	ʔəphaum	rəphaum
"five"	phan	—	—	phoan	phɔn

3.6.2 *tr-, *dr-

Although there are few examples, *tr-, *dr- can be reconstructed as the proto-phonemes of the following examples. In Lawa, there are no clusters such as tr-, ndr-, thr-, so the original *tr-, *dr- are apparently included in khr-, kr-, ŋgr- (< *N-gr-).

	Kmt.	MS.	Th.	BL.	UP.
"buffalo"	tʀaak	traak	trak	khrak	krak
"underneath"	tʀùum	ntrùum		ŋgraum	-ŋgrum

3.6.3 *kr-, *kh-

No doubt *kr- and *kh- can be reconstructed for the following examples, although I found no good examples of Khamu corresponding Khamet kʀ- and kh-.

	Kmt.	MS.	Th.	BL.	UP.
*kr-					
"bear"	kʀiis	—	—	khrɜih	kres
*kh-					
*kh-"month"	kheʔ	—	—	khɜiʔ	kheʔ
"tree"	-kheʔ	—	—	khɒuʔ	khoʔ

3.6.4 *sl-

I reconstruct *sl- for the following example. Thus, part of *hl- mentioned earlier might in fact be *sl-.

	Kmt.	MS.	Th.	BL.	UP.
"deaf"	luut	sluut	sluut	hlaɯk	hlaut

3.7 Final Consonants

Although final consonants have changed greatly in Lawa, they are quite stable in Khamet and Khamu so it is not difficult to reconstruct the proto-final consonants of the three languages.

3.7.1 *Stops and nasals*

Here I will not list the correspondence forms separately. Final *-p, *-t, *-c, *-k, *-ʔ and *-m, *-n, *-ň, *-ŋ could be reconstructed with little difficulty. Examples: "yawn" ŋaap, "cold" kɛt, "ant" ʀəmùuc, "tongue" pəltaak, "I" ʔɔɔʔ, "bird" siim, "child" kɔɔn, "shoot" puɯň, "bone" cəŋʔaaŋ, etc.[27]

3.7.2 *Liquids*

Final liquids do not exist in Lawa and only a final -l exists in Khamet, but two finals *-l and *-r can be reconstructed through Khamu forms. Namely, *-l for Kmt. -l: MS. -l, Th. -l (< *-l): BL. -#, UP. -# (< *-#), and *-r for Kmt. -l: MS. -r, Th. -r (< *-r): BL. -#, UP. -# (# *-#). Examples: "silver" kəmùul # *-l, "chicken" ʔɛɛl < *-r.

3.7.3 *Semivowels*

We can reconstruct *-j for the correspondence: Kmt. -j: MS. -j, Th. -j (< *-j): BL. -(i), UP. -(i) (< *-i).

	Kmt.	MS.	Th.	BL.	UP.
"fly (n.)"	-ʀɔ̀ɔj	rɔ̀ɔj	rɔɔj	roi	rua
"eye"	ŋàaj	—	—	ʔŋea	ʔŋai	etc.

---

27. Only the Khamet forms will be given in this section, to avoid repetition.

However, all cases where *-w seems to be the proto-phoneme are actually Thai borrowings, and it is not certain whether there was *-w at the common stage of the three languages.

| "cat" | mὲεw | mὲεw | meew(?) | meau | mεu | NT.mεεw |
| "foolish" | ŋàaw | — | — | ŋoa | ŋau | NT.ŋâaw |

3.7.4 *Fricatives*

I reconstruct *-s for Kmt. -s: MS. -ç[-jh], Th. -h (< *-s): BL. -h, UP. -s (< *-s); and *-h for the correspondence of -h in all dialects. Examples: "mushroom" tiis, "deer" poos, "wide" wàh, "wash" puh, etc.

3.7.5 *Open syllables*

Strangely enough, no word with an open syllable is shared by the three languages except for Thai borrowings. On the other hand there are many examples of the previously mentioned final *-ʔ and *-h. This fact suggests that either *-ʔ or *-h did not function as a final consonant in the common language.

GENERAL REFERENCES

W. Schmidt: "Die Palaung-, Wa-und Riang-Sprachen des mittleren Salwin" (Anhang an "Grundzüge einer Lautlehre der Khasi-Sprachen in ihren Beziehungen zu derjenigen der Mon-Khmer-Sprachen") *Abhandlungen der bayrischen Akademie der Wissenschaften* I. Kl., Bd. 22, Abt. 3, 1904, pp. 778–806.

R. Shafer: "Études sur l'austroasien" *Bulletin de la Société Linguistique de Paris* 48, 1, 1952. pp. 111–58.

W. Smalley: *Outline of Khmuʔ Structure*, 1961, xix + 45. pp.

6

The Glutinous Rice Zone in Thailand —Patterns of Change in Cultivated Rice

TADAYO WATABE

INTRODUCTION

The choice offered by the development of different types of rice, upland and paddy rice, glutinous and nonglutinous rice, and particularly *indica* and *japonica*, has influenced agricultural techniques and social structure. Widely different farming cultures have developed around the same crop, rice, as comparison of upland rice cultivation by slash-and-burn techniques and floating rice cultivation in riverine back-swamps clearly shows. Certain regions bear evidence of change in the type of rice cultivated, and this enables us to trace the development of agriculture. India and Southeast Asia in particular have intimate links with the origins of rice cultivation and are important areas of study, although there is limited documentation and archaeological data.

Since 1963 I have been engaged in fieldwork on rice crops in Thailand and feel that I have some reliable data to put forward. Here I will consider the development of rice cultivation in the area of Thailand that produces glutinous rice, the glutinous rice zone. My evidence dates back about fifteen hundred years, and covers the period which saw major changes in rice cultivation, especially that of glutinous rice.

THE AREA OF GLUTINOUS RICE CULTIVATION

1. Distribution

Most of the rice cultivated in the world today is nonglutinous, but in various Asian countries with a long history of rice, e.g. Japan, India and China, some glutinous rice is cultivated. In America, Australia and Europe, regions where rice cultivation is comparatively recent, there is almost no glutinous rice. In Africa, which also has a long history of rice cultivation, there is thought to be no glutinous rice (Nakao, 1969, p. 39). Thus glutinous rice cultivation seems to be characteristic of the Orient rather than a feature of a long history of rice. In most parts of Asia glutinous rice is a minor crop used for confectionary and alcoholic drinks, and not, as in Japan, a staple food.

But in Southeast Asia there exists a unique region where glutinous rice is cultivated as the major crop and is consumed as the staple food. The full extent of the region, lying in the high latitudes of Southeast Asia, is not yet known; but the glutinous rice zone of North and Northeast Thailand, and Laos, where 90 percent of rice is glutinous (Cho, 1963, p. 3), constitutes its center.

In Burma, we know from the works of Simmonds (1877, p. 323) and Copeland (1924; p. 120) that production of glutinous rice is widespread in the Shan states; it is also thought to be common in Lower Burma. According to Cheng Siok-Hwa (1968, pp. 38–39), the "Midon" group of varieties, which is widely cultivated in Lower Burma, has small, round grains and whitish-opaque unhulled rice,[1] and is mainly consumed in the home. From these characteristics it may be a type of glutinous rice, but is apparently not dominant in the region.[2] In Cambodia, glutinous rice is cultivated in a small area bordering Thailand and Laos, and in Vietnam, along the Laotian border (Hamada, 1965, pp. 544–563).

Figure 1 shows the general outline of the area of cultivation of glutinous rice, with North and Northeast Thailand and Laos as the center and parts of Burma, Vietnam, and Cambodia on the perimeter. The question mark in Yunnan indicates the paucity of information on this region. It may be necessary to revise this map following further investigations in Burma, Vietnam, Yunnan, etc.[3] Although there have been various researches on upland rice (slash-and-burn) cultivation in these regions, interest in glutinous rice has been extremely limited.

1.   The iodine—potassium iodide reaction is used for distinguishing glutinous and nonglutinous rice. And glutinous rice has the characteristic that if the water content of the unmilled rice is less than 14 percent it becomes white and opaque. It is easy to separate glutinous and nonglutinous rice by the color test if it is dry unmilled rice, but the two cannot be distinguished before harvesting.

2.   In a survey in this area in 1974 nonglutinous rice was found in the Midon group of varieties.

3.   In later surveys in Burma it was confirmed that glutinous rice is widely cultivated in the Shan and Kachin states. And it has also been authoritatively reported that in China glutinous rice is widely cultivated in the Kwangsi Chuang region as well as in Yunnan.

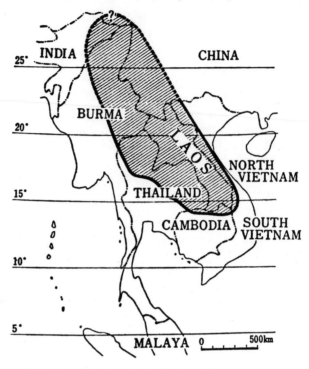

Figure 1.   *Distribution of glutinous rice in Southeast Asia*

Since this is the only region where glutinous rice cultivation is dominant, I feel that more research is necessary.

2. The Situation in Thailand

For several months I lived in the farming village of Sanpatong on the southern outskirts of Chiang Mai, the main city of North Thailand. This region is said to be moderately well-off in comparison with other farming villages in North Thailand, but the cultivation and use of glutinous rice by its people are representative of the entire glutinous-rice zone. About 84 percent of the paddy area of the village was devoted to glutinous rice in the rainy season (June to December), while in the dry season (February to June) nonglutinous rice occupied 94 percent of the cultivated land, although only 10 percent of the available land was under cultivation. Rice production in 1964 was approximately 80 percent glutinous to 20 percent nonglutinous. All villagers ate glutinous rice three times a day, every day. So a large part of the glutinous rice produced was consumed by the people as their staple

Plate 1.   *A glutinous rice steamer*

food, while the rest went to the domestic market or was exported to such countries as Laos and Japan.

Glutinous rice for the day is cooked once a day, normally in the morning. The utensil used is shown in Plate 1. The upper part where rice is placed is hollowed out of wood and has a loosely fitting wooden bottom which allows steam to pass from the wide-necked earthenware water pot below. The bottom part is an earthenware brazier. The cooked rice is transferred to a bamboo basket and at each meal a little is taken at a time, worked with the fingertips, and eaten.[4]

Of the Southeast Asian countries, only Thailand publishes figures on the areas of glutinous and nonglutinous rice cultivation. The table, based on these figures, shows the general picture of glutinous rice production in Thailand, and its concentration in the North and Northeast. Figure 2 shows the percentage of glutinous rice cultivated arranged

4.   The beginning of a trend away from the habit of having glutinous rice as the main food is observed, even in the villages, among the affluent classes and the intelligentsia. I wrote of this from Sanpatong in 1965.

It is not that the people of Northern Thailand do not eat nonglutinous rice at all. From observation it seems that in the affluent classes the amount of nonglutinous rice consumed is quite high. . . . In slightly wealthy households nonglutinous rice constitutes the evening meal. Poor people eat glutinous rice. If one asks members of the intelligentsia (educated classes) "Do you usually eat glutinous rice?" they pull a face and say "No, nonglutinous rice." It is possible that this is a craze for the 'Bangkok style' (like the 'Tokyo-style' in Japan), or maybe they are proud and regard glutinous rice as the food of peasants, or perhaps nonglutinous rice is a subsidiary food.

AREAS OF GLUTINOUS RICE CULTIVATION IN THAILAND (1962)

Region	Paddy Area (ha)	Area of Glutinous Rice Cultivation (ha)	Percentage
North	415,221	375,053	90.3
Northeast	3,139,220	1,944,044	61.9
Central	3,051,184	96,796	3.2
South	528,679	21,514	4.1
Total	7,134,304	2,437,407	34.2

(Rice Department, 1964: Table 9)

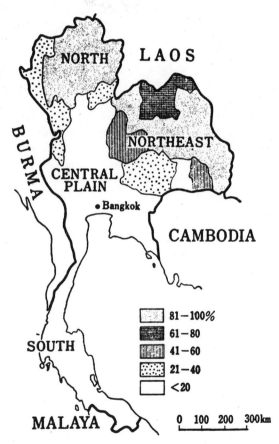

Figure 2.   *Proportion of land under glutinous rice to all paddy land, by region*

by province (*changwat*). In the Northeast, the percentage is generally high north of the river Mun, a tributary of the Mekong, and this area together with the North constitutes the center of the cultivation zone. Regions with a cultivated area of 21–40 percent are transition zones to nonglutinous rice. Here glutinous rice yields its place as staple food to nonglutinous rice, and its use in confectionary and alcoholic drinks increases. In the Central Plain where the Chao Phraya flows, nonglutinous rice is ubiquitous. Here and in Southern Thailand glutinous rice is a rare sight.

The dominance of glutinous rice in the North and Northeast has been recorded since early times, but few attempts have been made to explain this dominance. It is often said that glutinous rice suited the taste of the inhabitants of the region, but this explanation is merely superficial. Dobby (1958, p. 270) and de Young (1963, p. 78) both state that because glutinous rice is early maturing, it is suited to the short growing season of this high latitude zone. This explanation is, as far as I know, the only agricultural one put forward, but as neither of these authors is an agriculturalist this may be a hasty conclusion. Certainly in comparison with nonglutinous rice, the ratio of early-maturing varieties is high. And in Japanese studies it has been noted that many varieties of glutinous rice are resistant to low temperature. However, this argument is not persuasive as it ignores the fact that many types of nonglutinous rice are cultivated in higher latitudes with lower temperatures than Northern Thailand.

EVIDENCE OF CHANGE IN CULTIVATED RICE

1. Methods of Investigation: Two Problems

To learn more of the history of cultivated rice, it is desirable to investigate archaeological finds of unhulled and unpolished rice. In Japan such finds are accidental and sporadic and are not sufficient for a systematic investigation; in Thailand the situation is, if anything, less promising.

Therefore, I turned my attention to rice chaff which had been incorporated in the bricks used from early times in Thailand, particularly in stupas and in ramparts and city walls.[5] These bricks, like those of today, were made of clay and water with sizeable amounts of chaff. Fortunately they are found in remains all over Thailand and can provide material for a systematic and reliable investigation into cul-

---

5. I would like to add here that I received many useful suggestions from two friends, Mr. Kian Kongchatuk of Thailand and Dr. Yoshikatsu Takaya of Japan.

tivated rice that does not require archaeological finds of unhulled rice.[6]

In a preliminary investigation in 1967, twenty-two bricks representing each historical period were collected from ruins in the Chao Phraya basin and the shape of the incorporated chaff was examined. As previously reported (Watabe and Akihama, 1958, pp. 89–92), the chaff showed fairly accurately the type of rice cultivated at a given period and location. Thus by tracing the change in the shape of chaff the process of change in cultivated rice can be defined. The following year, bricks were collected from eighty-six sites throughout Thailand.[7] Of these, seventy-six contained sizeable amounts of chaff, as in Plate 2.

Two points relating to this method of investigation need some explanation. It is necessary to identify when and where the rice chaff in the bricks was cultivated. First, I have assumed the "when," that is, the actual period of cultivation, to be more or less the time of the construction of the monument for which the bricks were used. This assumes the coincidence of the period of cultivation of the chaff, the period when that chaff was incorporated into the bricks, and the period when those bricks were used in construction of the monument. The age of the remains was determined by discussion with specialists and consulting the literature.[8] In the case of recent buildings, particularly temples in Bangkok, the older Ayutthaya period temples were dismantled and the bricks taken to Bangkok and used there (Ishii, 1968, p. 36). There are also cases where a stupa has been enlarged, and the ages of bricks in the inner and outer layers differ. Such materials were excluded from this investigation.

Second is where the chaff was cultivated. I assumed that the chaff in the bricks came from rice cultivated not far from the site of the monument. To put it another way, I assumed that in days when transportation was not very advanced, the area of rice cultivation, the place where the bricks were manufactured, and the site of the monument would all be moderately close. Of course, there is no definite

6. As far as I know bricks incorporating rice chaff have been found in Laos, Burma, India, and parts of China, as well as in Thailand.

7. This collection was carried out in cooperation with Dr. Tomoya Akihama, technical officer of the Japanese National Institute of Agricultural Sciences of the Ministry of Agriculture and Forestry. The results and conclusions published here were largely based on discussion with Dr. Akihama, a specialist in rice classification.

8. For the identification of the age of ruins I am indebted to the specialists of the Thai Fine Arts Department and the National Museum. For some of the ruins C^{14} dating methods were applied to the wood from the same structure as the bricks. There were few cases where it was possible to identify a period precisely, but for this survey it was not necessary to inquire whether certain ruins could be dated 1320 or 1330, to say they were fourteenth century was sufficient.

Plate 2.   *A brick containing chaff*

proof that this is so. However, in saying "moderately close" I envisage distances of ten to twenty kilometers, or at most one hundred kilometers. As transportation facilities improved and the centralized nation state became more powerful, large national temples were constructed; it is possible that bricks for these were carried long distances. I, therefore, took care to avoid collecting bricks from this sort of national site, whether ancient or modern.[9]

Applying these criteria, ninety-six bricks were selected for study from the collections of 1967 and 1968. These bricks came from all regions of Thailand except the Pasak basin, and included samples from every period from the sixth to the nineteenth centuries.

Probably the first author to deal with the discovery of chaff in bricks is Ting Ying. He states that rice husks found in bricks of baked red clay excavated in the Hupei plain in China date from 4,000 years ago (Ting Ying, 1959, p. 31). In Southeast Asia and India it is generally thought that the widespread use of bricks does not date back so far. In the Indochina peninsula including Thailand there are very few remains, other than Oc-Eo, from before about the sixth century. The limitation thus imposed means that my materials probably include the oldest chaff obtainable by this method.

Perfect rice husks in the bricks were selected,[10] and for each brick

9.   The collection of bricks was carried out with the permission of the National Research Council. But in fact in many cases it was impossible to collect bricks from special large temples and ruins.

10.   Usually one type of rice chaff was incorporated in each brick (sample T68–01), but there were cases where two or more different types were incorporated (T67–12). In the latter cases it was assumed that two or more rice types were cultivated simultaneously in that area.

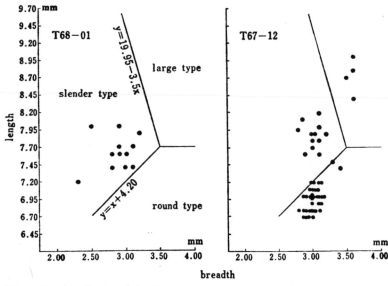

Figure 3.   *Classification of rice types*

the ratio of length to breadth of ten to fifty grains was measured. These were classified into three types: round, large, and slender, which corresponded to Matsuo's A type (*japonica*), B type (intermediate) and C type (*indica*), respectively, using his criteria for unhulled rice types (Matsuo, 1952, pp. 6–10).

Some of the bricks collected were fired, and some were adobe or sun-dried. As it was conceivable that chaff, particularly in fired bricks, might have shrunk, fresh unhulled rice was machine dried. The experimentally determined shrinkage was only 0.6–0.7 percent in length and about 1.5 percent in breadth, and this was considered to have negligible effect on deciding the type of unhulled rice.

2. Distribution of Types of Unhulled Rice by Period

The samples cover approximately fourteen hundred years from the sixth to the nineteenth centuries, in which the following four major historical periods are recognized:[11] (i) sixth to eleventh centuries,

11.   According to the simple book published by the Thai Fine Arts Department the sixth to the eleventh centuries are called the Dvaravati period. The eleventh to the fifteenth centuries were the time when various northern dynasties—Lopburi, Sukhodaya and U-thong—defended their autonomy, with some fluctations. The next period, from the fifteenth to the eighteenth centuries, was the Ayutthaya period. And the final period comprises the fall of the Ayutthaya dynasty (1767), the short Dhonburi dynasty, and stretches up to the present day and the Bangkok dynasty (Phya Anuman Rajadhon, 1957, pp. 5–10).

(ii) eleventh to fifteenth centuries, (iii) fifteenth to eighteenth centuries, and (iv) eighteenth century onward. Figure 4 shows the distribution according to these periods of the three types of unhulled rice—the round, large, and slender types of Figure 3.

From the sixth to eleventh centuries, the most common rice cultivated in Thailand was the round type, second was the large type. The slender type was sparsely distributed, mainly in the Northeast, the sole exception being found at U-thong (Sapanburi) in the Chao Phraya basin where the slender type otherwise was not found. Incidentally, the slender type was common in Cambodia at this time. Today the slender type is predominant in the Chao Phraya basin.

In the next period, the eleventh to the fifteenth centuries, the round type was found in every region, and as before was dominant in the Chao Phraya basin. During this period, however, the slender type became more common in the Chao Phraya basin. And the large type, although still found nationwide, tended to decrease. This change in the distribution of rice types, particularly the emergence of the slender type in the Chao Phraya basin, may be considered a turning point in the change in cultivated rice in Thailand.

From the fifteenth to the eighteenth centuries, the round type, centered as before in the Chao Phraya basin, was also widely found in the North and Northeast. And the slender type, now centered in the Chao Phraya basin had greatly increased. Its distribution was about half that of the round type in that region. The large type continued to decline and was no longer found in the Central Plain. The trend observed in the previous period continued.

In the last period, from the eighteenth century on, one can see a quite new development: the unilateral increase in the distribution of slender rice and its exclusive cultivation throughout the Central Plain. In contrast to this overwhelming increase in the slender type, both the round and the large types were found only in the North and Northeast in this period. The round type, which had been the most widely distributed from the earliest period, in fact, the representative type of rice in Thailand, underwent a distinctive change in distribution. Thus two important turning points emerge: one in the eleventh century, and one in the eighteenth century.

3. Conjectured Rice Types from the Distribution of Unhulled Rice

Next I would like to focus on the characteristics of these three types of cultivated rice. The round type, as just described, was most widely distributed throughout Thailand from the sixth to the eighteenth

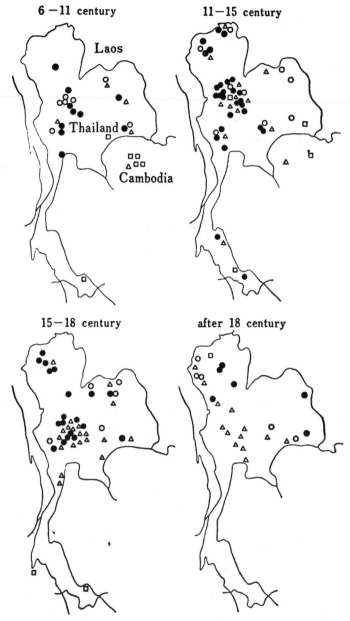

● : round type ○ : large type △ : slender type □ : no grain in brick

Figure 4.   *Distribution of rice types by period*

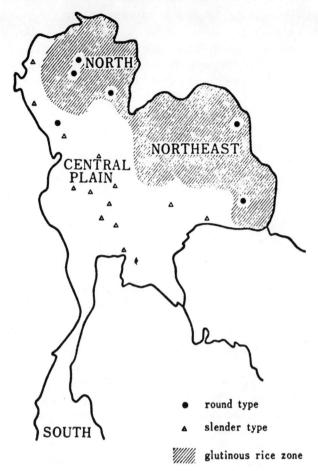

Figure 5.   *Distribution of round and slender types and the glutinous rice zone from the eighteenth century*

centuries. The ratio of grain length to breadth for this type of unhulled rice is generally about two, and its characteristics show great similarity to the *japonica* type.[12] This type disappeared completely from the Central Plain after the eighteenth century, and, as seen from Figure 4, remained only in the North and Northeast. Figure 5 shows rice distribution from

12.   We previously stated from these characteristics that this type is *japonica* (Watabe and Akihama, 1968). The *nuda* widespread in Laos at the present time is, according to Morinaga, very like *japonica* but with no husk hairs, and is a type with a very close affinity and relationship to *japonica*. From this Morinaga holds that the 'ecospecies *japonica*' is divided into 'ecotype *japonica*' and 'ecotype *nuda*'. Therefore it seems appropriate to redesignate the type mentioned earlier as '*japonica*-like'.

the eighteenth century superimposed on the glutinous rice zone of modern Thailand. It is clear that the round type occurs mostly in the glutinous rice zone, which implies that a large part of the round type is glutinous rice. Also it is probably no mere coincidence that the round type is confined to the Ping and Yom basins in the North and the lower reaches of the Mun and Song Khram in the Northeast, where water supply has always been good. Certainly the round type occurred in areas with flat paddy fields. This leads me to conclude that most of the round rice was probably glutinous paddy rice.

However, it is also known that varieties of the round type, which are thought to be *japonica*, occasionally occur in present-day upland rice in the mountainous areas of the North (Cho, 1960, pp. 10–13; Oka and Chang, 1963, pp. 163–168; Akihama, 1965, pp. 93–94), which means that there is a slight possibility of some of the round type being upland rice.

The large type was fairly widely distributed in all regions until around the fifteenth century, and subsequently disappeared from the Central Plain. Figure 6 shows the distribution of this rice from the sixth century onward superimposed on a contour map. Most large rice was found in the mountainous region of Kanjana Buri on the Northern border with Burma and the Khorat Plateau of the Northeast. From Figure 4 one can see that as time went on, the distribution of this type receded to comparatively high places and border areas. This suggests that most of the large type of rice was upland rice.

I do not have the materials to judge whether the endosperm of the large type, assumed to be upland rice, is glutinous or nonglutinous. Cho states that in upland rice at present cultivated by the Meo, Yao, and other tribes, both glutinous and nonglutinous varieties exist side by side in a ratio that differs from tribe to tribe, but with glutinous rice generally predominant (Cho, 1960, p. 3). Iwata states that most mountain tribes, other than the Meo and Yao, cultivate mainly glutinous upland rice (Iwata and Matsuoka, 1967, p. 309). In a Lawa village in the North I found that glutinous and nonglutinous varieties were usually cultivated together in the same field.[13]

Thus the following conjecture seems reasonable. In these regions of upland rice the main type of rice is glutinous, but sometimes natural hybrids of nonglutinous rice occur. Because the nonglutinous genes are dominant, the hybrids frequently recur; and as the generations of

---

13. From my experience it was pointless to try to judge whether glutinous or non-glutinous rice was cultivated in upland rice fields by examining small quantities of unhulled rice; misclassification has resulted from such attempts.

Figure 6. *Distribution of the large type from the sixth century on, superimposed on a contour map*

hybrids progress the proportion of nonglutinous rice gradually increases to the level where, as in the Lawa village, both types are intermixed. A shift in the other direction is not genetically possible. This type of process—that is, natural selection—occurs widely where little or no thought is given to selection of varieties. Hence I would like to postulate that glutinous rice predominated in the large upland rice of the earlier periods, while in the later periods nonglutinous varieties probably occupied a gradually increasing proportion. If this trend continues, nonglutinous varieties may predominate. To support this supposition more evidence is necessary on the distribution of glutinous and nonglutinous varieties in present upland rice. For the present I would like to point out the high probability that upland rice cultivated in early times in Thailand was glutinous.

Last, I will deal with the slender type. This was limited to the Northeast in around the eleventh century, and subsequently spread gradually to all regions. During the fifteenth to the eighteenth centuries it came to rival the round type in the Central Plain, and from the eighteenth century became dominant in this region. It must be noted that of the three types of unhulled rice only the slender type expanded its area of distribution in the fourteen-hundred-year period studied. Figure 5 shows clearly that the slender type occurs outside the limits of the glutinous rice zone in regions where today nonglutinous paddy rice is the focus of cultivation. This seems to indicate that most of the the slender type is nonglutinous paddy rice.

DEVELOPMENT OF THE GLUTINOUS RICE ZONE

1. The Process of Development

A pattern of development emerges from the findings for the three types of unhulled rice. Above I suggested that the round type is glutinous paddy rice, the large type, glutinous upland rice (possibly including more nonglutinous varieties as time progressed), and the slender type, nonglutinous paddy rice. Within the limits of this investigation, that is, beginning from the sixth century, the general outlines of the changes can be summarized as follows. In early times glutinous paddy rice and glutinous upland rice were dominant; but gradually the area of glutinous paddy rice cultivation shrank, while glutinous upland rice decreased everywhere. On the other hand, nonglutinous paddy rice increased. From the general trend of farming development in Southeast Asia, and the findings of Nakao, it seems that upland rice was cultivated earliest (Nakao, 1966, pp. 129–131). From the sixth to the eleventh centuries glutinous paddy rice (round type) and glutinous upland rice (large type) were both comparatively widespread (see Figure 4). This time can be regarded as a transitional period where glutinous upland rice is a relic from the older agricultural society, and glutinous paddy rice, the representative crop of the new.

Dividing the country into the Central Plain and the North and Northeast, a general theory can be formulated for the past fourteen hundred of change in cultivated rice.[14] In the Central Plain the dominant

14.   In the southern region materials for tracing the transition of rice cultivation were too few, and as I would like to make an accurate study I have not touched on that area here. The main feature of rice cultivation in that area is that it should be considered as part of that of the Malay peninsula. I have begun the collection of materials, and will deal with this on another occasion.

type is thought to have changed in the order: glutinous upland rice →
glutinous paddy rice → nonglutinous paddy rice. Thus nonglutinous rice
from this region, which we tend to view as representative of Thai rice,
is in fact a newcomer. Changes in the dominant type in the North and
part of the Northeast follow the same pattern from glutinous upland
rice to glutinous paddy rice, but the last transition, that to nonglutinous
paddy rice, is lacking. To put it another way, the change from glutinous
upland rice to glutinous paddy rice occurred throughout Thailand, but
only in the Central Plain did the transition to nonglutinous paddy rice
occur.

Originally, then, glutinous rice must have been cultivated virtually
all over Thailand. But beginning in the fifteenth century in the lower
basin of the Chao Phraya, cultivation gradually shifted to nonglutinous
paddy rice, and by the eighteenth century this covered the whole
Central Plain and part of the Northeast. The regions which did not
give way to nonglutinous paddy rice remain as today's glutinous rice
zone. The glutinous rice cultivation, which was characteristic of early
Thai agriculture, has been preserved in this region. So the clear boundary of today's glutinous rice zone, as seen from Figure 4, is at most
only about two hundred years old.

2. The Causes of Development

In connection with my idea that the early inhabitants of Thailand
were glutinous rice-eaters, it is interesting that Nakao (1966, p. 131)
indicated the existence of a glutinous type of starch, Job's tears (*Coix
ma-yuen* or *Coix lacryma-jobi*), in the development of root-crop farming
culture in Southeast Asia. The yams and taros of the society which, in
its early stages cultivated root crops, are thought to resemble glutinous
rice starch in taste. The change in the main food of Southeast Asian
agriculture from potatoes (roots) to Job's tears and glutinous rice is
the story of "sticky food." So it seems that glutinous rice cultivation in
Thailand was based on a continued attachment to this "sticky food" of
the ancient peoples of Southeast Asia.

Most regions have lost this attachment to "sticky food." Why does
it continue in the present-day glutinous rice zone? Why was it only
this region that nonglutinous rice did not enter? How did nonglutinous
rice gradually enter the Central Plain? The transition from glutinous
paddy rice to nonglutinous paddy rice in the Central Plain cannot be
explained by botanical factors. There is no doubt that the change was
instigated by man. So what were the human conditions at the time
when the Central Plain chose nonglutinous rice and the North and
Northeast did not?

One suggestion is that the pressure of population increase in the Central Plain was greater than in other regions and so the more productive nonglutinous type was chosen. However at the present time there is no great difference in productivity between the glutinous and nonglutinous rice produced in Thailand. Even if ancient and present rice varieties are not indentical, this argument is not persuasive. It is also suggested that rice production techniques, for example, methods of manuring, irrigation facilities, etc., developed markedly only in the Central Plain at a certain time; and this produced conditions more suitable to the cultivation of nonglutinous paddy rice. With today's knowledge of agriculture it is difficult to accept that there could be large enough differences in cultivation techniques and conditions to influence the productivity of glutinous and nonglutinous varieties of the same paddy rice. Therefore I think that neither of these points would be conclusive in the choice of nonglutinous rice by people who had long been attached to the characteristic taste of glutinous rice.

In the human field there is a clear possibility: that of ethnic or tribal differences. As shown in Figure 4, nonglutinous rice appeared in the Chao Phraya basin after the eleventh century, and it is possible that at this time a group of nonglutinous rice eaters immigrated to the area. If we allow this possibility the theoretically most simple assumption is that this people in due course made the Central Plain their domain and continued to cultivate nonglutinous rice. These circumstances are perhaps well known in historical and ethnological circles, but since ethnology is not my field I can only state that this explanation seems most appropriate.

As another possible reason for the development of the glutinous rice zone, we must consider the export of nonglutinous rice, which increased gradually from the eighteenth century. With the rice in external demand from various countries, particularly after the Bowring Treaty of 1855, and the improvement of facilities for transportation to Bangkok, the cultivation of nonglutinous rice in and around the Central Plain expanded rapidly. This great increase in nonglutinous rice production can only be explained by the fact that the people of the Central Plain already had experience in cultivating nonglutinous rice and that there was an external demand. The North and Northeast with generally poor transportation facilities are considered outside the limits of this economic demand. But the dominance of nonglutinous rice in the Mai Hong Son area in the northwest, remote from Bangkok and even today self-sufficient in rice, cannot be explained by this reasoning. Ethnological differences alone seem to offer some explanation.

So it seems difficult to explain all aspects of the long process of selection of glutinous or nonglutinous rice without considering the intricate interchange and migration of peoples in Thailand. In this article only the agricultural aspects of the development of the glutinous rice zone have been described. The main questions raised must be answered by ethnology and history.

REFERENCES

T. Akihama. "Classification of Cultivated Rice Varities—in Cultivated Plants in Some Ethnic Communities of Northwestern Thailand." *Nature and Life in Southeast Asia.* Edited by Matsuoka and Kira, vol. 4, Kyoto, 1965.

Cheng Siok-Hwa. *The Rice Industry of Burma 1852–1940.* Singapore: University of Malaya, 1968.

J. Cho. in "Symposium on the Synthetic Research of Rice Culture in Southeastern Countries" (in Japanese). *Minzokugaku Kenkyu,* vol. 22, nos.3:4. Tokyo, 1958.

Edward B. Copeland. *Rice.* Macmillan, London, 1924.

J. E. de Young. *Village Life in Modern Thailand.* 3d ed. Berkeley and Los Angeles: University of California.

Ernest H. G. Dobby. *Southeast Asia.* 6th ed. London, University of London, 1958.

H. Hamada. "Rice Cultivation in the Indo-Chinese Peninsula" (in Japanese). *Minzokugaku Kenkyu,* vol. 29, no. 1. Tokyo, 1964.

Y. Ishii. "An Introductory Note on the Thai Corvée System" (in Japanese). *Southeast Asian Studies,* vol. 6, no. 1. Center for Southeast Asian Studies, Kyoto University, 1968.

K. Iwata. and M. Matsuoka. "Agricultural Practices among Thai Yai, Thai Lu and Certain Hill Tribes in Northern Thailand." *Nature and Life in Southeast Asia.* vol. 5. Kyoto, 1967.

T. Matsuo. "Genecological Studies on Cultivated Rice" (in Japanese). National Institute for Agricultural Sciences Series, D3. Tokyo, 1952.

T. Morinaga. "Origin and Geographical Distribution of Japanese Rice." *Japan Agricultural Research Quarterly,* vol. 3, no. 2. Tokyo, 1968.

S. Nakao. *The Origins of Agriculture and Cultivated Crops* (in Japanese). Tokyo: Iwanami Shoten, 1966.

S. Nakao. *From the Niger to the Nile* (in Japanese). Tokyo: Kodansha, 1969.

H. Oka and W. Chang. "A Note on Rice Varieties of Japonica Type Found in Northern Thailand." *Botanical Bulletin of Academia Sinica,* vol. 4, no. 2. Taipei, 1963.

Phya Anuman Rajadhon. *Introducing Cultural Thailand in Outline.* Bangkok: Fine Arts Dept., 1957.

Rice Department. *Annual Report on 1962 Rice Production in Thailand.* Bangkok: Ministry of Agriculture, 1964.

Peter L. Simmonds. *Tropical Agriculture.* London: E. and F. Spon, 1877.

Ting Ying. "Notes on the Neolithic Rice Husks Unearthed in Hupei" (in Chinese). *Kaogu Xuebao,* no. 4. Peking, 1959.

Tadayo Watabe. "From Sanpatong" (in Japanese). *Southeast Asian Studies,* vol. 3, no. 3. Center for Southeast Asian Studies, Kyoto University, 1965.

Tadayo Watabe. *Glutinous Rice in Northern Thailand.* Tokyo: Yokendo, 1967.

Tadayo Watabe and T. Akihama. "Morphology of Rice Grains Recovered from Ruins in Thailand." *Southeast Asian Studies,* vol. 6, no. 2. Center for Southeast Asian Studies, Kyoto University, 1968.

7

Physiography of Rice Land in the Chao Phraya Basin

YOSHIKAZU TAKAYA

INTRODUCTION

Rice cultivation is found in various environments, ranging from mountain slopes to flooded deltaic basins. These rice lands in the Chao Phraya basin have been classified by Fukui into six categories, based on the simplicity of disseminating new varieties of rice.[1] This article gives a physiographic description of Fukui's six types of rice land.

AREAL DISTRIBUTION OF RICE LANDS

The six physiographic regions are the intermontane basins, the constricted river channel area, the old delta, the delta flat, the deltaic high and the fan-terrace complex areas. An outline of their distribution is given in Figures 1 and 2.

The upper reaches of the Chao Phraya contain rice lands that developed in small basins surrounded by mountains. These lands can be called intermontane basins. Rice land in the middle reaches of the river can be divided into a constricted river channel area and fan-terrace complex areas. The constricted river channel area develops as low-lying strips of land along major watercourses, while fan-terrace complex areas occupy gently sloping mountain-foot zones extending along the margin of the Central Plain. The lower reaches of the Chao Phraya have a deltaic landscape and have three kinds of rice lands corresponding to three physiographic regions—the old delta, the delta flat and the deltaic high. The area comprising the delta apex region has

---

1. H. Fukui, "Environmental Determinants Affecting the Potential Dissemination of High Yielding Varieties of Rice," *Tonan Ajia Kenkyu* [Southeast Asian studies] 9, no. 3 (Kyoto University, 1971): 348–374

a comparatively elevated and relieved ground surface and is called old delta in this article, because it dates from the Pleistocene era. A low-lying flat area south of the old delta is divided into two parts according to ground height; the slightly raised portion near the coast is called the deltaic high, and the rest is the delta flat.

The distribution of the six physiographic regions, and their cross sections, as shown in Figures 1 and 2, are constructed mainly from two topographic maps of 1 to 50,000 drawn by U.S. Army Map Service[2] and by Royal Thai Army Map Service.[3] No aerial photographs were available for this work.

The character of each physiographic region is described below.

INTERMONTANE BASINS

Physiography

Intermontane basins are situated in North Thailand, and correspond Fukui's traditional irrigation areas. They have high elevations, steep general slopes, strong local relief and small areas. The dimensions of a few typical basins can be tabulated as follows:

Area	elevation (m)	general slope (m/km)[1]	microrelief	acreage	
				gross[2]	net[3]
Chiang Mai basin	290 – 320	1.7	ʼ	12	10
Lampang basin	190 – 250	2.0	flat to	7	5
Phrae basin	150 – 170	2.5	undulating	4	3
Nan basin	190 – 210	2.5		2	2

1. General slope is calculated from the formula, $(a - b)/1$, where a and b are the highest and the lowest elevations in rice land, respectively, and 1 is the distance between the two.
2. Gross acreage means the acreage of a whole region. This is calculated on a 1 to 250,000 topographical map.
3. Net acreage means the acreage of rice land. This is adopted from H. Fukui, "Environmental Determinants Affecting the Potential Dissemination of High Yielding Varieties of Rice," *Tonan Ajia Kenkyu* [Southeast Asian studies] 9, no. 3 (Kyoto University, 1971).

The landforms of an intermontane basin are complex and varied. They may include Recent alluvial plains, Recent fans, fan-colluvial complexes, low and high terraces and Pliocene plains. An example is given in Figure 3. In the case of the Lampang basin shown in Figure

2.   *Topographical Map, 1 to 50,000 series L-708*, 1957.
3.   *Topographical Map, 1 to 50,000*–(mostly surveyed between 1910 and 1920), Bangkok.

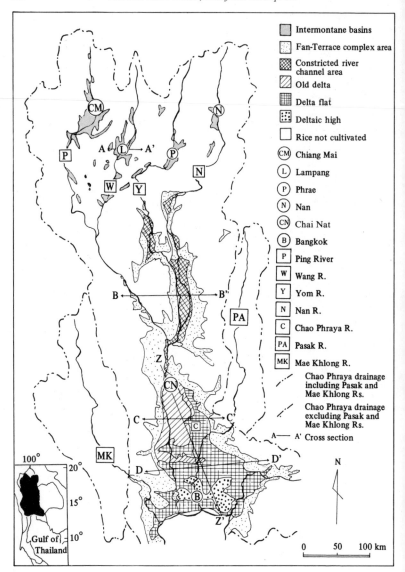

Figure 1. *Physiographic classification of paddy land of the Chao Phraya basin. The cross sections and profile are shown in Fig. 2*

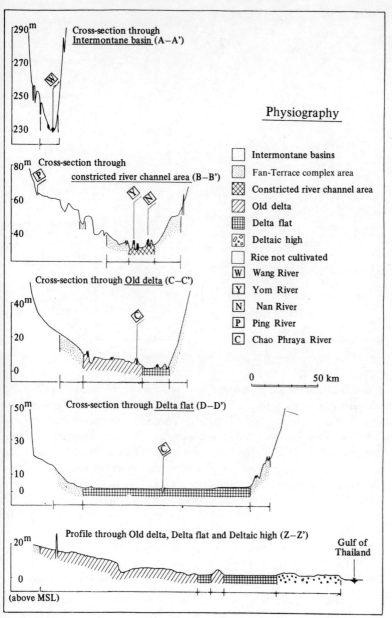

Figure 2. *Cross sections and a profile of the Chao Phraya basin. The locations are given in Fig. 1*

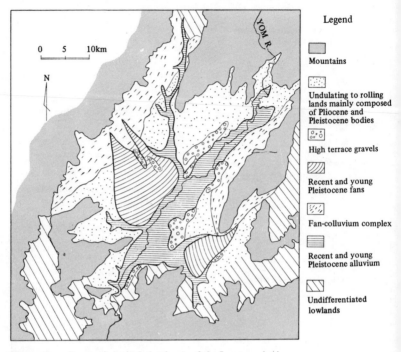

Figure 3.   *Geomorphological sketchmap of the Lampang basin*

3, the Recent alluvial plains and low terraces are dominantly composed of loamy materials with small amounts of sand in the natural levees. The Recent fans are sandy and contain considerable amounts of granules and pebbles. The fan-colluvial complexes are coarser in texture. High terraces are usually capped by thick gravel of cobble size and are occasionally lateritic. Pliocene plains are composed of varying geologic bodies ranging from clayey lacustrine strata to angular gravelly alluvium with various degrees of weathering. A more detailed description of the geology and pedology of the basin has been given by T. Hattori.[4] In these topographic units, most paddy fields develop either on the Recent alluvial plains, low terraces or on the Recent fans.

The water supply to paddy lands in the intermontane basins is ideal. The catchment/paddy area ratio[5] is usually large enough to

4.   "Some Properties of Soil and Substrata in the Lampang Basin," *Tonan Ajia Kenkyu* [Southeast Asian studies] 7, no. 3 (Kyoto University, 1970):527–547.

5.   The catchment area of a region is the entire area from which water drains to that region. The catchment of the Lampang basin, for instance, coincides with the entire drainage area of the Wang River above the southern end of the Lampang basin, while that of the delta flat includes the entire drainage area of the Chao

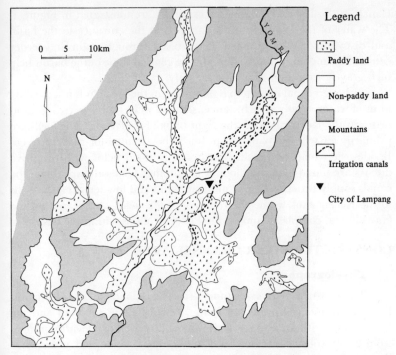

Figure 4.   *Distribution of paddy fields in the Lampang basin*

irrigate all of the basins. Moreover, the catchment areas of the basins have dendritic stream networks which effectively carry the rainwater into the basins. The condensation of atmospheric moisture in the mountain climate also means the basins have more chance of rainfall than open valleys or plateaus. These factors can be considered advantageous in growing a water-consuming plant such as rice.

Land use

The rice land distribution map indicates that the intermontane basins of Thailand can be considered a southern extension of the group of intermontane basins of South China. The affinity to South China is also suggested by the existence of such traditional agricultural techniques as Fai-irrigation.[6]

Current paddy growing relies largely on a modern irrigation system, which is in principle the same as the Fai-irrigation system.

Phraya, Pasak, Bang Pakong, and Mae Khlong rivers. These are determined from a 1:250,000 topographical map.

6.   A diversion irrigation dam made of bamboo and brushwood.

Canals in the Lampang basin, for example, are illustrated in Figure 4. The water of the Wang River is dammed at the entrance to the basin and distributed to many parts of the basin through main and feeder canals. The moderate size and moderate general slope of the basins help such gravity irrigation to work efficiently.

Although canal irrigation is dominant in the basin, it is not the only form of water supply. For instance, shallow wells mobilize rich ground water in the Recent fans on the right bank of the Wang. The wells are primarily for winter upland crops but some are used for rice crops too. Besides the canals and wells, patches of rain-fed fields with primitive ditches are found along the foot of mountains. Generally speaking, the canals supply water to Recent alluvial plains and low terraces, the wells to the Recent fans, while the rain-fed paddy fields are located on the fan-colluvial complexes and on the Pliocene plains within the basin.

CONSTRICTED RIVER CHANNEL AREA

Physiography

The constricted river channel area corresponds to Fukui's inland flood area, and comprises low-lying stretches along the Nan and the Yom rivers, with an average width of ca. 20 km. The elevation ranges from 23 m above mean sea level at the downstream end to 60 m at the uppermost end. The general slope is circa 0.2 m/km along its N-S axis. Despite the gentle general slope, the local relief reaches a height of more than 5 m because of the webs of natural levee and backswamp.

The area has an extremely high stream density, as shown in Figure 5. Geomorphologically this can be termed a Recent alluvial valley,[7] where silt-laden rivers often change course. The most important feature is the bottleneck gorge at the lowest reach of the valley, which holds back floodwaters causing deep and prolonged inundation. The constricted river channel area is so names because of this phenomenon.

The catchment/paddy area ratio is 32.8. This enormous ratio, together with the troughlike depressions and the gorge, causes the valley to suffer heavy flooding. Every year, the water level rises very rapidly after the first rain of the wet season and remains high long after the end of the rainy season, leaving only elevated natural levees above the water. No means of quick drainage is known except pumping. Slow run-off from the bottleneck is the only reliable way of lowering the flood level.

7.　T. Hattori, "The Quaternary Stratigraphy in the Northern Basin of the Central Plain, Thailand," *Tonan Ajia Kenkyu* [Southeast Asian studies] 9, no. 3 (Kyoto University, 1971): 398–419

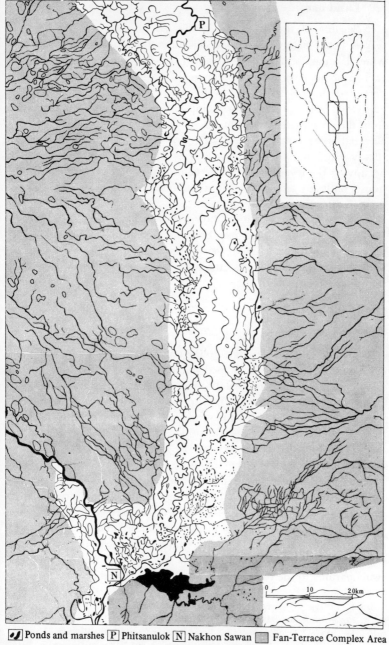

☙ Ponds and marshes P Phitsanulok N Nakhon Sawan ▨ Fan-Terrace Complex Area

Figure 5.   *Typical stream patterns of the constricted river channel area*

Land use

Because of the deep and prolonged flooding during the rainy season, land for human occupation is limited to natural levees. Figure 6, which is a map of part of the area in 1915, shows how houses were built exclusively on levees. Those along geologically active river courses were preferred, because of the convenience of transportation. Paddy was cultivated in the nearby backswamp areas which were easily accessible from the villages. Thus paddy was grown in depressions rather than on elevated land even in this easily flooded valley. Figure 7 is a map of a survey made in 1957. A similar type of land use is seen here too. After occupying the levees along active channels, people probably also built houses on levees along minor or abandoned channels with paddy fields in the adjoining backswamp areas.

The area's low elevation, however, will be a crucial handicap to the intensification of land use. Sophisticated water control is next to impossible in this trough. Moreover, once large irrigation schemes are adopted in adjoining areas, the valley is likely to become a water dumping ground.

OLD DELTA

Physiography

The old delta corresponds to the barrage irrigation area in Fukui's classification. The area is shaped like a distorted fan with its apex at Chai Nat. The radius is circa 100 km and the arc is circa 70 km. The elevation reaches 20 m near the apex and falls to 5 m near the arc. This is lower than the adjoining fan-terrace complex areas but higher than the delta flat. The general slope is circa 0.15 m/km in the N-S direction. The local relief reaches more than 5 m.

Geomorphologically the area is an Upper Pleistocene delta,[8] with superposed Recent levee deposits in parts.[9] The fanlike shape and the gentle general slope can be ascribed to the deltaic origin of this geological body, whereas the strong local relief results from the joint effect of normal erosion on the Pleistocene surface and the superimposition of the Recent levees. Another characteristic feature is ubiquitous bifurcation of streams, which provides the area with webs of swell and swale parallel to the ribs of the delta. This bifurcated channel system is

8. Y. Takaya, "Quarternary Outcrops in the Central Plain of Thailand," *Report on Research in Southeast Asia, Natural Science Series*, no. 3 (Kyoto University, 1968) : 7–68.
9. Y. Takaya, "Two Brackish Clay Beds along the Chao Phraya River of Thailand," *Tonan Ajia Kenkyu* [Southeast Asian studies] 9, no. 1 (Kyoto University, 1971): 46–57.

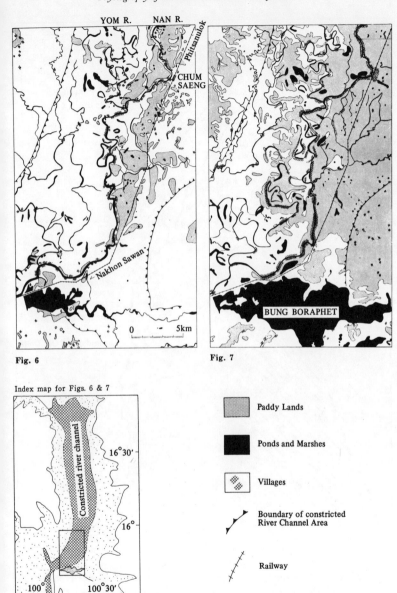

Figure 6.   *An example of land use in the constricted river channel area in 1915*

Figure 7.   *An example of land use in the constricted river channel area in 1957*

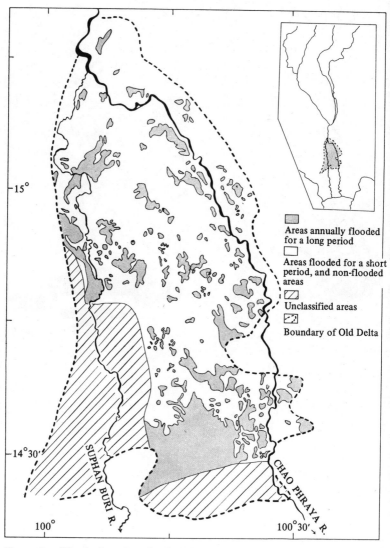

Figure 8. *Distribution of swales flooded annually for a long period This figure is compiled from the soil survey reports prepared by the Land Development Department, Ministry of National Development, Thailand.* Flooding is divided into five classes in these reports as follows:*

Class a: flooded for most of the year
Class b: periodic flooding of prolonged duration
Class c: periodic flooding for a short time
Class d: flooded only during exceptionally high floods
Class e: never or very seldom flooded

a vestige of the Pleistocene distributaries of the delta. These geomorphic characteristics are clearly shown on the flood distribution map in Figure 8. Chains of deep flooding are shown occupying the swales.

The physiographic peculiarity of the area is used to the best advantage in the layout of irrigation and drainage networks. One trunk river, the Chao Phraya enters the apex and bifurcates repeatedly to form a network of spreading distributaries. If a barrage were constructed at the point of the first bifurcation and feeder canals set on the levees of the distributaries, the whole area could be irrigated easily by gravity. The Greater Chao Phraya Project, which is a large scale irrigation and drainage project covering the whole of the old delta, is actually based on this idea.[10] Fortunately the ground surface has enough relative height and local relief to drain the water from the land. NEDECO estimates that if the system is managed skillfully water supply can be controlled completely for 60 percent of the area, while the remaining 40 percent, the depressions, will remain as a water dumping ground.

The catchment/paddy area ratio is 23.0. If a barrage or dam had the capacity to hold most of the runoff of the rainy season, the area could be irrigated during the dry season.

Land use

The old delta is thought to be one of the earliest inhabited areas in the Central Plain of Thailand, as is suggested by Dvaravati remains (provisionally thought to date from 700 to 1100 A.D.). Besides its long history of occupation, the area was the political and economic center of Thailand for more than five hundred years until the Bangkok plain developed as a rice-growing area in the 1850s.

10.   Y. Fujioka and Y. Kaida, "Irrigation and Drainage in the Bangkok Plain,"
      Tonan Ajia Kenkyu [Southeast Asian studies] 5, no. 3 (Kyoto University, 1967):
      572–600. (In Japanese.)

The "Areas annually flooded for a long period" comprise classes a and b, while the "Areas flooded for a short period, and non-flooded areas" comprise classes c, d, and e.

*Land Development Department, Ministry of National Development, Thailand, "The Boromdhart Tract," *Soil Survey Report*, No. 39, 1965.
———, "The Khok Krathiam Tract," *Soil Survey Report*, No. 40, 1965.
———, "The Maharat Tract," *Soil Survey Report*, No. 53, 1966.
———, "The Pholathep Tract," *Soil Survey Report*, No. 54, 1967.
———, "The Chong Kae Tract," *Soil Survey Report*, No. 57, 1967.
———, "The Channasut Tract," *Soil Survey Report*, No. 61, 1968.
———, "The Yang Mani Tract," *Soil Survey Report*, No. 66, 1968.
———, "The Tha Bot Tract," *Soil Survey Report*, No. 69, 1969.
———, "Report of the Detailed Soil Survey in the Channasut Land Consolidation Project Area," *Soil Survey Report*, No. 71, 1968.

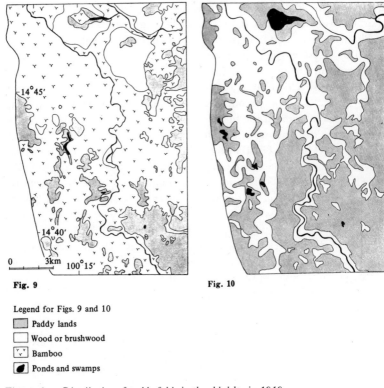

Fig. 9   **Fig. 10**

Legend for Figs. 9 and 10

▨ Paddy lands

☐ Wood or brushwood

ᵛ̣ᵛ̣ Bamboo

◢ Ponds and swamps

Figure 9.   *Distribution of paddy fields in the old delta in 1919*

Figure 10.   *Distribution of paddy fields in the old delta in 1957*

An earlier land use pattern can be seen in Figure 9, a map dating
from 1919. A fairly large area is still covered by grass, bamboo, and
trees, only a few depressions being used as paddy fields. Figure 10 is a
map of the same area in 1957. The paddy area has expanded greatly,
but the elevated parts are still uncultivated. Figure 11 shows the anticipated suitability of land for rice cultivation on successful completion
of the Greater Chao Phraya Project. On this map, portions which are
classified as "lands to be used for rice with irrigated dry-land crops as a
secondary crop in the dry season" correspond to NEDECO's areas of
high elevation with complete water-control. Comparison of the three
maps indicates that the earlier plots all occupy depressions, and this
preference for depressions lasts as long as irrigation techniques remain
primitive; however, once a modern irrigation scheme is introduced, the
choice shifts to the elevated parts which were previously considered

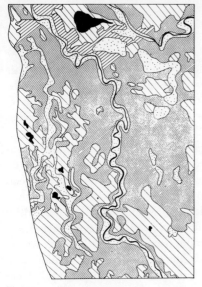

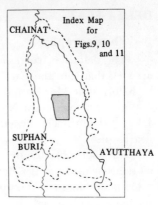

Fig. 11

Legend for Fig.11

⬚ Lands to be used for rice with irrigated upland crops as a second crop in dry season
⬚ Lands to be used for rice exclusively in two-crop pattern

⬚ Lands too high for paddy growing
⬛ Lands too low for paddy growing

Figure 11. *Part of the old delta showing suitability for rice growing*

barren. This transition involves the sacrifice of the traditional rice lands in the depressions, because they are expected to act as dumping basins. Tomosugi[11], who discussed the development of the irrigation works in the Chao Phraya delta, stressed this point. Kaida's careful analysis of the effect of environmental factors on rice yields in the Greater Chao Phraya Project area also suggests a similar conclusion.[12] This reversal brought about by the introduction of a modern irrigation scheme is a striking event in the history of the old delta's development.

11. T. Tomosugi, "Historical Development of Irrigation and Drainage Works in Chao Phraya Delta," *Tonan Ajia Kenkyu* [Southeast Asian Studies] 3, no. 4 (Kyoto University, 1966): 147–156. (In Japanese)
12. Y. Kaida, "An Analysis of the Effect of Environmental Factors on Paddy Rice Yields—A Case Study from the Northern Region of the Greater Chao Phraya Project," *Tonan Ajia Kenkyu* [Southeast Asian studies] 9, no. 2 (Kyoto University, 1971):220–251.

DELTA FLAT

Physiography

The delta flat, corresponding to Fukui's canalled lowland, is the area less than 2 m above mean sea level which, together with the deltaic high, forms the Mae Nam Chao Phraya delta. The area has an indented outline with maximum N–S length of circa 180 km and an area of 1.1×10^4 km². The general slope is 0.01 m/km, and local relief is nearly nil.

Physiographically, the delta flat comprises interdistributary basins on the Recent delta. It is dominated by brackish environments and has a monsoon climate. The downstream area of large rivers in monsoon regions is deeply inundated during the rainy season and becomes parched during the dry season. Though the cycle is occasionally disturbed by fickle tropical storms, the general pattern of flooding is regular. Monsoon deltas thus present a kind of amphibious terrain: neither land nor water.

The monsoon climate is one factor causing this amphibiousness. But the amphibiousness also has roots in another source: the mechanical properties of the deltaic sediments. Very often young deltas cannot support even their dead loads. Self-consolidation occurs in the substrata under normal conditions, and the ground surface subsides differentially depending on the subground structure and stress. A less-flooded plot of ten years ago is often found as a deeply flooded swale today, and this may form a nonflooded swell in the future because of differential vertical movement of the delta surface. In ten years, relative movement of one meter has often been recorded. Figures 12 and 13 demonstrate how the delta flat changed in a short period. An area which in 1914 was excellent paddy land is seen as swampy waste land in the map for 1957. So the Recent deltaic surface may be described as an unstable lowland with a large number of wandering marshes and swamps.

The depositional environments in which the delta flats were formed result in another peculiarity. The brackish to hypersaline depositional environment leads to the concentration of iron sulphide in the sediments. The very extensive distribution of acid sulphate soil in the area can be ascribed to the brackish environment in which the sediments were deposited.[13]

Land use

A vast land with ubiquitous swamps is most troublesome terrain to develop. The delta flat had been left untouched until in the 1850s

---

13.   F. R. Moorman, "Acid Sulphate Soils (Cat Clays) of the Tropics," *Soil Science* 95 (1963):271–279.

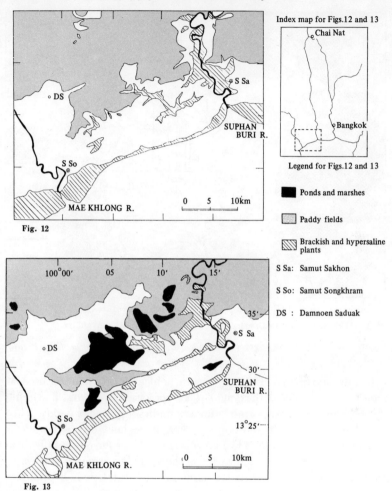

Figure 12. *Distribution of paddy fields and hypersaline plants in a part of the delta flat in 1914*

Figure 13. *Distribution of ponds and marshes, paddy fields and hypersaline plants in the same region, 1957*

people found rice was becoming a profitable export and started the reclamation of the land.

For reclamation it was necessary to secure a permanent means of access to the area. The best way was to canalize it. The delta flat under reclamation in 1915–1916 is seen in Figure 14. A considerable area near the northeastern corner of the delta flat is still covered by grass

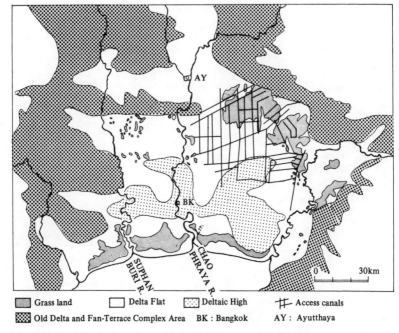

Figure 14.   *Distribution of grass lands in the Recent deltaic region of the Chao Phraya, 1915–1916*

with only narrow strips along natural and artifical channels used as paddy fields. Today all the delta flat, except for a narrow zone bordering the gulf, has been transformed into a boundless expanse of paddy fields.

The next step in development might be land consolidation for more intensive land use. This, however, would be far more difficult to achieve than the mere canalization of the area. The reason is that water control in such an extremely low-lying area is possible only by building flood-protecting levees along rivers or by making a polder of the paddy fields, but it is doubtful if such work is worthwhile. To cope with formidable subsidence large amounts of money would be required for maintenance. It appears that the delta flat will be increasingly and intensively utilized by the adoption of more intricate agricultural techniques. This intensification can be carried out profitably only through a thorough understanding of the character of the delta, especially its amphibiousness.

DELTAIC HIGH

Physiography

The deltaic high corresponds to Fukui's less-flooded delta and

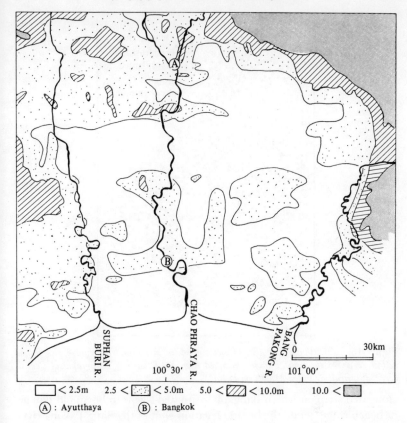

Figure 15. *Contour map of the Bangkok Plain (based on the U.S. Army Map Service's topographical map 1 : 50,000, 1957)*

comprises slightly elevated parts of the Recent deltaic plain. The ground height averages 3 m, which is about 1 m higher than the average height of the delta flat, but occasionally attains 5 m. The general slope is of the order of 0.01 m/km. The local relief is very slight, though it is stronger than that of the delta flat. The area is circa 2×10^3 km². The topographic relationship with the delta flat can be seen in the contour map shown in Figure 15.[14]

Though the area is apparently a part of the Recent delta, its detailed geomorphological nature is unclear. Probably the area consists of aggregates of elevated land of various geneses. For instance, the E–W

14. Y. Takaya, "Topographical Analysis of the Southern Basin of the Central Plain, Thailand," *Tonan Ajia Kenkyu* (Southeast Asian studies] 7, no. 3 (Kyoto University, 1969):293–300.

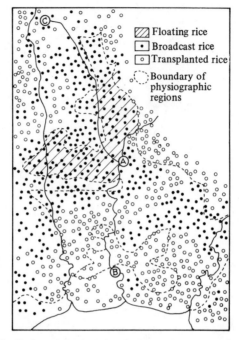

Figure 16. *Distribution of floating rice, broadcast rice and transplanted rice in the deltaic region of the Chao Phraya (modified from Y. Takaya, "Topographical Control over the Agriculture in the Mae Nam Delta.")*

elongated strip on which Bangkok is situated seems to be an old barrier or beach ridge, while the broad elevation west of the Bang Pakong river looks like a complex of natural levees produced by the river. Some portions may have been formed by local uplifting due to differential consolidation.

The deltaic high has a conspicuous physiographic dissimilarity to the delta flat: the former has higher ground elevation and greater stream density. And these topographic conditions promote shallower flood depth and quicker drainage in the deltaic high.

Land use

Figure 16 shows the distribution of broadcast and transplanted rice fields in the delta region. The physiographic divisions are reflected in the growing methods; the deltaic high is covered by transplanted rice, the delta flat by broadcast rice. Flood depth and drainage are the determining factors of the cultivation method.

Another physiographic control over rice culture is seen in the average area of cultivated land per farmhouse. The 1963 census of agriculture indicates that the average holding is roughly 20 to 35 rai[15] per farm house on the deltaic high,[16] while it is more than 35 rai on the delta flat.[17]

FAN-TERRACE COMPLEX AREA

Physiography

The fan-terrace complex area corresponds to Fukui's water-deficient foothills. Fan-terrace complexes have piedmont topography and have developed along the marginal parts of the Central Plain of Thailand. The general slope ranges from 1.0 m/km to 2.5 m/km. The local relief is usually strong, and streams are almost 10 m deep. The total area is estimated at circa 1.8×10^4 km².

Most of this area is composed of Recent and Upper Pleistocene fans. As is common in normal fan regions, the area shows evidence that the shifting of stream channels across the ground surface has been frequent. Streams are more or less straight and short. And active drainage lines are usually deep near the mountains but shallow down-slope, and occasionally vanish. These characteristics give the area a somewhat desolate landscape.

Because the area is a complex, it can be parcelled into many small fans and terraces of different nature. The differences result primarily from the geology of the corresponding hinterland. For instance, a fan with its catchment in a shale-dominated region will be rich in clayey fractions and nutrients, while fan fed by water from an arkose sandstone region will be coarse textured and poor. Given these differences, the whole fan-terrace complex area may be classified in terms of potential fertility. In Figure 17 a very rough classification of the area is given. The hinterland geology of course, is, not the only factor determining fertility. A better fertility map could be constructed by taking such factors as climate and age of the ground surface into account.

Hydrographically, the area cannot be said to be favorably situated. The catchment/paddy area ratio is as low as 5.1, and streams are all short and steep. This results in torrential flushes rather than steady flows. Another disadvantage lies in the porous substrata, which allow rapid sinking of water into the ground. Available water thus tends to be unstable and deficient. Because of these hydrographic features Fukui calls the area "water-deficient foothills."

15. 1 rai = 0.16 ha.
16. National Statistical Office of Thailand, *Census of Agriculture, 1963* (Bangkok, 1963).
17. Y. Takaya, "Topographical Control over the Agriculture in the Mae Nam Delta," *Japan Agriculture Research Quarterly* 4, no. 4 (1969):24–27.

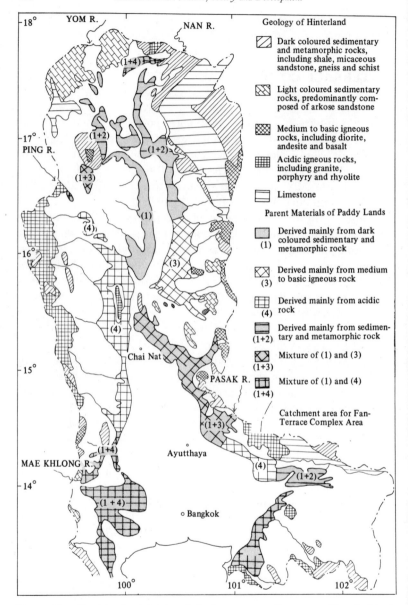

Figure 17. *Provisional subdivision of the fan-terrace complex areas with respect to the geology of the hinterland*

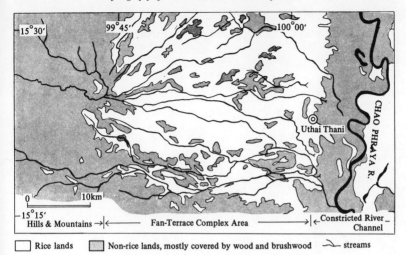

☐ Rice lands	▨ Non-rice lands, mostly covered by wood and brushwood	⌁ streams

Figure 18.   *Distribution of paddy lands in a part of the fan-terrace complex area*

Land use

Though the area appears rather desolate, the relief and sloped terrain offer ecological variety in comparison with flat monotonous land. People seem to have found suitable, if restricted, plots for growing food in this area from long ago. Archaeology suggests that the fan-terrace complex area is one of the earliest inhabited areas of Thailand. The most likely history of its development is that ancient people settled in the best spots, near the foot of the fans and extended their domain upslope along braided streams, using the streams as natural feeder canals. The typical layout of rice lands is seen in Figure 18.

The crucial limitation for paddy culture in the area comes from its small catchment/paddy area ratio. The capricious flow regime increases the disadvantages. The fact that both planted and harvested acreages change from one year to another is ascribed to these hydrographic conditions. This disadvantage cannot be overcome while rice growing relies on stream runoff only. The only way to solve the problem is to utilize water from the main tributaries of the Chao Phraya. It is thought that if barrages are constructed on main tributaries of the Chao Phraya and the water is carried from them to the upper slopes of the fan-terrace complex, the area can be effectively and constantly irrigated (personal communication, from Dr. Y. Kaida, Kyoto University). Topographically, the area has gravity irrigation potential. If fairly large initial investment were made for the proposed irrigation system, its maintenance would be comparatively simple.

TABLE 1

CHARACTERISTICS OF THE SIX PHYSIOGRAPHIC REGIONS

Physiographic region	Elevation m. above M.S.L	General slope (m/km)	Local relief (m)	Acreage × 1,000 ha	
				Gross[2]	Net[3]
Intermontane Basin	150–350	1.7<	<10	250	200
Constricted River Channel Area	23– 60	0.2	± 5	320	200
Old Delta	5– 20	0.15	< 8	490	400
Delta Flat	0– 2	0.01	negligible	1110	820
Deltaic High	2– 4	0.01	negligible	210	160
Fan-Terrace Complex Area	5–100	1.0–2.5	<10	1800	1350

2 and 3: see notes 2 and 3 to table on p. 115.

AND CORRELATION WITH FUKUI'S CATEGORIES

Soil Texture	Geomorphic setting	Catchment/ Paddy area ratio	Fukui's Category
Clay to gravelly sand	Complex of stream alluvium, fan and terraces	10~40	Traditional irrigation area
Clay with a little sand	Recent alluvial plain	32.8	Inland flood area
Clay with a little sand	Upper Pleistocene delta	23.0	Barrage irrigation area
Clay	Interdistributary low of Recent delta	15.6	Canalled lowland
Clay with a little sand	Relatively elevated parts of Recent delta		Less-flooded delta
Sand with a little clay and gravel	Recent and Pleistocene fans and terraces	5.1	Water-deficient foothills

Summary

The paddy land of the Chao Phraya basin in Thailand is classified physiographically into six divisions: the intermontane basins, the constricted river channel area, the old delta, the delta flat, the deltaic high and the fan-terrace complex area. These divisions correspond to Fukui's six categories of rice land, which are proposed primarily for evaluation of the feasibility of dissemination of new varieties of rice.

The description of the nature of each physiographic region and its correlation with Fukui's category are given in Table 1. The distribution of the six regions and their cross sections are as shown in Figures 1 and 2.

Acknowledgments

Two field surveys, carried out in 1966–1967 and 1968–1969, were under the auspices of the National Research Council of Thailand. I am grateful to the staff of Geology Department of Chulalongkon University for their kind assistance in supplying research facilities and valuable information. A series of instructive discussions held with H. Fukui, Y. Kaida, K. Kyuma, T. Hattori and Y. Ishii, members of the tropical agricultural study group of the Center for Southeast Asian Studies, is also very much appreciated. Financial support for the field surveys was granted by the Center for Southeast Asian Studies of Kyoto University.

8

Environmental Determinants Affecting the Potential Dissemination of High Yielding Varieties of Rice—A Case Study of the Chao Phraya Basin

HAYAO FUKUI

INTRODUCTION

High-yielding varieties (HYVs) of rice, such as IR-8, have a great yield-potential thanks to their high responsiveness to nitrogen. Various prerequisites must be satisfied, however, in order to realize their potential. These include physical environmental conditions which determine the magnitude of dissemination. Within the potential HYV acreage predetermined by environmental factors, other conditions related to technological, economical, and social factors further determine the rate of dissemination.

The object of this study is to examine, in terms of physical environmental conditions, the possibility of the dissemination of HYVs in the Chao Phraya River basin of northern and central Thailand. First, general environmental conditions are reviewed briefly in the following section. This discussion is based on various reports and my five-year study in Thailand. In the third section, a regional division of rice land in the basin is attempted, based on present physical environmental conditions and modes of rice cultivation. This work was carried out in close cooperation with a geologist, an irrigation specialist, and a soil scientist: each had fieldwork experience in the basin. In the fourth section, HYV dissemination possibilities and concomitant environmental obstacles are examined for each of the six rice-culturing regions. Finally, there is discussion on potential HYV acreage and possible processes of dissemination in the basin as a whole.

In this study, HYVs are taken to be a rainy season crop. The dissemination of HYVs as a dry season crop is not discussed for the following reasons. First, rainy and dry season environmental conditions are distinctly different; their bearing on dissemination should be discussed separately. Second, although dry season rice acreage is significant in such countries as West Malaysia and Ceylon, it is still very limited in continental Asia, including Thailand; furthermore, substantial increase in dry season rice acreage seems unlikely in the near future.

In this article, HYVs denote the semidwarf rice varieties characterized by short stature, stiff straw, and erect leaves of dark green color. They grow more slowly than native *indica* varieties (NVs) at the initial growth stage, and are usually insensitive to longer or shorter day-lengths. These basic morphological and physiological characteristics of HYVs are closely related to their ability to render high yield, and do not differ significantly between HYVs developed at different institutes despite differences in grain quality or resistance to disease.

GENERAL CONSIDERATION OF THE ENVIRONMENTAL CONDITIONS REQUIRED FOR DISSEMINATION OF HYVs

Climatic conditions

Among climatic factors, rainfall is the most decisive factor in the annual fluctuation and the regional differences in rice production. This is mainly due to inadequate water control. Even where the amount and distribution of rainfall are most suitable for rice cultivation, certain facilities are needed for stabilized rice production. This is particularly true of HYVs which require precise water control, as will be discussed in detail later. Where rainfall is less suitable, greater investment is needed for more sophisticated facilities on a larger scale. Technical and economic difficulties involved in effecting better water control depend not only on rainfall but also on other environmental factors, particularly topography. Therefore, rainfall as a determinant of HYV dissemination should always be discussed in relation to water control facilities.

Biologically, temperature and solar radiation are the basic climatic factors affecting plant growth. However, they do not seem vital to the question of the dissemination of HYVs. This is true, first because these two factors do not seem to differ significantly within tropical monsoon Asia insofar as the main season rice is concerned; temperature and solar radiation are generally suitable for any HYVs of rice developed in the region. And second, the effect of these two factors as well as of other climatic factors, though it might indeed be considerable, cannot be detected because the overwhelming influence of good or poor water conditions serves to conceal them.

One can conclude that, aside from rainfall, there seems to be no climatic obstacle that can seriously deter the dissemination of HYVs as the main season crop of tropical monsoon Asia.

Soil conditions and nutrient supply

Some soils have excessive salinity, toxicity, acidity, root development inhibiting texture, and other defects. These characteristics are difficult or often impossible to modify, and the application of fertilizers to these soils is ineffective. However, these soils occupy only a small portion of the present rice growing area of Asia. Soils presently under rice cultivation can generally be said to be suitable for NVs and for HYVs as well.

However, inherent soil fertility differs greatly from one place to another. High or low soil fertility affects the dissemination of HYVs because an ample supply of plant nutrients is one of the conditions necessary to realize the yield potential of HYVs. Nevertheless, the importance of inherent soil fertility is not necessarily great, because nutrients can be supplemented in the form of fertilizers. A brief explanation of the interrelation between inherent soil fertility, fertilizer application, and the amount of nutrients required by HYVs is given schematically below.

Under favorable environmental conditions with proper cultivation practices, fertilizer-supplied nutrients are efficiently absorbed by rice plants, increasing the size and number of plant leaves, thereby developing greater leaf area. This absorbs more solar energy, some of which is stored in the grain. In any variety of rice, the greater the leaf area, the smaller is the proportion of assimilated energy utilized for grain formation. Therefore, yield increase through the application of fertilizer is a synthesis of two conflicting components: (a) an increasing total assimilation due to enlarged leaf area, and (b) a decreasing proportion of energy channeled into grain formation.

The rate of total assimilation through the increase of nutrient supply rises greatly when the total amount of nutrients is below a certain level. The proportion of assimilated energy directed to grain formation remains high at a low level of nutrient supply but cuts off sharply when the nutrient supply exceeds a certain level. Therefore, when nutrients are supplied in limited amounts, rice varieties which can quickly develop greater leaf areas are advantageous. On the contrary, when nutrients are abundant, rice varieties which can direct a greater proportion of their assimilated energy to grain formation are advantageous. Schematically, NVs belong to the former category, and HYVs, to the latter. If the nutrient supply to NVs exceeds a certain level, they do not respond to further increments of fertilizer. HYVs do not necessarily outyield NVs if their nutrient supply is below that same cut-off level.

The critical level of nutrient supply cannot be expressed in terms of a set amount of fertilizer, because the actual amount of nutrients supplied to a plant is the sum of nutrients derived from the soil and from fertilizers. However, it can be expressed roughly in terms of corresponding yield levels. Reviewing numerous reports on fertilizer trials conducted in various countries, including those I conducted, one can say that most NVs cease to increase in yield when their nutrient supply results in a yield level somewhere between 3–4 ton/ha.[1] HYVs respond best to nutrient supplies that result in yields of 6 ton/ha or more.[2]

Therefore, where the present yield level of NVs is 3–4 ton/ha or more, either thanks to exceptionally high soil fertility as in the case of the experimental farm of IRRI, or due to the application of fertilizers, a further raise in yield seems very difficult without the adoption of HYVs. Where present yields are very low due to poor soil fertility, HYVs would not necessarily respond better than NVs when the yield level aimed at by fertilizer application is 3–4 ton/ha or less.

Water conditions

HYVs require much stricter water conditions than do NVs. First, water depth must be kept below a certain level, much shallower than that tolerated by NVs. This is because of the short stature and moderate rate of initial growth of HYVs. Excessive water depth at any stage of growth will ruin the adoption of HYVs. Farmers can plant only tall NVs where deep water prevents the planting of HYVs.

Second, the field must be submerged for the fixed duration of growth. The growth period of HYVs is not as long as that of many NVs because with HYVs the longer the growth period is, the smaller the proportion of total assimilated energy utilized for grain formation; an extended growth period would result in poor response to heavy fertilizer application. One hundred and twenty days, 20–30 days in the nursery and the rest in the main field, is the standard growth duration of HYVs. Due to the nonsensitivity of HYVs to day-length, their growth duration does not vary significantly with the time of planting.

Most paddy fields in tropical Asia are dependent on the southwest monsoonal or summer rains. The start of the rainy season is often very erratic. And even after it seems to have started, dry spells sometimes prevail. The water depth of paddy fields increases gradually with the

1.   In this article the yield per hectare is for paddy.
2.   In fact, very high yields have been reported with NVs and even with floating rice. But further study of those cases is necessary.

advancement of the rainy season and reaches a maximum at the end of the rainy season or just after. The time of water recession from the paddy fields seems relatively constant, partly because the end of the rainy season is more regular than the start and partly because water can be drained to rivers if the topography allows. Photoperiod sensitive NVs are well adapted to this variable duration of submergence.

When the coming of the rains is earlier than usual, planting must be done earlier. Otherwise deep water would make planting impossible, particularly in the case of short stature HYVs. Planting earlier than usual has very little influence on the date of maturation, whereas HYVs mature after a fixed number of days. This implies that HYVs must sometimes be harvested before the termination of the rainy season. Under heavy rain and deep water conditions, the harvesting, drying, and transport of grain, along with other necessary processing, result in high costs and a lower-quality grain product. When the coming of the rains is later than usual, planting is delayed. Or when a dry spell damages crops, farmers must begin their planting afresh. Yet while NVs can still mature in the face of water recession, HYVs may suffer from drought at the later growth stage.

Thus, besides damage from excessive water depth, excessively long water submergence owing to early monsoon rains or the undrainability of fields would discourage the adoption of HYVs. Farmers might encounter too many problems at the time of harvest and after. Too short a duration of submergence, arising in most cases from the late coming of the rains, totally prevents the dissemination of HYVs.

A drought during the course of plant growth damages a rice crop regardless of the variety used. However, actual financial loss differs according to the amount invested. The probability of drought once every few years would not rule out the planting of HYVs; they might temporarily be adopted in some areas. But fear of drought would inhibit the spending of large amounts of money on fertilizer application and other inputs, so the yield could not be expected to be as high as experimental trial results might suggest.

Present dissemination trends

Areas fully satisfying the environmental conditions stated earlier are very few. Yet HYVs are being planted in more and more areas where environmental and other factors are not necessarily favorable. Consequently, the average yield of HYVs in certain districts surveyed is disappointedly low, often below 3–4 ton/ha. From the biological point of view, such low yield levels with HYVs, though they might be higher than with NVs, as explained previously, cannot be attributed to their inherent yield potential.

However, for any given area planted with HYVs it is likely that about half the fields will have yields higher than the average. If their yield is 3–4 ton/ha HYVs can be considered successfully disseminated to about half their acreage. Lower average yields indicate smaller areas of successful dissemination.

Areas where HYVs are actually planted but their yield is lower than 3–4 ton/ha are considered to be unsuccessfully disseminated. There may be various reasons for the unimpressive yield of HYVs, for instance, insufficient fertilizers and other chemicals, poor water conditions, and improper cultivation. Regardless of the reasons HYVs have sometimes failed to realize their yield potential, sustained successful adoption of HYVs does not seem likely unless certain steps are taken to raise their yield.

This section is summarized below.

ENVIRONMENTAL CONDITIONS	SUITABILITY FOR DISSEMINATION
1. *Climate conditions*	
Rainfall	Water control facilities are necessary to ameliorate unfavorable rainfall patterns
Other climatic factors	Generally suitable
2. *Soil conditions*	
Defects unamendable by fertilizer application	Successful dissemination unlikely
Other soil properties	Generally suitable
3. *Nutrient supply*	
Sufficient supply due to rich soil or fertilizer application	Further yield increase difficult without HYVs
Insufficient supply due to poor soil or small amount of fertilizer application	NVs and HYVs are equivalent as long as the yield is below 3–4 ton/ha
4. *Water conditions*	
Excessive water depth	No dissemination possible
Duration of submergence	
Too long	Difficulties in harvesting and other operations
Too short	No dissemination possible
Occasional drought	Successful dissemination unlikely

AN ATTEMPT AT A REGIONAL DIVISION OF THE CHAO PHRAYA BASIN

Physiography

The big river basins of continental south and southeast Asia have a similar physiographical pattern. The Chao Phraya basin is no exception.

In the northern mountainous region are intermontane basins. In these relatively small basins, several terraces are formed on both sides of rivers. Rice is grown on lower terraces. Water flow slows down on leaving the mountains, and the resulting deposit of coarse particles forms alluvial fans of various sizes at the margins of the low-lying plain. The plain along the tributaries of the Chao Phraya is separated from the southern plain by hills close to the river between Nakhon Sawan and Chai Nat. These hills trap the water, causing floods upstream.

The plain south of Chai Nat and north of Ayutthaya is considered to have been a delta in the Pleistocene period. Today the plain is a large terrace slightly higher than the present delta further south. The Chao Phraya and its distributaries flow through this old delta, forming natural levees immediately beside the water channels with depressions behind these levees. Many streams have changed course, resulting in a complex surface configuration.

South of Ayutthaya, the topography is typically flat, except for higher elevations called barrier islands. These higher places develop near the coast and are considered to have been formed mainly through the effect of the sea.

For water control the most relevant physiographic feature is land gradient. The possibility of gravity irrigation and drainage depends on this factor. The cross sections in Figure 2 clearly show that the low-lying plains are distinctly flatter than the intermontane basins and fan-terrace complex area, while the old delta is intermediate.

Water conditions

Water conditions in the intermontane basins and in the peripheral areas of the low-lying plains are distinctly different from those in the other areas of the Chao Phraya basin in two ways. First, the mean gradient of land is steep enough that irrigation and drainage can depend solely on gravity. Second, any water control measures can but little affect water conditions downstream. Therefore, once irrigation water becomes available, it can be relatively easily distributed and cheaply managed. Drainage can be carried out without worrying about the influence of drainage water on the water balance of plains downstream.

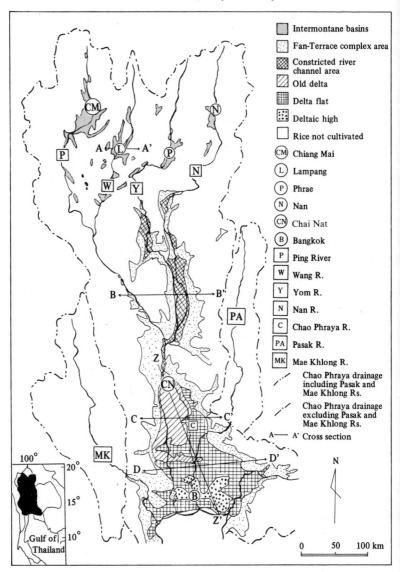

Figure 1. *Physiographic regions of rice land in the Chao Phraya basin (drawn by Y. Takaya)*

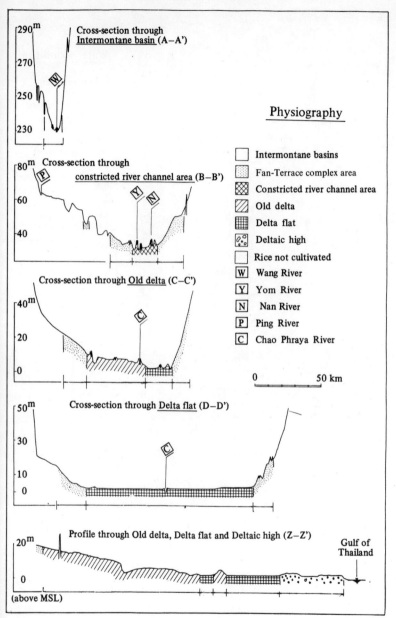

Figure 2. *Cross sections and a profile of the Chao Phraya basin (drawn by Y. Takaya)*

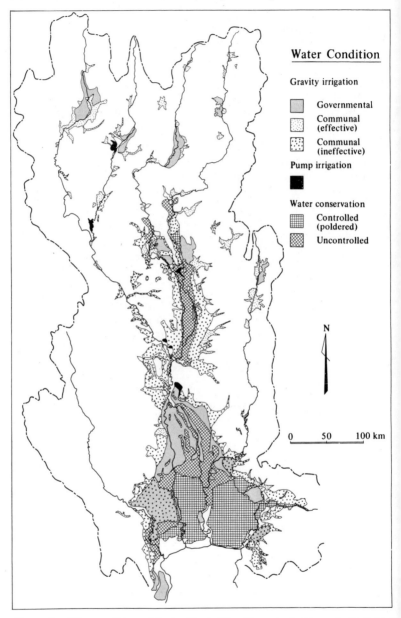

Figure 3.   *Water conditions of rice land in the Chao Phraya basin (drawn by Y. Kaida)*

Consequently, the primary problem in improving conditions in these areas is that of obtaining sufficient amounts of water.

Maximum irrigable area is roughly determined by the ratio of the area to be irrigated to the catchment area, which stores rainwater and eventually supplies it. The potential irrigable area suggested by this ratio exceeds the actual area of paddy land in most of the inter-montane basins and in some areas of the fan-terrace complex area. In these areas, a traditional system of water control, consisting of simple weirs made of stones, tree branches, and mud, and corresponding ditches, has been well developed and is still working effectively. The basic principle of modern facilities is the traditional one: diversionary barriers with corresponding canals.

In large areas of the fan-terrace complex areas, the actual area planted is more than the maximum irrigable area determined by the ratio explained earlier. Because of the coarse soil texture on the alluvial fans, surface water permeates deeply and flows down as groundwater. Though various community-operated water control devices are also seen in these areas, they are not effective because of the chronic water shortage. Effectiveness of modern facilities is similarly limited for the same reason.

In the low-lying plains, extremely flat topography makes it difficult or often practically impossible to control the water depth of individual fields by gravity. Rain water as well as water spilled over from natural levees remains on the plain until it is exhausted by evapo-transpiration and/or flows gradually to the sea. Thus, water conditions of the localities on the plain depend mainly on slight differences in relative elevation.

Measures undertaken until now to improve water conditions have aimed at obtaining a more uniform and more stable spread of flood water over a larger area in the plain. First, a huge storage dam on the upper Ping River has partially removed the problem of seasonal water-level fluctuation along rivers downstream. Second, the diversionary barrage at Chai Nat, which regulates water flow to distributary streams and the main canals, has resulted in wider dispersion of water over a greater area. Water from these channels can be gravity-irrigated to the higher places on the old delta between Chai Nat and Ayutthaya; general flatness, however, requires a very precise alignment of ditches for water distribution. Substantial areas remain which do not benefit from this scheme mainly owing to the poor alignment of lateral canals and ditches.

Third, water south of Ayutthaya is controlled by polders. The dikes of these polders are not very efficient at preventing seepage. The water is controlled by gravity drainage to the outer areas (there are no windmills or pumps), which is only feasible when the water level there is lower than that in the polder. Therefore, in practical terms the effect of the polders is limited to the prevention of extreme flood or drought. The higher elevation of the deltaic high area permits rice transplantation, though the basic water conditions are similar to those in the polder area.

There are two regions in the plain where even flood control is impossible. One is the narrow plain along the Nan and Yom rivers. The other is the deep-water area bordering the higher places of the old delta. Floodwater drains into these areas. Improved water conditions in higher-places has been made possible at the expense of these areas, which have become a sort of water-disposal area.

"Irrigated area" in the official statistics of the Thai government denotes areas equipped with facilities for water control which are under government supervision. Actual water conditions of the "irrigated area" differ greatly, depending on whether gravity irrigation or conservation irrigation is practiced. The latter, of course, refers to controlled flood-water irrigation. Yet, areas which are not included in the "irrigated area" do not necessarily lack irrigation facilities.

Soil

There are almost no defects in soil properties in the Chao Phraya basin which cannot be supplemented by fertilization. The major soil property affecting present paddy production and likely to affect the initial dissemination of HYVs is soil fertility.

Most paddy soils are located on alluvial deposits which were originally transported by rivers. As the parent rocks within the basin do not significantly differ in terms of soil fertility, differing soil fertilities can largely be explained in terms of weathering. Climatic conditions within the basin are quite uniform insofar as the weathering process is concerned, so the degree of weathering corresponds roughly to the time elapsed since the deposition of the sediment. Thus, the soils on older geological formations are generally more weathered and less fertile than those found on more recent sedimentations.

Soils on higher terraces in the intermontane basins are less fertile than those on lower ones. Soils developed on semi-recent alluvia in the fan-terrace complex area, similarly, are less fertile than most of those in the lower plain. Despite the age of the old delta south of Chai Nat, the fertility of its soils is moderate to high because the region has constantly received a fresh supply of sediment. Within the old delta, soils in depressions are more fertile than those on levees. Soils derived from brackish water sediments are young but infertile due to strong acidity caused by

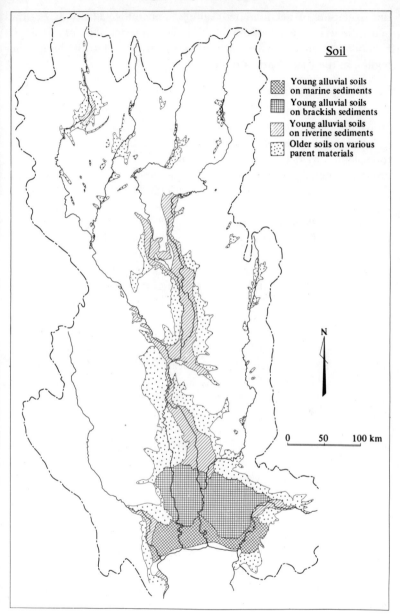

Figure 4.   *Soil conditions of rice land in the Chao Phraya basin (from "A Simplified General Soil Map of Thailand 1:2,500,000" by F.R. Moorman and S. Rojanasoonthon, with slight modification)*

the oxidation of accumulated sulfur compounds. The soils on the marine alluvium are the freshest and richest in terms of plant nutrients. Except for small areas where salinity is excessive, soil fertility here is the highest in the Chao Phraya basin.

Rice production

Seeds are directly broadcast in about one-third of the total rice-growing area of the Chao Phraya basin. Topography and water conditions bear a close relationship to the distribution of broadcast and transplanted rice fields. As shown in the accompanying map, the broadcast method is practiced in the constricted river channel area, in the low-lying part of the old delta, and in the delta flat. Lack of micro-relief and the uniform submergence of an extensive area in a short time make it difficult to manage a nursery properly or to keep the water depth of the main fields shallow enough for young seedings to be planted. These disadvantageous physical conditions aside, broadcast-rice regions satisfy minimum water requirements for the extensive cultivation of NVs of different plant height having variable growth duration characteristics. Consequently inherent soil fertility is the primary factor determining yield levels. The highest average yield is obtained in the extremely deep-water area where floating rice is grown. The great volume of flood water which enters these areas annually replenishes plant nutrients. The broadcast fields in the depression area of the old delta also give good yields for mainly the same reason. Strong acidity in the brackish alluvial soil accounts for the lowest-average yields in the delta flat.

The transplanting method is dominant in the remaining two-thirds of the total paddy area in the Chao Phraya basin. The highest yields are attained in the intermontane basins, followed by the coastal deltaic high region. The high yields in these regions can be attributed to stable water conditions and to high soil fertility. In the intermontane basins, various intensive cultivation⁻ techniques unique to the region are observed. The yields of transplanted fields in the fan-terrace complex area and the old delta vary greatly, mainly according to prevailing water conditions. Chronic water shortages and generally low soil fertility account for low yields.

The average paddy area per farm family is partially function of land productivity; the higher the yield, the smaller the paddy area per farm family. As shown in the accompanying map, total paddy production per farm family does not seem to be related so much to environmental conditons as to the following two factors. One is relative proximity to the centers of consumption and exportation, and the other is

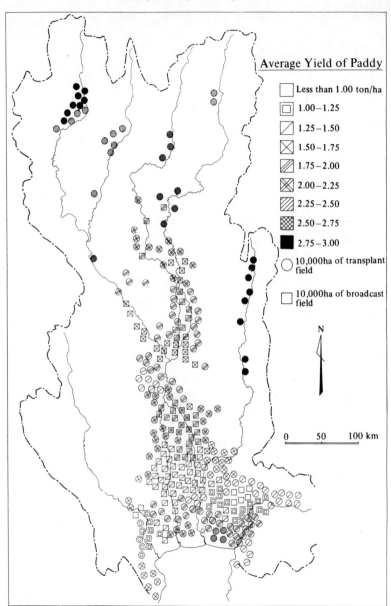

Figure 5.   *Average paddy yields in the Chao Phraya basin (by H. Fukui, based on the "Annual Report on 1964 Rice Production in Thailand", and the "Census of Agriculture, 1963")*

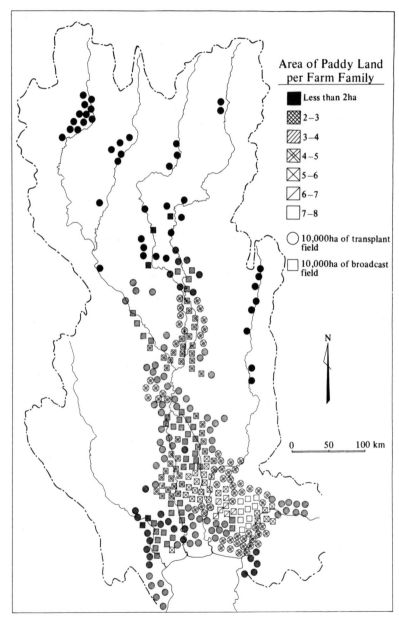

Figure 6.   *Area of paddy land per farm family in the Chao Phraya basin (drawn by H. Fukui, based on the "Census of Agriculture, 1963")*

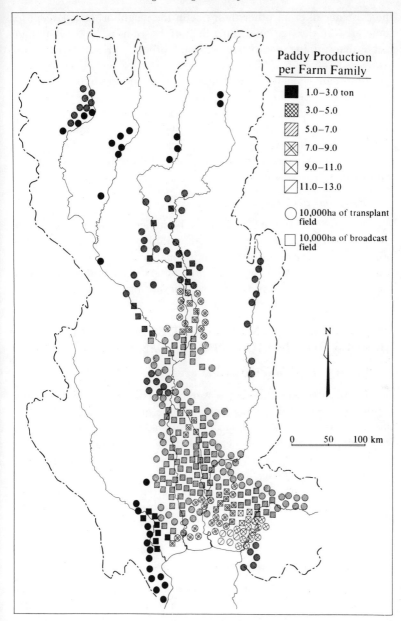

Figure 7. *Paddy production per farm family in the Chao Phraya basin (drawn by H. Fukui, based on the "Census of Agriculture, 1963")*

the existence of crops other than rice in the neighborhood. Except for some areas in the marginal zone, the former seems to be the dominant factor determining paddy acreage and production per farm family unit.

One can conclude that regional variations in productivity per unit area and per unit labor in the Chao Phraya basin are roughly explained by two things: such environmental factors as topography, water, and soil, and the relationship of demand to marketable production. Areas having higher yield levels, more intensive cultivation and/or more favorable physical conditions do not necessarily coincide with the major rice-producing areas.

Regional division

The rice land of the Chao Phraya basin here has been divided into six regions in terms of environmental and other aspects of present rice production. Description of each individual region is omitted here in order to avoid repetition. A map and a table are appended which give the regional divisions and summarize relevant production features and environmental conditions in each area.

HYV DISSEMINATION POSSIBILITIES IN THE SIX REGIONS OF THE CHAO PHRAYA BASIN

In the traditional irrigation area

In this area the drainage of water, to avoid both excessive water depth and prolonged submergence, can be managed relatively easily thanks to favorable topographical conditions. In most of the area, the water supply is ample and dependable, or at least potentially so. A gravity water-distribution system is also well developed. Thus, there are no physical obstacles to the dissemination of HYVs. But in order to carry out dissemination over the entire region, medium- to small-scale reservoirs and/or diversion barriers with an interconnecting canal system are necessary. Peripheral parts of the intermontane basins can then be irrigated.

In the water-deficient foothills

Just as in the traditional irrigation area, excessive water can be easily prevented. But water shortage is a more or less chronic hazard of the region. Water shortages in this region occur in two ways. One is a lack of water at the beginning of the growing season. If water is not available for 120 days before the time of water recession, HYVs cannot be planted. Day-length sensitive NVs, however, can mature within a

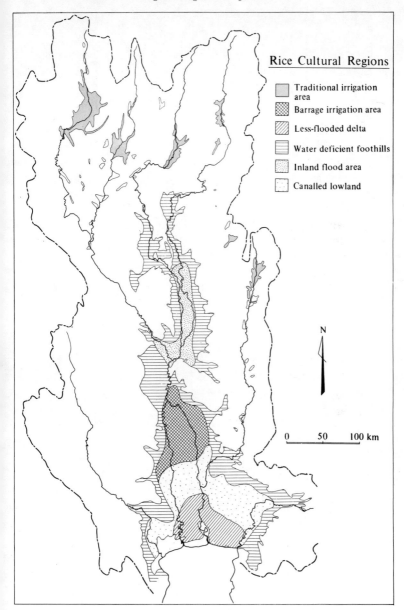

Figure 8.   *Rice cultural regions in the Chao Phraya basin (drawn by H. Fukui)*

TABLE 1

REGIONAL DIVISION OF THE CHAO PHRAYA BASIN

Rice-cultural regions	Physiography	Water conditions		Soil type	Soil fertility	Transplanted/ broadcast	Paddy yield ton/ha	Rice area cultivated per farm family ha	Paddy production per farm family ton	Approximate rice area × 1,000 ha
Traditional irrigation area	intermontane basin	Gravity Irrigation	Governmental Communal	Riverine Alluvial soils	Medium	Transplanted	2.5–3.0	1–2	2–4	320
Water-deficient foothills	Fan-terrace complex area	Conservation Irrigation	Effective Ineffective		Low	Transplanted	1.0–2.5	3–4	2–7	1,310
Inland flood area	Constricted river channel area	G.I.	Uncontrolled		Medium	Broadcast	1.5–2.0	4–5	6–8	200
Barrage irrigation area	Old delta	Conservation Irrigation	Governmental		Medium	Transplanted	1.8–2.2	3–4	5–7	80
			Uncontrolled		High	Broadcast	1.8–2.2	3–5	6–8	310
Canalled lowland	Delta flat		Uncontrolled Controlled	Brackish water Alluvial soils	Low	Broadcast	1.0–1.5	5–7	6–10	750
Less-flooded	Deltaic		Controlled		High	Transplanted	1.8–2.5	3–4	7–12	280

shorter period. Therefore, in areas where the coming of the rains tends to be late, NVs can be grown safely, while HYVs cannot.

The other type of water shortage in this region is caused by droughts after planting. In areas where the crop is likely to suffer from this kind of water shortage, HYVs may be adopted but the yield, as explained previously, will be low.

Therefore, in the case of the first type of water shortage, that caused by delayed rains, dissemination cannot occur. And in the case of the second type of water shortage, that caused by postplanting drought, successful dissemination is unlikely.

There are two ways to supply water to this region. Water can be diverted from a barrage constructed at the main river and transported through the adjacent foothills by a system of canals which parallel topographical contour lines. By this method, water supply can be made dependable, but the area that can be irrigated is restricted to the relatively low areas of the zone between the alluvial fans and the low-lying plain. An existing example of this type of irrigation is the Chai Nat barrage. Canals fed by this barrage supply water not only to the old delta but also to some water-deficient foothills to the east and west of the old delta. Similar projects are being planned and some are under construction. The major one to be completed in the near future is the Meklong project. Parts of the water-deficient foothills along the Nan river will also be supplied with water from a storage dam being constructed.

Areas which cannot be served by this type of barrage-canal system must be supplied with water by the other method; the collecting of water from local streams. But this presents a major difficulty. The streams are undependable, being much affected by the erratic geographical and seasonal distribution of rainfall in the area.

In the inland flood area

Under present conditions in this region, HYVs cannot be adopted at all because of the excessive water depth and/or sudden rise in water level that occur early in the rainy season. A storage dam now under construction on the upper Nan river will be able to improve this unfavorable situation only to a limited extent. This dam is intended mainly to stabilize river flow in the Greater Chao Phraya Project area south of Chai Nat and to supply water to some of the water-deficient foothills along the Nan river. As water from surrounding foothills will be drained into this region, the situation will eventually be similar to that of the depressions of the barrage irrigation area and the northern part of the canalled lowland: that is, it will become a water-disposal area.

In the barrage irrigation area

Depressions in this region as well as in neighboring regions, here included in the canalled lowland region, are planted with deep-water rice. The problem of deep water in these areas will not be improved by the construction of facilities to drain water from the higher parts of the barrage irrigation area. In fact, it will be physically impossible for HYVs to be planted here.

At higher elevations, further water-supply improvements, including construction of drainage ditches, are necessary before rice can be assured a submergence of fixed duration. Though both gravity irrigation and drainage are possible, they cannot be managed by individual farmers, because precise alignment of ditches and control of water balance over the entire region are needed. Improvements until now have aimed at the stabilization of water conditions for NVs. Further improvements are indispensable for the adoption of HYVs. These would depend on the refinement of present water-control facilities.

In the canalled lowland

As stated before, the northern part of this region, bordering on the barrage irrigation area, offers no hope of HYV dissemination. The rest of the region is not so deeply flooded as the water-disposal area, but it is still too deep for HYVs. Excessive water depth and too long a duration of submergence could be overcome only by poldering.

There are two kinds of polders. One can scarcely be called a polder in the strict sense. Piles of earth excavated for such various purposes as canals, roads, and railroads, form high dikes, each of which surround quite a large polder. This type of polder cannot guarantee the water conditions needed for HYVs.

The other kind of polder is one in the true sense of the word. Polders rarely exceed a few hectares and are cultivated quite intensively with high-value crops such as vegetables and fruits. The successful cultivation of HYVs is theoretically possible in these pump-equipped polders. There is no technical obstacle to such polders being built on the farmers' own initiative. Whether such polders will actually be used for HYVs, however, seems to depend on construction costs and anticipated profits from using them to grow HYVs. It is still too early to count on HYV dissemination by poldering.

In the less-flooded delta

In this region, time of planting is the problem which demands the most careful consideration in connection with possible HYV dissemination. Three periods of HYV cultivation are conceivable:

(1) May/June planting and August/September harvesting,
(2) August/September planting and November/December harvesting, and
(3) November/December planting and February/March harvesting.

The area where the first period is possible seems limited because of the relatively small area where water availability is assured for such an early rainy season planting. In cases where water is available, however, excessive water depth is unlikely because the crop is harvested before the time of maximum water depth which occurs in October. Various inconveniences accompanying reaping and other operations during the rainy season would have to be overcome.

The second period offers the advantage that possible damage by excessive water depth is avoided by making the time of maximum water depth coincide with the time of maximum plant height. However, this method is not practical unless the field is drained at the time of planting in August or September. Drainage at this time of the rainy season seems possible only in a limited area. Furthermore, drainage is difficult without the well-organized collaboration of farmers, since the water control of individual patches of fields is practically impossible without complete poldering. Water might still remain in the field at harvest time and might cause trouble in reaping, but the other operations could be carried out without difficulty thanks to dry weather in December.

The area potentially capable of employing the third period also seems limited, partly because of the difficulty of carrying out drainage at the end of the rainy season and partly because of the difficulty of obtaining enough water during the dry season. This period, however, does give a crop the decided advantage of receiving greater solar radiation throughout the growth period.

Using any of these three periods discussed briefly above, the area of potential dissemination of HYVs seems limited. Complete poldering is necessary for HYVs to be adopted widely in this region too.

Modification of water balance in the deltaic plain

Water-control projects thus far completed or to be undertaken in the near future will not basically alter the water balance of the basin. If the plain could be freed from annual flooding, the agricultural picture would change drastically. The water disposal area would disappear, and the cost of poldering would be greatly reduced.

The elimination of floodwater from the deltaic plain can be achieved by the following: (a) the construction of reservoirs upstream, (b) the complete diking of all water channels, (c) increasing the drainage capacity of rivers, and (d) the construction of bypasses to drain water directly to the sea. The combination of two or more of these measures is technically and economically more feasible than the adoption of any one single measure. In the case of the Chao Phraya basin, several alternatives have but recently come under consideration. However, practically speaking, the complete elimination of flooding seems impossible. Present proposed plans indicate the inevitability of a water-disposal area in combination with a large area maintained by conservation irrigation.

CONCLUSION

Environmental conditions affect the dissemination of HYVs in various ways. It seems impractical to classify environmental conditions simply according to their relative suitability to the dissemination of HYVs. While certain conditions will totally deter dissemination, others may permit it but with yields unexpectedly low in view of the high-yield potential of HYVs strains.

Generally speaking, HYVs will doubtless eventually be disseminated in the areas where gravity irrigation and drainage are possible. Whether such dissemination will be successful or not depends primarily upon potential water supply and the topographical conditions, which determine the relative difficulty of gravity irrigation and drainage. In the Chao Phraya basin, gravity irrigation is possible in three regions: the traditional irrigation area of the intermontane basins, the water-deficient foothills of the fan-terrace complex area, and the higher elevation areas of the barrage irrigation area on the old delta.

The traditional irrigation area, with total rice land of circa 320 × 1,000 ha, offers the best prospects for dissemination of HYVs thanks to the high potential availability of water and the relative ease of distribution and drainage. Actual dissemination seems influenced more by factors other than environmental ones: namely, the seemingly smaller demand for marketable surpluses, due partly to remoteness from the consuming center, and the fact that glutinous rice is the main product of northern Thailand.

The water-deficient foothills occupy quite a large area and include a total rice land of circa 1,310 × 1,000 ha. Although topography is suitable for irrigation and drainage, available water is very limited. HYVs will perhaps be adopted here; but their yields cannot be expected to be as high as their potential yield ability would suggest, because fear of drought will prevent large investments in fertilizer. Given this limited amount of fertilizer application and the generally poor, inherent soil fertility of this region, HYVs and NVs should remain competitive.

HYVs can be successfully adopted in paddy land supplied with water from barrage-canal systems.

Gravity irrigation and drainage is possible, but more difficult, in the higher parts of the barrage irrigation area than in the two regions just mentioned. Though the water supply here is abundant and becoming more dependable thanks to the construction of upstream reservoirs, facilities for irrigation and drainage must be further improved for HYVs to be successfully disseminated. HYVs could potentially be disseminated in the areas where rice growing by transplanting is presently practiced; this covers an area circa 80 × 1,000 ha.

Where gravity irrigation is impossible due to flat topography, HYV dissemination is practically impossible, even where flood water is controlled by conservation irrigation. In the Chao Phraya basin, conservation irrigation has been well developed and will be further improved and enlarged. Most of the less-flooded delta and about two-thirds of the canalled lowland are covered by this type of irrigation. In these areas, complete poldering is indispensable for the widespread dissemination of HYVs. But the construction of polders, while technically feasible, is economically impractical for less valuable crops such as rice. Even conservation irrigation is impossible in the water-disposal areas of the canalled lowland and barrage irrigation areas. Water conditions in the inland flood area are similar. As the drainage system of higher places is made possible only by sacrificing these lower ones, dissemination seems totally impossible. Only by drastically modifying the water flow of the whole Chao Phraya system could the general water supply and rice production conditions of the low-lying plain be improved. The completion of such a project lies in the distant future; yet even then, the complete elimination of floods cannot be expected.

As implied by the foregoing, paddy fields are distinctly different in deltaic and in nondeltaic regions. This is true also in their potential for HYV dissemination. Although the nondeltaic area is not the major rice-producing region, cultivation practices there seem to be more labor-intensive. Where inherent soil fertility is low, as is often the case in the nondeltaic region, farmers tend to increase their consumption of fertilizer. Thus rice cultivation in the nondeltaic region already seems to have become more intensive. While the degree of intensification is dependent largely on environmental conditions, HYVs offer a further new and great potential when intensification reaches a more advanced stage.

In the deltaic area, rice cultivation is quite extensive and stable, thanks to natural flooding and the modification of conservation irrigation. Except for the canalled lowland, yields are quite high due to generally rich soils. The deltaic region forms the "rice bowl" of Thailand. However, intensified rice cultivation, including the adoption of HYVs, seems extremely difficult here.

Methodology similar to that used in this study is being applied in dividing other river basins of continental Asia into rice-cultural regions. It cannot be said with certainty how well the regional division of other river basins will correlate to that of the Chao Phraya. However, I believe that the two broad categories of rice-growing areas, deltaic and nondeltaic, will be found there too. Clear differentiation between the two regions seems meaningful, not only in studying the possible dissemination of HYVs, but also in laying overall plans for agricultural development.

Acknowledgments

This paper is the product of the interdisciplinary cooperation of four researchers, one each from the fields of geology, irrigation technology, soil sciences, and crop sciences. The four are, respectively, Drs. Y. Takaya, Y. Kaida, and K. Kyuma of the Center for Southeast Asian Studies of Kyoto University, and myself. I would like to express my sincere gratitude to these cooperators. The encouragement and keen criticism throughout this study of Professors S. Ichimura, T. Motooka, and Y. Ishii of the Center for Southeast Asian Studies and of Professor K. Kawaguchi of the Faculty of Agriculture of Kyoto University is also appreciated. Thanks are also extended to Miss U. Nakaoku who typed the manuscript and prepared the maps.

References

High-Yielding Varieties in General

Asian Development Bank. *Asian Agricultural Survey.* University of Tokyo Press, 1969.

R. Barker. "Economic Aspects of New High-Yielding Varieties of Rice: IRRI Report," a paper presented at SEADAG seminar, Honolulu, June, 1969. (in *Agricultural Revolution in Southeast Asia*, vol. I)

L. R. Brown. *Seeds of Change, The Green Revolution and Development in the 1970's.* Praeger Publishers Inc., 1970.

ECAFE. "The Implications of Cultivating High-Yielding Varieties," as Chapter IV of Part One, *Economic Survey of Asia and the Far East, 1969.* Bangkok, 1969.

R. W. Cummings, Jr. and S. K. Ray. "1968–69 Foodgrain Production: Relative Contribution of Weather and New Technology," *Econ. and Pol. Weekly*, vol. 4, no. 39, Bombay, Sep. 1969.

FAO. *FAO/IWP Regional Study No.4.* (Asia and Far East).

FAO. "Raising Agricultural Productivity in Developing Countries Through Technological Improvement," as Chapter III of *The State of Food and Agriculture, 1968.* FAO, Rome, 1968.

W. David, Hopper and Wayne H. Freeman. *"India's Rice Development Moves from Unsteady*

Infancy to Vigorous Adolescence," unpublished mimeo. Rockefeller Foundation, New Delhi, March 1969.

Mekong Committee. *Amplified Basin Plan (draft).* Bangkok, 1970.

B. Sen. "Opportunities in the Green Revolution", *Econ. and Pol. Weekly,* vol. 5, no. 13, (India). March, 1970.

C. R. Wharton, Jr. "The Green Revolution: Cornucopia or Pandora's Box," *Foreign Affairs,* vol. 47, no. 3, April, 1969.

J. W. Willett. "The Impact of New Varieties of Rice and Wheat in Asia," *Spring Review of the New Cereal Varieties,* Agency for International Development (USA), 1969.

Performance of High Yielding Varieties and Native Varieties

J. C. Bunoan, Jr. *et al.* "Response of Rice to Fertilization in the Philippines," a paper presented at IRC meeting, Teheran, 1970.

M. F. Chandraratna. "The Fertilizer Response of Rice in the Philippines," a paper presented at IRC meeting, Teheran, 1970.

FAO. *Final Report on the Australian Ceylon Soil Fertility-Fertilizer Project,* vol. 1, 2, and 3. Rome, 1969.

R. W. Herdt. "Profitability of High-Yielding Wheat and Rice," *Econ. and Pol. Weekly.* vol. 4, no. 52, (India). Dec., 1969.

International Rice Research Institute. *Annual Report 1965, 1966, 1967, 1968, and 1969.* Philippines, 1965–1969.

M. A. Islam. "Fertilizer Trials on Paddy in Farmers' Fields in East Pakistan," *IRC Newsletter,* vol. 10, no. 2, June, 1961.

W. Ladejinsky. "Green Revolution in Bihar: The Kosi Area: A Field Trip," *Econ. and Pol. Weekly,* vol. 4, no. 39. Bombay, Sep., 1969.

Ministry of Food, Agriculture, Community Development and Cooperation (India). *IADP Second Report (1960–1965).* 1966.

Ministry of Food, Agriculture, Community Development and Cooperation (India). *IADP Third Report (1965/66 and 1966/67).* 1967.

P. K. Mukherjee. "The HYV Programme; Variables That Matter," *Econ. and Pol. Weekly,* vol. 5, no. 13, (India). March, 1970.

F. N. Ponnamperuma. "Fertilizer Trials in Cultivators' Fields in Ceylon," *IRC Newsletter,* vol. 8, no. 1, March, 1959.

G. Parthasarathy. "Economics of IR 8 Paddy: Factors Influencing Its Adoption in a Tank Irrigated District," *Econ. and Pol. Weekly,* vol. 4, no. 38, (India). Sep., 1969.

L. A. Paulino and L. A. Trinidad. "The Shift to New Rice Varieties in the Philippines," a paper presented at the seminar on economics of rice production in the Philippines, held at IRRI, Dec. 11–13, 1969.

Programme Evaluation Organization, Planning Commission (India). *Evaluation Study of the High-Yielding Varieties Programme: Report for the Kharif 1967.* 1968.

Programme Evaluation Organization, Planning Commission (India). *Evaluation Study of the High-Yielding Varieties Programme: Rabi 1967–1968.* 1969.

Programme Evaluation Organization, Planning Commission (India). *Evaluation Study of the High-yielding Varieties Programme: Report for the Rabi 1968–1969.* 1969.

Tanaka. *et al. Growth Habit of the Rice Plant in the Tropics and Its Effect on Nitrogen Response.* Technical Bulletin 3, IRRI, Philippines, 1964.

A. Tanaka. *et al. Photosynthesis, Respiration, and Plant Type of the Tropical Rice Plant,* Technical Bulletin 7, IRRI, Philippines, 1966.

R. N. Tripathy and B. Samal. "Economics of High-Yielding Varieties in IADP: A Study of Sambalpur in Orissa," *Econ. and Pol. Weekly,* Vol. 4, No. 43, Bombay, Oct., 1969.

J. G. Vermaat. *Report to the Government of Pakistan on Soil Fertility Investigations.* Rome, 1964.
N. Yamada. "Rice Production in Indonesia", vol. 7, no. 2. "Rice Production in Malaysia",
    vol. 7, no. 4. "Rice Production in Pakistan", vol. 7, no. 5. "Rice Production in
    Philippines", vol. 7, no. 6. "Rice Production in Thailand", vol. 7, no. 8. "Rice
    Production in South Vietnam", vol. 7, no. 9. *Agriculture, Asia (Ajia Nogyo),* Tokyo,
    1969.

Rice Cultivation in Thailand

Department of Rice (Thailand). *Annual Report on 1964 Rice Production in Thailand.* Bangkok.
H. Fukui and E. Takahashi, "Rice Culture in the Central Plain of Thailand (I), (II),
    (III), (IV), and (V)," *Tonan Ajia Kenkyu (Southeast Asian Studies),* vol. 6, no. 4
    (1969), vol. 7, no. 2 and no. 3 (1969), vol. 8, no. 1 and no. 4. (1970 and 1971).
    Kyoto University, Kyoto, 1969–1971.
S. Ishikawa. *Agricultural Development Strategies in Asia.* Asian Development Bank, 1970.
B. Lusanandana. *et al.* "Simple Fertilizer Trials on Rice in Cultivators' Fields in Thai-
    land," *IRC Newsletter,* vol. 12, no. 2. June, 1963.
National Statistical Office (Thailand). *Census of Agriculture, 1963.* Bangkok, 1963.
Y. Takaya. "Topographical Control Over the Agriculture in the Mae Nam Delta,"
    Japan Agricultural Research Quarterly (JARQ), vol. 4, no. 4, 1969.
Y. Takaya. "Topographical Analysis of the Southern Basin of the Central Plain, Thai-
    land," *Tonan Ajia Kenkyu (Southeast Asian Studies),* vol. 7, no. 3, Kyoto University,
    1969.
UNDP/SF Soil Fertility Research Project (Thailand). *NPK Fertilizer Experiments on
    Farmers' Fields 1967, 1968, and 1969.* Bangkok, 1968–1970.
T. Watabe. *Glutinous Rice in Northern Thailand.* Kyoto University, Kyoto, 1967.

9

Agro-Hydrologic Regions of the Chao Phraya Delta

YOSHIHIRO KAIDA

INTRODUCTION

This article aims at examining the various phases of water conditions in the cultivation of main season rice in the deltaic part of the Chao Phraya river basin in Thailand, to understand more clearly the "rice culture" in this delta. For this study the delta has been subdivided into several homogeneous agro-hydrologic regions, based on hydrological factors governing rice culture, so that a better evaluation can be made of present irrigation projects and a better perspective developed on the agriculture in this area.

In a previous publication, I made a statistical analysis of the effects of environmental factors on paddy rice yields, especially the effect of water conditions on yield.[1] However, this earlier study paid only minimal attention to the problems of areal extension of the various environmental factors. This article provides additional information on regional extension of these environmental factors, especially of water conditions, in relation to rice cultivation.

SOURCES OF DATA

The original data used in this analysis are taken from the "Crop Outlook Report" and "Daily Records of River and Canal Discharge and Water Gauge Readings" of the Greater Chao Phraya Project for the water year 1968, which were compiled by the Royal Irrigation Department. Detailed description of the methods of processing the original data from

---

1. Y. Kaida, "An Analysis of the Effect of Environmental Factors on Paddy Rice Yields, A Case Study of the Northern Region of the Greater Chao Phraya Project," *Southeast Asian Studies* 9, no. 2 (Kyoto: Center for Southeast Asian Studies, 1971).

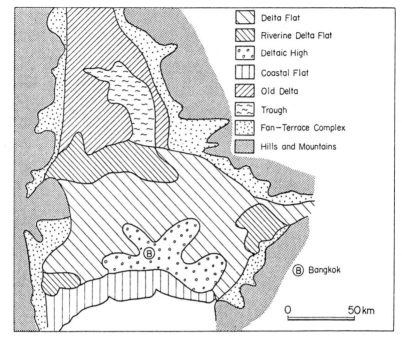

Figure 1.   *The physiography of the Chao Phraya delta (Takaya, "Rice Cropping Patterns in Southeast Asian Delta.")*

these sources was presented in a previous article. All data used were averaged for zones of the Greater Chao Phraya Irrigation Project,[2] thus the hydrologic factors and the demarcation lines of the following maps are accurate at the zone-scale.

Deficiencies in these data were partly supplemented by the author's own observations in April 1969 to January 1970, July 1973, and April 1974.

AGRO-HYDROLOGIC FACTORS

Results of the analysis of various phases of rice growth and hydrologic conditions are shown in Figures 2–9, which are drawn to the same scale. Reference will be made to Takaya's physiographic regions of the dalta in relating the agro-hydrologic factors to physiographic environment (Figure 1).[3] Discussion will focus on the regional distribution of water conditions in relation to rice cultivation.

2.   A zone is the smallest unit of land for regional operation of irrigation by the RID. The area of a zone averages 8,300 hectares, ranging from 800 to 23,300 hectares.

3.   Y. Takaya, "Physiography of Rice Land in the Chao Phraya Basin of Thailand," *Southeast Asian Studies* 9, no. 3 (Kyoto: Center for Southeast Asian Studies, 1971);

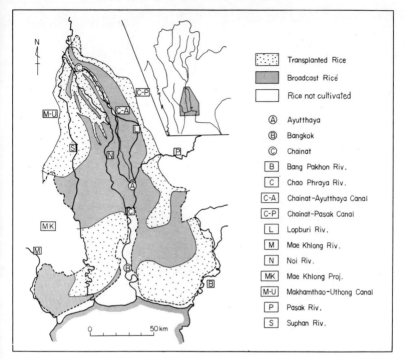

Figure 2.   *Area of transplanted and broadcast rice in the Chao Phraya delta*

Transplanted and Broadcast Rice

Areas planted with transplanted rice and broadcast rice are divided as shown in Figure 2. The "transplanted-rice area" represents the area where predominantly transplanted rice is grown, and the "broadcast-rice area," the area where broadcast rice is dominant; however, there may be some patches of appreciable size that are planted with transplanted rice in the broadcast-rice area and vice versa.

The transplanted rice area is restricted to (1) marginal zones of the delta comprising mostly the fan-terrace complex, (2) river levees of the old delta, and (3) a slightly elevated area toward the coastal zone, which is called the deltaic high. The west bank tract northwest of Bangkok is an exceptional area, where early season rice is grown quite extensively to avoid damage from possible floods in the later part of the

idem, "Topographical Analysis of the Southern Basin of the Central Plain, Thailand, "*Southeast Asian Studies* 7, no. 3 (Kyoto: Center for Southeast Asian Studies, 1969); idem, "Rice Cropping Patterns in Southeast Asian Delta," *Southeast Asian Studies* 13, no. 2 (Kyoto: Center for Southeast Asian Studies, 1975).

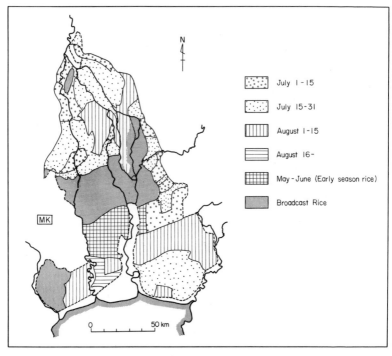

	July 1-15
	July 15-31
	August 1-15
	August 16-
	May-June (Early season rice)
	Broadcast Rice

MK

0   50 km

Figure 3.   *Date of transplanting in the Chao Phraya delta*

rainy season. The broadcast-rice area is (1) the trough, (2) the back-swamps in the old delta, and (3) the northern half of the young delta (the riverine delta flat in Figure 1).

Date of Transplanting

The transplanting date is a good indicator of the availability and stability of water supply in the early stages of the growing season, and is shown in Figure 3. Transplanting of main-season rice starts in early July in the areas serviced by the Suphan and the Chainat-Pasak canals in the old delta. In other parts of the old delta transplanting is finished by the end of July. Transplanting commences in August in patches of transplanted-rice fields in the "broadcast area." These fields are usually situated on raised land in lowlying areas, where there are no water supply facilities other than rainfall until the water table in the whole area rises substantially. The latest transplanting in the delta takes place toward the end of August on the right bank of the lowermost reaches of the Chao Phraya, in the Bang Yang area.

Early-season rice in the west-bank tract is usually planted between

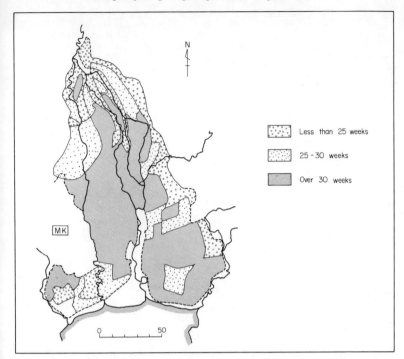

Figure 4.　*Inundation period in the Chao Phraya delta*

May 15 and June 10 and harvested before the period of deep flooding starts.

The transplanting date is largely controlled by the irrigation practices of the Royal Irrigation Department, which are based on a rotational supply of water from the main canal system. For example, the Chainat-Pasak canal receives water early in the season since it has to send water to an elongated area from Chainat down to the coastal zone on the left bank. Thus, certain zones in the area serviced by the Chainat-Pasak canal are the first to start transplanting in the delta.

Period of Inundation

As shown in Figure 4, the delta is divided into three zones with respect to the period of inundation of rice fields. Fields with a water depth of over 5 cm are considered "inundated." The levees and a large part of the marginal area of the delta have ponded water for less than twenty-five weeks, which approximately coincides with the growing season for transplanted rice. Most parts of the broadcast area are inundated for thirty weeks, which coincides approximately with the growing period for broadcast rice.

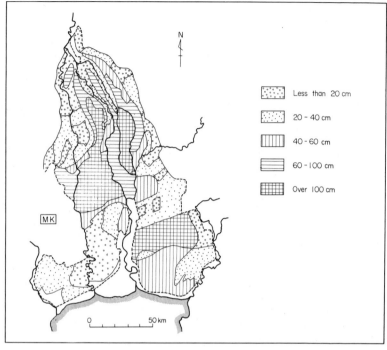

Figure 5.   *Maximum depth of inundation in the Chao Phraya delta*

Depth of Maximum Inundation

As shown in Figure 5, the delta is subdivided into five zones based on the maximum depth of inundation for the season. Shallow water, less than 20 cm, occurs in the fan-terrace complex, near levees at the upper reaches of such main distributaries as the Suphan and the Noi, and in the lowermost reaches of the Chao Phraya and the Suphan, in the west bank and the Bang Yang areas. These latter areas, however, are rather exceptional in that early-season rice is usually harvested before the beginning of the peak flood. The depression in the center of the delta is deeply inundated, with over 60 cm of water, and only broadcast rice can be grown. The deepest water, over 100 cm, occurs for a prolonged period in (1) the trough, (2) chains of depressional zones between the Suphan and the Noi, (3) the northernmost corner of the young delta (the riverine delta flat) and (4) the South Pasak Project area in the young delta northeast of Bangkok.

These deep-water areas can be considered "dumping places" for water from the surrounding levees and fan-terrace complex, as is clear when the maps showing the date of maximum inundation (Figure 6),

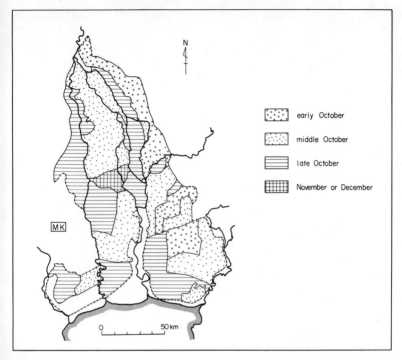

Figure 6. *Date of maximum inundation in the Chao Phraya delta*

the maximum rate of rise of the water level (Figure 7) and the maximum depth of inundation (Figure 5) are compared. A stable and comparatively shallow water-depth in the elevated areas can be sustained only at the expense of excessively deep floods in these lowlying areas.

Water depth in the coastal zones on both banks is fairly stable, and the maximum depth does not exceed 50–60 cm.

Date of Maximum Inundation

Maximum inundation in the trough and the huge depressional area at the northernmost edge of the young delta (the riverine delta flat) takes place from late October to November, sometimes even toward December, since these large areas receive water drained from the surrounding fan-terrace complex and the depressions of the old delta. However, the maximum depth in the chains of depressions in the old delta occurs in the middle of October, since its topography is of smaller scale, narrower, and of relatively sharp relief, compared with the huge depressional area of the young delta. This relatively early submergence takes place because the backswamps are filled with water from the levee

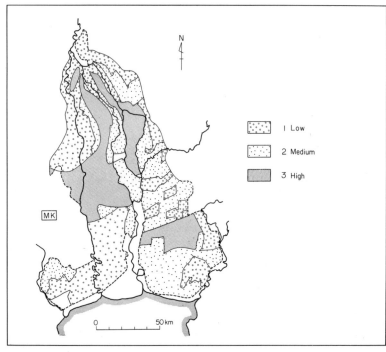

Figure 7.   *Rate of rise of water level in the Chao Phraya delta*

area shortly after the heaviest rainfall from late September to early October. The flood moves so slowly toward the coastal zones that the deltaic high attains its maximum inundation in late October.

Rate of Rise of the Water Level

The region is subdivided into three classes based on the maximum rate of rise of the water level in the paddy fields, as shown in Figure 7. Class 1 includes (a) most parts of the fan-terrace complex, (b) the northern part of the larger levees, (c) the lower reaches of the Chao Phraya on the right bank, and (d) the lower reaches of the Bang Pakong on the right bank. In Class 1 areas the water level rises very slowly, so shallow water can be maintained with very small fluctuations for at least twenty weeks. This area corresponds to the best rice area with respect to yield as demonstrated in earlier studies.[4] Class 2 includes

4.   Kaida, "An Analysis of the Effect of Environmental Factors on Paddy Rice Yields," and H. Fukui, "Environmental Determinants Affecting the Potential Dissemination of High Yielding Varieties of Rice, A Case Study of the Chao Phraya River Basin," *Southeast Asian Studies* 9, no. 3 (Kyoto: Center for Southeast Asian Studies, 1971).

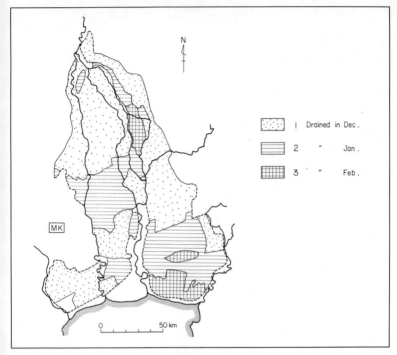

Figure 8. *Drainability in the Chao Phraya delta*

(a) the southern part of the Noi River levees, (b) the North Rangsit project, (c) the lower reaches of the Chao Phraya on the left bank, and (d) transitional zones between Class 1 and Class 3 areas. The rate of rise of the water level is medium, ranging from 2 to at most 5 cm a day. In this class, broadcast rice is dominant except in area (c). Class 3, which includes (1) the trough, (2) chains of depressions in the old delta, (3) the northernmost edge of the young delta (Phakhai, Phophraya, and the northern part of the west-bank tract), and (4) the South Rangsit project, usually suffers from a rapid rise of the water level, and these are the areas where no rice except tall varieties of broadcast rice can be grown. The transplanted rice area includes Class 1 and part of Class 2.

Drainability

The drainability of paddy fields is categorized into three simple classes as shown in Figure 8. Class 1 can be drained of ponded water completely by the end of December, Class 2 by the end of January, and Class 3 after the end of February. The main part of the old delta, including the fan-terrace complex, has good drainability, and is

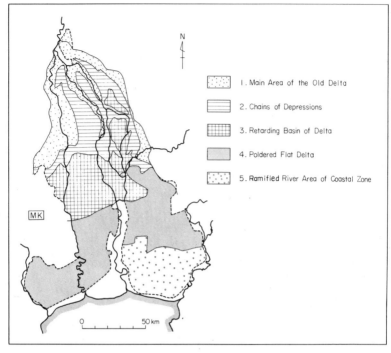

Figure 9.   *Agro-hydrologic regions of the Chao Phraya delta*

categorized as Class 1. A general slope of *circa* 1/5,000 and the relatively
sharp relief account for the good drainage. In most parts of the young
delta, ponded water remains on the fields until the end of January.
Drainability is poor in the extreme coastal zones on the left bank
because of the presence of a coastal embankment built against the
intrusion of seawater. The trough is the most difficult area to drain
completely; in some parts standing water remains until the middle of
March.

AGRO-HYDROLOGIC REGIONS

To illustrate the agro-hydrologic regions, the seven maps, Figures 2–8,
were combined to form a single map which indicates the regional
subdivisions of the delta based on hydrologic conditions in areas of
lowland-rice cultivation. This rough demarkation of the five agro-
hydrologic regions is shown in Figure 9. These are as follows:

Region 1 Main Area of the Old Delta

Region 1 comprises the fan-terrace complex, the main area of the
old delta marked by gentle slopes and relatively flat terrain, and the

narrow strips of natural river levees along the major distributaries. Relatively shallow water (not over 35 cm) can be maintained on the fields for at least twenty weeks. There is no risk of prolonged deep inundation, because the irrigation networks of the main-lateral-tertiary canal and ditch system have been well planned and operate efficiently. About 80 percent of the ditches function effectively owing to the appropriate topography for gravitational irrigation. Drainage is possible through natural and some man-made drainage canals into adjacent depressions.

Region 1 is solely a "transplanted-rice area" in the main season. The yield is generally slightly over 3 tons/ha. A schedule has been prepared for a crop diversification program for off-season cultivation, but this scheme seems unsuccessful so far, partly because the gravitational irrigation system does not function effectively in the dry season owing to a shortage of water relative to the dimensions of the canal system. This irrigation system is designed to meet the major requirements of both supplementary irrigation for the main-season rice and water dispersion during the flood season.

Region 2 Chains of Depressions

Region 2 comprises narrow strips of backswamps sandwiched between levees, relatively rugged terrain of raised land and depressions between major distributaries, and marginal zones of the trough. In short, Region 2 is a "dumping place" for water from the surrounding Region 1. Water conditions are very unstable, with a rapid rise in the water level shortly after heavy rainfall in the old delta. The average maximum water depth reaches 80–100 cm, the deepest being 140–160 cm. The rate of rise of the water level is usually very high, probably as high as 200 mm/day in certain localities. Region 2 is exclusively an area of broadcast rice, reflecting the unstable water conditions.

Region 1 can maintain advantageous water conditions only at the expense of Region 2. Drainage in the latter is rather difficult during the flood season. However, drainability in the late-growing season is fairly good as most of the water can eventually be drained into a huge depression, Region 3. The drainage scheme now underway will greatly benefit this region, transforming some areas into transplanted-rice areas.

Region 3 Retarding Basin of the Delta

Region 3 comprises the major part of the trough and the huge depression at the northwest corner of the young delta (the riverine delta flat in Figure 1). Region 3 can be said to be a huge retarding basin for the whole delta with a reserve capacity of more than 2×10^9 m^3.[5] The average maximum depth of water in the main season exceeds 100 cm, and the peak depth reaches 200 cm. The rate of rise of the water level is very high, but usually less than in Region 2 because of the buffering effect of this region. The period of inundation is extremely long, over eight months. These conditions make this region an acceptable habitat for the tall varieties of broadcast rice, as floating rice. Use of floating rice is the only feasible way of adapting to the water conditions.

The water conditions will not improve in the near future. A major construction program incorporating a flood protection scheme and a drainage project covering the entire delta would be necessary if water conditions in Region 3 were to be improved.

Region 4   Poldered Flat Delta

Region 4 comprises the main central area of the young delta including Rangsit, the west-bank tract, and the Bang Yang areas. The terrain in this huge area is characterized by flatness with very little relief. The average ground height is 1–2 m, and the general slope from north to south is from 1/20,000 to 1/25,000. The rate of rise of the water level in the high-water season is rather low, though the water depth reaches approximately 60 cm. General water conditions can be regulated to some extent by constructing large-scale polders and drainage canals. This has been confirmed in the Rangsit area and the west-bank tract where a system of polders has been developed with large man-made canals which serve both for transportation and for irrigation and drainage. A drainage and poldering scheme is also underway in the Bang Yang area as part of the Maeklong Irrigation Project.

Irrigation history shows that once the government provides a large main canal and some secondary canals in a sparsely populated area in the flat delta region, people begin to settle along the canals, and gradually expand their territory into the hinterland by digging tertiary canal networks.[6] They devise low lift pumps for irrigation, using reserve water in canals which is available perennially in certain areas. Early-season rice cultivation was started in this area when certain conditions of water availability were met and pumping facilities provided. In the Bang Yang area, one can see beautiful gardens of fruit

5.   NEDECO/RID, "Northern Chao Phraya Study, part III, Drainage and Flood Control," (The Hague: NEDECO, 1970).

6.   Y. Kaida, "Pioneer Settlement and Water Control Development in the west Bank of the Lower Chao Phraya Delta," *Southeast Asian Studies* 11, no. 4 (Kyoto: Center for Southeast Asian Studies, 1974).

and vegetables on land poldered on a smaller scale and surrounded by neatly maintained high dikes.

Region 5   Ramified River Area of the Coastal Zone

Region 5 roughly corresponds to the deltaic high. The region is characterized by a dense network of water courses, both natural and artificial. Some canals were constructed long ago (80–150 years) to supply water to the natural water network and to supplement irrigation for main-season rice. The arrival and departure of water in the region are later and generally more gradual than in Region 4. The feasibility of introducing new high-yielding varieties of rice of short stature is relatively high,[7] even in the main season, because of the good natural water conditions and relatively fertile marine-alluvium soils in most of this region.

GENERAL DISCUSSION

As is clear from the maps, water conditions for rice cultivation are governed largely by the geomorphologic framework. The Greater Chao Phraya Project, which aimed at supplementing irrigation water to give better and more stable cultivation of main season rice, contributed greatly to increasing the total production of rice as well as the paddy yield per unit area, in the following ways:

(1) It extended the irrigable area into the marginal areas of the delta by diverting water from the Chainat headworks.

(2) It changed much of the broadcast-rice zone to transplanted areas, especially in Regions 1, 4, and 5, by providing better water supply in the early-growing season. Improved cultivation can take place only in a transplanted rice field. The percentage of transplanted area to the total area in the delta increased gradually year by year after completion of the project, 22 percent before 1957, 35 percent in 1964, 37 percent in 1965, 40 percent in 1966, 42 percent in 1967, and 55 percent in 1970.

(3) It provided certain areas, especially in Region 1, with the possibility of implementing land consolidation projects in the near future, because of improved irrigation and drainage.

(4) It made possible the cultivation of early-season rice in the west-bank tract in Region 4 by providing better water supply in the early season.[8]

Nevertheless, it is recognized that certain parts of the delta have suffered because of this project. One example is Region 2, where water

---

7. Fukui, "Environmental Determinants Affecting the Potential Dissemination of High Yielding Varieties of Rice."

8. Y. Kaida, "Pioneer Settlement and Water Control Development in the West Bank of the Lower Chao Phraya Delta."

conditions have deteriorated. The canal network is designed so that water flows through a main and a lateral canal on the levee and down the levee-backslope to the backswamp. This means the levee areas (Region 1) benefit in two ways. They can receive irrigation water when necessary and can easily drain excess water into the backswamps through the irrigation and drainage systems. Region 2 thus suffers in the high-water season. Also, with the present irrigation and drainage system, improvement of water conditions in the main area (Region 1) can be accomplished only at the expense of Region 2 and Region 3.

Drainage of excess water from Regions 2 and 3 is the most important and the most urgent problem that must be solved in the delta, if any major improvement of the region's rice growing is to be realized. This will not be an easy task. Drainage from these regions can affect the delicate equilibrium of the water balance in Region 4 and Region 5, including Bangkok. Therefore, further improvement in the irrigation, drainage and flood control schemes of Regions 4 and 5 will have to be considered in conjunction with a master plan for the drainage of Regions 2 and 3.

10

An Approach to the Capability Classification of Paddy Soils in Relation to the Assessment of their Agricultural Potential

KAZUTAKE KYUMA and KEIZABURO KAWAGUCHI

INTRODUCTION

In comparison with soils cultivated for other crops, paddy soils are characterized by the following two features.

1. They occur on low-lying land which is naturally inundated or where water can be introduced by gravity. Therefore, most paddy soils occur on alluvia of the most recent geological periods (Holocene and uppermost Pleistocene).

2. As the soils are waterlogged, either naturally or artificially, for several months during the cropping season, their physical properties are relatively unimportant provided sufficient water is available.

The first feature means that most paddy soils are either Entisols or Inceptisols in the U.S. system of soil classification, or alluvial soils and low humic gley soils in conventional terminology. Vertisols (or grumusols) are not rare in the tropics but are less common than the above two types. For general discussion the other groups of soils are of minor importance.

Unlike other soils with a developed morphology, alluvial soils have undergone so little pedogenetic change that the nature of the soil is directly governed by the nature of the parent material. Thus, soil classification based on profile morphology alone has, even at the lowest categories, little value in assessing the fertility of alluvial soils.

From the second feature it follows that the productivity of paddy soils is heavily dependent on soil fertility, as the role played by soil tilth is relatively unimportant.

The preceding suggests that a capability classification of paddy soils in relation to the assessment of their agricultural potential should predominantly consider the chemical nature of the parent material. In this article, we put forward a concept of chemical potentiality which reflects the nature of the parent material and a method for its quantitative evaluation. Based on numerical scores, we can set up chemical potentiality classes, which will be an important factor in the capability classification of paddy soils.

METHOD AND DATA

To evaluate chemical potentiality the method of principal component analysis is used. It is one of the multivariate statistical methods for attaining a "parsimonious summarization of a mass of observation."[1] The n samples, each of which is defined by p characters, can be expressed as n points scattered in a p dimensional space. Principal component analysis aims at reducing the p axes to orthogonal m axes, where $m < p$, with a minimum loss of information. Mathematically this produces m new variates from the original p variates by an orthogonal transformation.

The procedure for obtaining principal components is as follows.[2]

1. A $p \times p$ correlation coefficient matrix (R) is prepared.

2. The following characteristic equation is solved

$$|R - \lambda I| = 0$$

where λ is the eigenvalue and I is a $p \times p$ unit matrix. The equation yields p real, nonnegative roots (or eigenvalues), rearranged in descending order: $\lambda_1 \geqslant \lambda_2 \geqslant \ldots \geqslant \lambda_p \geqslant 0$. An eigenvector corresponding to each λ is also obtained, that is, the normalized eigenvector, $l_{i1}, l_{i2} \ldots l_{ip}$, is determined for the eigenvalue λ_i. This eigenvector is the coefficient for linear transformation of the x-vector of the αth sample to a new variate $X_{i\alpha}$, or the ith principal component score of the αth sample.

3. As the sum of the λs equals p when started from the correlation matrix, the formula

$$(\sum_{l=1}^{k} \lambda_l / p) \times 100, (k: 1, 2 \ldots p),$$

gives cumulative percentages of the first k eigenvalues, from which one can decide the number of components (m) to be taken into consideration,

1. Hilary L. Seal. *Multivariate Statistical Analysis for Biologists*. London: Methuen & Co. 1964.
2. T. Okuno. "Tahenryo-kaiseki-ho (I–III) [Multivariate statistical analysis]," *Hinshitsukanri*. vol. 17, pp. 805–810, 983–989, 1439–1448. 1966. (in Japanese).

TABLE 1
Characters Used for Analysis

Character No.	Name	Description
1	pH	1 : 5 water suspension
2	T.C. (Total Carbon)	in % of air-dried soil, Tyurin's wet combustion method
3	T.N. (Total Nitrogen)	in % of air-dried soil, Kjeldahl digestion and steam distillation
4	NH_3-N	in mg N/100g of air-dried soil, after incubation for two weeks at 40°C
5	Bray-P	in mg P_2O_5/100g of air-dried soil, Bray-Kurz No. 2 method
6	Exch. K	in me/100g of air-dried soil, N NH_4−acetate extraction, flame photometry
7	CEC	in me/100g of air-dried soil, buffered neutral N $CaCl_2$ medium
8	Avail. Si	in mg SiO_2/100g of air-dried soil, pH 4 Acetic acid extraction at 40°C
9	T.P. (Total Phosphorus)	in mg P_2O_5/100g of air-dried soil, either $HF-H_2SO_4$ or $HNO_3-H_2SO_4$ digestion
10	Sand	in % of organic matter-free dried soil, sum of coarse and fine sands
11	Exch. Ca + Mg	in me/100g of air-dried soil, N NaCl extraction, EDTA titration

setting an arbitrary figure for the loss of information (usually about 20 to 30 percent of the total variance).

4. The principal component scores are calculated from standardized character values by the formula

$$X_{i\alpha} = \sum_{k=1}^{p} l_{ik} \cdot u_{k\alpha}/\sqrt{\lambda_i}$$

where $(\alpha: 1, 2 \ldots n)$, $(i: 1, 2 \ldots m)$, $(k: 1, 2 \ldots p)$ and $u_{k\alpha}$ is the standardized character value for the kth character of the αth sample. The $X_{i\alpha}$ values thus obtained are standardized component scores with respect to the n samples, having a mean of 0 and a variance of 1.

5. Correlation coefficients between a principal component and the p characters are also computed by the following formula

$$r(x_k, X_i) = \sqrt{\lambda_i} \cdot l_{ik}$$

where $r(x_k, X_i)$ is the correlation coefficient between the ith principal component and the kth character. This is to facilitate interpretation of the nature of the principal component or compound character.

TABLE 2

THE LARGEST THREE EIGENVALUES AND CORRESPONDING
EIGENVECTORS

Principal Component No.		1	2	3
Eigenvalue		3.9695	2.6177	1.3834
Cumulative Percentage		36.1	59.9	72.5
Eigenvector	1	0.274	−0.355	0.222
for	2	0.168	0.533	−0.013
Character	3	0.150	0.557	0.033
No.	4	0.161	0.404	0.102
	5	0.132	−0.074	0.639
	6	0.346	−0.073	0.129
	7	0.448	−0.078	−0.276
	8	0.412	−0.151	0.084
	9	0.250	0.161	0.447
	10	−0.309	−0.109	0.414
	11	0.428	−0.194	−0.242

These were all computed with a FACOM 230–60 at the Computer Center of Kyoto University.

The data used for the analysis are those for surface layer samples of 417 paddy soils taken by us in Cambodia, Sri Lanka, Bangladesh, India, Indonesia (Java), Malaysia (West), the Philippines, and Thailand. Eight soils from New South Wales, Australia, also are included for comparison.

The characters used for the analysis are listed in Table 1. These characters are commonly determined for paddy soil samples, and are clearly relevant to the fertility of a soil. In the present study the data were not transformed before principal component analysis.

RESULTS AND DISCUSSION

Starting from a correlation coefficient matrix of the 11 characters for the 417 soils, the largest 3 eigenvalues explained about 70 percent of the total variance of the data, as shown in Table 2. The correlation coefficients between the principal components and characters are given in Table 3.

The first principal component, which explains about 36 percent of the total variance, has high positive correlation with CEC, exchangeable Ca+Mg, available silica, and exchangeable K, and negative correlation with the sum of sands. It is also moderately cor-

TABLE 3
CORRELATION COEFFICIENTS BETWEEN PRINCIPAL COMPONENTS AND
CHARACTERS

Principal Component No.	1	2	3
Character			
1 pH	0.545	−0.575	0.261
2 T.C.	0.334	0.863	−0.015
3 T.N.	0.299	0.902	0.039
4 NH$_3$-N	0.321	0.654	0.120
5 Bray-P	0.263	−0.120	0.752
6 Exch. K	0.690	−0.118	0.152
7 CEC	0.893	−0.126	−0.325
8 Avail. Si	0.820	−0.244	0.099
9 T.P.	0.498	0.261	0.526
10 Sand	−0.616	−0.177	0.487
11 Exch. Ca + Mg	0.853	−0.314	−0.284

related with pH and total phosphorus. Total carbon, total nitrogen, NH$_3$-N, and Bray-P contribute only slightly to the first principal component. The first principal component is thus a compound character which reflects mainly the nature and amount of clay and the base status of the soil. We named this first principal component "Soil Chemical Potentiality," as it reflects the fundamental chemical nature of the parent material.

The second principal component is correlated with organic matter (total carbon and nitrogen, and NH$_3$-N) and with pH to some extent, but negatively. The third principal component is correlated with Bray-P, total P, and sand. These two components seem to be related, though crudely, to nitrogen availability and phosphorus availability, respectively. But they are not further elaborated here.

The standardized scores of the first principal component are computed for each of the sample soils. They are regarded as the relative measures of the chemical potentiality of each sample. As is evident from the computational procedure, all the characters used contribute to some degree to the score, but the original character values are weighted by the eigenvector, so that a character with a small absolute eigenvector value contributes relatively little to the score and vice versa. Thus, characters related to the nature and amount of clay and base status contribute more to the chemical potentiality score than do the characters related to organic matter.

The potentiality scores are standardized so that the mean is zero

TABLE 4
TWENTY HIGHEST-RANKED AND TWENTY LOWEST-RANKED SOILS AND THEIR CHEMICAL POTENTIALITY SCORE

Highest-Ranked		Lowest-Ranked	
Soil No.	Score	Soil No.	Score
I-62	2.76	T-72	− 1.89
Ph-36	2.71	T-78	− 1.87
In-33	2.57	T-3	− 1.83
Ph-29	2.45	T-75	− 1.83
I-58	2.38	T-79	− 1.75
In-32	2.35	T-82	− 1.74
I-65	2.27	T-22	− 1.73
Ph-45	2.25	T-17	− 1.71
I-4	2.25	T-76	− 1.67
T-95	2.17	T-68	− 1.64
I-56	2.17	Ca-9	− 1.62
In-20	2.17	T-77	− 1.60
Ph-38	2.15	M-36	− 1.56
I-60	2.12	T-80	− 1.55
M-18	2.11	Ca-15	− 1.55
In-31	2.11	Bd-20	− 1.53
In-43	2.08	T-69	− 1.53
Ph-7	2.02	Ca-14	− 1.51
Ph-40	1.99	Sr-18	− 1.50
I-55	1.96	T-6	− 1.49

Ca–Cambodia   In–Indonesia (Java)
Sr–Sri Lanka   M–Malaysia (West)
Bd–Bangladesh   Ph–Philippines
I–India   T–Thailand

and the variance is 1. The distribution of the score around the mean is as follows:

Score	No. of samples
> 2	18
2 − 1	50
1 − 0	115
0 − −1	162
−1 − −2	72

The distribution is slightly positively skewed. We do not know whether this is due to biases in our sampling (see below).

In Table 4 the soils with the highest twenty and the lowest twenty scores are listed. Those having the highest scores are grumusolic alluvial

TABLE 5

MEANS AND STANDARD DEVIATIONS OF CHEMICAL POTENTIALITY
SCORES

Country	No. of Samples	Mean	Standard Deviation
Indonesia (Java)	44	0.87	0.865
Philippines	54	0.76	0.871
India	73	0.31	1.030
Malaysia (West)	41	− 0.11	0.834
Bangladesh	53	− 0.33	0.684
Thailand	95	− 0.54	0.768
Sri Lanka	33	− 0.64	0.747
Cambodia	16	− 0.70	0.679
Australia, N.S.W.	8	0.40	0.659

soils, soils derived from recent marine clay deposits or those derived
from recent volcanic ejecta. The lowest-ranked soils are either sandy
soils or soils on old alluvia; many are from a specific parent material
group occurring in Northeast Thailand and Cambodia.

The sample soils were collected with the following considerations.

1. Area of distribution of the same kind of soil, with reference to
the results of soil surveys.

2. Accessibility of sites.

3. Specific soil characteristics of scientific and/or practical interest.

As the second and the third considerations bring about biases in
sampling, the samples used in this study cannot necessarily be regarded
as representative of the region from which they were taken. Nevertheless,
a rough estimate of the general potentiality level of each country or
region may be obtained by computing a mean of the scores of the sample
soils. Table 5 shows such a mean and standard deviation for each country.
As is evident from the table, the soils of Indonesia (Java) and the
Philippines have the highest potentiality, whereas the Sri Lanka and
Cambodian soils are generally of inferior chemical nature.

A similar calculation was done for the regions that can be defined
more or less discretely with respect to climate, parent material, and
area. The result, as given in Table 6, shows that the soils of the Godavari-
Krishna delta in India have by far the highest potentiality, and the
soils from the Northeast Plateau region of Thailand have the lowest.

It is possible to set up a chemical potentiality grouping of the soils
on the basis of the potentiality score. For example, by setting class

TABLE 6
MEANS AND STANDARD DEVIATIONS OF CHEMICAL POTENTIALITY
SCORES BY REGIONS

	Region	No. of Samples	Mean	Standard Deviation
1	Godavari-Krishna delta (India)	10	1.84	0.348
2	Gangetic alluvial region (Bangladesh)	15	0.46	0.511
3	Perlis-Kedah plain (West Malaysia)	10	0.28	0.491
4	Bangkok plain (Thailand)	35	0.04	0.609
5	Northern valleys region (Thailand)	36	− 0.60	0.501
6	East coast (West Malaysia)	12	− 0.66	0.602
7	Madhupur and Barind (Bangladesh)	9	− 0.73	0.553
8	Wet and intermediate Zones (Sri Lanka)	14	− 0.76	0.753
9	Northeast plateau region (Thailand)	20	− 1.36	0.630

limits at scores of $\pm$ 0.25 and $\pm$ 0.84 we can set up five potentiality classes of nearly equal size, if we assume a normal distribution. As the distribution of the potentiality scores of our samples cannot be regarded as normal, the actual number of samples falling into each of the classes is as follows:

Class	Class limits	No. of samples
I very high	> 0.84	88
II high	0.84 − 0.25	68
III intermediate	0.25 − −0.25	81
IV low	−0.25 − −0.84	92
V very low	< −0.84	88

Using twenty random samples from each of the five classes, linear discriminant functions were derived, with the assumption that variance-covariance matrices of the five groups are equal. The performance of the discriminant functions thus derived was not very good and mis-classification occurred in about 20 percent of cases. The computation is so involved that it is not practical, unless a computer is available, to use the discriminant functions for potentiality classification.

Therefore, in order to position a new paddy soil sample in the spectrum of soil chemical potentiality, use of the eigenvalue and eigenvector for the first principal component is recommended. Strictly speaking, this is not justified, because those parameters were determined with biased samples. But they should be good enough for an approximate potentiality evaluation.

The formula of computation is as follows:

$$Y = 1/\sqrt{3.9695} \times (0.274\,X_{pH} + 0.168\,X_{TC} + 0.150\,X_{TN}$$
$$+ 0.161\,X_{NH_3} + 0.132\,X_{Bray} + 0.346\,X_K + 0.448\,X_{CEC}$$
$$+ 0.412\,X_{Si} + 0.250\,X_{TP} + 0.428\,X_{Ca+Mg} - 0.309\,S_{Sand})$$

where Y: potentiality score

X: character value transformed by the following formula

$$X = (x - m)/s,$$

x: original character value (in the units given in Table 1)
m and s: transformation vectors as follows,

	pH	TC	TN	NH₃	Bray-P	Exch. K
m	5.93	1.44	0.129	8.63	3.54	0.38
s	1.11	1.26	0.106	9.26	8.62	0.36

	CEC	Av-Si	TP	Ca+Mg	Sand
m	18.5	26.6	84.2	15.7	32.8
s	11.8	25.7	64.6	13.1	25.1

There is a limitation to the utility of the concept of chemical potentiality. It is a relative measure of the potential supply of mineral nutrients in a soil, and, as such, does not reflect the consideration essential to the concept of soil fertility that the nutrients must be supplied "in proper amounts and in proper balance."[3] Accordingly, we cannot expect to establish a significant correlation between the chemical potentiality score and the yield of paddy. In this connection we have made a further attempt with some success to come to a better represen-tation of the concept of soil fertility by applying factor analysis in

3. Soil Survey Staff. *Soil Survey Manual*. U.S.D.A. Handbook no. 18. Washington, D.C. 1951.

combination with multiple regression to the soil data. The details of this are published in other papers.[4]

According to Moormann and Dudal[5] the major factors to be considered in the capability classification of paddy soils are the following:

1. water supply   3. soil horizons
2. soil characteristics   4. others (topography, climate, etc.)

Of these four, the last is related to the first factor of water supply; the factor of soil horizons is, as mentioned earlier, in our view not of primary importance for paddy soils. Because chemical potentiality covers the soil characteristics factor, if the water supply conditions could be evaluated in a similar manner, we should be able to establish a reasonably objective and reproducible capability classification by combining these two factors. This is, however, a task yet to be undertaken.

SUMMARY

The concept of soil chemical potentiality, together with a method for its numerical evaluation, was proposed as one of the factors to be taken into consideration in a capability classification of paddy soils.

A principal component analysis of eleven selected character data for 417 paddy soils from South and Southeast Asian countries yielded a compound character, which appeared to reflect the fundamental chemical nature of parent material. This compound character was called "Soil Chemical Potentiality," and its numerical evaluation for each sample soil was attained by computation of the first principal component score. Based on this score, a comparison of the chemical potentiality of the sample soils from different countries or regions was possible.

A formula was presented for chemical potentiality evaluation of a new paddy soil sample. Use of this formula would facilitate the objective location of the sample in the wide spectrum of the chemical nature of paddy soils.

4.   Kazutake Kyuma and Keizaburo Kawaguchi. "A Method of Fertility Evaluation for Paddy Soils (I), First Approximation: Chemical Potentiality Rating," *Soil Science and Plant Nutrition*. vol. 19, no. 1, 1973; Kazutake Kyuma, "A Method of Fertility Evaluation for Paddy Soils (II), Second Approximation: Evaluation of Four Independent Constituents of Soil Fertility," *Soil Science and Plant Nutrition*. vol. 19, no. 1, 1973; idem, "A Method of Fertility Evaluation for Paddy Soils (III), Third Approximation: Synthesis of Fertility Constituents for Soil Fertility Evaluation," *Soil Science and Plant Nutrition*. vol. 19, no. 1, 1973.
5.   F. R. Moormann and R. Dudal. *Characteristics of Soils on Which Paddy is Grown in Relation to their Capability Classification*. Soil Survey Report no. 32 Bangkok. 1965.

ACKNOWLEDGMENT

We wish to express our most sincere thanks to those who have contributed in various ways to the successful execution of our project, "A Comparative Study of Paddy Soils in South and Southeast Asia."

11

The Political Elite Cycle in Thailand in the Pre-1973 Period

TORU YANO

AUTOCRACY AND OLIGARCHY

Ever since the "revolution (*kaan-pathiwat*)" by the People's party in June 1932, the Thai political stage has been characterized by the cyclical emergence and disappearance of various power groups. Two distinctive patterns of leadership, arising from delicate changes in the character of oligarchic rule, can be discerned during this period. At times a particular individual has gained power with the oligarchy almost assuming the nature of an autocracy, while at other times plural power units, involved in conflicting or mutually restraining relations, have emerged within the political elite. These two patterns may be described respectively as the *autocratic* and *true* forms of oligarchy.

Typical examples of the former, or autocratic type of oligarchy, can be seen in the elite group of Phibuun Songkhraam during the first half of the 1950s and the leadership of Sarit Thanarat after 1957.

The autocratic nature of Phibuun's rule is well illustrated by the kinds of men who constituted the seventh Phibuun cabinet (March 24, 1952–1957). This cabinet included twenty-six ministers, most of them members of the so-called Phibuun clique. The clique included various subgroups, but all members had personal ties to Phibuun himself. Their relationships with him can be classified as follows: (1) members of the People's party at the time of the 1932 Revolution;[1] (2) friends and aides from the days when he was defense minister in the

---

1. For a list of the members of the People's party see Thibodii [pseud.], *Cotmaaiheet prawatsaat prachaathipatai khoong sayaam mai* [Documentary history of democracy in newborn Siam] (Bangkok: Daaraakoon, 1950), pp. 5–10.

late 1930s;[2] (3) those who helped in the 1947 coup d'état;[3] (4) those who secured his favor after 1947, through service in national affairs;[4] and (5) those introduced to him by mutual political acquaintances.

One is impressed with how few of the cabinet appointments came from outside these five categories. Phibuun obviously cherished and tried to perpetuate his personal relations.[5] And his subordinates (*luuksit*) in turn seem to have rewarded him with firm support and confidence as a result of their long association with him and the benefits he had bestowed upon them for their loyalty. The overall result was the emergence of an autocratic situation, a period whose stability allowed Phibuun's world tour and encouraged his bold lip-service to democracy. Phibuun, in short, occupied a uniquely superior position in an elite oligarchic group.

In contrast to this autocratic form of oligarchy, there also have been such periods of *literal* oligarchy as the years of civilian reign in 1945–1946[6] and the period of contention between the Phao and Sarit factions prior to the 1957 coup.[7] Both of these were characterized by tensions between a ruling group and a contending force, resulting inevitably in great political instability. This true oligarchical form,

2. Useful are biographies of Yutthasaatkooson and Fǔǔn Ronnaphaakaat found in Singthoong Siiphanom, *12 coomphon thai* [Twelve Thai generals] (Bangkok: Ruamsaan, 1963).

3. For a list of those who participated in organizing the Coup d'État group, see Bunchuai Siisawat, *Phantrii Khuang Aphaiwong—adiit naayokratthamontrii 4 samai* [Major Khuang Aphaiwong—former prime minister for four terms] (Bangkok: private publication, n. d.), pp. 480–481; and Wooraphong Sombuu, *Coomphon Sarit Thanarat* [General Sarit Thanarat] (Bangkok: Kaseemsamphan, 1964), pp. 383–385. A useful reference for studying the background of the 1947 coup is the court testimony of Navy General Luang Sin, who was later arrested during the incident of June 29, 1951. See article in *Bangkok Post*, 23 June 1956.

4. They share the characteristic of having served as cabinet minister a great number of times. For instance, Sukit Nimaanheemin was a minister from the 22nd to the 29th cabinets; Phrayaa Borirak from the 22nd to the 26th cabinets; Luang Phonsoophon in the 20th, 21st, 24th, 25th, and 26th cabinets; and Keemchaat Bunyaratthaphan in the 22nd through the 26th cabinets.

5. For instances of rewards given and kindnesses shown by Phibuun to his subordinates and friends, see Thai Nooi [pseud.], *10 naayok ratthamontrii* [Ten prime ministers] (Bangkok:Phrae Phitthayaa, 1959), p. 343.

6. For the most detailed account of the political situation under civilian control in 1945 and 1946, see Kiat [pseud.), *Phongsaawadaan kaanmǔang* [Political chronology] (Bangkok: Kiattisak, 1950).

7. For a detailed account of the confrontation between Sarit and Phao, prior to the 1957 coup, see Thai Nooi [pseud.] and Canthorasaan Kamon, *Wootoeluu khoong coomphon Plaek* [The Waterloo of General Phibuun] (Bangkok: Phrae Phitthayaa, 1957).

prone to political feuds and instability, however, has been short-lived, liable, at least until now, to be soon replaced by a new elite group under a strong autocratic leader. This process of oligarchic dissolution and transfer to more autocratic leadership has resulted from the seizure of power by the *khana*, or ruling circles. However, the autocratic situation also tends to give rise eventually to political confrontations and, in time, to a shift back again to the true oligarchy. The Phibuun autocracy of the early 1950s illustrated this cycle when it at last lost its autocratic nature and began struggling with the rising Sarit faction.

LINEAGE OF COLLECTIVE LEADERSHIP

The political elite of Thailand belong to *khana*, which have successfully sized power through a coup d'état. Such ruling circles normally remain in power for rather long periods of time. Indeed there have been only four such *khana* since 1932: the People's party (*khana raatsadoon*, 1932–1944), the Free Thai (*khabuan seeriithai*, 1944–1947), the Coup d'État group (*khana ratthaprahaan*, 1947–1957), and the Military group (*khana thahaan*, 1957–1973).

Each *khana* has a number of common features. First, having started as a secret society, it will have a small and limited membership. Second, there will be a clear line of distinction between core members, who first organized the circle, and the mass membership recruited later through personal ties, propaganda, professional relations, and other means. The core group is small, its members easily identified. Third, each *khana* ordinarily will have more than one subgroup. Plans for seizing power in an unstable political period often cause different revolutionary groups to join together into a unitary *khana*, but each group can be expected to retain a certain autonomy after the merger. Fourth, a strategic division of labor is effected in the actual execution of a coup, with a number of leaders forming the strategic center (*seenaathikaan*) and assuming posts as chiefs of the functional divisions. Fifth, each *khana* member is assigned a specific rank in his organization. Lists of names made public after the seizure of power are sacrutinized carefully by observers to see which of the principal leaders sign edicts, and in what order. It is not out of mere curiosity that the press describes a certain person as the *n*th-ranking member of a revolutionary group (*nak pathiwat maai leek-n*).

Let us now examine each of the ruling circles mentioned earlier within the framework of this general definition of a *khana*.

The People's party (*khana raatsadoon*)

The People's party is a secret association organized at the end of 1931 by a small number of people intent on toppling the existing monarchy.[8] On June 24, 1932 it succeeded in seizing power, thereby becoming the ruling circle. Its long history is so welldocumented that its organizational structure has become common knowledge among interested observers.

It consists of approximately seventy members belonging to four subgroups:[9] the veteran army officers (*naai thahaan bok chan phuuyaai*), the young army officers (*naai thahaan bok chan phuunooi*), the navy officers (*naai thahaan rŭa*), and the civilians (*phonlalŭan*). The actual organization and control of the party was initially effected by fewer than twenty men, the remainder being recruited immediately before the revolution from among the ranks of those who worked for or studied under those leaders.

The first subgroup, or the army veterans, is sometimes called the German group since its members all studied in Germany; their main goal in supporting the revolution was the modernization of the armed forces. The young army officers and the civilians on the other hand have been called the French group, their members having spent the early 1920s in Paris. Members of these two groups have tended to be motivated by ideals. The People's party actually was formed when these German and French groups merged, around December 1931. The last faction, the navy officers, was invited later for technical reasons, and not having a basic plan of its own, took its lead from the French group.[10]

The People's party successfully seized power on June 24, 1932. Its initial motivation was simply the narrow aim of bringing down the monarchy. Once this had been achieved, the unifying factor disappeared and tensions developed. The party was never able to become a stable ruling circle, nevertheless it remained crucial in Thai politics as the source of later political elites. As many as six premiers have come from this party (Phrayaa Phahon, Luang Phibuun, Luang Koowit, Thawii Bunyakeet, Luang Pradit, and Luang Thamrong). Its reign lasted from 1932 to about 1947, and two later *khanas*, the Free Thai and the Coup d'État group, were both offspring of the party. One may even claim that the reign of the People's party thus lasted until 1957 when the rule of Phibuun and his Coup d'État group was terminated.[11]

8. Study of how the People's party was founded is essential for understanding its characteristics, see Thai Nooi [pseud.], *Phrayaa Phahon* [Prayaa Phahon] (Bangkok: Phrae Phitthayaa, 1954), pp. 12–31.

9. Thai Nooi, *Phrayaa Phahon*, pp. 10–11.

10. On the establishment of the People's party, see Priidii Phanomyong, "Baang rŭang kiao kap kaan-koo tang khanaraasadoon lae raboop prachaathipatai," ["Background to the formation of the People's party and democracy"], *Rathasaat* no.14 (Bangkok: Thammasaat University, 1971).

11. Khathaa Dam regards the 1957 coup as signifying the political death of the politicians of the 1932 group. See his *Khaa bukkhon samkhan* [Assassination of important persons] (Bangkok: private publication, 1962), pp. 571–572.

The Free Thai (*khana seerii thai*)

This circle was conceived by the Priidii Phanomyong faction immediately following the outbreak of the Pacific War, and was carried on through the war years, both at home and abroad, as a large-scale secret society involved in underground resistance. It maintained military mobility and operated even in Great Britain and the United States.[12] When Phibuun resigned from the premiership in August 1944, it became the ruling circle and remained an important power group until November 1947, when Phibuun made a comeback through his coup d'état. The Free Thai continued effective resistance even after the coup, harassing and threatening the Phibuun administration for some time.

It is most difficult to obtain a clear grasp of the real nature of the Free Thai for various reasons, among them its complex and often covert history as an underground organization, its maintenance of both domestic and foreign organizations, secret cooperation with secret agents, and its hazy connections with numerous other organizations of a similar nature which sprang up toward the end of the war. According to the writer Naai Chanthanaa (pseud.), the Free Thai was also known as the X-O Group.[13] It was organized in the United States in 1941 by the Thai envoy to Washington, Seenii Pramoot, and in Great Britain by an army lieutenant colonel, Suphasawat Sawadiwat.[14]

The Free Thai started as essentially a military organization. During the period from 1942 to mid-1945, continuous efforts were made at military reorganization and further armament. As of July 1945 it had the support not only of its own voluntary corps but also of part of the national forces. Fairly well organized military corps were created throughout the country, including the metropolitan areas of Phranakhoon and Thonburii; and arms were flown in by the Allies to perhaps ten secret airfields throughout the country. More than twenty thousand Thais were involved in these Free Thai military organizations.[15]

---

12.   The most detailed account of the formation of the Free Thai is Naai Chanthanaa's [pseud.], *X-0 Group—ruang phaainai khabuan seerii thai* [X-0 group—inside story of the Free Thai] (Bangkok: Thaipaanit, 1946), which was written immediately after the end of World War II. Thai Nooi's *Prasopkaan 34 pii haeng raboop prachaathipatai* [Experience of democracy for 34 years] (Bangkok: Phrae Phitthayaa, 1966), takes up the Free Thai from a similar point of view and confirms the importance of Naai Chanthanaa's account.

13.   Naai Chanthanaa, *X-0 group*, pp. 357–358.

14.   For a description of the Free Thai in the U.S., see Chaiyanaam Direek, *Thai kap songkhraam look khrang thii 2* [Thailand and World War II], 2 vols. (Bangkok: Phrae Phitthayaa, 1966) pp. 472–474; for the Free Thai in Great Britain, see pp. 387–389.

15.   Naai Chanthanaa describes the military power immediately before the end of the war in his *X-0 Group*, pp. 400–418.

As a political organization, however, the Free Thai was restricted to a group of several dozen persons who seized leadership in postwar Thailand and remained at the center of political power through the autumn of 1947. It remains impossible, nevertheless, to clearly outline the nature of its organization or to stipulate its precise size since the Free Thai always maintained links with the large-scale military organization created during the war years.

The following three criteria are usually applied in identifying Free Thai members: (1) active involvement during 1941–1945 in the secret anti-Japanese organization formed by Priidii; (2) appointment to a ministerial post in one of the cabinets formed between the first Khuang administration (August 1944) and the second Thamrong government (May 1947), or selection to an important post, such as the national parliament, during the same period; and (3) involvement in resistance, in planning a coup, or flight to a foreign country during Phibuun's reign after November 1947. Many members received unduly harsh treatment from police superintendent Phao Siiyaanon.

The following two cautions also seem worthy of note. First, the Free Thai, during its underground military days, maintained a complex organization involved in nationwide propaganda as well as in military affairs; and as a result many observers have seen only a part of the entire organization, yet have mistakenly assumed that part to be the whole. Neet Kheemayoothin's description of the Free Thai is a good example of this tendency.[16] Second, the Free Thai as a political organization is sometimes called the Priidii-Khuang-Thamrong group,[17] as if it were composed of three factions whose bosses joined ranks without really forming a coherent organization. Such impressions are, however, misleading. Splits occurred only toward the end of the Free Thai's period of power, factional feuds were nonexistent during its initial period. And the eventual split resulted from personal antagonism between Priidii and Khuang,[18] leading to the creation of just two groups, with Thamrong belonging to the Priidii faction.

---

16. Besides *X-0 Group*, the following are standard works on the Free Thai: Kheema-yoothin Neet, *Ngaan tai din khoong phan-eek yoothii* [The underground work of Colonel Yoothii] (Bangkok: Phadungsŭksaa, 1957); idem, *Chiiwit naai phon* [Life of a general] (Bangkok: Phadungsŭksaa, 1956); Seenii, Praamoot, Moom-raatchawong, *Paathokthaa phiseet—khwaamsamphan rawaang thai-ameerikaa nai rawaang mahaasongkhraam look khrang thii laeo* [Special lecture—Thai-American relations during World War II] (Bangkok: Ruamsaan, 1966); N. Smith and C. Blake, *Into Siam— the Underground Kingdom* (New York: Bobbs-Merrill, 1946); John Coast, *Some Aspects of Siamese Politics* (New York: Institute of Pacific Relations, 1953).

17. Fred W. Riggs, *Thailand: The Modernization of a Bureaucratic Polity* (Honolulu, Hawaii; East-West Center Press, 1966), p. 233.

18. Kiat [pseud.], *Phongsaawadaan kaanmŭang* pp. 1–45.

The Coup d'État group (*khana ratthaprahaan*)

The Coup d'État group was a secret society of about forty members, most of them military personnel, founded under the leadership of Phin Chunhawan between the end of 1946 and November 1947 for the purpose of seizing power from the Free Thai.[19] Its successful 1947 coup made it the ruling circle, a position it maintained for a decade.

The basic unifying factor of the Coup d'État group was total loyalty to Phibuun Songkhraam. Indeed, the blind allegiance of so many of his political followers safeguarded this particular *khana* from the internal splits and factional feuds that had characterized other groups. Only with a new generation, less familiar with Phibuun, did criticism begin the decline, and eventual demise, of the Coup d'État group.

In contrast to the People's party or the Free Thai, the roots of this group lay not in idealism but in the severe hardships caused by postwar inflation, an experience rendered even more bitter because many military personnel had been stripped of power by the Free Thai clique after 1944.[20] A few made fortunes, for example, through real-estate dealings, but most military veterans found it difficult even to secure a livelihood. And when Rama VIII died an unnatural death in June 1946, the Free Thai's prestige fell sufficiently to offer the military an opportunity to attempt a comeback. With Phibuun hiding behind the stage, Phin Chunhawan planned the coup, and by early November the Coup d'État group was in power.[21] When several of Phibuun's powerful acquaintances, such as Yutthasaatkooson and Fǔǔn Ronnaphaakaat, subsequently joined the new government, it was able to establish a stable regime.

The Military group (*khana thahaan*)

This group was a semi-overt resistance organization against Phibuun and Phao Siiyaanon, formed by fewer than one hundred military supporters of Sarit Thanarat, when the feud between Sarit and Phao Siiyaanon grew fierce following the February 1957 general election.[22] In September of that year it successfully toppled the govern-

19.   For the most detailed account of the 1947 coup, see, Wichai Prasangsit, *Pathiwat-ratthaprahaan le kabot-calaacon* [Revolution, coup d'état, and rebellion] (Bangkok: private publication, n. d.), pp. 138–248.

20.   It seems that this point has been completely neglected to date. Confer, Singthoong Siiphanom, *12 coomphon thai*, pp. 123, 187.

21.   Wichai Prasangsit, *Pathiwat-ratthaprahaan le kabot-calaacon*, p. 141; idem, *Bǔanglang kaan-sawannakhot roo. 8* [Behind the death of King Rama VIII] (Bangkok: Thammaseewii, 1955), pp. 279–302.

22.   Udom Pramuanwit, *Naayokratthamontrii Coomphon Sarit* [General Sarit] (Bangkok: Kaseemsamphan, 1962), pp. 192–202.

ment and became the ruling circle, a position it maintained, in a sense, until the October Revolution in 1973.

The members of the Military group can be identified fairly easily from the lists of those who signed the several demands Sarit presented to Phibuun during the summer of 1957; for these lists included all of those who participated directly in the coup. If the group is defined in broader terms, however, one also might include those who assisted in the attack on Phibuun by other methods, such as anti-Phibuun parliamentary speeches. These included about ninety parliamentary members who submitted their resignations on September 12, 1957.[23]

The Military group differed from the others in maintaining a quasi-overt existence, a characteristic made possible by two factors. First, the group's strength was comparable to that of the Phibuun-Phao group. Second, its attack on Phibuun largely took the form of parliamentary debates. Phibuun had heard of the coup plan at an early stage but had been unable to take effective countermeasures due to the high level of Sarit's strength. And since Sarit fought publicly, the entire struggle was openly and keenly watched, both at home and abroad, with public opinion generally coming down in favor of Sarit and his followers.

The main leaders of the Military group were Sarit Thanarat, Thanoom Kittikhacoon, Phraphaat Caarusathian and, Chaloemkiat Watthanaangkuun, with Sarit in the dominant role.[24] This group maintained the most stable of Thailand's recent ruling circles for the following reasons. First, personal relations among core leadership figures were stable. Second, it was made up only of military personnel. Third, an effective division of labor was put into practice once it became the ruling circle. Fourth, by focusing on national issues in their policy formulation, its members raised the need for a flexible political system that would help them maintain a "fresh" political image.

SIXTEEN ELITE POLITICIANS

In the final analysis, any efforts to identify the genuine political elite among Thailand's pre-1973 ruling stratum must take into account both the individual's rank in the bureaucratic order and his role in a particular *khana* and in that *khana*'s power struggle. In concrete terms this means that a member of the Thai political elite should be expected to meet the following two essential criteria: (1) As an official, he must have been a

23. Witheetsakaranii [pseud.), *Coomphon Poo. liiphai* [General Phibuun's escape] (Bangkok: private publication, 1963), pp. 527–532.

24. Confer, Thai Nooi [pseud.] and na Nakhoon Rungroot [pseud.], *Naayokrat-thamontrii khon thii 11 kap 3 phuunam pathiwat* [The eleventh prime minister and three revolutionary leaders], 2d ed. (Bangkok: Phrae Phitthayaa, 1964).

TABLE 1
POLITICAL ELITE IN THAILAND

Name	Prime Minister	General	Phibuun Clique	Sarit Clique
1 Prayaa Phahon	×			
2 Phibuun Songkhraam	×	×	×	
3 Khuang Aphaiwong	×			
4 Thawii Bunyakeet	×			
5 Seenii Praamoot	×			
6 Priidii Phanomyong	×			
7 Thamrong Naawaasawat	×			
8 Pot Saarasin	×			
9 Thanoom Kittikhacoon	×	×		×
10 Sarit Thanarat	×	×		×
11 Phin Chunhawan		×	×	
12 Yutthasaatkooson		×	×	
13 Fǔǔn Ronnaphaakaat		×	×	
14 Chaloemkiat Watthanaangkuun		×		×
15 Phao Siiyaanoon			×	
16 Phraphaat Caarusathian				×

Note: × indicates that the person in question has served in the position indicated by the column heading.

general, a prime minister, or the occupant of a post equivalent to supreme commander of the army, navy, or air force; (2) and as a *khana* member, he must have helped lead a major incident in a power transfer, such as those which occurred in 1932, 1947, and 1957. The following generalizations also seem applicable to Thailand's supreme political elite groups of the past four decades: (1) membership of the People's party at the time of the 1932 Revolution seems not to have been a criterion; (2) with a few exceptions, prime ministers have been included in this supreme political elite group; (3) generals and admirals in the army, navy, and air force, including those granted the rank posthumously, have been considered among the top elite; (4) those who played important roles in the Phibuun circle from 1947 to 1957 have usually qualified; (5) most key members of the Sarit circle since 1957 also are numbered among the top elite.

Regarding the People's party. it should be noted that even though its members reigned over the Thai political world for some time following the 1932 Revolution, the party itself remained too weak to automatically propel its past members into the circle of the top elite. Moreover, frequent political feuds rising from the realities of power involved party statesmen in intense competition; and, as a result, membership of the party became a less important factor in achieving elite status than actual political accomplishment.

By applying the five criteria listed earlier, a group of sixteen persons becomes clearly identifiable as members of the elite. Their names are found (though not in order of importance) in Table 1. It should be noted that Chaloemkiat is an exception in that he was made general following his accidental death.[25] And among the former prime ministers Seenii Praamoot, Phot Saarasin, and Thawii Bunyakeet assumed the premiership under peculiar circumstances, and must be regarded in a somewhat different light from the others. The fact, however, that they were prime ministers demands that they be given due consideration.

TRENDS IN THE ELITE CYCLE

On examining these men in terms of social mobility (as seen in data of birth, hometown, and family occupation), they fall clearly into the older, intermediate, and younger generations.

Typical of the *old* pre-1932 generation was Phrayaa Manoopakhoon, the first prime minister following the revolution and a leader not included in the foregoing considerations.[26] Born in July 1884, the son of a commoner, he studied in a private village school, then attended the most modern and aristocratic schools of his time, Roongrian Suwankulaap and Roogrian Atsamchan.[27] He later entered the Law School of the Ministry of Justice, intending to go into government service, and graduated with honors. Following his studies in Great Britain, also under the sponsorship of the Ministry of Justice, he served as a judge and law school instructor; and on the merit of his work in those posts was selected to the House of Councilors by Rama VII. Thus can be seen from his career, his generation followed a pattern characteristic of absolute monarchies. Leaders went through a competitive process and served the monarchy's bureaucratic court, but they also remained loyal *khunnaang* officials of the king. They were allowed only to follow predetermined routes in ascending the bureaucratic ladder.

25. Singthoong Siiphanom, *12 coomphon thai*, pp. 354–355.
26. For a brief personal history of Phrayaa Manoophakoo, among others see Thai Nooi, *10 naayok ratthamontrii* and Preemcit Siri, *Prawatsaat thai nai raboop prachaathipatai 30 pii* [Thirty-year history of Thai democracy] (Bangkok: Kaseemban, 1962).
27. Detailed historical descriptions of the Thai school system can be found in Luang Kawiicanyaawiroot, et al., *Prawat kaan-sŭksaa kap prawat latthi kaan-sŭksaa le kaansuksaa haeng pratheet thai* [History of education, history of principles of education, and the Thai educational system], 3rd printing (Bangkok: Thai-watthanaaphanit, 1951), pp. 317–335; and Ankhong Sa-nguan, *Sing raek nai mŭang thai* [Advent of a new civilization Thailand] (Bangkok: Phrae Phitthayaa, 1959), *kaansuksaa* and *roongrian*. These works also comment on the modern aristocratic schools.

The 1932 Revolution brought about a fundamental change in this elite cycle by removing the inherent superiority of the royal family and opening the way for people of all social ranks to enter the elite by means of their own political abilities. Those who promoted the 1932 Revolution and tried to maintain exclusive political power thereafter thus represented a new generation of elite. They did away with the ascriptive principle of status and introduced new principles. The new patterns however, did not, become firmly established until well after 1932. Young new members of the People's party began at once to confront the older ascriptive patterns, but the social strata from which they came were conspicuously heterogenous. And as a result their generation constituted an intermediate stage, which fell short of qualifying as a genuinely new generation.

The mixed nature of this intermediate generation is seen in the three different social backgrounds from which came Khuang Aphaiwong, Thawii Bunyakeet, and Phibuun Songkraam.

Khuang, born in Battambang, was the son of a local governor-general,[28] and of royal blood. When the family moved to Phraachiinburii upon the annexation of his birthplace by the French, his father was allegedly accompanied by thirty wives. Khuang's primary education was in a school built by his father solely for the sake of children of his clan. He was sent to Bangkok at the age of five, studied at the aristocratic schools of Roongrian Theepsirin and Roongrian Atsamchan, then at the age of seventeen went to France as a private student with three of his brothers. In Paris he chanced to meet several members of the People's party, but they tended to remain aloof since he was from the privileged class.

Thawii Bunyakeet was the son of a *khunnaang* bureaucrat of *phrayaa* status,[29] and like other children of bureaucrats was sent to Roongrian Raatchawithayaalai. Success in his studies earned him a government scholarship abroad, so he went to France as the first government-sponsored student of agriculture. On returning to Thailand, he served in the Ministry of Agriculture, following a course typical of a capable commoner. Had it not been for the 1932 Revolution, he would have spent his life as a capable *khunnaang* officer.

Phibuun Songkhraam symbolized the emergence of a new category of elite. His father was an industrious, honest peasant, barely able to

28. A modest, detailed personal history of Khuang is found in Bunchauai Siisawat, *Phantrii Khuang Aphaiwong—adiit naayokratthamontrii 4 samai.*

29. A handy reference on Thawii's personal history is found in Kao Nŭng Saam [pseud.] *11 khon samkhan khoong thai* [Eleven important persons in Thailand] (Bangkok: Oodian Satoo, 1965), pp. 315–356.

maintain a solvent existence. After study at a private school in Nonthaburii, Phibuun entered a military academy of which he had learned
accidentally through the Governor of Nonthaburii.[30] Upon graduation
from the academy, he won a scholarship to the army artillery school and
subsequently to the army staff school, from which he was graduated at
the head of his class. Next he went to France on a scholarship from the
Ministry of Armed Forces in order to study modern artillery and other
military techniques. With his peasant background, Phibuun probably
would have joined the ranks of the middle-level military personnel
under an absolute monarchy; he might have become "a colonel with
the phrayaa's honor."[31] Following the revolution and the emergence of
military power, however, his became the course followed by most of the
political elite. He symbolized, in this sense, the rise of a new political
generation in the 1930s.

The mixed nature of this intermediate generation is seen in the fact
that three men of such varied social backgrounds could belong to the
same party. It is also manifest in each man's personal limitations and
ties to tradition. Most were given a name by the king, for example, and
went through the ceremony of pledging to him their allegiance. The
nature of the *new* generation on the other hand differed markedly.
Sarit, Thanoom, Praphaat, Chaloemkiat, and others of this generation
were born in the twentieth century and graduated from military
academies. Because their graduation coincided with the political and
economic unrest preceding and following the 1932 Revolution, few of
them had a chance to study abroad (Thanoom, for instance, was chosen
to go abroad but was prevented from doing so by the depression).[32]
Their education was solely military in nature and took place in Thailand.
Their origins also differed in that they were of peasant stock, their rise to
power being made possible by the military academy system. In the days
of Sarit and Thanoom, male children seven or eight years of age were
allowed to enter army academies and went through four years of preliminary education, six years of primary, and two years of secondary
school (twelve years altogether). They lived together in dormitories and
had all expenses paid by the government (except for their own clothing
and miscellaneous belongings).[33] Although sons of military personnel

---

30. Thai Nooi, *10 naayok ratthamontrii*, pp. 194–195.
31. Naai Honhuai [pseud.], *Caofaa Prachaathipok* [Prince Prachaathipok] (Bangkok:
    private publication, 1946), p. 217.
32. Kao Nŭng Saam [pseud.], *Coomphon Thanoom—naayok khon sŭŭ* [General Thanoom
    —honest prime minister] (Bangkok: Oodian Satoo, 1964), pp. 11–12.
33. For a brief account of the military academy system, see Udom Pramuanwit,
    Naayokratthamontrii Coomphom Sarit, pp. 30–33.

were granted the advantage of being allowed to attend without taking an entrance examination, anybody else was eligible if he passed the exams. Upon graduation they would become second lieutenants. Those who emerged from this open atmosphere to become members of the political elite shared social traits characteristic of the new political generation.

Phrayaa Phahon and the other nine former prime-ministers all have one thing in common: each occupied this top position during his early forties—a fact that bears evidence of the rapid pace of political ascendancy due to the existence of bona fide competition in modern Thai politics, competition which arose directly from the 1932 Revolution. Membership in the elite became extremely competitive and open, while the principle of status by ascription declined rapidly. That this revolution focused on a challenge to royal privilege is clear from the postrevolutionary attempt at a once-and-for-all eradication of all practices inherent in the status society. One also notes that the People's party, which monopolized the revolution, never won for itself a privileged existence of the kind the royal family had known. This was not, of course, due to intentional benevolence on the part of the party but because waning leadership and factional strife prevented a return of ascriptive principles. Competition among party members served as the means whereby men entered the elite after the revolution, though mere membership in the party was of no value in itself in the competitive process.

The first point to note in studying the elite cycles of the pre-1973 years is the *initial equality* of members contending for power. Along with a basic similarity in origins, nearly all contenders left their respective military academies as second lieutenants. Whether military or civilian personnel, they all started from low, *nonpolitical* ranks. Let us look, for example, at the careers of fourteen classmates of Thanoom Kittik-hacoon.[34] Thanoom, a 1929 graduate of the army military academy, had forty classmates, all of whom were appointed second lieutenants on April 10, 1930. Nearly all were then dispatched to various posts throughout the country, while a few went overseas to study. Despite these similarities, a few of these soldiers were to lead truly vicissitudinous lives. They may all have been merely loyal soldiers, but the twists of history brought them greatly varied careers. Three of the forty-one participated in the 1932 Revolution as members of the People's party. At the time of the rebellion by the Loyalist party in October 1933, twelve found themselves on the side of the rebelling party simply because of the posts

---

34.   Kao Nŭng Samm, *Coomphon Thanoom*, pp. 1–22.

TABLE 2
HIGHEST RANKS ACHIEVED BY THE CLASS OF 1929, ARMY MILITARY ACADEMY

General	1	Major	6
Major general	1	Captain	2
Brigadier general	3	First lieutenant	4
Colonel	3	Second lieutenant	13
Lieutenant colonel	4	Others/unknown	4

in which they were serving. As a result, they were later disgraced and labelled as rebels. Some lost their lives in this incident. Thanoom himself was fortunate in serving in the map section of the Ministry of Armed Forces in Bangkok at this time, thus avoiding disgrace. Others actually left the military and went into business. The pace of their promotions after 1933 thus shows marked differences. (See Table 2 for the highest ranks each had achieved by 1962.)[35] The fact that a large number only became second lieutenants reflects numerous early deaths or resignations. Posts above the rank of major general were won only by those who entered politics Thanoom, general and Lamaai, major general; none in purely military service had risen above brigadier general by 1962.

A second point regarding the elite cycle is that regular promotions based on official achievement gave way at times to political promotions— an eventuality that constituted a basic condition for entering the political elite. Personal histories of military-officers-turned-statesmen, men like Phibuun and Sarit, clearly indicate this point (see tables 3 and 4).[36]

Phibuun Songkhraam followed the ordinary course until he became a major, but all of his promotions from the rank of lieutenant colonel onward suggested political reward. What was more, Phibuun promoted himself after becoming major general. Thanoom Kittikhacoon belongs to a different political generation from that of Phibuun, but the same political factors influenced his promotions from the time he became a lieutenant colonel. His early political promotions were given by Phibuun, his later ones by Sarit. One should also note that Sarit Thanarat was promoted from colonel to major general following the 1947 coup, after which all his promotions were political in nature.

The reason these regular career promotions were eclipsed by political advancements lay in *politicization* of the person himself, and such promotions usually came from one of the following three develop-

---

35. Kao Nŭng Samm, *Coomphon Thanoom*, pp. 284–317.
36. For a personal history of Phibuun, see the material quoted in 5.

TABLE 3
PROMOTIONS OF THANOOM KITTIKHACOON

Rank	Year	Explanation for Promotion
Second lieutenant	1930	Graduation from the army military academy
First lieutenant	1935	No particular circumstance
Captain	1938	No particular circumstance
Major	1943	Activity at Lampaang Front
Lieutenant colonel	1944	Meritorious service at Phetchabuun
Colonel	1948	Meritorious service in organizing the Coup d'Etat group
Major general	1951	Commander of 1st Division
Lieutenant general	1955	Commander of 2nd Legion
General	1958	Meritorious service in coup by Military group
Five-star general	1964	Prime minister

TABLE 4
RECORD OF PROMOTIONS FOR PHIBUUN SONGKHRAAM

Rank	Year	Explanation for Promotion
Second lieutenant	1915	Graduation from the army military academy
First lieutenant	1922	Graduation as the top student from the army staff school
Captain	1927	Return from France
Major	1928	King bestows *luang* status and gives a name
Lieutenant colonel	1933	(June) Meritorious service in 2d coup of the People's party
Colonel	1933	(October) Meritorious service in suppressing rebellion of the Loyalist party
Major general	1939	Prime ministership assumed
Lieutenant general	—	(a jump of three ranks)
General	—	
Five-star general	1941	Meritorious service in annexation of French Indo-china

ments. First was the formation of an acquaintance with an influential politician. Phibuun in the 1930s was surrounded by several such acquaintance seekers. When he was almost poisoned to death in December 1938, as is well known, several military men—Captain Phao Siiyaanon, Lieutenant Colonel Luang Yutthasaatkooson, and Air Force Major Khun Ronnanphaakaat—risked their lives sharing the same table. As long as Phibuun retained power, they also wielded power as his aides. But when he went into exile in 1957, they, too, en masse lost their political life.[37] The second possible development was participation in a coup. One did not have to plan a coup; simple membership in a successful *khana* operation was sufficient. With a few exceptions, all sixteen elite politicians belonged to a *khana* and participated in a coup. Third, political promotion sometimes came when one suppressed counterrevolutionary activities and helped create political stability. The rebellion of the Loyalist party in October 1933, was a counterrevolutionary attempt against the People's party, and Phibuun Songkhaam's successful efforts to crush it made him the star of the armed forces almost overnight.[38] Sarit Thanarat and Phao Siiyaanon also achieved similar results by suppressing a series of counterrevolutionary and antigovernment attempts in the early 1950s. Both of them subsequently attained rapid political promotions through the favor of Phibuun.[39]

A third point with respect to the elite cycle is that the basis of power had shifted to the military. As long as power transfers were seen to depend on military intervention, the superiority of the military was almost inevitable. Consequently, at least three aspects of military rule in the pre-1973 Thailand need further examination: (1) the permanence of military rule; (2) the changes in the social character of the elite due to the military presence; and (3) the achievement of legitimacy for military rule.

Perpetuation of military rule seemed likely for the following reasons. First, the military rulers clung to power. They enjoyed their privileges and believed in their mission too much to be expected to forsake it.[40] Second, there seemed to be no growth of an alternative basis from which another political elite might seriously challenge the military. Khuang Aphaiwong and Seenii Praamoot, who once repre-

---

37. Their acquaintance with Phibuun was partly accidental, Phao while serving as a military officer attached to the minister of the army, and Yutthasaatkooson while serving with the secretariat of the same ministry. They subsequently rose to the rank of head of the police department and general, respectively (Fŭun also became a general).

38. Thai Nooi, *10 naayok ratthamontrii*, pp. 326, 329–341.

39. A clear account of Sarit's "achievements" and his political promotions is found in Singthoong Siiphanom, *12 coomphon thai*, pp. 206–212; and a detailed description is given in Phoothichaiyaa Raphin, *Coomphon Sarit Thanarat—naayokratthamontrii khon thii 11* [General Sarit Thanarat—the eleventh prime minister] (Bangkok: Kaseemsamphan, 1964), pp. 91–110. See Khathaa Dam, *Khaa bukkhon samkhan*, for a detailed account of Phao's case.

40. For an excellent comment on the Thai military, see David A. Wilson, "The Military in Thai Politics," in *The Role of the Military in Underdeveloped Countries*, ed. John. J. Johnson (Princeton, N. J.: Princeton University Press, 1962).

sented the nonmilitary elite, were regarded as "men of the past", both by the military itself and by the general public.[41] Neither had the generally recognized integrity or the respect to secure the full confidence of the public.[42] And with the fading of their prestige, the emergence of a capable civilian group seemed unlikely until the students revolted in 1973. For as these men grew older, no competent successors seemed to have arisen. Third, the military had often shown itself capable of skillful politics and adroit administration,[43] thus attaining a sense of social legitimacy. The military elite who succeeded Phibuun, men such as Sarit and Thanoom, had a supreme sense of confidence in their own abilities to maintain stable power relationships. At the same time they understood the pending issues quite clearly and were able to deal with them authoritatively, thus winning respect for running a responsible governing body.

The change in social characteristics of the political elite is an important concern in contemporary Thai politics. The large-scale change in the makeup of the political elite, which resulted from the coup of 1957, ultimately caused a significant shift in the social nature of the ruling circle. One historical significance of the 1957 coup was that it terminated the period of rule by former members of the People's party—a fact vividly symbolized by Phibuun's exile. Prior to 1957, central positions of power, whether civilian or military, were almost always occupied by past members of the People's party. And what determined the character of the rules was their social background. The period preceding 1957 may be justly called that of Phibuun's.[44] He first began to occupy an important place in the power structure at the age of thirty-five, assumed the premiership at age forty-one in 1938, and enjoyed a near-exclusive hold on power into the 1950s (except

41.   In January 1965, Kuang Aphaiwong spoke at Thammasaat University on the contemporary state of political affairs and criticized the form of government the military had adopted. His speech was followed by unhesitating criticism of Khuang by incumbent politicians, who labeled Kuang bluntly a "man of the past."

42.   Khuang's opportunistic behavior is broadly known. Immediately after the 1957 coup, when Phibuun exiled himself, Khuang started making numerous critical comments about Phibuun and even revealed past secrets. Khuang's personal integrity has been looked upon as rather doubtful ever since.

43.   For a positive evaluation of the Thai military, see, for instance, Amry Vandenbosch and Richard Butwell, *The Changing Face* (Lexington, Kentucky: University of Kentucky Press, 1966), pp. 310–311.

44.   One should never neglect the influence of Phibuun's personality on the development of modern Thailand. It is dangerous, for this reason, to deduce specifically Thai principles directly from events between the late 1930s and the 1950s. It is necessary to filter out that part which is directly due to the personality of Phibuun.

during temporary civilian control). He effected a kind of Phibuun autocracy until being forced into exile at the age of sixty. His reign was a long one, and the end of his political life signaled a chance for Thai politics to change qualitatively. Thus, it is not surprising that distinct social differences can be seen between the 1932 group of politicians and that of 1957.

The foremost feature of the 1932 group is that they grew up as so-called *nak-kaanmŭang* ("politicians") reared in a specifically Thai context. They had to equip themselves with an ability to struggle under fundamentally chaotic and fluid conditions in order to survive both politically and physically. As a result, they were flexible and highly opportunistic. Members of the 1957 group, on the other hand, were raised basically as soldiers (*thahaan*). Sarit, Thanoom, and Prapaat all awakened to political ambitions at a later age, remaining essentially nonpolitical and unselfish throughout their twenties and thirties. Consequently, they are not good at tactful political haggling; they prefer simple human talent or strategic guidance in achieving specified objectives. While former members of the People's party looked at political situations in the context of confrontation, the newer generation preferred to observe them in the context of harmony. One reason for the lack of divisive power struggles among leaders of the new generation is that a kind of harmony-orientation has become one of their norms. A second point of difference between the groups centers on the matter of self images—or self-confidence. The 1932 group was given to a kind of inferiority complex. While they challenged the absolute monarchy, they seemed to harbor hidden insecurities when they contrasted their new regime to its old stability and prestige. They also felt drawn toward—and inferior to—Western politics and culture, as a result of their studies in the West. In a way this complex was partly the natural destiny of the generation in which they lived. Through it, however, they came back again and again to the issue of political legitimacy, an issue that haunted them and increased their identity crisis. By contrast, the 1957 group was free of this complex—able to face its own past more coolly, to interact with foreign politics and cultures more rationally. Its members neither felt inferiority toward Western ideas nor paid lip-service to them. They sought justification in specifically Thai ideas and concepts. Moreover, they had a very clear understanding of what their strategic objectives should be, and how they might rationally be attained.

GENERAL REFERENCES

Thai Nooi (pseud.). *Bukkhon samkham thai* [Thailand's important persons] Bangkok: Khlangwitthayaa, 1962.

Yano Toru. *Tai-Biruma gendai seijishi kenkyu* [Studies in contemporary Thai and Burmese political history] Kyoto: Center for Southeast Asian Studies, Kyoto University, 1968.

12

The Dispute between Sukarno and Hatta in the early 1930s

KENJI TSUCHIYA

INTRODUCTION

For the Indonesian nationalist movement, the 1930s opened with the split of the Partai Nasional Indonesia (PNI) in 1931 and the continued dispute between the two factions, the Partai Indonesia (Partindo) and the Pendidikan Nasional Indonesia (PNI-Baru). This fission has been treated by J. S. Pluvier,[1] who has summarized the history of the 1930s nationalist movement, and by Bernhard Dahm,[2] who wrote Sukarno's political biography. Pringgodigdo of Indonesia and Masuda of Japan have also outlined the events of this period.[3] Here I would like to examine the dispute in more concrete terms, paying particular attention to Hatta's articles of this period, which neither Dahm nor Pluvier have dealt with. It is my intention to present the substance of the dispute as concretely as possible, since it is probably true that the confrontation between the Partindo of Sukarno and Sartono and the PNI-Baru of Hatta and Sjahrir, which is rooted in this period (1930–1934), constituted an important primary cause of antagonism on the Indonesian political scene from the time of independence to the present.

In the next section I shall summarize the situation of the Indonesian nationalist movement around 1930, against which background the

1. J. S. Pluvier *Overzicht van de Ontwikkeling der Nationalsitische Beweging in Indonesië in de jaren 1930 tot 1942* (The Hague, Van Hoeve, 1953), pp. 45–52.
2. Bernhard Dahm, *Sukarno and the Struggle for Indonesian Independence*, (Ithaca, N.Y.: Cornell University Press, 1969), pp. 127–173.
3. A. K. Pringgodigdo, *Sedjarah Pergerakan Rakjat Indonesia* (History of the Indonesian People's Movement) (Jakarta, 1950) (6th ed., 1967, pp. 105–110, 137–138); Atau Masuda. *Indonesia Gendaishi* [Modern history of Indonesia], (Chūō Kōronsha, 1971), pp. 85–88, 97.

dispute raged, in the third section I shall present the substance of the dispute, and in the final section I will attempt to establish what was the ultimate basis of the confrontation.

THE BACKGROUND OF THE DISPUTE

1. People's Associations

The reins of leadership of the nationalist movement, held in the second decade of this century by the Sarekat Islam (SI) or "Muslim Association," were taken over in the 1920s by the Indonesian Communist party (PKI). Under the great persecution which followed the uprisings of 1926 and 1927, however, the Communist party crumbled, leaving the crucial problem of who would succeed them. To take up the leadership of the nationalist movement meant, as Pringgodigdo has pointed out, reuniting the masses who had at one time joined the SI under the flag of Islam, and subsequently formed Sarekat Rakjat (People's Associations) under the guidance of the communists.

> The outlawing of Communist organisations by the government presented an opportunity to expand existing political structures or, better still, to establish a new organization. The opportunity arose not because the rank and file members of the People's Associations were true Communists who wanted to bring about fresh changes through underground Communist activity, but because they stood in need of a new guiding principle. They were a group composed of "petit-bourgeois," according to the Communist Party leaders, and some of the People's Association leaders were thought to be obstructing the Communist Party.[4]

Pringgodigdo went on to say that since the members of the People's Associations could essentially be called left-wing nationalists, the arrest of the Communist party leaders had deprived them of leadership; new leadership could not be expected from the existing nationalist organizations, since the Budi Utomo had not been with them from the outset while the SI had failed in its efforts to command them.[5]

2. Indonesian Students in Holland

In this situation, it was the so-called new elite of high school graduates, particularly those who had pursued their studies at universities in Holland, who emerged as new political leaders. In 1908, Indonesian students in Holland had formed an organization called Indische Vereeniging (Indies Association). In the 1920s, particularly after regrouping under the name of Indonesische Vereeniging (In-

4. Pringgodigdo, *Sedjarah*, pp. 55–56.
5. Pringgodigdo, *Sedjarah*, p. 56.

donesian Association) in 1922, they became increasingly aware of themselves as people of an Indonesian mother-land and embarked more and more on political activities. A few years later they changed the name of the organization from Indonesische Vereeniging to Perhimpunan Indonesia (PI), which was used officially thereafter. From around 1923, returning students set up propaganda organizations called study clubs and began to give instruction in European ideas and to agitate for national unity and liberation. In Holland, the influence to Tjipto Mangunkusumo and of Communist party leaders Tan Malaka and Semaun, and their location in the mainstream of international communism, drove the PI further to the left.

On December 5, 1926, the "Hatta-Semaun agreement" was concluded between these two as representatives of the PI and the Communist party. In this three-point agreement they declared that the Communist party would hand over leadership of the nationalist movement to the PI.[6] The PI's succession indicated not only that it was strongly influenced by communism at that time, but showed clearly where it would base its activities when it emerged as a political force in the "Indonesian motherland," namely, that it would direct its organizational efforts toward the People's Associations, the mass groups currently under the Communist party umbrella.

3. Formation of the Partai Nasional Indonesia

The Partai Nasional Indonesia (PNI) came into being on July 4, 1927, under the leadership of Sukarno. The party was not founded by Sukarno as an individual, but jointly by the PI and by Sukarno and fellow students of the Bandung Technical Institute. Earlier, in 1926, Sukarno had organized the Bandung study club (Algemeene Studieclub)

---

6. The substance of the agreement was as follows (Pringgodigdo, *Sedjarah*, pp. 50–51):

In view of the fact that a solid people's movement is necessary for the struggle towards Indonesian independence (and that it is necessary to build up the strength of the Indonesian nation), the following agreement was reached.
Item 1. The PI, which should emerge as the party of the people of the Indonesian nation, promises to act in political and social areas for the good of the Indonesian people. The PI will assume supreme authority over the entire Indonesian people's movement, and will bear full responsibility for that movement. The social area includes education of the people, national economy, health and welfare, and all other aspects beneficial to the raising of the national strength of the people.
Item 2. The Communist Party of Indonesia recognises the authority of the PI shown in Item 1, and must trust the PI completely. All organizations affiliated with the Communist Party of Indonesia must promise never to obstruct those nationalist movements lead by the PI, provided the PI carries out policies directed towards the achievement of Indonesian independence.
Item 3. All publications presently in the hands of the Communist Party of Indonesia must be transferred to the PI under terms to be decided later. The PI promises to publish a nationalist organ.

on the lines of the study clubs which were being set up all over Indonesia (Surabaya, Solo, Yogykarta, Bogor, Semarang, Jakarta) by students returning from Holland. At the Second National History Seminar of the Indonesian Republic held at Yogyakarta in August 1970, Sunario, a founder of the PNI, stated that the PNI did not arise from the developmental liquidation of the Bandung study club but was founded under the exclusive leadership of the PI, while the study club continued as a separate organization[7]. This is probably an accurate appraisal of the situation of the nationalist movement of the time, although the claim concerning the study club's independent survival needs futher investigation.

According to Sunario, there were nine founder members of the PNI: five were returned students from Holland and were originally members of the PI (Mr. Sartono, Mr. Iskaq Tjokrohadisurjo, Dr. Samsi Sastrowidagdo, Mr. Budiarto, and Mr. Sunario—Mr. being the title for holders of the Bachelor of Law degree), two were graduates of Bandung Technical Institute (Ir Sukarno and Ir Anwar) and the remaining two were Sudjadi, a former member of the finance department of the colonial government, and Tilar, a Jakarta bank official.[8] In addition, Tjipto Mangunkusumo attended the founding meeting, but refused to join, fearing that the colonial government would regard the new organization as a reformation of the Communist party.[9] Until Sukarno's emergence, Tjipto had been the most prominent leader of the nationalist left-wing and had enjoyed the confidence of the communists because of his good reputation. At the end of the year the government arrested him in connection with disturbances and exiled him to the island of Banda.

After its establishment the PNI stimulated national awareness by agitating for Indonesian independence through noncooperation and mass action. But leading the national unity and independence movements was, of course, Sukarno; and on December 17, 1927, he established a federation of seven political organizations (PNI, Budi Utomo, Sarekat Islam, Pasundan—the Sundanese Union, the Sumatran Union, the Batavian Union, and the Indonesian Study Club led by Dr. Sutomo) called the Permufakatan Perhimpunan-Perhimpunan Politik Kebangsaan Indonesia (PPPKI), "the Association of Political Organizations of the Indonesian People." With such slogans as "establish

---

7. Sunario. *"Perhimpunan Indonesia" dan Peranannja dalam Perdjuangan Kemerdekaan Kita* [The "Indonesian Association" and its role in our struggle for independence] (paper), Yogyakarta, 1970), pp. 49–51.

8. Sunario, *Perhimpunam*, p. 51.

9. Sunario, *Perhimpunam*, pp. 51–52.

the people's power," "state within a state," and "the brown front," he spread the feeling of national unity and aroused the people's fervor for independence. In an article published before the first PPPKI congress met, Sukarno announced that the meeting would be an extremely important national event that would mark a new era (*masa baru*) in the history of the nationalist movement.[10] Sukarno instilled into this new era the sense that the Sini party, those who would be reborn as "the Indonesian nation" from the "natives of the Dutch East Indies," had a mission to confront their opponents, the Sana party, and establish their own "power." This they would achieve on the common ground of a nationalism that embraced Islam (Sarekat Islam) and Marxism (the Communist party). Sukarno expressed his expectations of the PPPKI in these terms: "for us Indonesians, the struggle is a question of strength and of power."[11] "Because the PPPKI exists the split between the Sini and the Sana becomes clear and complete. With the existence of the PPPKI the strength of the organizations of the colored people is compounded and doubled. That is why the colored front will not merely carry the name of battle front, but will in essence be a front with strength and power."[12] This PPPKI was entirely of Sukarno's own conception. And even though the PNI was founded under the direction of the PI, as will be shown in the next section, Sukarno's future party activities were guided by what might be called his personal logic.

4. Sukarno's Arrest and the Dissolution of the PNI

Within three years of its founding the PNI had ceased its activities and within four it had been dissolved. On December 29, 1929, Sukarno was arrested with three other leaders of the PNI—Mankupradja, Maskun and Supriadinata. The reason given for the arrests was that the PNI intended to instigate a rebellion the following year and that Sukarno and his codefendants had plotted for that purpose.[13] However, this was merely a pretext to suppress the PNI, and with no concrete evidence against them the four were found guilty on charges of disturbing public peace and order in a trial which ran from August 18, 1930 to April 17, 1931. In court, Sukarno "faced the bench not as a defendant but, with the backing of four lawyers, Sartono, Sastromuljono, Sujudi,

---

10. Sukarno, *Dibawah Bendera Revolusi* [Under the banner of the revolution] vol. I, 4th ed. (Jakarta, 1959, p. 83).
11. Sukarno, *Dibawah*, p. 84.
12. Sukarno, *Dibawah*, p. 85.
13. In its decision, "the court manufactured an ingenious linkage of the PNI to the PKI and PI". (Dahm, *Sukarno and the Struggle*, p. 125).

and Idi Prawiradiputra, as the prosecutor of the charge against the Dutch for three centuries of colonial crimes. He became a legend in his time."[14] His address to the court was subsequently published as "Indonesia Accuses."

The party leaders who had escaped arrest held an emergency meeting under Sartono at which they ordered the suspension of party activities and discussed what further measures to take. Alamsjah, Sartono's biographer, had the following to say about the situation:

> ...at the emergency meeting, debate centered on whether the PNI should be continued or dissolved. Those present were divided into two groups. The first was opposed to the dissolution of the PNI; the other held the party's dissolution to be indispensable. According to the latter, the government's accusation amounted to the charge that the PNI was a reformation of the outlawed Communist party. The group centered on Sartono was of this opinion and attracted the most support. They believed that if the PNI continued, all leaders and members would be sent to Boven Digul (the penal settlement in West Irian where leaders of the Communist party and People's Associations had been exiled). Their opponents insisted that since the PNI had merely been accused and had not in fact been outlawed, it would be a mistake to dissolve the party. They must fight manfully, face the crisis bravely; no sacrifice could be meaningless. The debate continued during Sukarno's detention until finally the faction urging the continuance of the party was voted down. Simultaneously the decision was taken to establish a new party: the Partai Indonesia was born.[15]

When the government banned the PNI, about one week after its dissolution, the foundations of the split within the movement had already been laid. Groups opposed to the establishment of the new Partai Indonesia (Partindo, founded April 30, 1931) organized their own study clubs in each region centered on the Indonesian Study Club in Jakarta, and continued their activities under the name of Golongan Merdeka (Independent Groups—signifying their independence from Sartono).[16] These groups looked forward to Hatta's return from Holland. And on hearing of the dissolution of the PNI, in July 1931 Hatta dispatched a letter to various Indonesian newspapers criticizing the steps of Sartono and his associates.[17] He continued his criticism

14. Masuda, *Indonesia Gendaishi*, p. 85.
15. St. Rais Alamsjah, *10 Orang Indonesia Terbesar Sekarang* [The ten greatest Indonesians of today] (Jakarta, 1952), p. 158.
16. Pringgodigdo, *Sedjarah*, p. 105.
17. Dahm, *Sukarno and the Struggle*, p. 129.

of the Partindo in an article from Holland published in *Daulat Rakjat* (People's Sovereignty), the organ of the Independent Groups. In late December 1931, at a congress in Yogykarta the Independent Groups formed a new organization, the Pendidikan Nasional Indonesia, "Indonesian National Education." Its chairman was Sjahrir, who from 1929 until his return in the summer of 1931 was active in the PI in Holland and who became the leading disputant of the Independent Groups.[18] He is also said to have called for the establishment of the Pendidikan Nasional Indonesia,[19] abbreviated by its members to PNI-Baru, or "new" PNI.

Under the amnesty granted on the departure of the governor general de Graeff, Sukarno's sentence was reduced from four to two years, and on December 31, 1931, he left Sukamiskin Prison in Bandung.

5. The Split in the PNI and the Dispute between the Two Factions

The PNI, which had been the mainstream of the nationalist movement, split into two factions, the Partindo and the PNI-Baru. Both parties took up the manifesto of the PNI, calling for the achievement of Indonesian independence and noncooperation with the government. To this end the PNI-Baru stressed the need for education and training of cadres. The split marked a gloomy opening to the 1930s for the nationalist movement: the PNI, since its birth in 1927, had attempted to take over the powerful antigovernment movement formerly led by the SI and the PKI.

On his release from prison, Sukarno enjoyed the enthusiastic acclaim of the masses but was also greeted by the schism in the PNI. He immediately set about restoring unity. According to Dahm, Sukarno received an enthusiastic welcome from a crowd of six thousand in Surabaya on the eve of the Indonesia Raja (Greater Indonesia) Congress sponsored by the PPPKI early in 1932. At the congress he expressed his joy in the upsurge of the nationalist movement despite his arrest and imprisonment, and on the split in the PNI he likened himself to Kokrosono of the *wajang*, the rightful heir to the kingdom of Mandura, whose throne had been usurped, but who had retrieved his kingdom using the weapon Nanggala granted him by a god. At the same time Kokrosono was deeply distressed to see two of his children

18. Sjahrir's return has been cited as spring 1931 (H. Feith), summer 1931 (Dahm), and 1932 (Alamsjah). I follow Dahm here (Dahm, *Sukarno and the Struggle*, p. 135).

19. *Ensiklopedia Indonesia*, p. 1072.

in great danger. Sukarno wished to take up Nanggala again to save his children, to dissolve the misunderstanding between them and reunite the two factions.[20]

However, the criticism of the PNI-Baru shifted gradually from Sartono's dissolution of the PNI to bear directly on Sukarno's theories of unity and organization. As will be seen in the next section, these criticisms highlighted the fundamental differences between Sukarno and the Sjahrir group. Sukarno eventually realized that what he faced after his release from prison was not a "quarrel between brothers" but a dispute between himself and forces opposing him and on August 1, 1932, he joined the Partindo.

And in Holland, Hatta was announcing that he could not act politically within the Partindo after his return to Indonesia. Indeed, immediately after his return on August 23, 1932,[21] he joined the PNI-Baru, replacing Sjahrir as its chairman. The dispute then developed between Sukarno and the Partindo and Hatta and the PNI-Baru, and ranged over the problems of party organization, unity and the PPPKI, and the noncooperation policy.

By the 1930s, the Dutch had abandoned the "ethical" policy of the early years of the century and took exclusively coercive measures in the colony in dealing with the nationalist movement. This tendency became more marked with the advent of the new governor general, de Jonge, on September 12, 1932, and those groups which confronted the government openly with noncooperation (Partindo, PNI-Baru, Partai Sarekat Islam Indonesia-PSII or the reorganized Sarekat Islam, and the West Sumatran Permi[22] were countered with restrictions on assembly, raids, and the arrest and imprisonment of leaders. On August 1, 1933, the Partindo was forbidden to assemble, and Sukarno, Hamid Lubis, and Bujung Siregar were arrested. Sukarno was exiled to Endeh on the island of Flores from 1934 to 1938 and to Bengkulu in Sumatra from 1938 to 1942. Of the PNI-Baru, Hatta, Sjahrir,

20.   Dahm, *Sukarno and the Struggle*, pp. 133–135.
21.   J. S. Pluvier, *Overzicht*, p. 51.
22.   Permi (Persatuan Muslimin Indonesia, "Indonesian Moslem Unity") was established in 1930 as the branch of the PSII in Minangkabau, West Sumatra. From 1932 it advocated noncooperation and conducted the most radical campaign of resistance to the government in the Islamic movement of the 1930s. In 1934, Muchtar Luthfie, Iljas Jacub, and other leaders were exiled to West Irian and released in 1937. (J. S. Pluvier, *Overzicht*, pp. 76–77). In the early 1930s, Permi was strongly influenced by the Partindo, and in 1932, M. Yamin, a leader of the Partindo and native of West Sumatra, visited West Sumatra with Gotot Mangku-pradja and concluded an alliance with Permi. (Alamsjah, *10 Orang*, pp. 159–160).

Bondan, Burhanuddin, and others were arrested on February 26, 1934, and exiled first to Tanah Merah in West Irian, and from 1936 to the island of Banda (Bandanaira).

Following Sukarno's second arrest, the Partindo announced the abandonment of its noncooperation policy on December 1, 1934, withdrew from the PPPKI on February 9, 1935, and dissolved the party organization on November 18, 1936. The Partindo was succeeded by the Gerakan Rakjat Indonesia (Gerindo), the "Indonesian People's Movement," formed on July 24, 1937. The PNI-Baru also strove to rebuild after the arrests, but in 1936 the new leaders were also arrested and although for a time it maintained a slender existence through the activities of a few regional branches, in practice the organization remained in name only and died a natural death. In terms of party strength, the Partindo, in its heyday, had seventy-one branches (including twenty-four proposed branches) and embraced a membership of about twenty thousand; the PNI-Baru in 1932 had only about two thousand members.[23]

THE SUBSTANCE OF THE DISPUTE

The dispute between the two left-wing nationalist factions unfolded during the period 1931 to 1934 and centered on four main points: the dissolution of the PNI, the question of unity, party organization, and the policy of noncooperation. Some clue to these problems can be gained from examination of the writings of Sukarno, Hatta, and Sjahrir, which appeared in the respective party organs of the time and have subsequently been published in collected form.

1. Dissolution of the PNI

As described in the previous section, under the leadership of Sartono, the PNI was dissolved and a new party, the Partindo, was formed. But one faction of the old PNI was reluctant to follow the line of the new party, and set up Independent Groups. Giving sympathy and positive support to the groups was Hatta, who had been in Holland since 1922 and chairman of the PI since 1926. The PNI organ, *Persatuan Indonesia*, "Indonesian Unity," of April 10, 1930, carried Hatta's article "The PNI on Trial," in which he exhorted his readers not to be daunted by the fact that Sukarno and other leaders had been imprisoned by the government but to endure the ordeal bravely and continue the fight. He appealed to the party leaders who had escaped

---

23. Pringgodigdo, *Sedjarah*, pp. 105–110; Alamsjah, *10 Orang*, p. 20, 39.

imprisonment to intensify their activities and Press forward without despair or fear, emphasizing that the party (PNI) itself was the spirit of nationalism.[24]

Approximately one year later the news of the dissolution of the PNI prompted the critical letter from Hatta of July 1931. The rebuttal addressed to Hatta in far away Holland claimed his criticism was unjust and that he was estranged from the situation in Indonesia.[25] Hatta replied with further criticism in *Daulat Rakjat* on September 30, 1931. He claimed that the dissolution of the PNI had created two grave problems. First, the party executive had bound its own hands and surrendered the right to continue to lead the party. The action of the executive body in dissolving the party before the government had ordered it was tantamount to fleeing by night without offering the bravest possible fight. (In another article dated January 30, 1932, Hatta again took the executive body to task for their unprecedented political harakiri.[26]) He urged that even if part of the leadership were arrested, more resolute leaders would arise to carry on the movement. The present situation showed even more clearly the need to cultivate such indomitable leaders. The birth of such leaders would give meaning to Sukarno's words: "Even if one leader should fall, ten others will emerge to take over the PNI and continue the forward movement."[27]

The second problem was that the decision to dissolve the party had been taken without consulting the several thousand party members. This second point with its implied criticism of Sukarno's style of party organization was made as follows:

> . . . Is this (means of dissolving a party) democratic? Whether or not it is democratic concerns the basic principles of the independence movement. In the independence movement it is the people who are the spirit of the party. The people must be educated to become aware of the significance of the party and to believe firmly that the party is the flesh and blood of the people. The life or death of the party should be perceived as the life or death of the people. Only in this way can significant conditions be realised for a movement in which the people are aware of their own rights.
>
> But what are the realities? The (Nationalist) Party executive has issued a memorandum to the people ordering silence and non-activity from January 1930. Beyond that, all important party matters have been decided as the leaders think fit. The

24. Mohammed Hatta, *Kumpulan Karangan* [Collected articles], Vol., I, (Balai Pustaka, 1959), pp. 211–212.
25. Hatta, *Kumpulan*, p. 97.
26. Hatta, *Kumpulan*, p. 103.
27. Hatta, *Kumpulan*, pp. 98–99.

congresses at Mataram (Yogyakarta) and Jakarta were held without consulting the party members and without the discussion of all branch members. *Can we call such conferences valid?* (Italics mine.)

The word *kerakjatan* (democracy) comes easily to the lips of our leaders. But in reality democracy cannot be seen. The people are regarded as a doormat for the leaders to wipe their feet on. They are deemed necessary only to applaud the eloquent speeches of their leaders. The people have not been taught to bear responsibility themselves. If those fellows (the Dutch) call us immature we will probably get angry. But the attitude of the leaders who dissolved the PNI without first consulting the people who are party members itself amounts to nothing other than treating the people as immature. It is hardly surprising that the dissolution of the PNI was not approved by some of the party sympathisers. . . . [28]

As previously mentioned, Hatta went on in this article to say that his political activity after returning to Indonesia would lie beyond the limits of the Partindo. As I have indicated by italics, what Hatta basically called into question was the legitimacy of the Partindo's claim to the legacy of the PNI. The assertions of Sjahrir, who after his return became the focus of the Independent Groups and who criticized the dissolution of the PNI from the same standpoint as Hatta, underline this point. Sjahrir accepted the premise that the PNI, which advocated mass action and noncooperation, was the true party of the masses, and had the following to say of the dispute within the party. Generally when the left wing of a party becomes stronger the right wing uses its power to try to maintain its position. When the two factions are divided in ideas, principles, and aims, a split in the party becomes inevitable. The right wing becomes increasingly reactionary in suppressing the left, while the left wing takes up its new duties and attempts to deal with the future.[29]

And on the dissolution of the PNI and the establishment of the Partindo, Sjahrir commented as follows:

. . . The author does not consider the dissolution of the PNI to be a mere tactical error. It was a step taken from a false position [that of having suspended PNI activities in 1931]. . . . The party leaders yielded to external pressures [when they ceased their activities], and deviated from the line laid down by party principles and strategy. Thereafter they could not realise the strength

28. Hatta, *Kumpulan*, p. 99.
29. Sutan Sjahrir, *Pikiran dan Perdjuangan* [Thought and struggle], (Jakarta, 1947), pp. 21–22. This is a reissue (unfortunately not in chronological order) of Sjahrir's articles in *Daulat Rakjat* from 1931 to 1934.

(*kodrat*) of the people, did not accept their responsibilities, did not trust the people, and turned consistently to wait-and-see policies: thus the PNI began to move away from the people, to become estranged from the masses. . . . The dissolution of the PNI was the logical consequence of the false step taken earlier. . . . The dissolution of the party was not in line with the democratic spirit of the PNI, did not follow the principles and strategy of the PNI, and *was not carried out by the PNI.* (Italics, Sjahrir.) The "overmacht" (*fôrce majeure*) spoken of by those leaders at the time of the dissolution of the party tells only of the party's own "onmacht" (impotence). . . . But the people had a different aim: with the dissolution of the party . . . they returned to its former principles and spirit. Thus the question the newspapers are now asking about whether the Partindo is the successor to the PNI has already been answered. Even if all those presently in the Partindo were once members of the PNI, the Partindo . . . is not the PNI. The Partindo may well quote the old aims and battle plans. But their spirit and their promises are not those of the PNI. Thus the Partindo will almost certainly reach a point different to the goal aimed at by the PNI . . . .

The PNI was dissolved not because the party's principles were wrong. Even now many thousands of people have faith in the PNI's principles. And they believe that the PNI chose only what would bring independence as quickly as possible. The members of the old PNI who formed the People's Sovereignty faction (the Independent Groups) firmly believe that they will succeed to the heritage of the PNI, and then go on to carry through the policies of the PNI more thoroughly and more forcefully. They are firmly convinced that there is now no party which possesses the principled spirit that embraces mass action and noncooperation, and because of this they believe that there is no party with which they should unite. From this point of view, it was not they but that part of the PNI which abandoned the original party principles that broke away. They have held their position firmly throughout. They have been left (on their original ground) by those who flocked to the Partindo. . . .[30]

Thus Hatta and Sjahrir criticized the dissolution as a departure from the spirit of the PNI, the rightful successor to the independence movement. This was the basis of the Independent Groups' assertion of their legitimacy. But their criticism of the PNI leadership as undemocratic was not directed solely at Sartono's faction. Hatta, in particular, was also criticizing Sukarno, whose imprisonment had, in a sense, rendered him a "tragic hero," and Sukarnoist party activity and organization, as will become clear from the second point of the dispute below.

30.   Sjahrir, *Pikiran*, pp. 9–10, 12.

2. Unity—the *Persatéan* dispute

After his release from prison at the end of 1931, Sukarno endeavored without success to unite the Partindo and the PNI-Baru, and in the summer of 1932, with the drafting of his *Maklumat Dari Bung Karno Kepada Kaum Marhaen Indonesia*, "Announcement from Bung Karno to the Marhaens of Indonesia," he joined the Partindo. In this declaration Sukarno insisted that there were no fundamental differences between the Partindo and the PNI-Baru; both were parties of the Marhaens.[31] However, it was the question of which was the legitimate party of the Marhaens that was the bone of contention between the factions. Hatta's assertions on the question of unity were merely a vehicle through which to stress the "Marhaenness" of the PNI-Baru (Independent Groups). Subsequently Hatta's group turned their criticism against the unity that transgressed the Marhaenist principles that were the spirit of the PNI: they turned against the PPPKI.

Replying to charges that the emergence of the Independent Groups had disrupted unity, Hatta made the following comment on the PPPKI in *Daulat Rakjat* of April 20, 1932.

> This *Persatuan* (unity of the people) is really nothing more than *Persatéan* (pieces of meat skewered together for roasting). Goat, cow and water buffalo meat have all been brought together on the same skewer. But the ideas of the people and those of the bourgeoisie and the aristocracy can never be united. To unite all these groups will mean each sacrificing its own principles.[32]

Hatta developed his theory of unity further. The unity that he and his associates hoped for was not the *Persatéan* unity perpetuated by the PPPKI. For them, unity meant national unity, the unity of the indivisible Indonesian people. And the ideas of this united people should embrace diverse opinions; all should have the opportunity to act according to his own principles. There was no reason to stifle these activities with grumblings about "unity." The united front had not been questioned until it faced a crisis. The unity Hatta envisaged was quite distinct from the "unity" of the PPPKI. Although anathema to the noncooperators, elements within the PPPKI (for example, Thamrin) openly praised the government and adhered to such colonial agencies as the Volksraad (People's Council). This, Hatta asserted, strengthened the position of the nationalist cooperators in the PPPKI and carried the organization even further from the hearts of the people who had joined the PNI, a fact clearly demonstrated at the Indonesia Raja

31. Sukarno, *Dibawah*, p. 169.
32. Hatta, *Kumpulan*, p. 153.

Congress at Surabaya, January, 1931, led by the cooperation faction.[33]

Hatta's criticism of unity was closely echoed by Sjahrir, who in 1932 asserted that unity was not the aim of the movement but merely a condition for strengthening the battlefront.[34] In the history of the Indonesian nationalist movement he could count five instances where some degree of unity had been attained,[35] all of which, with the exception of the Radicale Concentratie of 1918, had occurred at a time of difficulty for the movement. But in every case the unity rested on equivocal attitudes, on concern only for the group; those who ventured to criticize were immediately branded dissolutionists and traitors to the cause. Undoubtedly nationalist sentiment demands unity in times of trouble, he argued, but viewed in context those critical situations that demanded unity had now passed and each party could carry out its own activities in accordance with its own principles. The clamorings for unity at this time were not based on a dispassionate understanding of practical politics, but on feelings alone, feelings that belonged in the realms of poetry.[36] To Sjahrir, the PPPKI was a combination of two forms of unity: that of the Radicale Concentratie, in which people who happened to have the same aims (self-government and the establishment of an assembly) came together for a fixed time, and that of the National Indisch Congres, in which organizations with mutually opposed aims cooperated as much as they could without losing their own independence for the sake of national unity. The result, he declared, was an *anak bantji*, "hermaphrodite child." In 1928, Mr. Sn (Sukarno) had stated that the PPPKI was born of "the desire to become one", but this was mere sentimentality and had no political meaning.[37] He had made "brotherhood" (*persaudaraan*) sacrosanct (*kramat*).[38] In this way the inner circle of the PPPKI had been forced to abandon the principles of the PNI, noncooperation and mass action, and as a result the PPPKI had linked the people of the PNI with the aristocracy. It was clear that the PPPKI's "unity" deviated from the principles of the PNI, and above all, that the Indonesia Raja Congress was merely an attempt to entrust the struggle for national independence to the hands of the aristocratic classes.[39] The mass action of the PNI meant education of

33.　Hatta, *Kumpulan*, pp. 153–154.
34.　Sjahrir, *Pikiran*, p. 22.
35.　Sjahrir, *Pikiran*, p. 34. The five examples of a united front cited by Sjahrir were: Radicale Concentratie, 1918; All Indische Congres, 1923; National Indisch Congres, 1924; PPPKI, 1927; and Congres Indonesia Raja, 1932.
36.　Sjahrir, *Pikiran*, pp. 35–39.
37.　Sjahrir, *Pikiran*, pp. 39–40.
38.　Sjahrir, *Pikiran*, p. 41.
39.　Sjahrir, *Pikiran*, p. 40, 42, 44.

the Marhaens; it was the politics of enlightenment (*politik Aufklärung*) aimed at awakening the people to their political duties.[40]

For Hatta and Sjahrir, unity ought not to have been an issue; in a sense unity already existed. Their understanding of unity, the unity of the Indonesian people against Holland, bypassed the difficulties involved in transition from the "natives of the Dutch East Indies" to "the Indonesian people," and consequently they treated unity solely in terms of a united front. But for Sukarno, who found his first, and highest, political stage since his release at the Indonesia Raja Congress—an assembly Hatta and Sjahrir termed "evil" (*djélék*)—the PPPKI was still very much "a part of my life."[41] The debate on unity continued in association with the question of whether priority should be given to class conflict among the people or to the racial conflict between Holland and Indonesia. This I shall examine later.

3. Party Organization

Hatta and colleagues held that the high-handed actions of the party leaders seen on the occasion of the dissolution of the PNI would destroy the democratic system of the party, would make a mockery of the masses who followed the party, and eventually would weaken the party's activities. In a critique of January 30, 1932, Hatta declared that the stated principles of the Partindo were merely a system for censoring party members, that they gave great authority to the leadership, and left the party sympathizers to follow like a line of ducks quacking in unison (*membébék*).[42]

On October 11, 1933, Hatta set forth the policies of the PNI-Baru in two articles entitled "Pergerakan dalam Rintangan" (the Movement under Pressure), and "Autonomi dan Centralisasi dalam Partai" (Autonomy and Centralisation of the Party). He explained that the PNI-Baru did not venture to call itself a party because this organization wanted a struggle of quality rather than quantity. Its primary objective was to educate a strong executive. He stressed the education of members rather than assembly and agitation. The troubled situation of the day (Sukarno was arrested in August of this year) demanded a sense of responsibility and autonomy in each branch organization and its members. Whether a branch could undertake its responsibilities would depend on the quality of its organization. The organization could not survive under a centralized system with orders passed down from above. Conversely if

40.   Sjahrir, *Pikiran*, p. 43.
41.   Dahm, *Sukarno and the Struggle*, p. 138.
42.   Hatta, *Kumpulan*, pp. 104–105.

the branch organizations agreed with the center on the principles of the struggle and acted on their own decisions with autonomy in all aspects the organization would continue to flourish.[43]

In a critique dated November 10, Hatta again mentioned the importance of organization, condemning as childish the intention to drive forward a movement by emotions alone. Since the feeling of unity had started to develop, and national unity been realized, the movement had passed from the stage of demonstration and entered the stage of organization.[44]

In summer of the same year, Sukarno announced from prison his withdrawal from the Partindo. In response, Hatta enquired whether the withdrawal of the leader regarded as the "head" of the movement could be said to show a responsible attitude toward the people, and whether such willful behaviour was not toying with the fate of the people.[45] While the Partindo, as described earlier, based its activities on mass assembly and agitation, the PNI-Baru stressed the training of cadres for the future struggle for independence, and criticized the nationalist movement, which relied solely on the personal qualities of its leaders (specifically Sukarno).

Comparing East and West, Sjahrir pointed out two areas in which the West was superior: organization and technology. He stressed that the age of capitalism, in particular, was an age of organization and that only organization could oppose organization.[46] He believed that organization was the only weapon with which to acquire independence, and that it would become the weapon of people who oppose capitalism and imperialism. Although morals were necessary for organization, (these morals must not be mystical or illogical), they were merely a prerequisite for organization. The strengthening of organization was the strengthen'ng of each part of the organization and the smoothing of relations between the parts and the whole. What was needed was not courage but the will to continue steadfastly. Only education could foster such an iron will.[47]

When Hatta and Sjahrir stressed "organization," "will," and "autonomy" rather than "fellings," "morals," and "courage" in reference to party structure, they were directly conscious of Sukarno's views. In his article "Mentjapai Indonesia Merdeka" (Toward Indonesian independence), of March 1933, Sukarno refuted the argu-

43.   Hatta, *Kumpulan*, pp. 173–175.
44.   Hatta, *Kumpulan*, p. 177.
45.   Hatta, *Kumpulan*, p. 177.
46.   Sjahrir, *Pikiran*, pp. 55–56.
47.   Sjahrir, *Pikiran*, pp. 55–62.

ments of Hatta's group on the issue of centralism in the vanguard party:

... party members that incline to reformism, ideas that incline to reformism, these must be thoroughly "washed out". If they cannot be "washed out" the offenders must be banished from the party without pardon or mercy.

You may well reply: if this is so, democracy will be lost within the party. It's inevitable! The party cannot be democratic in the sense that "all ideas are freely allowed." We cannot have a democracy that allows all "isms." The party is concerned with only one ideology and doctrine; one-hundred-percent radical ideology and doctrine. The democracy permissible within the vanguard party is no ordinary democracy. It is the democracy that abroad is called democratic centralism. It is the democracy which vests in its leaders the authority to punish deviation, to expel those members or factions that jeopardize the struggle of the masses. "The freedom of unlimited ideologies must not exist within the party. The pillar which unites the party is unity of belief." These are the teachings of a great leader on party organization and are worthy of note. Breakaway elements must not be tolerated. Deviation must be censured most severely or expelled immediately. A vanguard party that is disturbed by internal agitations can never become the vanguard of the masses.

This applies not only to deviation toward reformism. Deviation toward anarcho-syndicalism, unprincipled fanaticism, and blind actions and thoughts must also be redressed, must also be punished. It is this kind of deviation that screams traitor, by claiming that "leftism" is lacking in the party. It is this deviation that, because of its blindness, cannot distinguish between radical leftism and antisocial leftism. It cannot differentiate leftism that upholds nature and is upheld by nature from leftism that bears and is borne only by a feeling of hopeless rage. A sound party must continue to fight against this twofold deviation, in order that it can become the milestone showing clearly and firmly the radical course on which the giant wave of mass action rolls toward the ocean of independence.

For this reason, one requirement of the vanguard party is principle. A steely strong principle, a principle which punishes without forgiveness or mercy those party members who dare to depart from convention, this is the principle that will be the spirit of the vanguard party. It is not a principle which concerns only the ideology of radicalism, nor does it concern only the "theoretical side" of radicalism. It is a principle which relates to all aspects of the party. The theoretical principal, the organizational principle, the strategic principle, the propaganda principle —the party must have a principle consistent to the very last item, like the mechanism of a mechanical device that is flawless in both axle and machinery.

But the party must never be a heartless, unchanging machine. Such a party is lifeless and the storms of the age may blow it from

the face of the earth in an instant. The party which upholds
nature and is upheld by nature will be alive like nature itself and
will continue to evolve like nature itself. The party's life, the
party's evolution, the pace of the party's life, these must not be
obstructed or challenged. That which should be obstructed and
challenged is the party's disease, the disease of deviation, which
gnaws at the health of the body of radicalism in the party. Nature'
has never gone astray of its own accord, but has constantly
joined battle with all manner of diseases. The party must accept
cheerfully that which makes the body of its radicalism firm and
healthy, and for its diseases must immediately take its medicine,
"strictly" and without mercy. The centralism that ought to be at
the heart of the party must not be dictatorial, but the kind of
democratic centralism in which the party itself is the supreme
commander. But conversely, the centralism that ought to lie at
the heart of the party must not be a democracy which gives
freedom to anything, but a centralistic democracy which brings
to light the diseases infesting its radicalism.

Democratic centralism and centralistic democracy—these
are the internal conditions for the vanguard party . . . [48]

4. The Noncooperation Policy

Noncooperation in effect meant the rejection of compromise with
the colonial government, refusal to become a government official, and
boycotting the various assemblies in the colony (Volksraad and consulta-
tive committees). As early as 1922 the PI had announced a policy of
noncooperation in its manifesto, and this subsequently became a basic
plank in the PNI platform at the time of its founding in 1927. In the
early 1930s the two factions had clashed on this issue in their dispute over
party principles and strategy. The argument was occasioned by Hatta's
acceptance in November, 1932 of the offer from the Onafhankelijk
Sosialistisch Partij (Independent Socialist Party), to stand as candidate
for the Dutch Second Chamber. On December 10, *Persatuan Indonesia*,
now the organ of the Partindo, carried a criticism to the effect that Hatta
had exposed his true colors and that party members should be warned
against him.[49]

This issue revealed most clearly the basic differences in opinion
between Hatta-Sjahrir and Sukarno.

In an article in 1932, "Sekali lagi tentang Socio-Nasionalisme
dan Socio-Democracy" (Once again Socio-Nationalism and Socio-
Democracy), Sukarno repeatedly asserted that noncooperation is a
principle of the struggle.

48. Sukarno, *Dibawah*, pp. 305–307.
49. Dahm, *Sukarno and the struggle*, p. 159.

Noncooperation is a principle of our struggle towards Indonesian independence. In the struggle towards Indonesian independence we must always remember the opposition of interests between Sini and Sana, between the colonial masters and the colonial subjects, between the rulers and the ruled. Undoubtedly it is this opposition of interests that causes us to take this stand of noncooperation. Undoubtedly it is this opposition of interests that convinces us that we shall never achieve Indonesian independence if we do not carry out the policy of noncooperation. Undoubtedly it is this opposition of interests that prescribes, for example, *machtsvorming* (power formation), mass action and most of the other principles of struggle.

For this reason, noncooperation is not confined to the simple principle of struggle: "we will not sit in the masters' assembly." Noncooperation is a positive principle; it means we should not collaborate with the masters in any political field but should prosecute an unremitting struggle with the masters; it means an unmerciful struggle with the masters. Noncooperation is not confined within the walls of the conference hall but covers all areas of our principle of struggle. This is the reason that the policy of noncooperation is said to contain radicalism, to embrace radicalism. Radicalism means radicalism of the heart, radicalism of thought, radicalism of action, radicalism both internal and external. Noncooperation demands radical action.

One aspect of our noncooperation is nonparticipation in the masters' assemblies. And is the Dutch Second Chamber also included in the masters' assemblies? Yes, the Dutch Second Chamber is included in these masters' assemblies. This Second Chamber is for us one "illumination," one "body," one "embodiment" of colonist Holland; it puts us in fetters and is the "embodiment" of the authority which has deprived us of our independence. It is the Second Chamber which is the "symbol" of colonial Holland; it suppresses us and is the "symbol" of the conditions which have made us a wretched people.

Therefore, our noncooperation policy, on principle, must be directed against the Dutch parliament in general and the Second Chamber in particular. It must be directed against the "illumination" of systems like the League of Nations which fetter us and other Asian nations.

Then is this not anarchy? Is not the Second Chamber an assembly? Of course the Second Chamber is an assembly. But the Second Chamber is a Dutch assembly. If we reject all parliamentary institutions, then, of course, we are anarchists. If we reject an Indonesian parliament such as can exist only in an independent Indonesia, an Indonesian parliament that will light up the road to political democracy and economic democracy, then, of course, we are anarchists. Of course we are. If an Englishman boycotts the English parliament, if a German should fail to enter the Bundestag, if a Frenchman declines a seat in the French parliament, one may call him an anarchist. But if he rejects a seat in the assembly of a country that has fettered his country—if we the people of Indonesia

decline on principle to occupy a seat in the Dutch parliament—
that is not anarchy, it is the principle of struggle of the most ardent
noncooperator!

Look at the history of struggle through noncooperation in
other countries. Look, for example, at the history of noncooperation in Ireland. That is one of the original struggles through
noncooperation. Look at the activity of the "Sinn Fein" party in
that land. "Sinn Fein" was their slogan, it meant "we ourselves."

"We ourselves"! That portrayed their policy. It portrayed
the policy of not working with the English, of not cooperating with
the English, of not sitting in the English parliament. "Do not enter
Westminster. Quit Westminster. Build our own Westminster!":
this was the message and action of the Sinn Fein. Were they
anarchists? They were not anarchists, but principled noncooperative nationalists. Our noncooperation must also be principled
noncooperation.

There are those who support attendance in the Second
Chamber to carry out their policies of opposition and confrontation
against the masters, and who would make the Second Chamber a
stage to publicize their own struggle. They may carry out such a
policy. In fact, the Dutch Independent Socialist party, the
Communist party, and other leftist forces have repeatedly carried
out this policy. Even the faction of C. R. Das in India did not
oppose the English parliament. However, such a policy must not
be carried out by a noncooperative nationalist. In the instant the
noncooperative nationalist enters the masters' assembly, be it the
Second Chamber, be it the League of Nations, at precisely that
moment he will fling away the broad principle which is based on
the conviction that there is an opposition of interests between the
masters and his own group. In that instant he will carry out a
policy which is not principled, a policy which has essentially
abandoned the principle of noncooperation.

We must carry out a policy of principled noncooperation—we
must reject, on principle, seats in the Volksraad, the Dutch
parliament, and the League of Nations. And as I have already
made clear, this question of assemblies is only one side of our
noncooperation. The most important part of noncooperation is to
teach the people to rely on 'we ourselves'—to borrow a phrase from
the Irish noncooperators—and set in motion the organization of
the most fervent and vigorous mass action and of power formation
of the Marhaens.[50]

While Sukarno likened the relationship between the Sinn Fein
party and the English to that between Indonesia and Holland, Hatta
began his argument from the historical relationship between the United
Kingdom and Ireland, and pointed out that the Irish members of
parliament had always been elected by the Irish but had always been a

50.   Sukarno, *Dibawah*, pp. 189–191, 291–293.

minority in Westminster and been voted down by the English. They had, therefore, launched upon a policy of self-determination by "we ourselves," moved by their appreciation of *Realpolitik*.[51] This *Realpolitik*, which Hatta and Sjahrir long continued to expound, was the basis of their appraisal of the situation in Indonesia.

Sukarno responded with "Djawab saja pada saudara Mohammed Hatta" (My Reply to Comrade Mohammed Hatta), but developed his argument without regard to Hatta's point about the differing historical conditions.

> . . . . It is exactly as comrade Hatta says. The Irish people had for a long time been voted down. They were continually defeated in divisions. They were continually repressed and oppressed by the English capitalists. However, they did not establish the Sinn Fein only on account of that. They did not establish "we ourselves" for only that reason. They established "we ourselves" and persued a policy of "we ourselves" primarily to teach the spirit of Irish independence. They established "we ourselves" and persued a policy of "we ourselves" to perfect the material and spiritual conditions essential for an independent existence. They established "we ourselves" and persued a policy of "we ourselves" not with the negative desire to withdraw from the parliament in which they would always be voted down, but with the positive desire above all to educate the minds and bodies of the people.[52]

Sukarno went on to quote the patriotic message of Sir Arthur Griffith, the leader of the Sinn Fein movement, who urged his compatriots to forget the English people and believe in themselves. Then he continued:

> . . . . It is indeed a crime if comrade Mohammed Hatta regards the policy of the Sinn Fein as mere *Realpolitik*.
> Recently, though, comrade Hatta has developed a taste for *Realpolitik*. Needless to say, comrade Hatta has criticised us for "viewing affairs through only sentimentality and emotion, rather than building our foundations on *Realpolitik*." Undoubtedly comrade Hatta's argument has been forcefully defended by someone (perhaps Sjahrir?-Sukarno) calling himself "realpolitician" in *Utusan Indonesia* (Indonesian mission).
> *Realpolitik* means practical politics. So let me ask comrade Hatta some questions. If Ireland is continually defeated in divisions in the Westminster parliament, utterly defeated by the English, will not Indonesia be beaten down even more by Holland in the parliament in the Hague? If the Irish people who have their own seats in parliament, who have the right to vote and the right

---

51. Sukarno, *Dibawah*, pp. 209–210.
52. Sukarno, *Dibawah*, p. 210.

to be elected, who have the right to participate both actively and passively in government, if they have boycotted Westminster, should not we Indonesians boycott the parliament in the Hague? Even though we have the right to be elected, we have no right to vote. In effect we have only the right to participate passively in government. And if the people of Ireland will not willingly attend the Westminster parliament where they occupy over a hundred seats, should not comrade Hatta—comrade Hatta who declares *Realpolitik* to mean practical politics—boycott the parliament at the Hague, where he and several other radical groups would occupy only a handful of seats?"[53]

Sukarno went on to deal with Hatta's assertion that: "In parliament one can overthrow the government and dismiss ministers" by saying if that were so would Ireland withdraw from parliament and act as Sinn Fein? He continued:

What is more, the downfall of the government in the Hague, the dismissal of ministers and the shattering of the Dutch cabinet would not mean that Indonesia would become independent. The downfall of the government in the parliament in the Hague would merely be the destruction of the present political organisation. As long as Indonesia is Holland's "basket of fate," as long as Indonesia is "the cork of that basket in which Holland is drifting," as long as it is said that "Holland will be brought to ruin if Indonesia becomes independent," as long as just such a situation prevails, Indonesian independence cannot rely on the vagaries of this and that administrative power in Holland, nor on the appointment and dismissal of ministers in the parliament in the Hague. If we act upon considerations of *Realpolitik* while the situation is such, for us Indonesians a seat in the Second Chamber can never be more than just a seat in the Second Chamber.

This must be so. Whatever the nation, whatever the people, the independence of the nation—and this applies not only to Ireland—depends on the degree of "autonomy—Sinn Fein" of the nation and the people....

Comrade Hatta agreed "in principle" to stand for the Second Chamber. He did not agree as a tactic or an "expedient," but on the foundation and basis of the question. This is the very reason that we stated that if comrade Mohammed Hatta's noncooperation is not principled noncooperation then neither is it noncooperation which respects one-hundred-percent noncooperative nationalists. This is the very reason that we stated that "comrade Hatta has already essentially abandoned his noncooperation..."

Noncooperation is not merely a question of struggle. Non-cooperation is also a principle of struggle. It is this principle of struggle that we must grasp as firmly as possible. It is this principle

53.   Sukarno, *Dibawah*, pp. 210–211.

of struggle that forbids a noncooperative nationalist to go to the
Hague. . . .

We must build up our own strength. We must place the
greatest importance on our own strength, our own *machtsvorming*
(power formation). Only through this sort of power formation, an
indomitable Indonesian power formation, an Indonesian power
formation that will forge spiritual and material power, a power
formation which can be achieved in the midst of the Indonesian
people, only through this can we make our voices roar like thunder,
can we build our strength to shake the earth, in order to overthrow
capitalism and imperialism. For this reason I will say again: we
must continue to refuse to sit in the Hague. . . .[54]

Hatta's response appeared in *People's Sovereignty* of January 30,
1933 under the title "Sekali lagi Noncooperasi dan Tweede Kamer"
(Once again Noncooperation and the Second Chamber). The argument
of Sukarno cited above and the following reply by Hatta show clearly
the differences in their fundamental views:

The differences of opinion on "noncooperation and the Second
Chamber" relate to the individual's personal experience, not to
whether he is principled or nonprincipled. For those who criticise
us, noncooperation has been interpreted as a dogma and it has
already become a metaphysical belief (a mystic belief). But for us,
noncooperation is one weapon of the struggle, a rational means of
struggle, a sound logical conclusion. . . .

Politics is frequently associated with a culture. (But here) it is
not associated with the Marhaen culture that will arise in due
course but with the old dying culture, the old culture which is
concerned with Heaven and Nirvana.

Political theories which set out to reform the present and the
future have, in practice, often become figures of speech through
wajang stories of events that never happened. Pictures with no
history are held up as examples of the national type. Before they
know it the people are forced to look backwards, they are taught
to live and die in an illusion. N.B.

If today's theories of struggle are built on the illusions of
antiquity, they can never become weapons of struggle but will be
reduced to mystic beliefs.

Even though mythology and dogma may intensify the feeling
of struggle they cannot give a sound view of *Realpolitik*.

For us, the greater part of the national struggle is taking place
on the West European continent. The eleven years that we (that is,
Hatta) of necessity spent in Western Europe has decided our fate.
While maintaining the struggle over there, we have been able to
learn the ways in which Western Europeans fight. With just a few
tools these means can be applied by us of this land. We have learned

54. Sukarno, *Dibawah*, pp. 211–214.

that the Western European, be he a worker or a capitalist, bases his struggle on a rational foundation.

They have used every possible place to attack and weaken the enemy and to spread propaganda. They have employed reason and resourcefulness in the struggle, not self-indulgent sentimentality and emotion. Thus they were well able to adapt their real aspirations to their principles. Surely none who have read Marx's "Historical Materialism" can deny that his teachings are based on the most rational of principles. According to these teachings of Marx, tactics must be adapted to the circumstances. When Marx said this, had he abandoned his principles? He certainly had not.

We frankly accept that we have been influenced by the rational spirit (*rationele geest*) of Western Europe. For this reason, noncooperation does not mean dogma and mystic belief to us, but a rational means of struggle, a rational weapon of struggle. And by chance our opinions agreed with those of the PNI-Baru. And no small wonder. Most of the PNI-Baru group are poor Marhaens without even the time to dream of Nirvana. Their spirit is affected by their day to day life, and by their thoughts of a rational, simple and clear struggle.

But we don't want you to think we are applauding the correctness of character of the European struggle. You must not think that we have already become completely Western European, or that we have taken on Western European characteristics. This is far from the truth.

What we are commending is merely the way Western Europeans use their strength when they set about achieving a certain purpose. This is the rational method. We are not praising the Western Europeans' greed or avarice. On the contrary, we cannot criticise them enough. Thus in our morals we have never been enamoured by the West, but rate Eastern morals as highly as we ever did.

We inferiors will not hesitate to accept learning from Westerners. What reason can we have for hesitating to follow the Western Europeans' rational methods of struggle? How much more so if it is Western Europeans we are to fight! None who are fanatical about our culture and sentimentality will want to admit that the Western Europeans are more advanced than us and that there are many matters which we might imitate. For them there is nothing to surpass the East.

For the Marhaen movement a rational means of struggle is most important. Thus the noncooperation conceived by the PNI-Baru is the weapon of struggle with which to oppose those fellows. The Second Chamber is also a good place to confront colonial imperialism. That place can be used in principle.

Some say that our noncooperation policy took the form we have just elaborated only after our invitation from the Independent Socialist Party to stand for the Second Chamber.

We know that in the arena of the Indonesian nationalist movement there are many who have little experience, that there are very many children who have become bosses of the movement, having been taught only to applaud. Consequently, if those who stand for noncooperation state that merely to seek a seat in the Second Chamber does not mean the violation of their principles, then the question of noncooperation and the Second Chamber is settled. Below we will clarify how this will never become an issue.

The most radical of all groups founded on noncooperation, namely *the PI, decided in 1929 that to occupy a seat in the Second Chamber for the purpose of fighting against colonial imperialism did not conflict with the basis of noncooperation* . . . . (Italics mine.)

. . . Such a strategy was linked to the general interests of the working class. The heart of imperialism and capitalism lies in the colonies. In the opinion of the leaders of Europe's left wing, it would be highly significant if colonial capitalism and imperialism could be overthrown in parliament by the leaders of the people who are themselves oppressed. This strategy was endorsed by the PI of 1929. . . .

. . . Here, too, the difference of opinion which arose from this experience can be seen. This is the difference between the mystic beliefs of some of the noncooperators of this land and the rational methods of struggle of the old PI faction. . . .

N.B. We do not for one moment forget that *wajang* and the like even now provide entertainment for the majority of the masses. However, we cannot agree to combining the policy of opposition to imperialism with the *wajang*.[55]

Subsequently Hatta met great difficulties in supplanting sentimentality with realistic policies. He reemphasized the need for rational struggle, citing the example of the PI which had acquired international solidarity and gradually rid itself of national sentimentality and racial sentimentality and adopted rational methods of struggle.

THE MEANING OF THE DISPUTE

Running through the dispute described in the previous section is the issue of legitimacy of succession to the nationalist movement. What emerged clearly from the dispute on the right of leadership were the basic differences in the mode of thought of Sukarno and of Hatta and Sjahrir. In 1932, all were still young: Sukarno was 31, Hatta 30, and Sjahrir 23; all had little experience in politics. But each went on to develop a coherent mode of thought and to establish himself as a leader of opinion in modern Indonesian history. Even after 1934 when both parties had exited from the political stage, the points of their dispute were taken up, in particular, in the "cultural-debate" on the ideal type of the Indonesian people, between the Taman Siswa national

55.   Hatta, *Kumpulan*, pp. 166–170.

education movement and the Pudjangga Baru literary movement.

In the following I will consider the substance of the dispute and its political background in an attempt to interpret the meaning of the dispute.

1. The legitimacy of succession to the nationalist movement

The dispute between Hatta and Sukarno originated in the dissolution of the PNI and was closely linked to the controversy over the right of succession to the nationalist movement.

As described earlier, the Indonesian nationalist movement began in the early years of this century. The most radical opposition to the colonial government came first from the Sarekat Islam, which at one time boasted more than a million members, and subsequently from the Communist party and its mass organizations, the Sarekat Rakjat (People's Associations).

After 1927, however, as Pringgodigdo has pointed out, the People's Associations were deprived of their leadership. At just that time, among the new elite being raised under the "ethical" policy, the group of Indonesian students in Holland were seeking an arena for their political activities in the old country. And the Hatta-Semaun agreement signed at the end of 1926 indicates that the PI intended to direct its activities primarily at the People's Associations. In 1927, the PI founded the PNI, together with Sukarno and others who were emerging as political figures in the colony and chose to place Sukarno in the forefront. They intended that the PNI should reorganize the masses in the People's Associations and thereby take over the mainstream of the Indonesian nationalist movement. And in fact Sukarno and the PNI quickly established their right of leadership of the whole nationalist movement.

When the PNI split up, the legacy of the PNI of 1927 was first challenged by the Hatta-Sjahrir group, as described previously. At that time both Hatta and Sjahrir recognized fully the significance and the legitimacy of the PNI of 1927 as leader of the nationalist movement, the role it had inherited from its founding organization, the PI, and ultimately from the PKI whose "transfer of sovereignty" of the nationalist movement to the PI was symbolized by the Hatta-Semaun agreement. Such was the reasoning behind their claims that the Independent Groups, which had broken away from the Sartono faction, and their successor, the PNI-Baru, should rightfully inherit the spirit of the PNI and the right to leadership of the nationalist movement. Hatta's response to questioning on his stand on noncooperation, in connection with his candidacy for the Dutch Second Chamber, that his action was in line with the decision of the 1929 PI and that there was therefore no further need of discussion, also indicates his views on the line of succession to the leadership of the nationalist movement.

The PNI-Baru's claim to be the rightful successor to the PNI was also shown in the abbreviation of its name. The Pendidikan Nasional Indonesia attached the word *baru*, "new," to its initials, not only to distinguish itself from the Partai Nasional Indonesia but to associate itself with that organization.

Viewed in this way it seems as if the claims of Hatta and Sjahrir in the face of, first, Sartono (he also belonged to the PI at one time), and, later, Sukarno were based merely on considerations of the legitimacy of the PNI-Baru, a matter which ultimately hinged on the written agreement concluded at Leiden in Holland between Hatta and Semaun, and left aside the question of how they proposed to reorganize and strengthen the independence movement in Indonesia. But the continued assertion of Hatta and Sjahrir of the right of the PNI-Baru of a mere thousand or so members to lead the nationalist movement was not based soley on considerations of legitimacy, but on their confidence in the new ideas of leadership that they intended to introduce into Indonesia.

In his eleven years in Holland, Hatta had become completely conversant with Western European society and had adopted many Western ideas, particularly those of socialism. Sjahrir was not disappointed when he finally reached the Holland that he had dreamed of and yearned for since childhood and declared "I feel almost as if it were my home".[56] Hatta and Sjahrir had complete confidence in their social consciousness and ideas of leadership, which they ardently believed they should introduce into Indonesian society. It was this sense of mission that allowed them to assert their claim to the leadership of the independence movement. As shown previously, they felt their ideas of leadership provided a rational perception of reality by rejecting sentimentality and emotion and would enlighten the masses to the realities of world history by sweeping away the delusions of the *wajang* and of the glory of ancient kings. This assertion was made most intensely by Hatta in his "Kearah Indonesia Merdeka" (Toward an Independent Indonesia) written in 1932, an article used as propaganda by the PNI-Baru.

56. Sjahrir, (Sjahrazed) *Renungan Indonesia* [Indonesian meditation], (Djakarta, 1947), p. 163. The original title of these notes (in Dutch) of Sjahrir (Sjahrazad) was *Indonesische Overpeinzingen*, 1945. Translation into Indonesian was by H. B. Yasin.

Sukarno's thoughts, on the other hand, appeared in *Mentjapai Indonesia Merdeka*, (Toward Indonesian Independence), written in 1933. This brochure became the propaganda of the Partindo and includes the assertions of Sukarno in the period between his court speech in 1930 and his rearrest in the summer of 1933.

I would like to examine these two manifestoes to determine the ideas on nationalism of Hatta and Sukarno and the basic differences between them. Both are long articles, and detailed scrutiny would probably disclose further problems, but here I would like to arrange, under headings, the differences which emerge from the articles taken as a whole.

2. Sukarno and Hatta

In these articles, both Hatta and Sukarno advocate a nationalism aimed at Indonesian independence, and both stress that independence should be founded on democratic principles, to which end the masses should be educated. Their democracy was both political and economic; Sukarno called it sociodemocracy and stressed the need for economic equality.

Despite this general agreement, both sides opposed each other bitterly, as seen in the third section. In a preliminary study, I arranged under headings the points of difference that were exposed during their dispute. At that time I cited Sukarno's principles of struggle as the doctrine of independence for its own sake, the universal negation of Holland, and faith in the laws of progress. Sukarno adhered to these principles through the dispute of the early 1930s and went on to establish the concept of Marhaenism, while gradually shifting the focus of his discourse from the city intellectuals (in a sense his own circle) to the *desa*, "village communities".[57] Below, as a restatement of that study, I would like to deal with the differences and the bases of confrontation between Sukarno and Hatta.

1. *The nation*

Both sides agreed that independence was the most immediate and the highest objective, and both attached importance to how society should develop once that goal was achieved. Both cited the example of the French revolution, underlining its failure to achieve economic equality, and both set the goal of "socialism" for postindependence Indonesia. In this context, independence could be regarded as a bridge. And it was on whether the bridge itself or the other side of that bridge

57. Kenji Tsuchiya, "Sukarno no Kenkyū" [Studies on Sukarno], *Tōnan Ajia Kenkyū* [Southeast Asian Studies], 8, no. 4, pp. 566–579.

was more important that the factions of Sukarno and Hatta were divided. The ideas of "People's Sovereignty" propagated by the PNI-Baru were, as Hatta explained, important not only in the movement of the day, but in the days to come when they would constitute the basic principles of the nation. Thus it was necessary to spread these ideas through education. On the other hand, Sukarno likened independence to a "golden bridge".[58] Independence was undoubtedly a bridge, but for Sukarno it was golden. Consequently it was of paramount importance to him to forge the "national spirit" that could reach the bridge. Sukarno's "national spirit" was subsequently formulated as *Gotong Rojong* (mutual help), a phrase Sukarno first used at the end of his 1933 article,[59] although at this time it was apparently not identified with the "national spirit" itself. Neither Hatta nor Sjahrir mentioned "national spirit"; instead they spoke exclusively of "People's Sovereignty" as a concrete expression of the "national spirit."

The differences in their attitudes toward independence were closely linked to their differing concepts of the nation. Hatta's discussion of nationalism in the opening of his article treats nationalism in contrast to internationalism. And when he spoke of democracy, Hatta began by describing the history of development of Western European democracy after Montesquieu, and went on to link it to the democracy advocated by the PNI-Baru.[60]

In his article, Sukarno gives a schematic representation of Indonesian history: glorious past→wretched present→future filled with promise. For Sukarno the people meant simply the people of Indonesia. Hatta's view was wider: he also thought of the people in abstract terms, in terms of the theories of "imperialism and the repressed peoples," as well as in terms of the Indonesian people. Thus for Hatta and his associates, the Indonesian people as a people already existed in theory. This consideration probably influenced the theory of national unity, which formed one basis of the assertions of Hatta's group concerning the PPPKI.

2. *Holland*

Sukarno, whose supreme aim was independence, continued to advocate unity and solidarity of the people, a stance which assumed the absolute opposition of the colonial governors and the governed people. Sukarno understood this as the irreconcilable conflict between Sana and Sini, and in his long pamphlet, *Mentjapai Indonesia Merdeka* he

58. Sukarno, *Dibawah*, p. 314.
59. Sukarno, *Dibawah*, p. 322.
60. Hatta, *Kumpulan*, pp. 61–74.

repeatedly emphasizes the absolute opposition of the two. And at the basis of his universal negation of the Sana is his rejection of the theory of "the duty of the white man" (the essence of the "ethical" policy). Why, Sukarno demanded vehemently, did the white man not go to the Eskimo people of the North Pole if he was motivated by his duty to teach his lofty culture, rather than first coming to the places of peoples with advanced civilizations like India and Indonesia?[61] Until the Sana vanished from the sight of the Sini, they would continue to confront each other like the lion and its prey.[62]

On the other hand, when Hatta and Sjahrir spoke of a rational perception of reality, it is clear they were advocating Western European rationalism. Hatta's Western European outlook as expressed in his response on the problem of noncooperation clearly bears this out. Hatta and Sjahrir based their perception of the situation on the fact that there were also inequalities in Dutch society, and accordingly pressed their own claims against Holland from a position of equality with Dutchmen, a position of having a thought process and logical framework which could appreciate Western culture and institutions on equal terms and which were mutually understandable. And it was this position, this Western European mode of thought, that they intended to introduce into the home country as the basis of their ideas of leadership.

In later years when Hatta and Sjahrir were in exile in Bandanaira, Sjahrir made extensive notes, which show clearly his (their) mode of thought.[63] In his notes of March 7, 1938, Sjahrir expressed his appreciation and understanding of Hatta in the following terms:

> Formerly he was a noncooperator by political conviction, and yet in many respects he still had faith in the conventional morality and humanity of colonial government. . . . In other words, in the background of his thoughts he still maintained a high opinion of the respectability and methods of the colonial rulers against whom he made a stand. He now thinks quite differently about these things, thanks to Digoel. He is no longer as grim a non-cooperator as he used to be, but in a moral sense he was perhaps more of a cooperator then than he is now, because formerly he regarded the government with unconscious faith in its reason-

61. Sukarno, *Dibawah*, p. 276.

62. Sukarno, *Dibawah*, p. 290.

63. Bandanaira was a trade center in the Banda islands where Western and Asian cultures met, and it had a (new) "cosmopolitan" culture. This "cosmopolitan" character imparted to Sjahrir far more "peace of mind" than any other part of Indonesia. Sjahrir expresses his feeling of intimacy with the un-Indonesian society of Banda in *Renungan Indonesia*, pp. 92, 102, 112–115, 149–152, 164.

ableness and respectability. *He thus had an unconscious respect for the rulers, and certainly much more than a cooperator such as Thamrin ever had.*

The same is true in my case, as well. In those days, we cooperators propagated suspicion toward the government, but we did not realize that we ourselves regarded it with a measure of moral trust. At one time, Hafil (Hatta) did not believe that he would be banished, and certainly never dreamed that he might be sent to Digoel. . . .

It was really a revelation for Hafil, and he has learned more from it than he did during all his years of 'political life' in Europe. . . .

. . . the young noncooperators had such a high opinion of the same rulers that they considered it natural that frankness and openness, even if troublesome to the administration, would be tolerated by the government as long as they remained within the bounds of the law.

Hafil had a great deal of this faith in the human and democratic disposition of the colonial government. While he attacked and criticized colonial conditions in his articles, and while he expressed his disbelief in the good intentions of the government and in the possibility of cooperation with that government in order to lift the Indonesian people to a really national status, *nevertheless in his heart he was still a Netherlander. He was still a Netherlander in the sense that he did not really regard that government as a foreign and enemy element, but considered it in the same way that, for example, a left-wing socialist opponent considers the Netherlands government in Holland.* Hafil thus unconsciously accepted many of the same mutual norms and recognized one very important common basis for cooperation with the Dutch: namely, an internal faith in the humane, democratic, and reliable methods of a government that outwardly he called unreliable.[64] (Italics mine.)

As Sjahrir clearly states, for Hatta it was the Dutch who "spoke the same language," and consequently he regarded his candidacy for the Dutch parliament "as an honour".[65] In Sukarno's view this "honour" was scarcely tolerable, while in Hatta's opinion the *persatéan* of the PPPKI which was "part of my life" for Sukarno, and the *membébék* of the leader who had sung the praises of the "spirit of the Indonesian people," and the masses who were intoxicated with the idea were hardly more tolerable. At this point, both sides had to accept that their positions were, emotionally, mutually incomprehensible.

Hatta and Sjahrir, in commenting on the PPPKI, asserted that a united front was only necessary, in fact only effective, when the move-

---

64. Sjahrir, *Renungan*, pp. 174–175. Soetan Sjahrir, *Out of Exile*, trans. Charles Wolf (New York, 1949), pp. 202–204.
65. Dahm, *Sukarno and the Struggle*, p. 161.

ment faced a crisis. It was not until the eve of World War II that they called for unity of the nationalist movement, and at that time their sense of danger was alerted to the threat to democracy from Fascism.[66] At the beginning of the century, in connection with the "ethical" policy, Snouck Hurgronje had envisaged that stable spiritual unification of the Dutch and Indonesians would be realized through the introduction of Western European thought. After almost forty years, Hatta and Sjahrir responded to this idea in its purest form, but the echoes resounded only faintly from the seclusion of their exile in Bandanaira. When Sjahrir declared flatly in the 1930s that the responsibility of the PNI was "Aufklärung," he, an Indonesian, was reiterating the views held formerly by Hurgronje. When Sjahrir called for the defense of Dutch democracy from his exile, the Marhaens, in fact, were fully expecting the Sini and Sana to split decisively, a fact which Sjahrir himself confirmed in Bandanaira.[67] This made Sjahrir feel keenly the distance between himself and the Marhaens, and added to his and Hatta's fears that the modernization of Indonesia, which since the days of the PNI-Baru they had entrusted to the ideas of "People's Sovereignty," was ever more distant.

3. *Marhaenism*

The word Marhaen was used frequently by both parties in these articles. Originally the name of a self-sufficient but poor farmer of West Jawa, it first appeared in Sukarno's speech before the court in 1930, but it was limited to use alongside the term *Kromo* (little man). After Sukarno's release from prison, the Partindo preferred the term Marhaen to indicate all the poor people of Indonesia, while Hatta's group also used it often.

And Sukarno wholeheartedly urged the unity of Marhaens and the strengthening of their battlefront. At this time Sukarno had not actually suspended the activities of the PPPKI, but he seldom mentioned that organization in his articles. He now attempted to charge Marhaenism with the synthesis which in 1927–1929 he had expected of the PPPKI. According to Sukarno (and subsequently to the ruling of the Partindo), the word Marhaen was defined to include the Indonesian proletariat, poor farmers, and other poor people of Indonesia, while Marhaenism meant socionationalism and sociodemocracy.[68]

By definition the proletariat formed the nucleus of the Marhaens,

---

66.   Sjahrir, *Renungan*, pp. 103, 121, 129–133, 161–163, 168–169, 177–183.
67.   Sjahrir, *Renungan*, pp. 162–163.
68.   Sukarno, *Dibawah*, p. 253.

but in Sukarno's own mind, as he repeatedly pointed out in his 1933 article, they were the farmers who constituted the greater portion of the Indonesian people. In 1927, Sukarno had presented national unity as a unity of political ideas and political forces, while with Marhaenism he sought the unity of the structural elements of Indonesian society.

On this concept of the Marhaen, there was no dispute between Sukarno and Hatta and Sjahrir. In an article, written in 1932 as propaganda for the PNI-Baru, Hatta cited three of the characteristics of the *desa* (village community) pointed out by van Vollenhoven, a scholar of customary law: the right of the community to oppose (outside pressures), the desire for consensus, and mutual help (*tolong-menolong*). He suggested that these could form the basis of a future democratic Indonesian society.[69] This, however, requires further examination in the light of Hatta's theory of cooperatives and Boeke's theory of Indonesian villages.

As this article has shown, and as Dahm has pointed out, Hatta and Sjahrir took a "European" standpoint; the PNI-Baru itself was a "European" organization.[70] By comparison, Sukarno and his party could be called Indonesian and nationalistic, although the term Indonesian here requires further investigation.

69.   Hatta, *Kumpulan*, pp. 75–76.
70.   Dahm, *Sukarno and the Struggle*, p. 142.

13

A Study of Philippine Manufacturing Corporations

KUNIO YOSHIHARA

INTRODUCTION

Most Asian countries are poor and underdeveloped. Unfortunately, the Philippines falls in this category. Before World War II, there were only a few industries in the Philippines, and most industrial goods were imported from her "mother country" at that time, the United States. In the postwar period however, the Philippines began to industrialize by restricting the import of "unessential" goods, while encouraging domestic production. Visitors from industrial countries to the Philippines readily note the large number of manufactured goods that are imported; this reinforces their preconceived notion that the country is not industrialized. Compared with other countries in Asia, however, the industrial base of the Philippines is broad.

For underdeveloped countries, "industrialization" essentially means increasing manufacturing activities. Industrialization, in other words, means "manufacturization." This view is historically justified. All developed countries today were originally agricultural; their development started with the increase of manufacturing activities. One can argue, however, that increase in productivity is the key to development and that it therefore does not matter where the increase takes place. In this case, it is important to undertake activities which yield the largest increase in productivity; it is possible to develop a country by concentrating on agricultural and extractive industries. But this view is not well received, for development is usually considered synonymous with industrialization.

The task of industrialization is difficult. Shortage of capital and lack of human skills are often cited as obstacles. Nor should we forget cultural and institutional barriers to industrialization. As successfully demonstrated by Japan, industrialization can take place within the institutional framework of Asian societies as well as in the West. Apparently, then, industrialization is possible within a broad institutional framework. Industrialization, however, is built on certain premises such as rationalism and economic calculation, and in certain cultural contexts it may not be possible.

A number of papers and monographs have been written on the topic I will deal with in this paper. The reader unfamiliar with Philippine industrialization would profit from consulting John Power and Gerardo Sicat,[1] Amado Castro,[2] Frank Golay,[3] and G. Hicks and G. McNicoll.[4] All of their work approaches the problem of industrialization by analyzing government policies and examining aggregate data. Although the reliability of aggregate data can be questioned, the macro approach is important in order to gain an overall view of the problem. To study Philippine industrialization, however, I took manufacturing corporations and examined them from various aspects in an approach that has not been previously undertaken. I hope that this article will contribute to a better understanding of Philippine industrialization and provide some useful insights.

THE RESEARCH DESIGN

Since it would be too time-consuming to study all corporations in the manufacturing sector, I have limited them to a manageable number for the purposes of this article. This could have been accomplished by means of random sampling, but since the data for small corporations are of low reliability, I decided to take all corporations above a certain size. Value added is the ideal indicator of the manufacturing activity of corporations, but this data was not readily available. The most available indicator was the amount of sales.

I also limited my study to 1968, the last year for which data were readily available, and which was, in general, a normal year. Athough it is more informative and useful to study corporations over a longer period of time, due mainly to data limitations this was not undertaken here.

1. John Power and Gerardo Sicat, "The Philippines: Industrialization and Trade Policies," *The Philippines and Taiwan* (London: Oxford University Press, 1971).
2. Amado Castro, "Import Substitution and Export Promotion: Trade and Development," *The Structure and Development in Asia*, Proceedings of a conference held by the Japan Economic Research Center, Tokyo, 1968; idem, "Philippine Export Development, 1950–65," *Economic Interdependence in Southeast Asia*, ed. Theodore Morgan and Nyle Spoelstra (Madison: University of Wisconsin Press, 1969).
3. Frank Golay, *The Philippines: Public Policy and National Economic Development* (Ithaca: Cornell University Press, 1961).
4. George Hicks and Geoffrey McNicoll, *Trade and Growth in the Philippines* (Ithaca: Cornell University Press, 1971).

First, I obtained a list of 1,000 corporations.[5] These corporations recorded sales of at least 1.9 million pesos in 1968. From among the 1,000, I took only those in the manufacturing sector which sold over 5 million pesos. This cut-off point netted a total of 254 corporations.

There are many aspects of corporations which are not apparent to an outsider. Therefore, I had to rely on information submitted by the corporations to government agencies or published by the corporations themselves, such as financial statements, lists of stockholders, and brandnames.

The lists of stockholders and financial statements were obtained, insofar as possible, from the Securities and Exchange Commission (SEC). Although I was able to obtain all the desired financial statements, information on ownership was not complete for some corporations. Corporate files at the Board of Investments helped supplement this. Brand names were studied for the light they throw on licensing agreements.

The information collected at government agencies was supplemented by interviews with the corporations when more data were needed. Not all corporations granted me interviews. I had particular difficulties with Chinese and Chinese-Filipino corporations.

Other data on corporations were not systematically collected, although I did gather additional fragmentary information on corporations through interviews or from articles in various newspapers and journals.

THE SAMPLE

The sample consisted of the 254 largest manufacturing corporations in the Philippines.[6] The names of individual corporations are listed in papers witten at University of the Philippines.[7]

5. *Business Day Special Report: The 1000 Largest Corporations* (Quezon City: Enterprise Publication, 1970).

6. The distinction between manufacturing and commercial firms is not very clear-cut for the Philippines. This probably holds true for most underdeveloped countries. I interpreted commercial firms to be those engaged in the sale of goods that do not undergo transformation in their hands. Thus assembling, packaging, and bottling I considered to be manufacturing operations. In cases where firms are engaged in both manufacturing and commercial activities, those whose manufacturing operations accounted for more than 5 million pesos were included in my sample.

7. See Kunio Yoshihara, "Foreign Business Interests in the Philippines: The Compilation of Data on Ownership by Nationality," revised, mimeographed (University of the Philippines, School of Economics) (April, 1971); idem, "Philippine Manufacturing Corporations: The Compilation of Financial and Ownership Data,"

The distribution of corporations by sales is shown in Table 1. Since one dollar was worth four pesos in 1968, 5 million pesos, the amount of minimum sales, were worth about $1.25 million. The largest sales recorded, 532.9 million pesos, were made by a conglomerate firm engaged in a variety of manufacturing operations. The median was in the range of 10.0–19.9 million pesos.

The distribution of corporations by industry is given in Table 2. The scope of manufacturing activities is surprisingly wide. Although one finds no integrated steel mills, no modern shipyards, and no petro-chemical complexes, the list is nonetheless impressive. It is true that many of these corporations are "turn-key" projects or are engaged merely in assembly or similar operations using imported materials, but it would be unfair to categorize all of these corporations as "assembly" or "packaging" industries. For example, although the steel industry is without an operational integrated mill, there are cold mill and metal fabrication facilities.[8]

FOREIGN PARTICIPATION

Foreign corporations started operations in the Philippines for two different reasons. First, they came to the Philippines to maintain and expand their supply of raw materials and to obtain mineral resources and plantation crops. In the case of manufacturing companies, these local items undergo light processing before being sent back to the parent companies. In the case of pineapple, foreign companies operate plantations and canneries and ship the finished product back to the home market.

The second reason concerns exports. Foreign corporations set up subsidiaries when it proved cheaper to undertake certain stages of manufacturing in the Philippines than to ship the finished products themselves from the home country. Transportation costs could be a determining factor, as in the case of beverages. The availability of

---

mimeographed (University of the Philippines, School of Economics) (March, 1971); idem, "The Control of Philippine Manufacturing and Mining Corporations: Data Compilation," mimeographed (University of the Philippines, School of Economics) (May, 1971). These studies list 256 corporations; 2 of them were later found to be commercial firms.

8. One should note that the wood industry is not classified here. This is because the wood industry in the Philippines consists mostly of logging and lumbering. There were fifty corporations in this industry with gross sales of over 5 million pesos in 1968. Some have facilities to produce plywood as well as lumber, but an even larger part of their sales comes from logging. The wood industry therefore is better classified as an extractive rather than a manufacturing industry, thus excluding it from the scope of my study.

TABLE 1
DISTRIBUTION OF MANUFACTURING CORPORATIONS
BY AMOUNT OF SALES

Sales (million pesos)	Number of corporations
5.0–5.9	27
6.0–6.9	24
7.0–7.9	8
8.0–8.9	13
9.0–9.9	6
10.0–19.9	81
20.0–39.9	50
40.0–59.9	16
60.0–99.9	15
100.0–199.9	11
Over 200	3
Total	254

major raw materials in the Philippines could be another. In cases where technology can be transferred fairly easily, it is uneconomical to ship raw materials abroad only to have the finished products sent back again. Also, foreign corporations began to set up packaging and assembly operations when the importing of finished products was made difficult and when foreign producers were forced either to lose the market or to develop later stages of production in the Philippines.

Tables 3 and 4 give the ownership of corporations by nationality. Table 3 breaks down corporations by industry and by nationality of ownership. Nationality control of a corporation is determined by which nationality owns the largest number of common stocks.[9] Since control is based on the largest number of shares, Filipino corporations may have foreign equity investment. Similarly, foreign corporations may have Filipino capital. Therefore, the table does not give much information on the extent of foreign capital participation in Filipino manufacturing corporations.

Table 4 divides corporations into "domestic" and "foreign."

9. According to the Philippine Corporation Law (P.A. No. 1459 [1906]), as amended in 1956, all shares have voting rights without distinction. Their votes determine (1) changes in the number of directors, (2) changes in the amount of capital, (3) amendments to the articles of incorporation, (4) the adoption of bylaws, and (5) the voluntary dissolution of the corporation. Shares classified as voting stock (usually common stock), however, have the exclusive right to determine the election of directors. The owners of such voting stocks control corporate policy.

TABLE 2
The Distribution of Corporations by Industry

Industry	No.	Percentage
Food, beverages and tobacco	80	31.50
1. dairy products	4	1.57
2. sugar	20	7.87
3. flour	6	2.36
4. other foods	18	7.09
5. beverages	4	1.57
6. liquor	6	2.36
7. tobacco	12	4.72
8. copra	10	3.96
Textiles	34	13.39
1. textiles	31	12.21
2. industrial textiles	3	1.18
Chemicals	50	19.69
1. petroleum	4	1.58
2. paint	6	2.36
3. fertilizer	3	1.18
4. drugs	14	5.51
5. soap and cosmetics	5	1.97
6. batteries	3	1.18
7. matches	2	0.79
8. others	13	5.12
Metal fabrication	25	9.84
Household appliances	11	4.33
Machinery and equipment	17	6.69
1. general machinery	7	2.76
2. transport	10	3.93
Others	37	14.56
1. paper and paper products	11	4.33
2. rubber	7	2.76
3. glass	3	1.18
4. cement	9	3.54
5. construction materials (not classified elsewhere)	4	1.57
6. animal feed	2	0.79
7. others	1	0.39
TOTAL	254	

"Domestic" corporations are those with a majority of shares owned by Filipino citizens, and "foreign" corporations are those with a majority of shares owned by aliens. Domestic corporations are divided into "Filipino" and "Chinese-Filipino." This division was motivated by the desire to examine the extent of the participation of Filipinos of Chinese ancestry in the Philippine manufacturing sector. A Chinese-

TABLE 3
The Distribution of Corporations by Industry Showing Ownership by Nationality

Industry	Number of Corporations	Control				
		Filipino	American	Chinese	Japanese	Others
Food, beverages and tobacco	80	53	16	5		6
1. dairy products	4	1	2			1
2. sugar	20	15	3			2
3. flour	6	6				
4. other foods	18	11	6			1
5. beverages	4	1	3			
6. liquor	6	5		1		
7. tobacco	12	8		2		2
8. copra	10	6	2	2		
Textiles	34	29	1	2		2
1. textiles	31	27		2		2
2. industrial textiles	3	2	1			
Chemicals	50	20	27			3
1. petroleum	4	0	3			1
2. paint	6	3	3			
3. fertilizers	3	3				
4. drugs	14	2	12			
5. soap and cosmetics	5	2	2			1
6. batteries	3	2	1			
7. matches	2	1				1
8. others	13	7	6			
Metal fabrication	25	18	4	2	1	
Household appliances	11	6	5			
Machinery and equipment	17	10	7			
1. general machinery and equipment	7	3	4			
2. transport	10	7	3			
Others	37	30	7			
1. paper and paper products	11	9	2			
2. rubber	7	4	3			
3. glass	3	2	1			
4. cement	9	9				
5. construction materials (not classified elsewhere)	4	3	1			
6. animal feed	2	2				
7. others	1	1				
TOTAL	254	166	67	9	1	11

TABLE 4

THE DISTRIBUTION OF CORPORATION BY TYPE OF OWNERSHIP
AND INDUSTRY

Industry	Number of Corporations	Foreign		Domestic	
		Subsidiary	Non-subsidiary	Filipino	Chinese-Filipino
Food, beverages and tobacco	80	16	11	32	21
1. dairy products	4	3			1
2. sugar	20		5	15	
3. flour	6			4	2
4. other foods	18	7		3	8
5. beverages	4	3			1
6. liquor	6		1	4	1
7. tobacco	12	1	3	1	7
8. copra	10	2	2	5	1
Textiles	34	2	3	16	13
1. textiles	31	1	3	14	13
2. industrial textiles	3	1		2	
Chemical	50	28	2	14	6
1. petroleum	4	4			
2. paint	6	1	2	2	1
3. fertilizer	3			3	
4. drugs	14	12		1	1
5. soap and cosmetics	5	2			2
6. batteries	3	1		2	
7. matches	2	1		1	
8. others	13	6		5	2
Metal fabrication	25	5	2	7	11
Household appliances	11	3	2	5	1
Machinery and equipment	17	6	1	7	3
1. general machinery and equipment	7	3	1	3	
2. transport	10	3		4	3
Others	37	5	2	19	11
1. paper and paper products	11	2		4	5
2. rubber	7	3			4
3. glass	3		1	1	1
4. cement	9			9	
5. construction materials (not classified elsewhere)	4		1	2	1
6. animal feed	2			2	
7. others	1			1	
TOTAL	254	65	23	100	66

Filipino is defined as a Filipino citizen who bears a Chinese name. A Filipino is defined as all other Filipino citizens, thereby including Europeans and Americans who have acquired Filipino citizenship. Foreign corporations are divided into "subsidiary" and "nonsubsidiary" categories. A subsidiary corporation is one owned by a foreign corporation engaged in a related line of business. Corporations controlled by foreigners whose primary business is in the Philippines are included under the heading nonsubsidiary. The latter operations are owned mostly by Chinese, Spaniards, and Americans who were either born in the Philippines or who have lived there for a long time.

The existence of nonsubsidiary foreign corporations reflects the colonial experience of the country. Chinese were brought, by colonial rulers, to the Philippines to act as middlemen in economic transactions and to help the economy run smoothly. Many have stayed on in the country since the Philippines gained independence but have not taken citizenship. The Spanish first came to the country as rulers, and many decided to remain when the Philippines became an American colony. Probably out of pride, many chose not to become Filipino citizens. Americans came at the end of the nineteenth century. Under American control, Americans had more privileges and rights than Filipinos and other nationalities. After independence, they remained the most privileged foreigners. In the economic sphere, their rights and privileges are the same as those of Filipino citizens. They control various businesses in the country.

Of the 254 corporations treated here, 88 are foreign owned. These 88 corporations are spread over different areas of the manufacturing sector. The flour milling, animal feed, and cement industries are the few areas where foreign controlled corporations are absent. There are more foreign than domestic corporations in the dairy, petroleum refining, drug, soap and cosmetic industries. All corporations engaged in the refining of petroleum are foreign owned.

Among foreigners, Americans are dominant; of eighty-eight foreign corporations, sixty-seven are American owned. This dominance is related to the "special" relationship between the two countries in this century.

The Philippines were ceded to the United States with the defeat of the Spanish in the Spanish-American War at the end of the nineteenth century. The American period lasted until 1946, interrupted only by the comparatively brief Japanese occupation. Although the postwar period has not been a colonial period, the Philippines extended to Americans rights and privileges enjoyed only by Filipinos. This is the parity clause in the U.S.-Philippine trade agreement which necessitated an amendment to the Philippine Constitution. According to the clause, no law can give Filipinos any advantage not afforded to Americans. This clause has provided a favorable political environment for American business.[10]

Some American corporations came to the Philippines before World War II, but the majority came afterward. This was in response partly to the trade and exchange restrictions imposed by the Philippine government. Starting in the early 1950s and lasting until 1962, the country was under exchange controls. Imports were available only to those who received exchange allocations. Thus, American corporations which had been exporting their products to the Philippines faced the possibility of losing the Philippine market. They had to choose between losing the market or setting up subsidiaries in the country. Since American companies did not want to risk a large amount of capital, and because Philippine trade and exchange policy discouraged the importation of "unessential" consumer goods and placed priority on the import of component parts and raw materials, American investment in assembly and packaging firms assumed a fixed pattern.[11]

Not all American investment in the Philippines can be explained in this way. Some subsidiaries were set up to supply processed goods to the parent company. Some would have been established irrespective of Philippine trade and exchange policies when the export of finished goods would not pay or manufacturing abroad proved more profitable. A large number of American corporations set up in the postwar period, however, were designed to import parts and raw materials from the parent company and assemble or package them for the Philippine market. Under the commerical and exchange policies of the postwar period, this investment offered an alternative to the export of commodities. This type of investment, of course, did not contribute to Philippine foreign exchange earnings.[12]

10. Another advantage for Americans has been the investment guarantee program run by the Agency for International Development of the U.S. government (now administered by the Overseas Private Investment Corporation). This program provides insurance for the loss of investment funds due to expropriation and exchange restrictions. Thus American investors are assured that they can convert local currency into dollars and that they will run little political risk. This insurance is provided for a premium of less than 1 percent of the guaranteed coverage. The insurance program may not play a crucial role in determining investment, but it does help in eliminating a large part of the uncertainty facing an outside investor.

11. This pattern was first pointed out by B. G. Bantegui "Memorandum to Staff Secretariat of NEC Working Committees on Laurel-Langley Agreement," September 26, 1968.

12. The possibility of setting up efficient firms using technologies available in developed

(*Continued on p. 254*)

What is surprising is that only one corporation of the 254 is controlled by a Japanese firm. Japan's economic relations with the Philippines began late in the postwar period. Recently Japan passed the U.S. in the total amount of external trade with the Philippines. Japanese products are found in abundance in department stores and supermarkets, and billboards displaying Japanese brand names are ubiquitous. Yet there is only one corporation controlled by Japanese, and it does not even produce for the Philippine market; it processes raw materials which are sent back to the parent Japanese company. Thus there are no Japanese-owned corporations or subsidiaries producing goods in the Philippines for the domestic market. Rather, Japan's business interests take the form of commodity trade, licensing, and joint ventures with minority equity participation.[13]

DOMESTIC CORPORATIONS

Filipinos own 166 of the 254 corporations in this survey. The existence of a Filipino majority seems to refute the allegation that the economy is dominated by foreigners. Of the 166 corporations, however, 66 are owned by Chinese who have acquired Filipino citizenship. Many Filipinos say of them, "Filipino by citizenship, Chinese at heart" and do not consider them real Filipinos.

The majority of immigrants from China and their descendants, whether they have acquired Filipino citizenship or not, keep their "Chineseness" and do not intermarry with other nationalities. Since they carry Chinese names and look distinctly Mongolian, there is no problem identifying them. We therefore considered all Filipinos with Chinese names to be Chinese-Filipinos. In countries such as the Philippines, however, where there are many *mestizos* of mixed blood, it is sometimes difficult to determine whether or not a person is Chinese-

---

(*Continued from p. 253*)

countries is not very promising. Developed countries have a large domestic market, and their industrial technology is often oriented to mass production. Furthermore, a large number of skilled workers is often required. Underdeveloped countries have neither large domestic markets nor large numbers of skilled workers. As a consequence, foreign manufacturing in underdeveloped countries tends to be a half-hearted operation.

13.　As of June 30, 1970, direct Japanese investment amounted to $11.3 million and went to twenty-four Philippine corporations. A large part of the $11.3 million was invested in the mineral and mineral-processing industry. More recently, however, several Japanese firms have begun joint ventures in the manufacturing sector. These firms are Aji-no-moto (26.7), Matsushita Electronics (40), Toshiba (31.2), Hitachi (30), and Teijin (40). The number in parentheses indicates the percentage of shares held by the Japanese corporation.

Filipino. Some Chinese want to become assimilated into Philippine society and therefore adopt non-Chinese names or intermarry with Filipinos. Others, however, observe Chinese customs and traditions and belong to the Chinese community. A non-Chinese name may have been adopted in many cases to escape harassment rather than to become integrated into the society. Several people in this latter category were listed in my survey; I based my classification of their "nationality" on their degree of closeness to the Chinese community.

If Chinese-Filipino corporations are excluded, the number of Filipino corporations is reduced to 100. These 100 corporations cover the range of Philippine industries. Industries dominated by Filipinos are sugar, liquor, textiles, fertilizers, batteries, cement, and animal feed. These industries are all capital intensive except for liquor and batteries. This gives rise to the hypothesis that the amount of invested capital, on the average, is highest for Filipino corporations. This hypothesis is supported by the fact that industries which require a large amount of capital also need political connections—and politics is monopolized by Filipinos. The government has large investment funds and can guarantee loans from international agencies. A large part of government funding comes from reparations payments from the Japanese government, which roughly average $28 million a year. Funds also come from the sale of P.L. 480 agricultural surpluses. Those with political connections are able to take advantage of these funds since decisions on who receives government loans or guarantees are largely political. In all underdeveloped countries where capital is scarce, capital intensive industries seem to be closely associated with politics.[14]

Some of the 100 "Filipino" corporations are under foreign management or have a substantial amount of foreign investment. Corporations with foreign minority shareholders are treated in this article as domestic, but their control (in terms of who determines corporate strategy) may be in the hands of foreigners. Passive Filipino stockholders and those who follow policies mapped out by foreigners are sometimes referred to

14. The following quotation makes a similar observation on the importance of political acumen in Philippine business operations. ". . . in the Philippines . . . entrepreneurs have been recruited from the political dominant cacique class and . . . their success as entrepreneurs is highly dependent upon their skill in combining political acumen with entrepreneurial initiative. Their viability as businessmen frequently was more dependent upon their capacity to manipulate politically factors influencing the distribution of credit and foreign exchange resources, than upon their skill as managers and entrepreneurs." Frank Golay, *Underdevelopment and Economic Nationalism in Southeast Asia* (Ithaca: Cornell University Press, 1969), p. 451.

as "our kind of people" by foreign executives; Filipinos call them "dummies." Foreigners can control corporations even with a minority of shares if they can find enough of "their kind of people." Going through the lists of stockholders which were available to me, I found that about 15 out of this group of 100 corporations were managed completely or to a considerable extent by foreigners. This reduces the number of Filipino controlled corporations to about 85, and as I could not examine the stockholders of all corporations, 85 may be considered the maximum number of corporations owned and managed by Filipinos.[15]

In hopes of excluding foreigners, particularly the Chinese, from retail businesses, Filipinos passed a retail nationalization law. In spite of the law, they were still unable to break into the retail business. Control of the commercial network of the country remains in the hands of the Chinese community. Filipinos fare better in the manufacturing sector, but not much. They control and manage about 35 percent of the 254 largest manufacturing corporations. Although they control national politics, they are doing poorly in the economic sphere, which piques the pride of Filipino nationalists.

THE RATE OF RETURN

A Filipino businessman is quoted as saying, "A 25 per cent annual return on investment in the Philippines is considered a minimum; a 35 per cent return ordinary; a 50 per cent return far from unknown"[16]. Since capital is scarce in underdeveloped countries, one would expect the rate of return on invested capital to be higher than in developed countries. This view is partially supported by the high interest rates on deposits and loans. A 10 percent annual interest rate is not particularly high in the Philippines. Since invested capital involves risk, a rate of return reflecting the risk factor is necessarily higher than the normal interest rate. The above quotation is no exaggeration.

15. I determined the nationality of stockholders and executives on the basis of their citizenship, but some of those I classified as foreigners identify strongly with Filipino society and culture. Also, many Filipinos are reluctant to identify their corporations as foreign. For example, about a dozen corporations are managed by Soriano y Sia. Soriano y Sia is operated by Andre Soriano, Jr. and Jose Maria Soriano, the sons of the late Andre Soriano, Sr. They are ethnically Spanish, but following World War II, they acquired United States citizenship; many Filipinos consider them Filipino entrepreneurs rather than American. The fact that Soriano enterprises are publicly held corporations may also add to the comparative mildness of the nationalistic feeling directed against them. Such feelings are usually directed most intensely toward American corporations.

16. Eugene Lang, "Mission Finds the Philippines a Land of Opportunity Seeking Joint Ventures," *International Commerce* (December 17, 1962): 6.

TABLE 5

THE DISTRIBUTION OF THE RATE OF RETURN TO NET WORTH

Rate of Return (in percent)	Foreign		Domestic	
	Subsidiary	Nonsubsidiary	Filipino	Chinese-Filipino
Loss	7	0	25	4
0 – 5.0	2	5	20	16
5.1–10.0	5	3	10	17
10.1–15.0	8	3	19	11
15.1–20.0	9	4	10	5
20.1–30.0	9	6	12	7
30.1–50.0	15	1	2	5
Over 50.0	10	1	2	1
TOTAL	65	23	100	66
Median (in percent)	21.5	15.3	7.5	8.9
Maximum (in percent)	297.3	55.1	57.2	51.6

Table 5, however, would seem to indicate the contrary. This table shows the distribution of the rate of return for the four groups of corporations: subsidiary, nonsubsidiary, Filipino, and Chinese-Filipino. Rate of return is defined as the ratio of net income to net worth. Net income is profit after corporate income taxes inclusive of dividends on preferred stocks. Net worth is the sum of paid-in capital and accumulated surplus. The median rate of return is 21.5 percent for the subsidiary group, 15.3 percent for the nonsubsidiary one, 7.5 percent for the Filipino group, and 8.9 percent for Chinese-Filipino corporations. None of these exceed the 25 percent stated as the minimal rate of return by the Filipino businessman. Corporations which earned the "ordinary rate of return" of 35 percent were at most 15 percent in 1968.

It may be argued that my choice of the year 1968 is arbitrary. Since this was not a recession year and was normal in several other respects, it is unlikely that the picture would be radically different for other years. This is partly supported by Castro's study.[17] He computed the rate of return for mining, agriculture, and manufacturing during the period 1955–1962 and found that none of these sectors exceeded a 25 percent rate of return. The maximum was 23 percent for the mining sector.

A rate of return of 21.5 percent for subsidiary and 15.3 percent

17. Amado Castro, "Import Substitution and Export Promotion: Trade and Development," The Structure and Development in Asia, Proceedings of a conference held by the Japan Economic Research Center, Tokyo, 1968.

TABLE 6
THE PERCENTAGE RATE OF RETURN BY INDUSTRY AND OWNERSHIP (MEDIAN)

Industry	Number of Corporations	Foreign		Domestic	
		Subsidiary	Non-subsidiary	Filipino	Chinese-Filipino
Food, beverages and tobacco					
1. dairy products	38.4	43.6			9.2
2. sugar	13.4		16.4	10.8	
3. flour	5.2			5.2	
4. other foods	11.0	13.1		4.7	8.3
5. beverages	45.4	58.3			32.3
6. liquor	16.7		16.4	22.8	8.7
7. tobacco	15.8	2.7	16.7	49.6	14.3
8. copra	10.5	0.0	29.0	10.5	6.0
Textiles					
1. textiles	3.1	11.5	3.1	negative	9.0
2. industrial textiles	15.2	11.1		19.7	
Chemicals					
1. petroleum	9.9	9.9			
2. paint	17.5	15.9	19.6	0.0	21.6
3. fertilizer	negative			negative	
4. drugs	18.5	30.3		16.0	28.3
5. soap and cosmetics	19.8	19.8			15.5
6. batteries	12.5	32.8		10.2	
7. matches	25.0	36.6		13.4	
8. others	12.0	16.5		16.4	0.0
Metal fabrication	7.5	16.0	7.2	7.9	4.8
Household appliances	13.0	33.3	24.7	3.1	3.3
Machinery and equipment					
1. general machinery	11.3	34.1	5.6	5.9	
2. transport	14.1	15.1		15.2	13.2
Others					
1. paper and paper products	9.5	0.0		6.9	9.6
2. rubber	11.1	28.4			9.4
3. glass	10.8		12.9	10.8	6.7
4. cement	5.1			5.1	
5. construction materials (not classified elsewhere)	14.8		14.3	9.6	20.3
6. animal feed	0.0			0.0	
7. others	negative			negative	
TOTAL	11.5	21.5	15.3	7.5	8.9

Note: 0.0 indicates that as many coporations lost money as recorded positive returns.

for nonsubsidiary businesses may not be as high as originally expected, but it can be accepted as a reasonable return. The return rate is higher than that of domestic corporations due largely to superior management, marketing know-how, and technology. These are well advanced in highly developed countries where a high return rate reflects not only the return on capital but also the effect of the intangibles brought in from abroad. One reason a corporation seeks direct investment in another country is to further utilize funds already expended on research and development.

According to Table 6, which shows the rate of returns by industry and ownership, the average rate of return for foreign subsidiaries exceeds 30 percent in the following industries: dairy, beverages, drugs, batteries, matches, household appliances, and general machinery. For foreign nonsubsidiaries, there is no industry in which the rate of return exceeds 30 percent; only the copra industry comes close to this figure. There are, however, industries in which foreign companies do not earn a good return. In the tobacco industry, for example, foreign subsidiaries earned returns of only 2.7 percent; for copra and paper products, there were as many companies which lost money as recorded positive returns. In the case of industries producing paper products, however, the divergence between two foreign subsidiaries was large: one company had been losing money for the past few years, whereas the other earned returns of over 30 percent. Both are well-known American firms. Another thing we should note in Table 6 in connection with foreign corporations is that the petroleum-refining industry, which is monopolized by foreign companies, is not doing particularly well. Their average return of 9.9 percent is not low but much less than one would expect for such big international companies.

It is hard to ask in meaningful terms whether foreign corporate earnings are too high since it is difficult to ascertain what a reasonable rate of return is, but emotion runs high on this issue. Filipino nationalists feel that foreign companies are withdrawing too much from the country by way of high returns. When we examine Table 7 showing the rate of returns to paid-in capital, the difference in earnings between foreign and domestic corporations becomes more pronounced. Foreign subsidiaries in one year earn a full one-third of the amount of capital originally brought into the country. A high rate of return is a reward for superior know-how and entrepreneurship; however, one can legitimately question whether it is not reasonable to regulate the overseas remittance of profits and to force corporations earning high returns to use part of their earnings for domestic social development.

Returns for domestic corporations seem too low. Witness the 7.5

TABLE 7
THE RATE OF RETURN TO PAID-IN CAPITAL

Rate of Return (in percent)	Foreign		Domestic	
	Subsidiary	Nonsubsidiary	Filipino	Chinese-Filipino
No information	3	0	0	0
Loss	7	0	25	4
0 – 5.0	2	3	20	14
5.1–10.0	1	4	8	15
10.1–15.0	3	1	10	7
15.1–20.0	4	3	10	9
20.1–30.0	9	6	9	7
30.1–50.0	12	4	9	8
Over 50.0	24	2	9	2
TOTAL	65	23	100	66
Median (in percent)	32.8	21.8	8.7	9.7
Maximum (in percent)	720.0	184.6	118.6	81.4

percent rate of return for Filipino and 8.9 percent rate of Chinese-Filipino corporations. These figures appear low, not so much in comparison with the return rate of foreign corporations, but simply because the interest rate on time deposits apparently is higher than the return on invested capital. Capital here would appear to earn more money in banks than in corporations.

In cases of disequilibrium, the return on invested capital can be theoretically lower than the interest rate, but the real reason for this situation in the Philippines is that the financial statements from which I computed the returns are not reliable. Most corporations are owned by a single family or a small number of closely related families. A corporation is not a purely economic institution whose sole aim is to maximize the rate of return. Its main purpose is to increase the welfare of family members. The rate of return in Philippine manufacturing corporations cannot therefore be strictly compared to that of developed countries where management and ownership are separate.

One factor resulting in a low rate of return is the unnecessary expenditure often lavished on family members occupying high positions in corporations. This often includes foreign travel once or twice a year, large salaries for wives and other family members, expense accounts for automobiles, food, restaurants, and night clubs, as well as expenses for prestige items not strictly needed for business transactions such as helicopters and airplanes. These expenses must be added to earnings when comparing the rate of return with interest rates.

A second factor is the underreporting of earnings. This is illegal, but investigation by the Bureau of Internal Revenue is often lax and besides, there is a tremendous incentive to underreport profits. The corporate income tax rate is roughly 30 percent which is low compared with the rate for developed countries. Many Filipino businessmen try to pay as little tax as possible. Although this may be true of all national-ities, in developed countries such offenders may be caught and have to pay a heavy penalty, but this possibility seems unlikely in the Philip-pines. If an offender does pay, the money goes to the political friend who saves his neck.

These factors reduce the reliability of the rate of returns shown in Table 5 and contribute to the low rate of return for domestic corpora-tions. Foreign corporations are less likely to underreport earnings, and their unnecessary costs also seem to be much smaller. But foreign corporations may resort to legal maneuvering to maintain or enlarge remittances to the parent company. As pointed out earlier, they exist in order to provide increased sales to the parent company, so they often resort to a variety of procedures to make this possible. It does not matter whether the rate of returns in the Philippines is low or high; subsidiaries can be sacrificed for the benefit of the parent company. If the remittance of profits is difficult owing to government restrictions or to a high tax rate, they can afford to reduce their profits in the Philippines as long as it does not injure the interests of the parent company. If a corporation is set up to supply raw materials to the home country, it can underlist export prices in order to reduce its paper profits in the Philippines. If a subsidiary buys raw materials and parts from a parent company, such items can be overpriced so that the profits of the subsidiary business decline, in effect draining would-be profits out of the country.

"One large U.S. manufacturer, for example, concedes that it penalizes some of its overseas subsidiaries for the good of the total corporation by forcing them to pay more than necessary for parts they import from the parent and from other subsidiaries. Says one of the company's executives: 'We do this in countries where we either antici-pate or already face restrictions on profit repatriation. We want some way to get our money out.'"[18] Foreign subsidiaries which are losing money or have a low return may resort to such operations.[19]

Figures should be interpreted with care. The 7.5 percent rate of

18. "Multinational Companies," *Business Week*, April 20, 1963.
19. For the practice of underpricing canned pineapple, see Frank Golay, *The Philip-pines: Public Policy and National Economic Development* (Ithaca: Cornell University Press, 1961).

return for Filipino corporations and 8.9 percent rate for Chinese-Filipino corporations may be fictitious. One important question is raised, however, by Table 5. Even if the median seems low, is it not possible that there are many corporations which are inefficient and which should eventually be phased out? There are twenty-five Filipino and four Chinese-Filipino corporations listed which lost money and twenty Filipino and sixteen Chinese-Filipino Corporations listed which has less than 5 percent earnings. Even if we take into consideration underreporting and unnecessary costs, there seem to be a number of corporations which can be considered potential failures.

I cannot offer a good explanation for the losses and low returns in Chinese-Filipino corporations, except to note the possibility that the scope of their underreporting is considerably greater than that of Filipino corporations. This cannot be substantiated by evidence, however. For many Filipino corporations, these losses or low returns seem to be genuine. Many companies which lost money are in capital intensive or crowded industries. As shown in Table 6, the median return was negative in textiles and fertilizers, whereas the median was only 3.1 percent for household appliances and 5.1 percent for cement.[20]

Textiles and cement are political industries in the sense that, being capital intensive, owners obtain large loans from government financial institutions or from the Reparations Commission. Such money is given to the friends of politicians or, at least, is secured through politicians. In the case of textiles, the major raw material is cotton, which is sold to the Philippines by the U.S. under P.L. 480. Cotton is allocated to textile manufacturers by a government agency in charge of the program; who gets what amount is mainly a political decision.

Cement and household appliances are faced with the same problem: the market is crowded. There are nine cement and eleven appliance companies in our list, and many smaller ones. Two cement corporations suffered losses and two more earned only 1 percent on invested capital in 1968. In appliances there were only two Filipino corporations which earned more than a 10 percent return; the rest either suffered losses or earned returns of less than a 3 percent.

Most industries with a low rate of return were set up in the postwar period. The government apparently had no consistent policy to regulate or give assistance to the private sector. As a consequence, there are

20.   In 1968, the median of fixed assets was 4.4 million pesos for foreign subsidiaries, 3.3 for foreign nonsubsidiaries, 8.4 for domestic Filipino, and 4.6 for domestic Chinese-Filipino corporations. Among domestic Filipino corporations, the textile, cement, fertilizer, and sugar industries were capital intensive; the median was 21.2 million pesos for textiles, 31.3 for cement, 22.9 for fertilizers, and 15.0 for sugar.

many corporations whose utilization of capital is at a very low level owing to too much competition.[21]

It may be unfair to say that no one in the government realized the grave consequences of too many corporations being set up in the same industry. If anyone did, however, he was overriden by politicians or high-ranking government officials who had something to gain from establishing new firms. It was therefore in their interest to establish as many firms as they could. Gain was not solely restricted to them, however. Incorporators also profited and gains were sometimes so large initially that there was no strong incentive to make a firm a going concern. When machines were bought from foreign sellers using government loans or reparations money, kickbacks were demanded which sometimes amounted to considerable sums.

LICENSING AGREEMENTS

Corporations can enter the foreign market by any of three methods. One is to export a commodity produced in the home country to the foreign market. Another is to set up a subsidiary in a foreign country to produce the same commodity for the foreign market. The third way is to find a foreign company which will produce the company's commodity and to receive payments in the form of royalties and fees for the technical skills, marketing, management knowhow, and trademark rights granted to the company. A corporation which wants to increase its sales in a foreign market has to choose the best alternative under these circumstances.

When the third method is chosen, licensing agreements are drawn up between two corporations. The licensee produces a commodity taking advantage of the rights granted, and the licensor abstains from exporting the commodity to that country's market. This seems the fastest way to get into a foreign market or to enter a market too small to justify larger investment. Most staffing problems are avoided and advantage can be taken of the licensee's sales capabilities and relations with local governments. This may be better than direct investment for small and medium-size companies whose capital and managerial staffs are limited, but for multinational corporations moving aggressively into an overseas market, a subsidiary may be preferable.

There are three government agencies in the Philippines which

---

21. In underdeveloped countries where capital is scarce relative to labor, it is natural to expect that its utilization rate be high. In capital intensive industries in these countries, however, the utilization rate is low. This is because a large part of the capital used to purchase machinery is obtained at low interest rates from governmental or international financial institutions.

have information on licensing agreements: the Patent Office, the Central Bank, and the Board of Investments. None of these agencies had complete information on licensing in the early part of 1971, when this research was conducted. The number of licensing agreements registered in the Patent Office is small. I have cause to believe, from information gained from other sources, that most licensing agreements entered into by corporations are not to be found in the records. Patents and trademarks are registered in the Patent Office for protection, but the registry of a licensing agreement evidently does not offer much legal advantage. The Board of Investments has information on licensing agreements of those corporations registered to take advantage of tax incentives, but most of our 254 corporations do not appear in the list of registered enterprises. The Central Bank should have the most comprehensive information on licensing, but from 1962 to 1970 there were no foreign exchange controls, so there was no need for Filipino licensees to provide the Central Bank with copies of their agreements in order to obtain foreign exchange. Since foreign exchange is now once again under government control, corporations will need foreign exchange to pay for royalties and fees, so they will eventually have to supply such supporting documents as licensing agreements to the Bank. At the time of my research, the Central Bank was the ideal place to obtain this information, although I was told that the information was incomplete. Access to corporate files at the bank was not granted, however, and the study had to rely on other sources. One source of information was the financial statement submitted to the SEC. Another was a report by the UNCTAD secretariat on restrictive business practices.[22]

In the financial statements submitted to the SEC, items such as royalty and technical service fees are included. For 154 of the 254 corporations, I was able to determine whether such payments were being made by examining their financial statements. For the remaining 100 corporations the statement is consolidated, and it was not clear whether such payments were being made. Of the 154 corporations, 35 were paying either royalties or fees.

Surprisingly, eleven of the thirty-five corporations paying such royalties or fees were subsidiaries. Since a subsidiary is set up with the capital and most or all of the intangible assets of the mother company, there would seem to be no need to draw up a licensing agreement stipulating the terms of payment. Apparently this is often done in

22. UNCTAD Secretariat, "Restrictive Business Practices," (January, 1971), incorporates Finance Secretary Virata's report on the Philippines.

underdeveloped countries, however, as a precondition for defending patent and trademark rights against third parties, for tax purposes, or for foreign exchange regulations.[23] In the Philippines, however, the tax on royalties is 30 percent, which is about the same as the corporate income tax rate. Therefore, there does not seem to be any tax advantage which would motivate a subsidiary to enter into a licensing agreement paying royalties to the parent company. Tax advantage is to be found, instead, in obtaining payment as a technical service fee rather than as royalty, for there is no tax on the former. The eleven subsidiaries mentioned above paid 4.4 million pesos in royalties and 2.4 million pesos in technical service fees, a total of 6.8 million pesos in 1968.

The remaining twenty-four corporations paid 22.6 million pesos in royalties and 0.7 million pesos in technical service fees, a total of 23.3 million pesos. The total amount of payments made by the thirty-five corporations was 30.0 million pesos, equivalent to $7.5 million. Since total imports for the Philippines in 1968 were $1.133 billion, government foreign expenditures nearly $21 million, and other invisible payments $676 million, the royalty payment of $7.5 million seems to have been only a small part of total foreign exchange payments.

Large subsidiaries tend to make consolidated financial statements, so they might include large amounts for royalties and fees. These are alternative forms of profit remittance, however, and do not particularly concern me here. What I was really interested in was payments made by domestic corporations. For these corporations, however, payments do not seem to amount to a large sum.

Of the above twenty-four corporations, six are in cigarettes, four in household appliances, three in paints, three in food, two in synthetic textiles, one in batteries, one in drugs, one in flour, one in cosmetics, one in the match industry, and one in the metal fabrication industry. As pointed out, the royalties and fees for these twenty-four corporations amounted to 23.3 million pesos. Among the twenty-four, only two are in intermediate industries not involving foreign brandnames. Their payments were for patent or know-how rights, and the payments amounted to only 7 thousand pesos. The other domestic corporations paying substantial amounts in royalties or fees are involved with foreign brand names and can be readily identified by examining the brand names of domestic corporations.

Of the 189 nonsubsidiary corporations in our list of 254, 35 use foreign brand names. Eight are in household appliances, six in tobacco, four in transportation, four in paints, three in flour, two in foods, two

---

23.   UNCTAD Secretariat, "Restrictive Business Practices," (January, 1971): 33.

in synthetics, two in liquors, one in drugs, one in batteries, one in chemicals, and one in cosmetics. One brand name in food, two in transportation, and two in household appliances are Japanese; most of the others are American.

The largest royalties were paid by the cigarette industry followed by the flour industry. The only industry for which there was no indication of royalties was transportation machinery. Of the four domestic corporations assembling cars or motorcycles, two gave detailed financial statements, and two gave consolidated ones. According to the two detailed statements, the corporations did not pay royalties. There are probably no royalty payments under licensing agreements in the transportation machinery industry. This raises the question, then, of why some industries use foreign brand names without making any payments while others make payments?

In the case of both the cigarette and the flour industry, raw materials are not purchased from the trademark owner. The cigarette industry blends domestically grown tobacco leaves with imported Virginia leaves. Flour millers use imported wheat. Virginia tobacco leaves and wheat, however, are sold to the Philippines by the U.S. government under P.L. 480 and are not supplied by the brand name owner. Therefore the only way the owner of a band name can be paid in such cases is to receive money for the use of the name. However, in the transport machinery industry, the owner of the brand name sells parts, and there is no need for royalties if the agreement is written in such a way that the licensee is forced to buy overpriced parts. A licensor normally relies on royalty payments, then, if there is no possibility of tied purchasing. If tied purchasing is possible, the sale of parts or raw materials can be regulated to increase profits. In such cases, royalties are not necessary.

Although no royalties appear to be paid in the transport machinery industry, the household appliance and paint industries present a mixed picture. Some companies pay royalties while others do not. Of the seven household appliance corporations which use foreign brand names, four corporations paid royalties and one did not; there is no information on the remaining two. In the paint industry, three paid royalties and one did not. This gives rise to the hypothesis that when no royalty is paid, the substitution of local parts or raw materials for imported ones is made difficult by the licensing agreement. Such substitution is probably easier if royalties are paid.

The difficulty of substituting domestically produced parts for imported ones is illustrated in the case of transport machinery by the practice of "deletion allowance." Under this practice a licensor sells a package of various parts needed for assembly with the price of these parts itemized. The licensor might charge, for example, $50 for a certain part in a package deal, but if the assembler substitutes a local product for the imported part, he will get only a fraction of the $50 refunded, which is often lower than the cost of local production. There is therefore no incentive on the part of licensees to purchase local parts. Many of those who argued for setting up assembly plants in the initial stage of industrialization hoped that "backward integration" would gradually proceed and that parts would eventually be produced locally, but the "deletion allowance" does not permit such a gradual transition.

Since the Philippines is in an early stage of industrialization and needs various types of assistance in the form of expertise, the question remains why royalties and technical service fees are of such small importance to intermediate industries. One explanation might be that Filipino corporations cannot afford to pay these fees, but this is not the whole story. There are two additional important explanations. One is purchasing tied to the provider of assistance. For example, a chemical corporation might need instruction on production processes as well as foreign technicians; these may be provided "free" if the corporation buys raw materials from the foreign company giving the assistance. These fees are included in the price of the raw materials. The second explanation is that technical expertise is wrapped up in the capital equipment provided, so that fees for patents and technical assistance are included in the price of the equipment. Technicians to maintain and repair machinery may also be provided "free" for an extended period of time.

CONCLUDING REMARKS

Many other aspects of corporations would have to be studied in order to fully understand Philippine industrialization. For example, the socio-logical background of Filipino entrepreneurs, the sources of industrial capital, and Philippine industrial groupings should be inquired into, but such questions must be left for future research.

Our knowledge of Philippine corporations is far from perfect. This study, however, has hopefully helped point out several problems which must be taken into consideration by Filipinos when seeking to determine future industrial strategy for their country. They would seem to be as follows. (1) Import substitution often leads to inefficiency and the misallocation of resources. What possible alternatives are there? (2) What should be the balance between import substitution and export promotion? (3) Is it not desirable to allow joint ventures with foreign majority equity in the export industry? (4) What benefits are to be gained by setting up capital intensive factories which are run most efficiently in markets far larger than any offered by the Philippines? (5) Is it not preferable to restrict the number of firms in the same industry and permit oligopolistic competition?

Industrialization is not directed solely toward economic welfare but is pursued with a variety of goals under several constraining influences. For example, in the Philippines the strong promotion of domestic industrialization has led to various nationalistic measures. At the same time, the Philippines has a number of pressing economic problems such as malnutrition, unemployment, and a low level of income. From a purely economic point of view, free trade and capital movement are the best policies for solving these problems while increasing the living standards of the country as a whole. Such policies, however, have to be modified because the Philippines, naturally enough, want to exist as a politically and culturally distinct entity. Some of the policies aimed at this latter goal have resulted in a slowing down of economic growth: economics alone is too imperfect a guide to determine optimum, balanced industrial planning.

I would like to emphasize that because of their rapidly growing populations, such underdeveloped countries as the Philippines do not have enough time to pursue industrialization at their own pace. Even if population growth slackens in the near future, a large number of people must still find gainful employment. To accomplish this, the country will have to become involved in international trade to a considerable extent. Success will not be accomplished by duplicating the industrial experience of developed countries. Instead, an attempt should be made to foresee the pattern of future world trade and to place priority on the development of those industries which can compete successfully in the international market.

AUTHOR'S NOTE: The research for this article was undertaken during my stay at the University of the Philippines as a visiting professor of economics during the 1970–1971 academic year. I would like to express my appreciation to Amado Castro and Leon Mears who were helpful in various stages of the research, to Commissioner Yabyabin at the Securities and Exchange Commission for his cooperation, to Elizabeth Ong and German Palabyab for their competent assistance, and to the Rockefeller Foundation for financing this research. A part of this article was presented to the Conference on Agriculture and Economic Development of the Japan Economic Research Center, held at Tokyo and Hakone in September 1971.

14

The Conditions Governing Agricultural Development in Southeast Asia

TAKESHI MOTOOKA

INTRODUCTION

In order to develop the agriculture of Southeast Asia many obstacles must be overcome. Southeast Asia, composed of nine countries, possesses aspects both of unity and of diversity, but in this article I propose to disregard the conditions peculiar to each country and to elucidate the basic conditions common to all the countries of Southeast Asia.

DECISION-MAKING UNITS IN AGRICULTURAL DEVELOPMENT

It need hardly be reiterated that in agricultural development the relevant decision-making units are most important. In Southeast Asia we may cite three such units—the planters, the peasantry, and the governments.

The Planters

Until World War II, the plantation entrepreneurs played an extremely important role in agricultural development in Southeast Asia. In particular, in the peninsular and island countries of Malaysia, Indonesia, the Philippines, etc., such tropical crops as rubber, sugar cane, coconuts, palm oil, sisal, tea, coffee and cotton were developed under plantation management. The role performed by the colonial governments in these regions consisted in assisting the development of these plantations by providing legal backing for the acquisition of land, and carrying out experimental research on agricultural technology by making available the required labor force. On the other hand, the colonial authorities hardly paid any attention to the development of native agriculture; it was placed in a subordinate position within a dual structure of colonial agriculture consisting of foreign commercialized plantation agriculture and native subsistence agriculture.

In the rice-producing countries of mainland Southeast Asia, Burma, and Thailand, and in Indo-China, the influence of the planter was limited, as were the functions performed by the government. However, the role of plantations in prewar agricultural development in peninsular Southeast Asia was extremely large.

The most marked change in the postwar agricultural structure in Southeast Asia has been the decline of the plantation. This is despite the fact that in Malaya the greater part of the rubber plantations, formerly run by white men, has passed into the hands of overseas Chinese and in Indonesia some plantations, formerly run by the Dutch, are under the management of Indonesians or overseas Chinese. In South Viet-Nam plantations run by the French have been confiscated. In postwar Thailand two Japanese sugar companies, Shibaura Seito and Osaka Seito entered the field of sugarcane cultivation. The planter may be regarded as having lost his position as one of the basic decision-making units in agricultural development as a result of management factors which have rendered the cultivation of tropical crops by native peasants more profitable than plantation agriculture and as a result of the political factor, represented by the sharp decrease in the numbers of foreign planters, which has accompanied the formation and development of the new nation states. It seems unlikely that the planters will ever recover their lost position.

The Peasantry

Those directly concerned with agricultural production are the cultivating peasants themselves. Investments by landlords to bring new land under cultivation by coastal, riverine, and lacustrine reclamation and by land improvement works are few. An exception is the role of landlord capital in the development of rice cultivation in the Rangsit area of the Central Plain in Thailand at the beginning of the present century. Landlords also played a major role in the development of rice cultivation in the Irrawaddy delta in Burma. Both of these instances are historical, and at present landlords have very little to do with agricultural development.

It is said of the cultivating peasantry of Southeast Asia that "they are never in desperate want of food because bananas, coconuts, and so on grow wild in that region, that the very simplest of housing, enough to deep out wind and rain, is sufficient for them and that since it is warm they need not worry about clothing; consequently, there is no obstacle to their making a livelihood, even if they be lazy and extremely deficient in the will to work." It is even thought that it may not be possible to treat them as *homines economici* at the level of economic theory. From my own on-the-spot investigations, I feel that such general theories concerning the peasantry of Southeast Asia are apt to lead us into error. Considering only the question of the "will to work," for example, there is a marked difference between the peasantry of Malaya and that of Thailand, although these two countries are adjacent. What I wish to stress here are the results obtained from my village surveys in alluvial plains, such as those of the Irrawaddy in Burma and the Chao Phraya in Thailand. In particular the peasantry of the Central Plain in Thailand treat new consumer goods such as clothing, food and condiments, beer, tobacco, etc., as a matter of course and there is an influx of transistor radios, motorcycles, and other durable consumer goods. However since they do not have the income to pay for these articles frustration has set in. Recognition of the necessity for an increase in income in order to accompany the change in the pattern of consumption and a positive desire to improve the management of holdings in order to produce this increase in income, are the necessary conditions for their qualifying as *homines economici*.

It is abundantly clear, however, that such conditions as tradition, religion, education, technology, and the level of knowledge have prevented them from becoming *homines economici* in the fullest sense. For example, let us consider the question of the low degree of social consciousness among the peasantry. In Thailand, in times of water shortage, it is normal practice for the peasants to break down common embankments and draw water into their own fields. They also ignore the damage to common embankments caused when their water-buffaloes cross irrigation canals and ditches. Both these features cause problems for the maintenance of irrigation installations in the country. As a countermeasure, the government has appointed supervisors of irrigation canals and ditches, but it is next to impossible for them to administer all the irrigation canals in this extensive plain.

However, we must not conclude from the peasants' lack of social consciousness that "no matter how much effort governments may put into agricultural development it will be no good, because they will not cooperate." The peasants desire development, but they lack technological inputs and expertise, so while they fulfil some of the necessary conditions of a decision-making unit in agricultural development, they are deficient in others.

At this point there arises the question of peasant education or educational investment. This may be divided into school education (particularly elementary) and agricultural or rural extension work.

School education contributes indirectly to agricultural development, but agricultural improvement and extension work are more urgent as they have direct results; and the consciousness, level of knowledge, and technology of the peasantry would no doubt increase. Of course some time would have to elapse before these objectives are realized. The position of the peasantry as a decision-making unit in agricultural development will depend to a large extent on government policies.

The Government

The agricultural improvement and extension work just mentioned is a task which falls to the government. In the future, advances in agriculture will not depend on the peasants themselves but will be initiated by governments. In this connection the government has two functions. One is that of basic policy, of deciding in which direction to advance development, and the other is to provide financial backing sufficient to implement the basic policy. In other words, the government must perform an entrepreneurial role which includes innovation in agricultural development. I shall discuss the provision of funds later as part of this entrepreneurial role. For the present I wish to examine the formulation and execution of agricultural development plans by the government as a decision-making unit.

What is demanded of the government before all else is political stability. Agricultural development is not easily advanced in those countries in postwar Southeast Asia which have been in a continuous state of political confusion such as North and South Viet-Nam and Indonesia. In contrast, Thailand is a model case of economic development, not only in Southeast Asia but among the developing countries in general, and this has been due in very great measure to the political stability of the country since the war. Rapid development took place under the influence of the Sarit regime which came to power in 1958. Its policy was to unify by reorganizing national mechanisms, and to introduce foreign capital for joint investment, with state capital, in development. There are also differences between the countries of Southeast Asia with regard to their governments' "positive posture" as decision-making units in agricultural development. It would seem that Thailand and Malaysia have enjoyed political stability and a dynamic government attitude toward agricultural development, while Indonesia had neither until toward the end of the 1960s.

Apart from these basic conditions, there are also a number of problems in administration. The first is inefficiency, coupled with the lack of the will to work on the part of government officials. Malaysian officials, influenced by the British, are very capable and industrious, but as a whole it is doubtful whether the administrative efficiency of the governments in the region is sufficient for effective agricultural development. Studies of administrative efficiency and inservice training are urgently required.

The second problem is that of administrative centralization, which has a strong influence on agricultural development. The most extreme example of this is to be found in Thailand where the experimental stations in the provinces act entirely on instructions from the Ministry of Agriculture in Bangkok. They do not even keep the data obtained from their studies; instead these are sent to Bangkok to be kept at the ministry. Under such circumstances researchers have no enthusiasm to press forward with their experiments to meet the needs of agriculture. It is, of course, natural that the central government should have a great say in such matters as the formulation and implementation of development plans, but the delegation of responsibilities to the provinces would seem to be necessary in order to render administration more efficient. The tendency for government officials to dislike working in the provinces or the rural areas is also a great obstacle to agricultural development.

The third problem is that, because of such social conditions as the influence of class or caste systems or an "elite consciousness" among government officials, even those whose business it is to deal with agricultural matters stick firmly to office work and have little contact with the peasants. Because of this gap between officials and peasants, it frequently happens that planned agricultural development policy is divorced from reality and the means for its implementation do not fully penetrate the peasantry.

Another problem is that of administrative sectionalism accompanying the bureaucratic system, and the more underdeveloped a country, the worse the sectionalism. In the case of Thailand, it is no exaggeration to say that not only is there no coordination between the various ministries, but the departments within each ministry are independent of one another. For instance in encouraging cultivation of other crops on land use only in the rainy season for rice, the Ministry of the Interior, the Department of Rice, the Department of Agriculture in the Ministry of Agriculture, the Department of Irrigation and the Department of Land Cooperatives in the Ministry of National Development, all act independently. As a result of this sectionalism startling instances of losses have come to light.[1]

1. T. Motooka, "Tai nōgyō ni okeru seisan kiban no seibi" [Basic Requirements for Agricultural Development in Thailand] *Southeast Asian Studies* 4, (Kyoto: Center for Southeast Asian Studies, Dec., 1966): 525.

One cannot overlook corruption and graft in some governments of Southeast Asia. Such countries as Burma and Malaysia enjoy "clean" government, but where corruption and graft have made their way into the administrative system, extending from the center to the provinces, planning at the center is subject to extraordinary distortions, as is its execution at the periphery of the administrative network.

CAPITAL FOR AGRICULTURAL DEVELOPMENT

Capital for agricultural development may be divided into two broad categories. First is individual or private capital for the purposes of forming and developing individual agricultural holdings. This includes fixed capital for irrigation and drainage, for heavy agricultural machinery and implements, and for the larger domestic animals, as well as liquid capital for seed, fertilizers, agricultural chemicals, small agricultural machinery and implements, the smaller domestic animals and so on, in addition to which some quantity of circulating capital is also necessary. Second is the social capital required to provide the basis for the individual agricultural holding. This is "capital for the infrastructure," and in the broad sense of this term investment in education can be included. This must be borne by the state.

I will now consider private or individual capital investment which, in principle, should be carried out by the cultivating peasants, insofar as agricultural development is carried out by individual farms. However, in the developing countries this is not an easy task. It is necessary to know actual savings and investments among the peasants to understand the Southeast Asian peasant economy, but regrettably up to the present time practically no wide-ranging and detailed surveys of this nature have been made. Reliable figures on the rates of savings and investment must await further study. I should like to draw attention, however, to the following three points from my own field surveys.

First, the Southeast Asian peasant economy is more or less self-sufficient and static. The typical peasant maintains an economic balance in times of normal havests, not only in subsistence but also in cash income, but practically no surplus is produced. In times of bad harvests, however, the capital required for planting the next year's crops and, in the majority of cases, capital for living expenses, is borrowed at high interest rates, principally from commercial middlemen, some of whom are landlords, on the security of future assets. This indebtedness oppresses the peasant economy, although frequently these loans can be repaid in times of good harvests. Consequently, in the long term the peasant economy is static and cyclical, it being practically impossible to produce a surplus for the investment required for new development.

Second, approximately 10 percent of the household expenditure is given to religious establishments by both Mohammedans and Buddhists in the rural areas. The offering of gold leaf to pagodas in Burma is a well-known example, and these religious disbursements are frequently considered to be an absolute expenditure. The peasants, therefore, run their agricultural holdings and maintain their livelihood with balance after the deduction of their religious contributions. Increased investment prospects could be expected if the peasants were to cease to subsidize religion and divert the money to economic development instead, but this is impossible for peasants who are bound by the obligations of a religious society.

Third, the increase in cash expenditure accompanying changes in the pattern of consumption has a positive aspect in that it stimulates the peasant's desire to produce, but at the same time it causes a disturbance in the static condition of peasant holding. In Thailand, which has been proud of being a "country of peasant proprietors," the peasants are now buying new consumer goods, sometimes financed by loans, regardless of the balance between their income and expenditure. One is often witness to the tragedy of their giving up their land because they are unable to repay these loans, with the result that the number of tenant farmers is gradually increasing.[2] A rapid development from self-sufficiency to production for the market is the normal developmental process of the agricultural economy, but the functions of merchant usury capital in this developmental process become a serious problem in a different sense from that implied in the static agricultural economy.

As is clear from these considerations, state investment for rapid agricultural development must be made not only in relation to the infrastructure, but must also be partially substituted for the individual and private investments which properly should be borne by the peasant economy. Consequently, state capital comes to play a leading role as agricultural development capital.

While it is clear that the introduction of state capital is urgently required, many complicated problems are involved.

The first is the ability to make state capital available. Many students of the subject take up the economic development of Japan since the Meiji Restoration of 1868 in reference to the economic development of Southeast Asia. Japan's modernization and economic development in the last hundred years have been extraordinarily successful, even

---

2. T. Motooka, "Problems of Land Reform in Thailand with Reference to the Japanese Experience", in M. Inoki, ed., *Japan's Future in Southeast Asia*, (Kyoto: The Center for Southeast Asian Studies, Kyoto University, 1966), pp. 15–28.

when viewed on a world scale. In the early Meiji period, the land tax accounted for approximately 80 percent of national tax revenue,[3] and this must be considered as the major financial factor in the "take-off" of Japan's economic development. In contrast, in Thailand in the 1960s we find that the tax and premiums on exports of rice made up approximately 10 to 15 percent of national revenue, and a figure of roughly the same order is inferred in the case of Burma. No more than this could be made available from the agricultural sectors. Both early Meiji Japan and present-day Thailand are agricultural countries; but Thailand, unlike Japan, had little ability to make state capital available for economic "take-off." The same can be said of the other countries in Southeast Asia.

Second, the state must supply capital to the cultivating peasants for the improvement of their farms. In addition there are public investments for agricultural development, headed by large-scale irrigation and drainage works, technical development, research in agricultural technology and education aimed at the introduction of new technology into the peasant economy. How this immense volume of capital is to be made available is the most serious question in the developing countries. The most important means presently used are indirect taxes, particularly taxes on imports, and consumption taxes on tobacco, alcoholic beverages, etc. As a result, consumer prices increase and a rise in the levels of consumption is impeded. However, there are limits beyond which indirect taxes cannot be raised. As an accompaniment

---

3. In Japan, the land tax as a proportion of total national tax revenue was 72.8 percent in 1875, gradually rose to 82.0 percent in 1885, and thereafter declined continuously, reaching 19.3 percent in 1915. T. Ogura, ed., *Kindai ni okeru Nihon nōgyō no hatten* [Agricultural development in modern Japan] (Tokyo: Research Committee on Agricultural Policy, 1963), p. 22.

In a recent work containing his principal papers, published on the occasion of his retirement, Barter, who has served the FAO for many years, evaluates in the following terms the role of the land tax in the process of the modernization of Japan's economy.

Much attention has been given lately to the early development of Japan as the first example of an advanced economic and agricultural development in an Asian country. In Japan the main source both of government revenue and of investment was initially the land tax. Land tax alone accounted for 86 percent of the total tax revenue in the mid-1870s, 45 percent by the mid-1880s, and still 22 percent by 1907. Taking into account the burden of excise and other taxes, it is estimated that agriculture's share of taxes exceeded 80 percent as late as the mid-1890s and was still over 50 percent at the time of the First World War. Much of this taxation was used for investment, and government investment in Japan exceeded 50 percent of total investment throughout the period 1895–1910. This is a remarkable example of the classical pattern.

P. G. H. Barter, *Problems of Agricultural Development* (Geneva: Librairie Droz, 1966), p. 30.

to the progressive growth of the economy increased direct taxes must be levied, particularly on corporate and private incomes. But it is no easy matter to establish satisfactory tax-collecting systems.

A further source is such foreign capital as gifts or loans from other countries or international organizations, but such capital can cause serious problems of both a social and an economic nature. The Japanese indemnity payments can be cited as bad examples in Southeast Asia. In Indonesia and the Philippines, for instance, they were used to finance luxury consumption, and in Burma, for the construction of large power stations irrelevant to her economic development at that time. Little importance was placed on a goal-oriented or rational utilization of funds supplied by foreign countries.[4]

Aid of this nature should be given on the principle of "help for those who help themselves." In concrete terms the projects carried out with foreign capital should have a "counterpart" contribution supplied by the recipient country. Furthermore, in order for foreign capital to produce the desired results, parallel technical aid must be sought and necessary attention paid to the administrative ability of governments.

THE SOCIOECONOMIC CONDITIONS GOVERNING AGRICULTURAL DEVELOPMENT

Many socioeconomic factors of an institutional, social, religious, traditional, and racial nature impede agricultural development. These differ to an extraordinary degree in the various countries of Southeast Asia, and the principal ones are discussed below.

The first concerns the conditions of land tenure, an important cause of the social and political unrest in that area.[5] However, there are marked differences in this respect as between one country and another.[6] Thailand, for example, is relatively underpopulated, and since the squatter's right which provides that state-owned land brought under cultivation by peasants reverts to their ownership has been assured since the nineteenth century, the cultivating peasant proprietor system is predominant at present, and the land-tenure system is not impeding agricultural development. (Of course, as has already been stated, it is

4. T. Motooka, "Political, Economic, and Social Factors in the Development of Water Resources in Southeast Asia," in Y. Fujioka, ed., *Water Resource Utilization in Southeast Asia* (Kyoto: The Center for Southeast Asian Studies, Kyoto University, 1966), p. 17.

5. E. H. Jacoby, *Agrarian Unrest in Southeast Asia* (New York: Columbia University Press, 1949).

6. T. Takigawa, "Tonan Ajia ni okeru tochikaikaku no kihon seikaku" [Basic characteristics of land reforms in Southeast Asian countries] *Azia Kenkyu* [*Asian Studies*] 13, no. 2 (July 1966).

extremely important as a matter of future agricultural policy to devise some countermeasures in the light of the fact that the system of cultivating-peasant-proprietorship is tending to break up, although at a slow pace.)[7] In contrast, in the Philippines the tenancy system is predominant because of the geomorphic conditions of the country as a collection of islands, high population pressure, the persistence of the system of large landholdings, the legacy of Spanish rule, and the fact that the landlord system is involved in the administrative mechanisms of the country. What is more, not only is there absentee landlordism, but these absentee landlords display practically no interest in the improvement of agriculture, avoid the investment of capital in agriculture, and impede any reform of the land tenure system with their political power. It can scarcely be denied that this landlord system is an obstacle not only to the agricultural development of the Philippines but also to the economic development and political stability of that country.

It does sometimes happen that a large landholding system possesses highly advantageous aspects from the point of view of agricultural development. As already noted, the reclamation of the Rangsit area of Thailand was carried out by landlords. Again, the development and increased production of tropical cash crops in Malaya and Indonesia, and in Indo-China, was undertaken by means of plantation agriculture, in which the unit of management is based on large-scale land ownership. However, the importance of the plantation has sharply diminished in present-day Southeast Asia. Landlords do not carry out agricultural investment, and have no functions except that of levying rents. It is no exaggeration to say that the merits of the landlord system have practically disappeared, and that only its evil effects remain. Consequently, reform of land-tenure systems is normally an important prerequisite for agricultural development.

The implementation of land reform is a complicated process. The success of those carried out in postwar Japan and Taiwan is frequently cited, but we must remember that in Japan a land-tenure policy was developed as long ago as the 1930s, as a means of dealing with the depressed condition of the rural areas at that time, and that with this background reform was enforced at a stroke as a part of postwar American-occupation policy. The reform of the land-tenure system in Taiwan was also enforced by conquerors, from mainland China. In both cases the government's ability to overcome the resistance of the

---

7.   T. Motooka, "Problems of Land Reform in Thailand with Reference to the Japanese Experience."

landlord class was an essential condition. However, in Southeast Asia, government authority and the interests of the landlords are very closely related, except in the socialist countries.

The mechanisms for credit and marketing throughout the rural areas of Southeast Asia, which are closely related to agricultural development, are in the hands of the overseas Chinese. (In Burma they are joined by the Indians and Pakistanis.) I personally evaluate the credit and marketing functions performed by these Chinese particularly highly, especailly for their achievements in the introduction of cash crops into agriculture. The censure that they exploit the peasants is not necessarily justified if looked at from the point of view of economic efficiency. The truth would seem to be that the commercialization of rice production in mainland Southeast Asia and of cash crops in the islands would not have been accomplished without the overseas Chinese.

Nevertheless, their presence has created a number of serious problems from the economic point of view alone. In Thailand, the Chinese problem produced a great deal of tension from the latter half of the nineteenth century on into the first years of the twentieth century, but since then the "Thaiization" of overseas Chinese has been skillfully and successfully advanced by the government, one of the reasons for Thailand's political stability. In Malaysia the Moslem Malsys do not intermarry with the Chinese. The Chinese live not only in the towns but also form Chinese settlements in the rural areas. Furthermore, the overseas Chinese are not a racial minority, but account for approximately 38 percent of the total population. Inasmuch as Malaysia is a multiracial state, racial conflicts are more severe, which may prove to be a source of trouble for the country. The presence of overseas Chinese has also led to extraordinarily troublesome racial problems in Burma and Indonesia, but generally it is more a political problem rather than an economic one.

The agricultural cooperative movement appears as an agricultural development measure aimed at excluding middlemen and transferring credit and marketing functions from the hands of the overseas Chinese to those of the peasants. In practice, however, the movement is the responsibility of the government, for the peasants do not have the social consciousness or the ability to manage it themselves. This movement is in a state of uncertainty,[8] and furthermore, managers are needed for the agricultural cooperatives, if they are to be developed. When the cooperatives are directly run by the government, that is to say, when the managers of the cooperatives are government officials, the efficiency

8.   T. Motooka, "Tai nōgyō ni okeru seisan kiban no seibi."

of management is markedly inferior. On the other hand, a considerable period of time will be required for the social consciousness and spontaneity of the rank-and-file to be awakened. The nurturing of capable cooperative managers must be a chief policy measure for the immediate future.

Thirdly, we may cite the traditional village structure. It is said that in comparison with other developing countries, the peasants of Thailand are independent in character and their communal organizations and social consciousness are not strong.[9] This weakness in communal organization constitutes a barrier to the development of communal utilization of watersupplies, as in irrigation and drainage works. Such factors as the traditional character of the village, the power of the headmen, and the influence of the Buddhist temples also impede the progressive introduction and proper use of new technology.

In Indonesia, however, communal consciousness is strong within a village society, while strong antagonism exists between villages, constituting a great obstacle to the implementation of agricultural development projects affecting areas larger than a single village.

As an agricultural development policy, particularly in connection with agricultural production, "package programs" have been adopted in various places, in order to have the whole village simultaneously and comprehensively adopt new forms of technology, such as new varieties of seed, fertilizers, agricultural chemicals, and agricultural machinery and implements. This may prove to be a powerful means for breaking up the traditional institutions of the village.[10]

Community development programs are frequently employed as agricultural development policies. These aim at full-scale and comprehensive development, not only of agricultural production, but also of transportation and communications, or of education, medical services, etc., as parts of the infrastructure. These may be expected to be more efficacious than development projects directed at farming alone. But even in the case of such development plans as these, the manner in

9. H. P. Philipps, *Thai Peasant Personality, The Patterning of Interpersonal Behavior in the Village of Bang Chan* (Berkeley and Los Angeles: University of California Press, 1965), p. 17.

10. For example, the Package Programme at Tegalega in western Java is said to be extremely successful. In this case, fifty-seven households of peasants increased their yields of maize approximately five times from 800 kg. per hectare to nearly 4,000 kg. per hectare by adopting new strains of seed, recommended fertilizers (both as regards types and quantities applied), making changes in the depth of sowing, carrying out disease and pest control measures, etc. A. T. Mosher, *Getting Agriculture Moving* (New York: The Agricultural Development Council, 1966), pp. 77–78.

which the village reacts to them is the most important condition for success. We frequently see instances in which the plans are forcibly carried through without the autonomous cooperation of the village. In the case of the community development programs in northeast Thailand, for example, the programs have been imposed "from above," and the villagers fail to respond as had been hoped for. It is the community development program carried out by means of substantial and long-term cooperation with the villagers that is likely to prove successful in overcoming the bonds of tradition.

Fourth, movements of labor between sectors of production and between regions are necessary for the purpose of economic development. It is one of the characteristics of developing countries that they lack a "social ladder" and that their labor force is generally immobile. The stronger the communal institutions of the village, the more immobile the labor group. Thailand is an exception to this general rule. The key to the development of Indonesia lies in transferring population from Java, which is suffering from overpopulation, to the outer provinces where development has made hardly any progress because of the paucity of population. Under the present political and economic situation in Indonesia, however, movements of population, though desirable, are very difficult to bring about, but regional redistribution must certainly become a feature of future planning. Even within Java itself there are serious interregional antagonisms between the eastern, central, and western areas. A telling fact is the occurrence of ten thousand deaths from starvation on the island of Lombok in the spring of 1966. It was said that the deaths were confined to certain localities and that other areas were entirely free from food shortages.

The question of labor immobility is deeply involved with such social conditions as language, race, tribe, history, etc. If the restrictions on labor mobility associated with these conditions are to improved to any degree, such steps as the dissemination of peasant education and the strengthening of the central government will be necessary.

Movements of population within a country, whether for the cultivation of new land, settlement on coastal, riverine, and lacustrine reclamations, or the resettlement schemes, to which particular importance is attached in Malaya, will raise the mobility of labor in the agricultural sector.

THE TECHNOLOGICAL CONDITIONS GOVERNING AGRICULTURAL DEVELOPMENT

On all sides attention is drawn to the low level of agricultural technology in Southeast Asia. This is most strikingly demonstrated by the yields of

TABLE 1
Yields of Rice (Unhulled) Per Hectare in the Countries of Asia

Country	1948/1949–1952/1953 (A)	1958/1959–1962/1963 (B)	Percentage $\left(\dfrac{B - A}{A}\right)$ increase
Burma	14.6	16.3	12
Cambodia	11.7	10.1	−14
Ceylon	12.9	17.9	39
Mainland China	21.7	26.9	24
Taiwan	22.1	31.2	41
India	11.3	14.5	28
Indonesia	16.1	17.8	11
North Korea	29.4	...	...
South Korea	27.5	29.3	7
Laos	6.4	7.9	23
Malaysia: Malaya	18.6	23.7	27
Saba	12.6	20.4	62
Sarawak	4.5	9.4	109
Pakistan	13.8	15.1	9
Philippines	11.8	11.8	0
Thailand	13.1	14.0	7
North Viet-Nam	...	20.4	...
South Viet-Nam	13.6	20.4	50
Japan	40.0	49.1	23

Source: *ECAFE Economic Survey of Asia and the Far East, 1964*, Bangkok, 1965, p. 106.
Note: Yields in 100 kg.

rice per unit area. As shown in Table 1, the yields of unhulled rice in the countries of Southeast and East Asia fall into three groups. The first comprises Japan, with a yield of five tons per hectare, the second the former Japanese colonies, Korea and Taiwan, with yields of around three tons per hectare, and the third group has yields of between one and two tons per hectare—comprising Malaysia, Viet-Nam, Indonesia, Ceylon, Pakistan, Burma, India, Thailand, and the Philippines, in that order. Whereas the increase of the five-year average from 1958–1959 to 1962–1963 over that from 1948–1949 to 1952–1953, that is, the rate of increase in yields over this ten-year period, was 23 percent in Japan, it was in general low in the countries of Southeast Asia, and lay between 12 percent and 14 percent. This low productivity was influenced, as I shall show later, not only by the level of technology but also by price considerations, but for the present I shall confine my attention to the levels of agricultural technology.

First there is the fact that we cannot find in the countries of Southeast Asia anything analogous to the technology of the "conscious and earnest agriculturalists" (*tokunōka*), which contributed to the early development of Japanese agricultural technology. Agricultural technology that has been improved by the peasants themselves is practically nonexistent, and, consequently, new agricultural technology must be nurtured outside the peasantry and introduced into their economy. Experimental research of this nature carried out by the government, and the diffusion of the results of this research to the peasants are particularly important for the countries of Southeast Asia. In the prewar colonial period, experimental research on commercial crops for export from the colonial countries was carried out at the request of the planters and was frequently pursued with their financial backing. The botanical gardens of Bogor and Singapore carried out basic studies of tropical plants, and the Rubber Research Institute at Kuala Lumpur is the finest rubber experimental station in the world. On the other hand, the colonial countries did not study crops other than the important commercial crops; and even for rice, the staple food of the natives, little experimental research was carried out. After the war the countries of Southeast Asia recognized, as a matter of agricultural policy, the necessity for agricultural experimental research on crops other than those grown on the plantations, and they set up appropriate experimental stations. The most advanced country in this respect is Thailand, where more than seventy stations have been set up in practically every province. These stations cover the principal crops, such as rice, field crops and rubber, and the organization for linking experimental stations to the center and in provinces has more or less been established. Unfortunately, however, great results have not been produced to date. The reasons are that agricultural experimental research takes time, and it is only in recent years that this organization has been established. The number of technologists engaged in this research is limited, the quality of the personnel is not high and the technologists are not fond of field-work. The equipment for experiments is also poor. Moreover because of the extreme sectionalism of the government bureaucracy, agricultural experimental research as a whole is not well organized. Because of this centralization of administration, no autonomy is accorded to the provincial experiment stations. Even in Thailand, the most advanced of these countries, this is the case, and the situation is still worse in the other countries.

The tasks of agricultural experimental research are numerous and varied: the breeding of new plant varieties, introduction of new crops, fertilizer application, irrigation and drainage, disease and pest control, improvement of methods of cultivation, introduction of agricultural machinery and implements, establishment of rotational or multiple-cropping systems, improvement of methods of husking and threshing, and the improvement of methods of storage and transportation. The situation with regard to every one of these is that practically no results have been forthcoming from Southeast Asian countries to date.

In contrast, in 1964, as the result of several years' cooperation in Malayan rice-improvement technology, Japan produced *Malinja*, a variety of rice for winter cropping, and in 1965 *Mashli*, a variety strongly resistant to rice blight; and at present these varieties are being rapidly diffused in Malaysia.[11] Outstanding research results were achieved by the International Rice Research Institute at Los Baños in the Philippines. This Institute has already succeeded in breeding the new varieties IR8-288-3, IR9-60, and IR5-47-2.[12]

---

11.   *Rice Culture in Malaya* (Kyoto: The Center for Southeast Asian Studies, Kyoto University, 1965).

12.   Dr. R. F. Chandler, Jr., the Director of the International Rice Research Institute, reports as follows:

One of the important achievements of the year [of 1965] was the identification of certain selections from the Institute's breeding program which were sufficiently outstanding to warrant testing throughout the tropical and sub-tropical rice-growing regions. Most of the selections sent to other areas have been in the F6 or F7 generation. Although by the end of 1965 more than 570 crosses had been made, it was only the progeny of crosses made in 1962 that had become sufficiently stable to permit appropriate evaluation and widespread testing.

The three selections which seemed particularly outstanding under Philippine conditions and, at this stage, especially on the Experimental Farm, are IR8–288–3, IR9–60, and IR5–47–2. It happens that each of these three lines have the variety Peta as one of the parents. Peta is a tall, tropical *indica* variety with high vigour, seed dormancy, and resistance to certain important diseases. It was developed in Indonesia but is now one of the Seed Board varieties in the Philippines.

In light of the results produced by this large-scale International Rice Research Institute and by the contrastingly very small-scale Japanese Rice Technology Aid Plan in Malaysia, I am convinced that the breeding of new varieties is by no means difficult. To raise the level of technology, steps must first be taken to develop agricultural experimental research in a positive manner. For this purpose the following points should receive particular attention.

(1) At present the returns on investment in agricultural technical development are widely recognized—from the United States to Southeast Asia. I wish to stress that from the point of view of investment, the basic measures to secure agricultural development in Southeast Asia are to be found in the development of new forms of agricultural technology.

(2) For the present we cannot expect the peasants of Southeast Asia to undertake technical development for themselves, and now that the plantation is in decline, technical development on the basis of private enterprise has become impossible. Consequently, practically all technical development in agriculture will have to be carried out by the governments.

(3) For agricultural experimental research, time in particular is required, inasmuch as the objects studied are crops. In the breeding and fixation of new varieties, for example, trials covering several generations are necessary. Nevertheless there is an urgent demand for new forms of technology for agricultural development.

(4) In order that results may be produced, a high level of research and the latest research equipment are desirable. Though the most sophisticated agricultural technology is unnecessary for the peasants of Southeast Asia, we must not confuse this with the need for more advanced studies in agricultural technology. The fullest consideration

---

One of the best selections resulting from the crossing of Peta with Dee-geo-woo-gen (a short *indica* variety from Taiwan) was IR8–288–3. This line has high yielding ability, some resistance to the tungro virus disease, is short and nitrogen responsive, and has desirable cooking and eating qualities. The crossing of Peta with I-geo-tze, another short *indica* from Taiwan, also produced a promising selection, IR9–60. It has fairly high seed dormancy, is short (95 cm. high), in early trials, appeared to be vigorous and nitrogen responsive. In many trials it has yielded between 6,000 and 7,000 kg./ha. under good management. The IR5–47–2 selection is a cross between Peta and Tankai Rotan, a relatively tall *indica* variety from Malaysia selected as a parent because it was not as tall as most *indicas*, and, in early trials, appeared to be vigorous and non-photoperiod-sensitive. The IR5–47–2 is a line of medium height (138 cm.) and maturity (132 days), and appears to be rather resistant to the tungro virus disease and to bacterial leaf blight. In recent preliminary yield trials it has produced over 6.5 metric tons per hectare in the monsoon season. It is now being widely tested in Southeast Asia.

The International Rice Research Institute, *Annual Report, 1965* (Los Baños, Laguna, Philippines, 1966), p. 15.

TABLE 2
POLISHED RICE REQUIRED FOR PURCHASE OF 1 KG. OF FERTILIZER IN THE PEASANT ECONOMY, 1964

(in Kg.)

		AMMONIUM SULPHATE	CALCIUM CYANAMIDE	UREA	SUPER-PHOSPHATE P_2O_5 LESS THAN 25 PERCENT	SUPER-PHOSPHATE P_2O_5 MORE THAN 25 PERCENT	SULPHATE OF CALCIUM	CHLORIDE OF POTASH
Absolute Figures	Japan	0.996	1.347	0.913	0.921	0.826	0.543	0.366
	Philippines	2.762	—	—	2.114	—	—	1.173
	Thailand	5.129	5.643	4.430	3.824	3.180	2.261	1.654
As percent of Japan	Japan	100.0	100.0	100.0	100.0	100.0	100.0	100.0
	Philippines	273.3	—	—	231.5	—	—	320.5
	Japan (Thailand)	515.0	418.9	485.2	415.2	385.0	416.4	451.9

Note: Since only wholesale prices for polished rice appear in the statistics for the Philippines and Thailand, prices 20 percent lower have been taken as producers' prices.

Source: Compiled from FAO, *Production Yearbook, 1965* (Rome 1966), pp. 344–346, 415–417.

—: None, in negligible quantity (less than one half of the unit indicated) or entry not applicable.

must be paid to the quality of research personnel and equipment if the desired results are to be obtained at an early date. It is clear that at the present stage positive foreign aid for studies of agricultural technology is necessary for the countries of Southeast Asia.

(5) Last, levels of agricultural technology in the field will be raised only when the new forms of technology have been introduced among the peasantry. Extension work directed at the peasants and the investment of capital in agricultural holdings are necessary conditions to meet this objective.

THE PRICE RELATIONS GOVERNING AGRICULTURAL DEVELOPMENT

Whether a new form of technology will be profitable for the peasants will depend on whether it will produce higher net returns. The introduction of technology is determined by the connection between input and output prices. The most striking example is the case of the introduction of fertilizers. If the application is profitable, the peasants may be expected to apply it. In concrete terms, the question is not how many kilograms increase in the yield of rice can be produced by the application of 1 kg. of fertilizer; it is necessary that the price of 1 kg. of fertilizer should be less than the price of the rice represented by the increase in the yield. The amount of rice (converted into terms of polished rice) considered necessary for the purchase of 1 kg. of fertilizer in the peasant economy is the determining condition. From Food and Agricultural Organization (FAO) statistics I have drawn up the data in Table 2. The statistics give figures for only the Philippines and Thailand of the countries of Southeast Asia, and there are also many doubtful points regarding the figures themselves. Taking the example of ammonium sulphate, a representative nitrogenous fertilizer, in Japan peasants consider an output increase of 0.996 kg. of polished rice necessary to warrant the purchase of 1 kg. of ammonium sulphate while in the Philippines 2.762 kg. and in Thailand 5.129 kg. are necessary. In other words, while a Japanese peasant has only to get a yield increase equivalent to 1 kg. of polished rice for 1 kg. of ammonium sulphate, the Thai peasant must get a yield increase equivalent to 5 kg. of polished rice if it is to pay. The question arises whether fertilizer prices in Thailand might be too high. According to FAO statistics, however, ammonium sulphate prices in the year 1964–1965 were $27.9 per 100 kg. in Thailand as against $26.4 in Japan. There is practically no difference. It is the farm prices for rice which produce the difference between the two countries. Taking FAO statistics and converting them to those for polished rice, the peasant's sale price per 100 kg. in 1964 was $5.44 in

Thailand as against $26.5 in Japan. Thai peasants get only approximately one-sixth of the price which the Japanese peasants receive for their produce. The price relation between rice and fertilizer places the Thai peasant in an unfavorable position and thereby impedes the increased use of fertilizer.[13]

As is shown by these input-output relations, an important determinant of agricultural development is to be found in the size of the net returns based on prices.

Two aspects of the peasant's net return need to be considered. The first is the increase in this return, and the second is its stability. The factors necessary for an increase in net returns are found in increases in the price of outputs and decreases in the price of inputs. However, in the rice-producing countries of Southeast Asia, headed by Thailand, a policy of low prices for rice is being enforced by means of taxes and premiums on rice exports. There are two bases for this policy of low prices for rice—making the peasantry an important source of state revenue through indirect taxation and keeping down the consumer's price of rice on the home market. Basically, however, this runs contrary to the principle of progressive taxation and, from the point of view of international trade, to the principle of world trade liberalization. Furthermore, considering rice consumers as the nonagricultural population, since this amounts to no more than 20 percent of the total population in the case of Thailand, this policy cannot be expected to keep prices low on the home market. It is, therefore, necessary that the current policy for agricultural products be carefully reexamined.

All are agreed on the necessity of keeping down the prices of investment goods. As concrete measures to this end, some advocate taking steps to make the latest producers' goods at home, as opposed to the present situation in which practically all of these—fertilizers, agricultural machinery and implements, agricultural chemicals, and so on—must be imported. One example is a urea factory set up in Bangladesh, with the plant imported from Japan. But it is very doubtful whether self-sufficiency in producers' goods would, in fact, be cheaper than imports. The revenue from import taxes on these goods would be

13. I find these FAO statistics difficult to accept. That is because the prices for rice in the FAO statistics are lower than in reality, especially in the case of Thailand. It also seems true, however, that the peasant purchase prices for fertilizers given here are lower than they really are. Considering both these facts, I see no reason to change my belief that in terms of farm prices the purchase of 1 kg. of ammonium sulphate requires an increase of 1 kg. of polished rice in Japan and 5 kg. of polished rice in Thailand.

lost. Efforts should be made to economize in the process of distributing these goods to the peasant population.

Furthermore if self-sufficiency is the aim, capital and technology will be required in the construction of new factories for these producers' goods. Should not the limited capital and technology at the disposal of the countries of Southeast Asia be allocated rather to the improvement of the infrastructure? Again, when factories for the new producers' goods are to be built, this is done by the introduction of large sums of foreign investment. In many cases these are low-interest long-term loans, but the ability to repay them nevertheless must be carefully looked into.

We must also consider price-stabilization policies, another important aspect of policy. Monoculture for the export market is an outstanding characteristic of Southeast Asian agriculture. Apart from rice, most cash crops are semiperennial or perennials, and the price elasticity of their supply is low. The prices for agricultural products and consequently peasant cash incomes, are exceedingly unstable. As a countermeasure there is price stabilization based on international agreement, as in the case of coffee, but these do not have much real effect. In the future it will be necessary to devise measures on an international scale in the interests of agricultural development in the developing countries throughout the world.

One form of price stabilization which each country can put into effect and which is practical at the present time, is development from monoculture to diversified agriculture, on the individual-holding scale and on a national one. The introduction of diversification on the individual holding is also highly regarded as a means of introducing rationality, particularly on the self-sufficient, small-scale agricultural holding. The introduction of other crops on land used for growing a single crop of rice in the rainy season, is an example of the principle of diversification. The most successful venture into diversification of agriculture on a national scale is that of Thailand where field crops have been incorporated into a system of agriculture in which rice cultivation predominates. This has developed markedly since the war, more in the form of the introduction of field crops in newly reclaimed areas unsuitable for rice than by the introduction of field crops on land primarily used for rice cultivation. It has contributed greatly not only to the raising of agricultural incomes in Thailand but also to their stability.[14]

14. L. R. Brown, *Agricultural Diversification and Economic Development in Thailand: A Case Study* (Washington, D. C.: United States Department of Agri culture, 1963).

CONCLUSION

I have considered the decision-making unit concerned in development, capital, socioeconomic conditions, technology, and prices, as conditions governing the development of agriculture in Southeast Asia. I have omitted consideration of the natural basis of agriculture, and this is an important problem for the future. In particular one must recognize that the natural conditions of the tropics possess both advantageous and disadvantageous aspects in relation to agricultural development. New land can be expected to be developed spontaneously if the necessary infrastructure is provided.

Although the conditions impeding the agricultural development of Southeast Asia are matters of great difficulty, it seems that development is possible if all Southeast Asian countries could concentrate their efforts on achieving such objectives and could receive the requisite aid from foreign countries. Accordingly, the most urgently needed policies should be given priority and carried out as soon as possible. These policies have to be decided on the basis of comprehensive research on the economic and agricultural situation of each Southeast Asian country.

15

Economic Analysis of the Rice Premium Policy of Thailand

HIROSHI TSUJII

INTRODUCTION

The rice premium, a specific export duty which constitutes an appreciable part of the export price of Thailand's rice,[1] has greatly influenced Thailand politically and economically. In fact, the rice premium policy has been one of the most controversial economic policies in postwar Thailand. Research on the policy began to appear while the controversy continued, but most was not based on thorough theoretical and empirical investigation of the mechanism and function of the policy in Thailand and in the world rice market. Consequently, the theories widely disseminated by the opponents of the rice premium are founded on the mistaken assumption that the world market for Thai rice is prefectly competitive, and many economists who have studied the policy have accepted this claim.

In this article I intend to analyze and evaluate the establishment of Thailand's rice premium policy, the mechanism and function of the policy, and the controversy surrounding the policy, based on thorough theoretical and empirical investigation of this and related policies and of the Thai and international rice markets. The most important conclusions drawn from this approach are that the world market for Thai rice is imperfectly competitive, and that the Thai government's rice premium and export quota policies place it in an oligopolistic position vis-à-vis the world rice market. The opponents of the rice premium policy base their arguments on the assumption of perfect

---

1. The rice premium has constituted 21–35 percent of the export price from 1956 (excluding the periods 1971 to 1973, and 1975). From 1946 to 1955, total levies on rice exports ranged from this level to considerably higher.

competition in the world rice market, and their criticism either does not hold true or is in need of large-scale revision. In contrast, the opinions of the policy's supporters who assume that the world market for Thai rice is imperfectly competitive are largely confirmed.

In the first section, the historical reasons for the establishment of the rice premium policy are described briefly, and its economic and political background is discussed. Second, the details of the rice premium policy, the export quota policy and the reserve stock policy, the implementation of these policies, the policy objectives, and the degree of attainment of these objectives are investigated. The special characteristics and the organization of government and private exports are also discussed. In the third section I offer a theoretical and empirical appraisal of the dispute on the rice premium policy.

CHANGES IN RICE EXPORT POLICIES IN THAILAND— THE ORIGIN OF THE RICE PREMIUM POLICY

After the Bowring Treaty of 1855 between Britain and Thailand, which opened the Thai economy to the outside world, the export of rice from Thailand increased rapidly. In the middle of the nineteenth century, exports of rice from Thailand were about 100,000 tons a year; at the beginning of the twentieth century they exceeded 1,000,000 tons and continued to grow rapidly until about 1940.[2] From the middle of the nineteenth century to just before World War II the export of rice was carried out with little interference from the government except for the low export tax fixed by the Bowring Treaty at four baht per kwien (1.5 tons) of white rice and the provision for halting rice export in the event of a domestic shortage.[3] The government encouraged the export of rice by stimulating rice production through public investment and the land tax system.[4]

Thai fiscal policy at the beginning of the twentieth century aimed primarily at increasing revenue through import tariffs. With the revision of the Bowring Treaty in 1926, through which Thailand regained autonomy over tariff determination, the proportion of government revenue derived from import taxes rose rapidly. But the proportion of revenue derived from export taxes decreased from that year because many export taxes were discontinued. However, the rice export tax

2.　J. C. Ingram, *Economic Change in Thailand, 1850–1970* (Stanford: Stanford University Press, 1971), p. 38.

3.　Ingram, *Economic Change*, p. 75.

4.　Ingram, *Economic Change*, chapters 3, 4, and 8.

was retained, reflecting the traditional importance of rice export taxation to the government.[5]

In 1938, with the establishment of a constitutional monarchy, new tax laws were promulgated. The land tax and the head tax, traditionally heavy levies on the farming population that had provided between 10 and 22 percent of total tax revenue, were abolished; corporation tax was newly introduced and the income tax system reformed. However, these direct taxes brought extremely poor returns up to the end of the 1950s.[6] From 1946 to 1970, returns from rice export levies have constituted a large proportion of government revenue. This percentage matches that of the land and head taxes before 1937. Thus it would seem that eight years after the rice producers were relieved of the burden of the land and head taxes, rice export became a vital source of government income which compensated for the loss of revenue from these other taxes.

In January, 1942, Thailand entered the Second World War on the Japanese side. As the war progressed rice exports fell to approximately 200,000 tons per year. Postwar development of the rice export policy and of the rice exportation system, and the recovery of rice exports were partly prescribed by the outcome of the war. I have divided this development into periods as follows:[7]

January 1946–August 1947	1st period (war reparations)
September 1947–December 1949	2d period (international control)
January 1950–December 1954	3d period (state control)
January 1955–December 1955	4th period (private exports)
January 1956–present	5th period (concurrent government and private exports)

The war ended with the defeat of Japan, and immediately afterward Thailand proclaimed state monopoly of rice exportation.[8] At this time there was a severe worldwide rice shortage. On January 1, 1946, Thailand made a formal peace agreement with Britain and India. One clause stated that Thailand would deliver for export, free of charge, 1,500,000 tons of first-class white rice, as reparation for her cooperation with Japan during the war. This marked the beginning of the first period. The machinery for dealing with these rice reparations was first the "Mixed Committee," and then the "Rice Purchasing Bureau" on

5. Ingram, *Economic Change*, chapter 8, pp. 180–183. Before 1926, tax on rice exports was treated differently from tax on other exports.

6. Ingram, *Economic Change*, pp. 184, 300.

7. Sura Sanittanont, *Thailand's Rice Export Tax: Its Effects on the Rice Economy* (Bangkok: National Institute of Development Administration, 1967), chapter 2. I have followed Sura's divisions up to the third period.

8. Ingram, *Economic Change*, p. 87.

the Thai side, and on the British side, the "Siam Rice Unit." The delivery of the rice reparations was arranged by these bodies under the direction of the British. On May 6, 1946, an agreement between Thailand and Britain and America was concluded and the "Combined Siam Rice Committee" was established. This committee, following the advice of the British and American "Combined Food Board," encouraged the export of Thai rice and made recommendations for and cooperated in the recovery of the Thai economy.[9]

At the beginning of the first period, the extremely low price offered by the government prevented it from collecting enough rice to meet its obligations, and the zero reparation export price probably prohibited the government from increasing its procurement price. To promote rice exports the following measures were taken: the export price was increased to a low positive level, the domestic buying price was raised, domestic distribution and storage were controlled, a bounty was offered on rice sold to the government, and rice merchants were allowed profit on the private export of a small amount of rice and on a small amount of foreign exchange proportionate to the amount of rice delivered to the government. Even so, the amount of rice exported hardly increased.[10] In the first period Thailand was required to export 2,250,000 tons of rice, but only managed to export 762,000 tons. At the end of August, 1947, the tripartite agreement ended, the Combined Siam Rice Committee was abolished, and Thailand was exempted from its unfulfilled export obligations.[11] The main reason for the extremely small amount of rice exported was the low government procurement price compared with the domestic market price. And it has been suggested that the Thai government deliberately sought to avoid the obligations of reparation exports.[12]

In the first period the government had a monopoly on rice exports and bought rice at a low price, forcing down the farmers' selling price. It could be said that the reparation exports were made at the expense of the farmers. On the other hand, except for the period from January to March 1946 when the export price was zero, the government gained considerable revenue from reparative rice exported at about twice the

9.　Yoshihiko Hasegawa, *The Rice Situation in Thailand* (in Japanese) (Tokyo: The Institute of Developing Economies, 1962), pp. 473–476.

10.　Hasegawa, *The Rice Situation* pp. 474–481. The policy of allowing private exports and profits from foreign exchange to encourage rice exports is called the 3 percent and 10 percent Inducement Scheme. The policy was to allow those who sold rice to the government to export 3 percent of that amount privately and to keep 10 percent of the foreign exchange from their transactions.

11.　Sura, *Thailand's Rice Export Tax*, p. 19.

12.　Ingram, *Economic Change*, p. 87.

domestic procurement price.[13]

In this period the Rice Purchasing Bureau, with its legal monopoly of rice exports, was not yet corrupt.[14] But the control of rice exports by the bureau and the government was not perfect, and with the incentive of high black-market prices in Singapore and Kuala Lumpur, rice smuggling was rife.

The second period began on August 31, 1947, with the termination of the tripartite agreement. Management of rice export passed from the Combined Food Board to the International Emergency Food Committee (IEFC) and the Rice Purchasing Bureau was reorganized as the Siamese Rice Office. In this period too, only intergovernmental rice export was permitted in accordance with IEFC quotas. Rice exported from Thailand had the same base price as that from other rice exporting countries,[15] and any hint of war reparations was removed. The Siamese Rice Office controlled the domestic rice market by buying up all surplus rice. In 1947, the government's domestic procurement price, at 50 dollars a ton, was almost twice the 1946 level, and in 1948 and 1949 rose to 63.1 dollars. The export price in 1947, at 95.1 dollars, was also almost twice the 1946 level, and in 1948 rose to 138.8 dollars.[16] Thai rice exports quickly returned to prewar levels.

At the end of 1949, the IEFC was dissolved and Thailand became completely autonomous with regard to rice exports. From this time to the end of 1954 is designated as the third period (state control). Thai rice export, which from 1946 to 1949 had been a state monopoly under outside control, from 1950 to 1954 became an independent state monopoly. Thailand decided to control rice export after 1950, agreeing with Britain that an attempt should be made to impose some degree of stability on the still unstable world rice market.[17] Domestic control of rice distribution and storage continued as in the previous period.

In this third period the rice export system became more complicated and was deeply involved with domestic politics through political funding. Under the stable market conditions of 1950, Thailand exported 1,500,000 tons of white rice under government-to-government contracts. In 1951 the prices of primary products rose because of the Korean War, foreign reserves of rice-importing countries such as Indonesia were strong, demand for rice was high, and the international price of rice rose.

13. Sura, *Thailand's Rice Export Tax*, p. 18.
14. T. H. Silcock, *The Economic Development of Thai Agriculture* (Canberra: Australian National University Press, 1970), p. 216.
15. This price was still lower than the free market price.
16. These prices are taken from Sura, *Thailand's Rice Export Tax*, pp. 18–19.
17. Hasegawa, *The Rice Situation*, p. 488.

In the same year, Indonesia bought rice from Thailand outside government-to-government contract for the first time since the war, and for these reasons the price of rice on Thailand's domestic market rose.[18] The government held steady it rice procurement price, and this caused financial problems for the traders who sold rice to the government.[19] At the same time countries importing Thai rice had to contend with the problems of low quality and incomplete fulfillment of contracts. To counter these problems the two main importing countries, Britain and Japan, took the following measures. Japan indemnified rice dealers for their losses, and Britain suggested the Inducement Scheme whereby the rice dealers were allowed to export one ton of rice privately for every 4.5 tons sold to the Siamese Rice Office. This scheme followed the lines of the 3 percent and 10 percent Inducement Scheme of the first period.[20] In 1952–1953 the international price of rice again rose, and the Thai government adopted a policy of increasing the proportion of highly priced private exports at the expense of low-priced government rice.[21] So in these years, rice was exported in the three ways first seen in 1951: government exports, private exports under the Inducement Scheme, and private exports authorized at the government's discretion. Rice export by the third method started in 1951 with the Indonesian purchases outside government-to-government contracts.

In the third period, as in the second, the Thai government received large sums of revenue from the state control of rice exports and the system of multiple exchange rates.[22] In these periods most rice was exported under government auspices. The Siam Rice Office bought white rice from millers and sold it to exporters who were authorized representatives of the importing countries at a price almost 20 percent higher than the procurement price. The only expenses were in documentation and profits were enormous. And all foreign exchange from rice export had to be sold to the Bank of Thailand at an official rate that ensured large profits for the government when it was sold on the free market.[23] Thus government control of rice exports gave it two sources of revenue.

The government also profited in the same ways from private

18.   Hasegawa, *The Rice Situation*, p. 491.
19.   Sura, *Thailand's Rice Export Tax*, p. 21.
20.   Hasegawa, *The Rice Situation*, pp. 491–492. For the 3 percent and 10 percent Inducement Scheme, see note 10.
21.   Hasegawa, *The Rice Situation*, p. 493.
22.   Paul Sithi-Amnuai, *Finance and Banking in Thailand* (Bangkok: Thai Watana Panich, 1953), pp. 74–75.
23.   This was about twice the rate in the free market, in terms of baht.

exports. In both types of private export mentioned earlier, exporters had to buy from the government, which held all surplus rice, at a price 15 to 20 percent higher than the government procurement price,[24] and all foreign exchange from rice exports had to be sold to the Bank of Thailand at the official rate. In 1951, the government instituted a special levy, the "rice premium," on the issuance of export licenses for private rice export with government discretionary permission. This reached fifteen to thirty dollars a ton on occasion,[25] and was the forerunner of the rice premium policy brought into effect in 1955. Licenses themselves were also traded, and in 1951 their price reached thirty-five dollars a ton.[26] Some government officials also sold licenses for private gain.[27]

Thus the Siam Rice Office obtained a large amount of revenue from rice exports. Its contribution to the Treasury in 1948, 1949, and 1950 respectively was 14.4, 19.5, and 6.6 million dollars, amounting to 19, 22, and 6.5 percent of total revenue.[28] However, it is said that these figures are not the total revenue from rice exports. At the beginning of the fifties, Thailand enjoyed a seller's market for rice, and accounts of the Rice Office were not made public. Ingram has the following to say in his study of the revenue of the Rice Office.

> Government profit on rice trading is one large new source of revenue. . . . It is frequently alleged that part of the rice profits are being siphoned off by high officials. . . .[29]

Silcock has this to say on Ingram's comment and on the establishment of the rice premium policy.

> If he [Phibul] wanted to derive profit from rice for the ruling army group, he had to gain control of the Rice Bureau. . . . The Rice Bureau was taken over by the politicians, and throughout the sellers' market of the Korean War its accounts were never published. It was an open secret that the profits from rice were one of the main sources of the dictator's power to buy support.
> The Thai politicians thus had both a personal and a political interest in keeping the internal price of rice low during the whole

---

24. Sura, *Thailand's Rice Export Tax*, p. 21.
25. Sura, *Thailand's Rice Export Tax*, and Hasegawa *The Rice Situation*, pp. 493–494, 504. According to the latter, the income from this levy did not become national revenue but was used as political funds.
26. Ingram, *Economic Change*, p. 91.
27. Ingram, *Economic Change*, p. 91.
28. Ingram, *Economic Change*, p. 185; Sura, *Thailand's Rice Export Tax*, p. 20. These figures do not include the income from the multiple foreign exchange rate policy. Sura estimates this at about 15–20 percent in the period 1951 to 1954.
29. Ingram, *Economic Change*, p. 186.

period of the Korean War, when the international price of rice was high. This is the main reason for the present pattern of the Thai economy, with low internal prices of rice keeping the cost of living low.[30]

Thus Silcock holds that the system of rice exports in the late forties and fifties, a system closely involved with politics, formed the basis for the rice premium policy after 1955. I cannot deny this, in that politicians attempted to perpetuate the system for their own ends, but find it difficult to accept as the reason for the formal establishment of the rice premium policy, since all revenue from the policy went into the national coffers after 1955. I believe that a more fundamental basis for the rice premium policy lies in the importance of economic activities connected with rice, and the tradition of taxing these activities. The export tax on rice has continued from the middle of the nineteenth century to the present and is traditionally regarded as important by the Thai government. The production, marketing, and export of rice has been and still is the most important form of economic activity in Thailand, and is naturally subject to taxation. In fact, as stated earlier, revenue losses incurred by abolition of the land and head taxes on rice-producing farmers, taxes which until 1938 had provided a large part of Thailand's revenue, were recovered by tax revenue from rice exports after 1946.

After reaching a peak in 1951, the prices of most primary products other than rice started to fall, and in 1953 (the end of the Korean War) and in 1954, they fell violently. Many countries exporting these products imported rice; and because their foreign currency reserves plunged their demand for rice declined. Moreover, while the international price of rice had continued to rise from 1950 to 1953, that of wheat was generally stable, and demand shifted to wheat. Under these conditions the Thai rice trade gradually got into difficulties and by 1954 there were 800,000 tons of rice stored in Bangkok warehouses. The private export price of rice also declined, and with strict government control and multiple exchange rates the incentive for private export decreased. Faced with these difficulties the government gradually simplified procedures for rice export and liberalized the rice trade.

In January 1955, the Thai government relinquished its monopoly of rice trading and established a new system of private rice export, under which the rice premium was levied. The government was looking to private rice export to stimulate the rice trade. This was the start of the fourth period. Until July of that year, the multiple exchange rate system continued alongside the rice premium, but from August this was

---

30.   Silcock, *Economic Development*, p. 216.

simplified to the rice premium only.[31] So in 1955 the postwar government monopoly was replaced for one year by the private rice trade. The rice premium per ton of exported rice averaged about half that of the third period (for example, approximately 1,160 baht on 5 percent rice) and the amount of rice exported increased to 1,250,000 tons, an increase of 22 percent over the previous year.[32]

The rice premium policy is generally said to date from 1955, the fourth period, for the following reasons: (1) The extremely complex system of levies on rice exports under the multiple exchange rate system of the third period was simplified to a single specific tax called the rice premium in 1955. (2) The large portion of profit which had been misappropriated politically and privately in the third period was, under pressure chiefly from the Bank of Thailand,[33] diverted to accounts newly established at the Ministry of Economic Affairs,[34] and so became national revenue. However, as mentioned previously, the term "rice premium" had been used since 1951 to refer to the special levy on private rice exports.

RICE EXPORT POLICY IN THE FIFTH PERIOD (CONCURRENT GOVERNMENT AND PRIVATE EXPORTS)

In the fourth period—that is, 1955—rice exports from Thailand were all carried out privately, but in 1956 the government began to export rice again, and the fifth period of concurrent private and government exports has extended from 1956 to the present. For the following economic analysis of the rice export system, in particular, the rice premium policy, I will use primary data from my investigations in Thailand and the relevant literature.

Government exports of rice increased gradually from 1956, and in the sixties accounted for 26–46 percent of total exports. But government reentry into the export market has not involved reintroduction of the system of government control of the third period. Private exporters can export rice simply by paying the rice premium and other duties to the government. The Director General of the Department of Foreign Trade, Ministry of Commerce, Mr. Suthee Natvaratat, gave the following reasons for the coexistence of government and private exports: importing countries require government exports, private exporters cannot handle the large orders characteristic of government-

31. Hasegawa, *The Rice Situation*, pp. 509–510.
32. Hasegawa, *The Rice Situation*, p. 510, and Sura, *Thailand's Rice Export Tax*, pp. 22–26.
33. Silcock, *Economic Development*, pp. 217–219.
34. So named before 1972. From 1972 it was renamed the Ministry of Commerce.

to-government contracts, and government exports supplement private exports.[35]

I first want to investigate the mechanism of government rice exportation, which is basically similar in the fifth period to that in the first three periods. The government makes contracts with foreign governments specifying the price and amount of rice to be exported, then procures the rice from the private domestic market and allows private exporters to export it. This government export is actually all handled by private firms for a commission; the Department of Foreign Trade's management is only on paper. The domestic price of rice is lower than the export price because of the rice premium, as discussed later, and the government makes vast profits on its exports. The difference between the price at which the government buys rice and the export price is also called the rice premium.[36] Earlier in the fifth period, as in the first three periods, the government bought up rice for export at an official price,[37] but recently the price has been decided by tenders from private firms and has reached the market price.

Next I want to look at the system of private exportation, which follows a basic pattern. The exporter independently makes a contract with a foreign importer, then obtains export permission from the government, pays the rice premium and other duties, and exports the rice. The rice premium is calculated according to the grade and quantity of rice and is paid in full at the time of export by the exporter, who is licensed by the government.

According to the Board of Trade of Thailand, there are 126 rice exporting companies.[38] However, many are not exporting rice at present. Of those who are, many are also involved in internal distribution and operate rice warehouses and mills. The top five companies handle 30 percent of exports and are said to control the domestic rice market to some extent.[39]

In examining the structure of Thailand's rice export policies, I will first discuss the rice premium policy. As pointed out in the preceding section, the policy is based on the traditional characteristics of Thailand's

35.   Interview with the author, July, 1974.
36.   Jittima Pookkachatikul and D. E. Welsch, *Thai Rice Premium Data, 1954–1973*, Staff Paper No. 12 (Department of Agricultural Economics, Kasetsart University, 1974), p. 2.
37.   Sura, *Thailand's Rice Export Tax*, p. 26. This price was adjusted at intervals according to supply and demand.
38.   Board of Trade of Thailand, *Annual Report for 1973*, (Bangkok, 1974).
39.   According to my interviews with rice exporters.

economy and public finance and emerged in its earliest form in 1951. The policy proper was established in 1955, in which year the rice premium per ton of exported rice was about half of all taxes levied per ton of exported rice in the third period. The rice premium policy has continued from 1955 to the present (periods four and five).

At present there are three types of tax on exported rice:

(1) Rice export premium (here called the rice premium)
(2) Rice export tax
(3) Local tax on exported rice[40]

The rice premium (1) is a specific export duty.[41] As shown in the table, except in 1971–1973 and 1975, the premium contributed 21–35 percent of the total value of rice exports. Before 1965, the rice premium contributed between 9 and 17 percent of total government revenue, and was thus important to Thailand's finances. This proportion fell after 1966, rose to 8 percent in 1974 in response to strong world demand for rice, then fell again in 1975. The premium differs for each of the many grades of rice, and on the average it is higher for private than for government exports.[42]

The rice export tax (2) is the same as the prewar general export tax, and is an *ad valorum* duty of from 3.2 to 10 percent on the official export price.[43] The local tax on rice exported (3) is collected by the Ministry of the Interior and distributed to the towns and villages, in contrast to (1) and (2), which become national revenue. Of these three types of levy, the rice premium is the most important in terms of the revenue per unit weight of rice exported and the percentage of government revenue.[44]

First I will show in a simple figure, the influence of the rice premium policy on the export price P^x, the domestic price P^d, the amount exported Q, and domestic supply and demand. D^w is the world demand curve for Thai rice and X^t is the Thai rice export curve (excess supply curve). In this figure the domestic supply and demand curve corresponding to X^t could be drawn in the quadrant to the left of $\overline{OP}$, but is

40. Anan Lewchalermwong, *Taxation and Tax Reform in Thailand* (Bangkok: Kurusapha Ladprao Press, 1972), p. 96.

41. Ingram, *Economic Change*, p. 247. Faced with the prospect of a domestic rice shortage and a sharp rise in the domestic price, in January 1967 the government made the rice premium an *ad valorem* duty based on an official price for each grade of rice. Even after the situation eased, the rice premium continued on an *ad valorem* basis until September 1969, when it was made specific again.

42. Ingram, *Economic Change*, p. 247.

43. From Anan, *Taxation*, p. 96, and my interviews.

44. Anan, *Taxation*, p. 96, and Bank of Thailand, *Monthly Report*.

RICE EXPORTS AND THE RICE PREMIUM

YEAR	RICE EXPORTS			RICE PREMIUM				Wholesale price of 100 percent white rice (Bangkok)(baht/ton)
	(1) Volume (1000 tons)	(2) Value (million baht)	(3) Price (baht/ton)	(4) Total receipts from premium (million baht)	(5)ᵃ Average premium (baht/ton)	(6)ᵇ percent of export value	(7) percent of total government revenue	
1950	1,418	1,672	1,179					1,738
1951	1,474	1,824	1,237					1,912
1952	1,549	2,629	1,697					1,718
1953	1,359	3,747	2,757					1,705
1954	1,001	3,087	3,084					1,880
1955	1,236	3,133	2,535					1,858
1956	1,265	2,861	2,262	842	666	29	17	1,771
1957	1,570	3,622	2,307	840	535	23	16	1,963
1958	1,133	2,968	2,620	812	717	27	15	1,800
1959	1,092	2,576	2,359	756	692	29	13	1,641
1960	1,203	2,570	2,136	745	619	29	11	1,731
1961	1,576	3,598	2,283	872	553	24	12	1,992
1962	1,271	3,240	2,534	753	592	23	9	1,799
1963	1,418	3,424	2,416	819	578	24	9	1,680
1964	1,896	4,389	2,315	1,238	653	28	12	1,649
1965	1,895	4,334	2,281	1,192	629	28	11	

1966	1,507	4,001	2,650	995	660	25	8	2,189
1967	1,482	4,653	3,144	995	671	21	7	2,532
1968	1,068	3,775	3,534	1,268	1,187	34	8	2,110
1969	1,023	2,945	2,879	1,037	1,014	35	6	2,377
1970	1,064	2,517	2,366	540	508	21	3	2,103
1971	1,576	2,909	1,846	225	142	8	1	1,787
1972	2,112	4,437	2,101	158	75	4	0.7	1,976
1973	849	3,594	4,233	333	392	9	1	3,007
1974	1,029	9,778	9,502	3,123	3,072	34	8	3,921
1975	953^P	5,851^P	6,140^P	371	389^P	6^P	1	3,925

N.B. a: (4) ÷ (1) b: (4) ÷ (2) p: estimate

Source: Bank of Thailand, *Monthly Report*; Bank of Thailand, *IMF Consultations*, 1960, 1970; Department of Customs, *Annual Statement of Foreign Trade*.

THE RICE PREMIUM AND THE EXPORT QUOTA

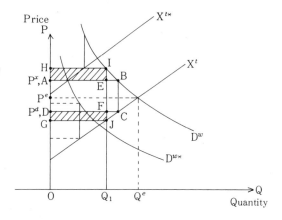

omitted for simplicity.[45] Rice marketing costs are assumed to be zero for the same reason. The slope of D^w or price elasticity of world demand for Thai rice is an important point and will be dealt with in detail in the next section. The figure shows that if there were no rice premium, the amount exported would be Q^e, and the export price and domestic price would be the same, P^e. But when there is a rice premium of $\overline{BC}$ per unit weight of exported rice, the amount exported becomes $\overline{DC}$, the export price P^x and the domestic price P^d; in other words, with a rice premium of $\overline{BC}$ and *ceteris paribus*, the amount of rice exported decreases from Q^e to $\overline{DC}$ and the export price and domestic price differ by $\overline{BC}$, the export price P^x being higher and the domestic price P^d lower than P^e. Although not shown on the figure, because the domestic price falls in accordance with the rice premium $\overline{BC}$, domestic rice supply decreases and demand increases. These changes in domestic supply and demand correspond to the fall in the amount exported from Q^e to $\overline{DC}$.

Since the war, export quotas have been adopted intermittently in Thailand. The figure shows the relationship between this system and the rice premium $\overline{BC}$. When the quota is $\overline{OQ_1}$ and the rice premium is $\overline{BC}$, the quota is effective (the quota determines the amount of rice

45.   This figure is based on the figure on p. 78 of my dissertation, Hiroshi Tsujii, "An Econometric Study of Effects of National Rice Policies and International Rice Trade among Less Developed and Developed Countries: With Special Reference to Thailand, Indonesia, Japan, and the United States", (Ph. D. dissertation, University of Illinois at Urbana-Champaign, 1973).

exported, the export price and the domestic price), and the rice premium is ineffective. In the sharing of excess profits (rectangle GHIJ) the rectangle AEFD becomes public revenue from the rice premium and the two shaded areas accrue to the exporters. But if the quota is greater than $\overline{DC}$, only the rice premium is effective: the Thai government receives the premium revenue and no excess profits accrue to the exporters.

Next I will investigate the mechanism by which the rice premium is determined. This has not been touched on by other writers, but relates to many important issues connected with the rice premium policy. The rice premium is under the jurisdiction of the Department of Foreign Trade, Ministry of Commerce, and the premium levels are decided on the basis of daily consideration of supply and demand in the international and domestic rice markets.[46] For such short periods as a week, and for longer periods when the quota is effective, the amount of exports can be considered constant. In this case the premium levels are decided on the basis of the difference between the export price of the different grades of rice and the sum of the domestic wholesale price, exporters' expenses, and normal profit. The idea is to guarantee normal profits for the exporters. But for longer periods when the export quota is not effective, the premium cannot be determined by this method, because the world demand for rice and the amount of rice exported are a function of price. In this case the rice premium is decided by the Department of Foreign Trade on consideration of the following points. First, the highest wholesale price and lowest farmer's price considered politically and socially acceptable at a given time should not be exceeded. Second, considerable revenue should accrue from the rice premium. And third, existing stable export markets for Thai rice should be safeguarded.[47] Thus in this second case the rice premium levels are determined by the government's evaluation of the political power relationship between itself, the consumers, and the farmers, and of financial and export market problems.

The rice exporters can also influence the process by which the government decides the rice premium. A Rice Committee at the Board

---

46. This explanation of the decision-making process is based on interviews with Mr. Suthee in July, 1974, and with other people connected with the rice trade, and also on various related materials.

47. In my interviews with the people responsible for the rice premium policy, I received the impression that the acquisition of foreign exchange from rice exports is not considered very important in the determination of the rice premium. This is worth noting in connection with the fact that the relative price elasticity of demand for Thai rice in the world market approximates to unity.

of Trade investigates the rice premium, and if it decides the levels should be changed the board of directors requests this of the government.[48]

At the Department of Foreign Trade there is no formal committee concerned with the rice premium, and the Director General of the department has a considerable say in deciding the premium. The department may not change the premium without the cabinet's agreement, and if this is not forthcoming the ministers concerned form a temporary committee to investigate the levels of the premium.

The problems in this decision-making process lie in the determinant factors of the premium: the export price of rice and its domestic wholesale price. These prices are quoted by the group of rice exporters who form the Rice Price Subcommittee of the Rice Committee of the Board of Trade. A quotation is made each Monday for that week, and the prices are approved by the Department of Foreign Trade. The Board of Trade of Thailand is a private organization set up to facilitate liaison and coordination between the government and traders and industrialists, to encourage foreign trade, and to mediate in commercial disputes. According to my interviews in the summer of 1974 with people connected with rice exports, the export price quoted by the Rice Price Subcommittee is the price the exporters can offer but it does not necessarily agree with the actual export price, which is frequently higher. If the quoted and the actual price differ, then in the short run or when the quotas are effective in the long run, rice exporters may make large profits or losses. When the quotas are not effective in the long run, the exporters make dynamic adjustment of their economic activities, which influences their profits or losses. In either case it is difficult for the government to carry out an appropriate rice premium policy. For these reasons it seems that the Department of Foreign Trade ought to use independently surveyed prices rather than the export price and domestic wholesale price quoted by the rice exporters.

As supplements to the rice premium policy, export quotas and the reserve stock policy, which is linked to rice exports, have been adopted intermittently since 1955.[49] Export quotas have been introduced

---

48. According to interviews at the Board of Trade of Thailand.
49. For the intermittent application of the export quotas, see Silcock, *Economic Development*, p. 217; Sura, *Thailand's Rice Export Tax*, p. 27. For the reserve stock policy, see Ammar Siamwalla, "A History of Rice Price Policies in Thailand," in *Finance, Trade and Economic Development in Thailand*, ed. Pratheep Sondyauvan (Bangkok: Sompong Press, 1975), pp. 141–165. The export quotas and the reserve stock policy of July 1974 began in 1972.

recently, from 1966 to 1968 and 1972 to 1974, when world and domestic supply were limited, there was excess demand, and the international price rose rapidly. At these times the rice premium policy, which has been in force continuously since 1955, and the export quotas were executed concurrently. Leaving aside the question of whether the difference between the export price and the domestic price accrues to private entrepreneurs or to the government, the export quotas and the export tax are, in international economic theory, interchangeable policy instruments for adjusting the price and amount of exports. In theory, either should be sufficient to fully achieve a given policy objective, so why are the rice premium and the quotas enforced simultaneously? I interviewed officials of the Department of Foreign Trade, rice exporters and people connected with the embassies of rice-importing countries, and offer the following analysis.

In practice the rice premium alone is not sufficient to achieve policy aims on price and export quantities. Rice is the staple food and wage good of the Thai people, so stabilization of the domestic rice price is a very important consideration for the government. When world demand for Thai rice increases rapidly (D^w in the figure shifts violently to the right), the rice premium, as a specific duty, would require numerous adjustments over a short period if the domestic price were to be maintained by this means alone. However, adjustment of the rice premium needs the agreement of the cabinet and this takes time. Moreover frequent change of the premium provokes strong opposition from the exporters (because of the uncertainty it creates).[50] Also, the position of the world demand curve for Thai rice, which is necessary in determining the rice premium, is extremely difficult to estimate accurately, especially when it is shifting rapidly. However, the quotas allow domestic prices to be held stable when acute increase in world demand prohibits estimation of the demand curve and many adjustments of the rice premium are difficult. For example if Q_1 is the amount of the export quota in the figure then the domestic price can be held at $\overline{OG}$.

The export quota alone is also not sufficient. First, if export amount and price are determined solely by the quota, all excess profits accrue to the exporters. This benefits the exporters unfairly. Concurrent use of the rice premium divides the excess profits between the government and

50. According to people connected with rice export, contracts for private export are made two to three months before export, whereas the rice premium has to be paid at the time of export. If the rice premium is changed every month, for example, the exporters have difficulty in estimating returns.

the exporters as just described. This is important to the Thai government, which until recently has lacked good sources of revenue. By proper management of the rice premium and the quotas the government can ensure fair profits for the exporters, which it hopes might be reinvested in the export trade.[51] Second, the rice premium can be adjusted faster than the export quotas. So if D^w or X^t shifts rapidly to the left, for example, to D^{w*} and X^{t*}, respectively, in the figure, and price and export quantity have to be adjusted rapidly, the rice premium is a better instrument than the quotas.

Thus the rice premium and quota policies are skillfully employed in concert to stabilize domestic prices and assure public revenue in the face of an extremely changeable world demand for Thai rice.

The export quotas are decided by the Department of Foreign Trade. At the beginning of the year rice production is predicted, the surplus for the year is estimated, and the year's quotas, which represent the export target, are fixed.[52] Until the end of 1973 the quota for each exporter was based on his past export quantities, but from January 1974 the amount held in warehouses was also considered.[53] This quota is decided on a monthly basis and each month's quota is effective for three months.[54]

Next I will briefly explain the second supplementary policy, the reserve stock policy, which together with the rice premium and the export quotas has been dealt with theoretically by Professor Chihiro Nakajima ("Theoretical Analysis of Rice Export System in Thailand," *Southeast Asian Studies* 13, no. 3, December, 1975). Under this policy, rice is purchased compulsorily from exporters at a low official price and is sold to consumers at less than market price when the domestic price rises greatly.[55] The amount purchased from an exporter is a specified proportion (the reserve ratio) of the amount he exports privately. This policy began in March 1962 with a reserve ratio of 15 percent and was in effect intermittently up to March 1973 at a reserve ratio of between 5 and 15 percent. The 1972/1973 rainy season crop was poor, some 18 percent less than the previous year, and from 1972 to 1973 the world

51.   In my interviews with people connected with rice export in summer 1974, the opinion that the premium and the export quota were being used for this purpose was put forward.

52.   According to interviews at the Department of Foreign Trade in 1974. The total quota for white rice in 1974 was 1,200,000 tons.

53.   According to interviews at the Department of Foreign Trade.

54.   As in note 53.

55.   According to an interview at the Department of Foreign Trade in July 1974, the government bought rice from the exporters at about 99 dollars a ton, and sold it to consumers at about 164 dollars a ton, under the reserve stock policy. At that time the market price was 197–213 dollars a ton.

market for cereals tightened considerably and the international trade prices of cereals soared. Domestic rice prices in Thailand started to rise rapidly at the end of 1972 and reached a peak in June 1973. From June to August 1973, Thailand faced a "rice crisis."[56] In this situation much of the rice collected under the reserve stock policy was soon sold to consumers at a low price, and the reserve ratio was increased rapidly from March of that year to 200 percent in August. In this way the reserve stock policy, together with the export quota adopted from 1972, was used to mitigate the acute domestic supply and demand situation from the end of 1972 to 1974.

This high reserve ratio provoked strong reaction from the rice exporters, and from October 1973 it was gradually lowered through a shift in emphasis to the rice premium policy.[57] However, the 1974 domestic price remained higher than that of 1973, and the reserve ratio rose to 50 percent in July 1974 and to 100 percent on December 27.[58] The reserve stock policy was abolished in January 1976.

Lastly I will look at the objectives of the rice premium policy and see to what extent they were achieved. These objectives are: to secure government revenue, to stabilize the domestic rice price by maintaining the domestic supply in the face of fluctuating world prices and changes in domestic supply and demand, and to control the excess profits of the exporters which result from the rice export quota and the licensing of exporters.[59] Judging from the process by which the policy was established and from the taxation tradition underlying it, the first objective was probably regarded as more important when the policy was introduced. Recently this objective had become secondary to the maintenance of domestic supply and stablization of domestic prices. This change in emphasis is described below.

As mentioned in connection with the table, income from the rice premium constituted from 9 to 17 percent of the total revenue before 1965 and was thought of as an important source of revenue by the government. After 1966 the importance of the premium as a source of revnue declined rapidly. In 1974, with the sharp rise in world rice prices, the premium on one ton of exported Thai rice rose to an unprecedented height, but government receipts from the premium reached only 8 percent of the total revenue (see the table). This resulted

---

56. From June 12 to July 30 1973 rice exports were prohibited.
57. For the reserve stock system and the "rice crisis," I used my interviews with the policy makers and rice exporters in Thailand, the FAO, *Rice Trade Intelligence* and Ammar, "A History of Rice Price Policies," p. 164.
58. As in note 57.
59. For example, Sura, *Thailand's Rice Export Tax*, p. 20.

from the recent structural change in government revenue, namely, the shift in emphasis to direct taxation.

From 1955 to 1965, as reflected by the average export price for Thai rice in the table, the world rice price was comparatively stable. In this period it was not necessary to stabilize the domestic rice price by adjusting the rice premium to absorb fluctuations in world rice prices. The average rice premium changed only slightly from 1955 to 1965 and the domestic rice price was stable in this period (see the table).

From 1966 to 1975 the world rice price indicated by the average export price for Thai rice in the table fluctuated wildly. In 1967 there was a severe drought in Thailand and rice production fell steeply, and in 1967 and 1968 the international rice price rose greatly. As a result, the average rice premium per ton of rice exported in 1968 and 1969 increased to more than 1,000 baht, almost double the previous level, and the rice premium for different grades changed frequently from 1967 to 1969. From the end of 1966 to about 1968 the rice export quota was in operation. Unfortunately there is no detailed material on the quota policy, but it is thought to have been effective alternately with the rice premium from 1966 to 1968.[60] As a result of these government measures rice exports fell sharply to about 1,000,000 tons per year in 1968 and 1969. Wholesale prices of white rice in Bangkok, which indicate the state of domestic supply and demand, fell in 1968 when world prices were at a peak. This illustrates the use of the rice premium with the help of the export quota policy to ease domestic demand and stablize the domestic price of rice.

In 1971 both world and domestic demand for rice became extremely slack and the export price for Thai rice fell suddenly. In response the government began to lower the rice premium on all grades of rice except the two highest (100 percent and 5 percent). As shown in the table the average rice premium per ton of rice exported fell to 142 baht in 1971 and 75 baht in 1972. By making the rice premium extremely low, rice exports were encouraged and a sharp fall in the domestic price was checked.

From 1972 to 1974, the domestic and international rice markets were extremely tight, the rice price rose sharply, and in 1973 the

---

60.   The rice premium is decided for each grade of rice, but the export quota is applied to the total quantity of rice exports. It is comparatively easy for exporters to alter the grade of rice through mixing and sifting. So even when the quota is effective, changes in the rice premium can have some effect on wholesale prices and on export prices and amount exported of the various grades of Thai rice. Also according to Ingram, *Economic Change*, pp. 247, 250–252, from January 1967 to September 1969, the rice premium was an *ad valorem* duty.

government stepped up its compulsory purchases under the reserve stock policy in order to supply consumers with low-priced rice. The average price of exported rice, as seen from the table, was 9,502 baht a ton in 1974, almost four times the average price after the war. The rice premium had also been increased greatly and averaged 3,072 baht a ton in 1974. As previously mentioned, the rice export quota was in operation from 1972 to 1974; and from June 12 to July 30, 1973, rice exports were prohibited. I think that there were months when the quota was effective and months when it was not, during this period from 1972 to 1974.[61] The rice premium policy and its supplementary policies succeeded in keeping rice exports at a low level in 1973 and 1974, as seen from the table, and they stopped the rise of domestic prices in 1974 at a little over twice average postwar prices.[62]

The preceding discussion of the aims of the rice premium and supplementary policies has shown that from 1965 procurement of government revenue became subordinate to stabilization of the domestic rice price, and that the latter aim was largely accomplished. In an interview in July, 1974, the Director General of the Department of Foreign Trade, Mr. Suthee, told me, "The important aims of the rice premium policy are firstly to keep the rice price for domestic consumers at a reasonable level, and, secondly to provide a fair rice price for the farmers. The rice premium is not regarded as very important as a source of government revenue." This corresponds with the change in emphasis of the rice premium policy aims stated above. But, as is also clear from the method of determination of the rice premium described earlier, it is generally difficult to achieve simultaneously a "reasonable" consumers' rice price and a "fair" farmers' price by the premium alone, since adjustment of the premium shifts the farmers' price and the consumers' price in the same direction.

Although the export price of rice changes frequently (about weekly), in the eleven years from 1956 to 1966, the premium for the main grades of rice changed only between two and nine times. As a

---

61. Data are partial, but, for example, in 1974 the quota for private exports was 80,000 tons in January; 100,000 tons in February; 65,000 tons in August; and 65,000 tons in September, whereas actual exports in these months were about 74,000; 144,000; 23,000; and 56,000 tons, respectively. Private exports in February used a quota carried over from 1973. For 1974 the quota for the year was 1,200,000 tons and the actual amount exported was 1,050,000 tons. See the FAO, *Rice Trade Intelligence* and the Bank of Thailand, *Monthly Bulletin* (various issues for 1974).

62. In interviews, Thai rice exporters often mentioned that the rice premium policy together with the export quota had prevented the internal price rising rapidly.

result fluctuations in the export and wholesale prices of Thai rice showed high positive correlation, on a weekly or monthly basis. Thus some scholars have concluded that the rice premium has little stabilizing effect on the domestic price.[63] After 1967 the rice premium was adjusted more often, though still infrequently compared with the movement of export prices. Thus the view that the rice premium has little stabilizing effect in the short term (weekly or monthly) is probably correct. However, as my analysis of the results of the rice premium and its supplementary policies demonstrates, from 1966 to 1975 the rice premium was employed chiefly on a longer term (yearly) basis with the aim of stabilizing domestic rice prices.

DISPUTES ON THE RICE PREMIUM POLICY

The rice premium policy has been the most discussed and researched economic policy in postwar Thailand. Here I would like to present a theoretical and empirical analysis of the dispute.

Before investigating this dispute the relationship between the rice premium policy and supplementary policies, the export quota, and the reserve stock policy should be clarified. This has not been attempted in previous studies of the dispute. Before March 1973 the reserve stock policy had little influence on the domestic and international rice markets since the reserve ratio was very low, and, therefore, it was not considered in the dispute on the rice premium policy. For this reason I shall not deal with the relation between these two policies in this section. However, when dealing with recent export policies the relationship between these two must be considered, because from 1973 the reserve ratio rose steeply and remained high throughout 1974 and 1975.

As explained, when the export quota system is effective the rice premium does not influence the export price, the amount exported, or domestic wholesale prices.[64] However, it does influence the division of the excess profits that accompany the quota system between the government and the rice exporters. But this question of profit distribution concerns the quota system and the relationship between the two policies rather than the rice premium policy itself, and has not previously featured in the rice premium dispute. The quota system has only been applied at times of very tight supply and demand, and the data in note

63. For example, see Sura, *Thailand's Rice Export Tax*, p. 28; Ingram, *Economic Change*, pp. 247, 253; Chaiyong Chuchart and Sopin Tongpan, *The Determination and Analysis of Policies to Support and Stabilize Agricultural Prices and Incomes of the Thai Farmers (With Special Reference to the Rice Premium)* (Bangkok: Ministry of National Development; Kasetsart University; SEATO, May 1965,) pp. 37–41.

64. This is not necessarily true for each grade of rice, as explained in note 60, but is true for Thai rice as a whole.

61 indicate there were many months when the quota was ineffective. For these reasons I will look at the dispute in cases where only the rice premium was effective and the quota system was not.

Most opponents of the rice premium policy are economists or agricultural economists[65] and the gist of their argument is as follows. They hold that both the international and domestic rice markets are competitive. And when the rice premium is levied, the domestic wholesale price and the farmers' price are forced down by almost the same amount. Because farmers are responsive to price changes, rice production falls, and the income of farmers, who make up more than 70 percent of Thailand's population, is greatly reduced. And the small group of city dwellers, whose income is higher than that of the farmers, can purchase rice, their staple food, more cheaply thanks to the rice premium. Consequently the rice premium is a policy of heavy taxation of the farmers and results in the unfair transfer of income from the majority of poor farmers to the minority of relatively affluent city dwellers. And from the point of view of rice exports, the decrease in Thailand's rice production decreases the amount of rice exported. As the opponents of the rice premium policy hold that the world rice market is competitive, they point out that this decrease in exports brings a proportional decrease in foreign currency receipts and is undesirable. And although they admit that the rice premium is an important source of government revenue, they hold that alternative sources can be found easily. So the opponents of the rice premium policy are of the opinion that the rice premium should be abolished or greatly reduced.

The supporters of the rice premium policy are Thai government officals.[66] One group holds that the domestic rice market is not com-

65. The views of the opponents of the rice premium policy are to be found in, for example, Chaihong and Sopin, *Determination and Analysis of Policies*, pp. 56–57; Dan Usher, "The Thai Rice Trade," in T. H. Silcock, ed., *Thailand: Social and Economic Studies in Development* (Canberra: Australian National University Press, 1967), pp. 206–230; Sura *Thailand's Rice Export Tax*, Phairach Krisanamis, *Paddy Price Movements and Their Effect on the Economic Situation of Farms in the Central Plain of Thailand* (Ph. D. dissertation, Indiana University) (Bangkok: National Institute of Development Administration, June, 1967), pp. 20–24; J. R. Behrman, *Supply Response in Underdeveloped Agriculture: A Case Study of Four Major Annual Crops in Thailand, 1937–1963* (Amsterdam: North-Holland Publishing Co., 1968), pp. 10–13, 337; Virach Arromdee, "Economics of Rice Trade among Countries of South East Asia," (Ph. D. dissertion, University of Minnesota, 1968).

66. The report of the World Bank on Thailand, International Bank for Reconstruction and Development, *A Public Development Program for Thailand* (Baltimore: John Hopkins Press, 1959), pp. 68–69, also endorses the policy.

petitive, and that if the rice premium is abolished the profit will all be absorbed by middlemen and the farmers' price will not rise. This assertion rests on their belief that the domestic market is not competitive because the rice merchants are in coalition, and this seems to be supported by the licensing of exporters, which limits numbers and competition in the rice trade. At the present time I do not know to what extent competition is limited by licensing and will leave further discussion of this point to the future. I will now investigate the opinions of another group of proponents of the rice premium policy who hold the domestic market to be competitive.

This group of supporters asserts that "because the rice premium had raised the export price of rice in comparison with when there was no premium, part of the premium is being paid by the countries importing Thai rice."[67] Namely, they view the world market for Thai rice as imperfectly competitive.

These supporters of the policy do not deny that the rice premium has increased government revenue and forced down farmers' income by lowering the farmers' rice price. But, they assert, farmers are ultimately compensated for loss of income by government-financed development and diffusion of farming techniques and investment in irrigation and road construction. In this way the increased government revenue from the rice premium is considered to be restored to the rice farmers. They also say that the rice premium is an important source of revenue, and it would not be simple to find an appropriate tax base to replace it. Thus they hold that payment of part of the rice premium falls on rice-importing countries and that the fall in rice farmers' income is compensated for by government expenditure on agriculture.

Part of this group consider that the farmers do not respond to rice prices and that rice production does not fall despite a decrease in the farmers' price when the rice premium is in operation. So these supporters of the rice premium hold that it does not repress domestic production or rice exports.

The other part of this group who hold that rice production does respond to price argue in the following way. Because the rice premium stablizes the domestic rice price at a low level, first, it promotes the development of Thai agriculture by encouraging crop diversification as it makes rice less profitable vis-à-vis other crops. Second, as rice is the staple food of the Thai people, a low price is useful in stablizing the wages of workers in the towns and so offers favorable conditions

67.   Ingram, *Economic Change*, p. 248.

for Thailand's industrialization. And third, a low rice price is one of the prerequisites of political stability in Thailand.

The following four main questions emerge from this dispute.[68]

(A) Who bears the export tax, the rice premium?
(B) To what extent are the domestic and export markets for Thai rice competitive?
(C) How responsive are the rice farmers to prices?
(D) How should resources and the burden of taxation be allocated between agriculture and other industries?

First I will treat question (B). I consider the world market for Thai rice to be imperfectly competitive, for the following reasons.

(1) The relative export price elasticity of world demand for Thai rice at the averages, calculated from my econometric model of the international rice market,[69] is about unity. This elasticity is calculated from the world rice model estimated from time series data for the fifties and sixties, with respect to world demand for Thai rice and the relative price of the Thai rice export price index and the world export price index. Because this relative price was used, the elasticity can be thought of as a long-term elasticity. According to the figure, this elasticity is the approximate value of the long-term elasticity of the export amount Q with respect to the export price P^x, and for the demand curve D^w, and for this reason it can be said that D^w slopes steeply down to the right in the vicinity of the average values of P^x and Q.

(2) The Department of Foreign Trade, which controls Thai rice export, is clearly aware of competition among the main exporting countries of Burma, China, America, and Japan, and these competitive conditions are important considerations in decisions on rice export policies.[70]

(3) The Thai share of the world rice export market is very large (from 1966 to 1972 it averaged about 20 percent) and the domestic rice market in most countries is kept separate from the world market by each country's rice policies.

(4) The Department of Foreign Trade can use the rice premium policy and the export quota as devices to control export price and quantity.

(5) The established reputation of Thai rice as high quality rice in Asia and the long relations between Thailand and various importing countries mean that Thai rice is favored.

68. Hiroshi Tsujii, "An Econometric Model of the International Rice Market and Analysis of the National Rice Policies in Thailand, Indonesia, Japan and the United States," Discussion Paper No. 75, The Center for Southeast Asian Studies, Kyoto University, 1974, p. 44.

69. Tsujii, "An Econometric Model," p. 52.

70. Based on my interviews in Thailand.

Points (2) to (5) imply that the Thai government behaves as an oligopolist in the world rice market.

Next under question (B) I want to look at competition in the domestic rice market. The works of Udhis and Usher on rice marketing in Thailand come to the conclusion that rice marketing is efficient and competitive.[71] And my investigations of rice producers, millers, and the markets in the areas of production, showed that the rice trade was fairly competitive. For these reasons I conclude that the domestic rice market in Thailand is competitive.

As for who must bear the rice premium, question (A), the considerable downward slope to the right of the long-term world demand curve and the rise to the right of the long-term Thai rice export curve together indicate that both rice-importing countries and the rice-producing farmers bear the rice premium.

Next, I wish to discuss the response of the farmers to prices, (C). Many works on this topic, for instance Behrman's study on Thailand,[72] and my previously mentioned econometric study, indicate positive response. This point is not disputed by scholars.

I will now evaluate the dispute on the rice premium policy based on the preceding examination of questions (A), (B), and (C). The basic assumption of the opponents of the rice premium that the world rice market facing Thailand is perfectly competitive is not supported by the evidence, (1) to (5), which shows that this market is imperfectly competitive. And the main views of the opponents, which follow from this assumption and its corollary that the export price for Thai rice is an exogenously determined constant, are either not substantiated or must be greatly revised. These views are (i) the rice premium is borne by the farmers only, (ii) there is an unfair transfer of income from the majority of poor farmers to the minority of relatively affluent town-dwellers, (iii) the domestic rice price is forced down by the same amount as the rice premium, (iv) because of this rice production is reduced and (v) rice exports decrease and important foreign exchange is lost. Views (i) and (iii) are not substantiated and the others should be moderated. Because the basic assumption of the policy's supporters that the long-term world demand curve for Thai rice slopes downward to the right is correct, their opinion that part of the rice premium is borne by importing countries is upheld. Both supporters and opponents hold that in the long-term the domestic rice price will be forced down by the rice premium. Thus the part of the rice premium not borne by

71.   Udhis Narkswasdi, *Farmers Indebtedness and Paddy Marketing in Central Thailand* (in Thai) (Bangkok, 1958); Dan Usher, "The Thai Rice Trade."
72.   Behrman, *Supply Response.*

the importing countries will be borne by the domestic rice producers through lower rice prices.

Assertions (ii), (iv), and (v) of the opponents of the rice premium policy are exaggerated, as the long-term world demand curve for Thai rice is fairly steep. In particular, claim (v) that foreign currency receipts are lost under the rice premium is in error near the averages if, as described above, the price elasticity of the long-term world demand curve for Thai rice approximates to unity at the averages. In this case, even if the rice premium is levied, foreign exchange revenue will hardly alter.

Last, I wish to examine question (D), taxation and expenditure patterns and the allocation of resources, in relation to the rice premium dispute. First, the position of supporters of the rice premium policy that receipts from this policy eventually return to the rice producers seems to be well supported by the emphasis placed on irrigation and road investment in past development plans and their implementation.[73] Government ideology in connection with the rice premium policy is along these lines.[74] Second, Sura and Anan have studied alternative tax bases to the rice premium policy.[75] They agree that increased revenue is possible with direct taxes. These research results, together with the recent shift in emphasis in public finance towards direct taxation, support the views of policy opponents that an alternative tax base can be developed. Third, according to Silcock, Ayal, Marzouk and others the rice premium has been effective in diversifying agriculture.[76] Thai agriculture has recently diversified rapidly while the rice premium policy was in force, and this means that the supporters of the policy were probably correct on this point. And fourth, the supporters' proposition that the rice premium has stabilized domestic rice prices and thus contributed to industrialization and political stability is supported.

73. The same opinion is found in Ingram, *Economic Change*, p. 259 in connection with the Central region of Thailand.
74. According to Silcock, *Thailand*, p. 217. In my interviews with the Director General of the Department of Foreign Trade, in July, 1974, I was told that about three billion baht of that year's revenue from the rice premium had been officially earmarked for the stabilization of the rice price and for the encouragement of rice production.
75. Sura, *Thailand's Rice Export Tax*, pp. 128–130 and Anan, *Taxation*, pp. 108, 142–160.
76. T. H. Silcock, "The Rice Premium and Agricultural Diversification," in *Thailand: Social and Economic Studies in Development*, ed. by T. H. Silcock, pp. 231–257; E. B. Ayal, "The Impact of Export Tax on the Domestic Economy of Underdeveloped Countries," *Journal of Development Studies*, (July, 1965): 344–345; G. A. Marzouk, *Economic Development and Policies* (Rotterdam University Press, 1972), pp. 135–144.

As previously stated the rice premium stabilizes domestic rice prices over a long-term period, that is, annually; and in view of the importance of rice to the Thai people, it cannot be denied that the stabilization of the rice price has contributed to industrialization and political stability.[77] Thus the proponents of the policy are correct in three of their assertions pertaining to the taxation and expenditure pattern and the allocation of resources, but mistaken on the feasibility of finding alternative sources of revenue.

The results of this analysis of the dispute on the rice premium policy are that, with the exceptions of the response of the rice producers to the rice price and the feasibility of finding alternative sources of revenue, the views of the opponents of the policy are mistaken or need large-scale revision, and the opinions of the supporters of the policy are mostly correct.

CONCLUSION

The rice premium policy is one of taxation of rice exports. It officially began in 1955, from which year the complex postwar system of rice exports was simplified and all revenue from rice exports accrued to the treasury, although a rice premium had been levied on private exports since 1951. Silcock sees the establishment of the rice premium in 1955 as a continuation of the political and economic machinery of the early fifties for taxing rice exports. However, I think that the rice premium has a more traditional basis. To support this I pointed out that rice export taxes have been important to the government since the nineteenth century, and that eight years after the abolition of the land and head taxes in 1938, two traditionally important sources of revenue borne by rice farmers, a system of export taxes on rice was introduced to compensate for these taxes.

From 1956, rice has been exported from Thailand both privately and by the state, the government regarding its exports as complementary to private ones. Rice for state export is bought at a price considerably lower than the contracted export price, and the difference between these prices, which becomes national revenue, is also called the rice premium. Usually, however, the rice premium denotes the specific duty paid by private rice exporters to the government at the time of export according to the grade and weight of rice exported. It is sometimes supplemented with export quotas and the reserve stock policy. Together the rice premium and the export quotas are employed as complementary policy measures aimed at stabilizing domestic rice

77.   Ingram, *Economic Development*, p. 258.

prices and guaranteeing government revenue in the face of violently fluctuating world demand for Thai rice and unstable rice production in Thailand.

Of the three levies on rice export, the rice premium, the rice export tax, and the local tax, the rice premium's contribution to government revenue is greatly preponderant. The rice premium is decided by the Department of Foreign Trade, Ministry of Commerce, with cabinet approval, in the short run, or in the long run when the export quota is effective, by consideration of domestic and export prices, in order to give normal profits to rice exporters. When the quota system is not effective in the long run, the premium is decided by the Department of Foreign Trade and the cabinet to balance the following political and economic considerations: the consumers' demand for a low rice price; the farmers' demand for a high paddy price; the desirability of high tax receipts from the rice premium; and the maintenance of existing stable export markets for Thai rice. Rice exporters can request changes in the rice premium through the Board of Trade of Thailand. The weakness in the process of deciding the rice premium is that domestic and export rice prices are supplied to the Department of Foreign Trade by the Board of Trade's Rice Price Committee, which is made up of rice exporters.

The policy aims of the rice premium policy are to secure government revenue and to guarantee domestic rice supplies and stabilize the domestic rice price. The first aim was paramount until the middle sixties but became secondary with the shift in emphasis of the taxation structure which accompanied economic development. The second aim became dominant after 1966. From 1955 to 1966 international rice prices had been comparatively stable, but from 1966 to 1975 they fluctuated violently. In fact the rice premium and its supplementary policies have been applied more promptly since 1966, with the aim of stabilizing domestic rice prices and, judging from yearly average domestic rice prices, have had a considerable stabilizing effect.

The rice premium policy is the most researched and disputed economic policy of postwar Thailand. Except in the periods 1971 to 1973 and 1975 the rice premium has constituted 21 to 35 percent of the export price of rice, and consequently is an important source of government revenue which greatly influences the Thai economy. This analysis of the rice premium dispute has dealt only with times when the quota system was not effective and has ignored the reserve stock policy, for the reasons stated earlier.

The opponents of the rice premium assume the international rice market to be perfectly competitive. They believe that the rice premium forces the domestic price of rice down by an amount cor-responding to the premium, and thus is borne only by the rice farmers, and that the rice premium reduces rice production and farmers' income, results in unfair transfer of income from the majority of poor farmers to the minority of relatively affluent town dwellers, and reduces foreign currency earnings by curtailing exports. However, the assump-tion of perfect competition is not upheld. The international rice market facing Thailand is imperfectly competitive: the Thai government occupies an oligopolistic position from which it can, to some extent, control the price and amount of rice exported through the rice premium and the export quota. So the points put forward by the opponents of the rice premium, based on the supposition that the market is perfectly competitive, are mistaken or in need of considerable revision. In particular, the suggestion that the rice premium reduces foreign currency earnings from rice export is not upheld near the averages, since the relative price elasticity of world demand for Thai rice ap-proximates to unity as shown in my econometric study.

The opinion of the rice premium policy's supporters that part of the premium is paid by importing countries is correct, because the rice premium raises the export price of Thai rice, that is, the long-term world demand curve for Thai rice falls to the right. But the assertion of part of the supporters that the rice-producing farmers are not responsive to the price of rice is not vindicated. From these conclusions it can be seen that the rice premium is borne by both importing coun-tries and Thai rice producers. The opinions of the supporters that revenue from the rice premium is returned to the farmers through government agricultural expenditure, and that the rice premium policy contributes to political stability and promotes agricultural diversification and industrialization are also upheld. But their proposi-tion that the development of an alternative source of tax revenue to the rice premium is extremely difficult is not supported. So the result of this analysis of the rice premium policy dispute is to endorse most of the views of the supporters of the rice premium policy and to suggest that it is necessary for its opponents to greatly revise some of their views and abandon others.

16

On the Two-Gap Analysis of Foreign Aid

MITSUO EZAKI

INTRODUCTION

The objective of this article is to clarify the welfare implications of the two-gap analysis of foreign aid, concentrating on the model developed by Chenery and Strout,[1] and to provide related numerical examples for four Southeast Asian countries (Republic of Vietnam, Thailand, Indonesia, and the Philippines), where the real series of national income statistics are available.

The two gaps are, of course, the investment-saving gap (*IS* gap) and the import-export gap (*ME* gap), both of which are used in the *ex ante* sense and must be consistent with the target growth-rate of output. Two-gap analysis of foreign aid means that the required amount of foreign aid should be determined by whichever is the dominant gap. Synthesizing previous works on the macro-analysis of foreign aid— Rosenstein-Rodan, Chenery and Bruno, Mckinnon, Fei and Paauw, Adelman and Chenery, etc.—[2] Chenery and Strout made an extensive

---

1. H. Chenery and A. Strout, "Foreign Assistance and Economic Development," *American Economic Review* 56 (September, 1966): 679–733. The welfare implications of their two-gap analysis of foreign aid are also discussed from a different point of view by Deepak Lal, "The Foreign Exchange Bottleneck Revisited: A Geometric Note," *Economic Development and Cultural Change* 20 (July, 1972): 722–730. A short survey of foreign aid theories is given in Raymond F. Mikesell, *The Economics of Foreign Aid* (Chicago, 1968), chapter 3. A comprehensive study of two-gap analysis, theoretical and practical, is made by J. Vaneck, *Estimating Foreign Resource Needs for Economic Development: Theory, Method and a Case Study of Colombia* (New York, 1967).
2. P. Rosenstein-Rodan, "International Aid for Underdeveloped Countries," *Review of Economics and Statistics* 43 (May, 1961): 107–138; H. Chenery and M. Bruno,

(*Continued on p. 322*)

theoretical and empirical study of foreign aid using the two-gap approach incorporating analysis of absorptive capacity limit, and showed that most of the developing countries would pass through three phases in order to reach and maintain a constant target rate of growth. The three phases, whose order was determined empirically, are: Phase I where the absorptive capacity limit and one of the two gaps are effective; Phase II where the *IS* gap is dominant; and Phase III where the *ME* gap is dominant.[3]

The essence of the Chenery and Strout two-gap analysis lies in determining the amount of foreign aid required for the constant target growth-rate of output. From the welfare point of view, however, the target growth rate need not be constant and must be determined in such a way as to maximize the social welfare function. The optimal or required amount of foreign capital inflow will be determined correspondingly. This approach was adopted by Chenery and MacEwan,[4] in their linear programming analysis of the Pakistani economy using a slightly more elaborate framework than Chenery and Strout. In this article I will apply the same procedure to the framework of Chenery and Strout and try to obtain general results on the welfare implications of their two-gap approach.[5] The main result derived from this optimization procedure is that if the optimal solution exists, it must occur where the two gaps are made equal throughout the planning period (except for very special cases). This means that if either the *IS* gap or *ME* gap is dominant, even for a very short period along a certain growth path of the economy, that time path cannot be optimal. From

---

(*Continued from p. 321*)

"Development Alternatives in an Open Economy: The Case of Israel," *Economic Journal* 77 (March, 1962): 79–103; R. McKinnon, "Foreign Exchange Constraints in Economic Development and Efficient Aid Allocation," *Economic Journal* 74 (June, 1964): 308–409; J. C. H. Fei and D. C. Paauw, "Foreign Assistance and Self-Help: A Reappraisal of Development Finance," *Review of Economics and Statistics* 47 (August, 1965): 215–267; I. Adelman and H. Chenery, "Foreign Aid and Economic Development: The Case of Greece," *Review of Economics and Statistics* 48 (February 1966): 1–19.

3. Note that in Phase I the target growth rate is not attained due to the absorptive capacity limit, while in Phase II and Phase III, where the absorptive capacity limit is no longer effective, the target growth rate is attained and maintained.

4. H. Chenery and A. MacEwan, "Optimal Patterns of Growth and Aid: The Case of Pakistan," in I. Adelman and E. Thorbecke, eds., *The Theory and Design of Economic Development* (Baltimore, 1966).

5. The scope of this analysis will be limited Phases II and III only, that is, to cases where the economy has been released from the absorptive capacity limit. This limitation, however, will not lead to the loss of any essential features of their two-gap approach.

the point of view of maximizing social welfare, therefore, I conclude that the required amount of foreign aid may better be determined by the one-gap approach rather than by the two-gap.[6] As an illustration of this conclusion, I will provide numerical examples on the one-gap and the two-gap approaches for four countries, the Republic of Vietnam (South Vietnam), Thailand, Indonesia, and the Philippines, concluding with a brief discussion on the relationships between foreign aid and economic growth in these countries from the 1970s to the 1980s.

BASIC FEATURES OF THE CHENERY-STROUT MODEL

It seems worthwhile to summarize here the basic features of the Chenery-Strout model in preparation for the later analysis of its welfare implications. I have adopted the same notation:

V_t = Gross National Product (in year t)
I_t = Gross investment
S_t = Gross domestic savings
$\overline{S}_t$ = Potential gross domestic savings
M_t = Imports of goods and services[7]
$\overline{M}_t$ = Required imports of goods and services
E_t = Exports of goods and services
F_t = Net inflow of foreign capital
C_t = Consumption
$\overline{r}$ = Target rate of growth of GNP
α' = Marginal savings rate ($\Delta \overline{S}/\Delta V$)
β = Maximum rate of growth of investment
k = Incremental gross capital-output ratio ($I/\Delta V$)
μ' = Marginal import rate ($\Delta \overline{M}/\Delta V$)
ε = Rate of growth of exports.

Then the most comprehensive formulation of their model can be expressed as:

6. The term "one-gap approach" was first introduced by T. Fukuchi in "The One Gap Approach versus the Two Gap Approach," *Developing Economies* 8 (December, 1970): 3–15. However, it must be noted that my use of the term is a little different from his. Here the two gaps are defined in terms of *consistent minimums*, and my one-gap approach applies to the case where these two gaps are equalized (or made equal). On the other hand, Fukuchi formulates a model with the two gaps equalized a priori for the reason that consistent parameter estimates must be dervied from the *ex post* data where the IS and the ME gaps are always equal. He does not allow for the two gaps based on the concept of consistent minimums. He shows that it is possible to attain the target average rate of growth and/or the target foreign capital inflow by changing the parameter values of the model. The concept of consistent minimums is treated in the next section of this article.

7. Note that interest payment on foreign debt is either neglected completely or included in this variable.

1. $V_{t+1} = V_t + (1/k)I_t$ (more generally, $V_{t+1} \leqslant V_t + (1/k)I_t)$[8]
2. $V_t = S_t + C_t$
3. $S_t \leqslant \overline{S}_t = \overline{S}_0 + \alpha'(V_t - V_0)$
4. $M_t \geqslant \overline{M}_t = \overline{M}_0 + \mu'(V_t - V_0)$
5. $E_t = E_0(1 + \varepsilon)^t$ (more generally, $E_t \leqslant E_0(1 + \varepsilon)^t)$
6.7. $F_t = I_t - S_t = M_t - E_t$
8. $F_t = \max\{I_t - \overline{S}_t, \overline{M}_t - E_t\}$
9. $I_t \leqslant (1 + \beta)I_{t-1}$
10. $V_t \leqslant (1 + \overline{r})V_{t-1}$.

Here we must note that potential savings $(\overline{S}_t)$ means the maximum amount of domestic savings potentially available at the income level of V_t; required imports $(\overline{M}_t)$ means the minimum amount of import required to support the output level of V_t; and the absorptive capacity limit is identified with the skilled-labor limit, which leads to a maximum growth rate of investment (β).

In this formulation, the essence of the two-gap approach is represented by equations 8 and 10. Equation 8, in particular, indicates that the required amount of foreign capital inflow should be determined by the dominant gap of the two, that is, either $(I_t - \overline{S}_t)$ or $(\overline{M}_t - E_t)$. On the other hand, from equations 1, 3, and 4, the two gaps must be consistent with the growth of GNP, which is determined by the target growth rate (equation 10), though the target rate must be replaced by the maximum feasible rate under the skill limit when equation 9 holds with equality. Now it seems clear that our two gaps are *minimum consistent*, according to Vanek's terminology,[9] because they are consistent with GNP growth and because they are feasible minimums due to the fact that, under the given GNP growth, $\overline{S}$ and E are feasible maximums while I and $\overline{M}$ are feasible minimums.

In the preceding model, one can understand easily (with equations 6 and 7 in mind) the fact that equation 8 is equivalent with and therefore replaceable by

8'. $S_t = \overline{S}_t$ and $M_t > \overline{M}_t$, or $S_t < \overline{S}_t$ and $M_t = \overline{M}_t$.

In the first equation of 8', the potential savings are realized $(S_t = \overline{S}_t)$ and the *IS* gap becomes dominant $(F_t = I_t - \overline{S}_t)$, while the amount of imports is determined at above the minimum required level $(M_t = F_t + E_t \geqslant \overline{M}_t)$ by some adjustment process.[10] On the other

8. To generalize further $V_t \leqslant V_0 + (1/k)\sum_{\tau=0}^{t-1}I_\tau$.
9. See J. Vanek, *Estimating Foreign Resource Needs for Economic Development: Theory, Method and a Case Study of Colombia*, chapter 6.
10. Concerning the expost adjustment of gaps, see Vanek, Estimating Foreign Resource Needs for Economic Development, pp. 108–111.

hand, in the second equation of $8'$, the amount of imports is realized at the minimum required level $(M_t = \overline{M}_t)$, and the ME gap becomes dominant $(F_t = \overline{M}_t - E_t)$, while the level of savings remains below the potential maximum $(S_t = I_t - F \leqslant \overline{S}_t)$. The relation $8'$ together with skill limit 9 and target growth constraint 10 leads us to the three phases as shown in Table 1. Note that in each phase there exist seven equalities which determine the time paths of the seven variables in the economy, that is, $V, S, C, I\ M, E,$ and F. Each phase lasts as long as the characteristics of that phase (expressed in Table 1) remain unchanged. Changes in the characteristics will result in a transition from one phase to another. Based on a very extensive empirical study of many developing countries, Chenery and Strout showed that the most typical transition would first be from Phase I (to be more specific, Phase IA) to Phase II and then from Phase II to Phase III.

WELFARE MAXIMIZATION UNDER THE CHENERY-STROUT MODEL

As the summary of the previous section clearly illustrates, the leading principle implicit in the two-gap analysis of Chenery and Strout consists in the fact that the required amount of foreign aid is determined to realize maximum GNP growth. That is to say, when the target rate of GNP growth is attainable, the dominant gap consistent with that growth rate determines the amount of foreign aid. On the other hand, when the target growth rate is not attainable due to the absorptive capacity limit, the amount of foreign aid is determined by the dominant gap consistent with the GNP growth rate, which is the feasible maximum under the absorptive capacity constraint. It must be noted, however, that under the framework for the national economies of developing countries adopted by Chenery and Strout, there exists the possibility that the economy grows faster than the assigned target rate. There is no reason, except for the purpose of simplifying planning targets, why the economy should remain on the growth path with constant target rate after it is freed from the absorptive capacity limitation. This, however, is not the main point. The main point is that maximum GNP growth does not always imply maximum welfare. Therefore, it seems worthwhile to clarify the welfare implications of their two-gap analysis, which is the main objective of this article. For this purpose, the scope of the analysis was limited to cases where the absorptive capacity limit is no longer effective without losing the essential features of their two-gap approach. Continuous rather than discrete time was used to make calculations easier, and the social welfare function of Chenery and MacEwan was adopted.

TABLE 1
THREE PHASES OF THE CHENERY-STROUT MODEL

	Phase I (Phase IA)	(Phase IB)	Phase II	Phase III
Growth limit	$V_t \leqslant (1 + \bar{r})V_{t-1}$		$V_t = (1 + \bar{r})V_{t-1}$	$V_t = (1 + \bar{r})V_{t-1}$
Skill limit	$I_t = (1 + \beta)I_{t-1}$		$I_t \leqslant (1 + \beta)I_{t-1}$	$I_t \leqslant (1 + \beta)I_{t-1}$
Savings limit	$S_t = \bar{S}_t$	$S_t \leqslant \bar{S}_t$	$S_t = \bar{S}_t$	$S_t \leqslant \bar{S}_t$
Import limit	$M_t \geqslant \bar{M}_t$	$M_t = \bar{M}_t$	$M_t \geqslant \bar{M}_t$	$M_t = \bar{M}_t$
Equalities	(1) (2) (3) (5) (6) (7) (9)	(1) (2) (4) (5) (6) (7) (9)	(1) (2) (3) (5) (6) (7) (10)	(1) (2) (4) (5) (6) (7) (10)
Dominant gap	IS gap	ME gap	IS gap	ME gap

The welfare function adopted by Chenery and MacEwan for the case study of Pakistani development planning has the following form (expressed in terms of continuous time) :[11]

$$W = \int_0^T C(t)e^{-it}dt + \eta V(T) - \gamma \int_0^T F(t)e^{-it}dt$$

where T = Terminal year of the plan; i = Rate of discount; η = Weight for terminal year income incorporating discount procedure for future consumption; γ = Cost (or price) of foreign capital, which varies according to the supply conditions for the country concerned.

Then the strategy for planners will be to maximize social welfare with respect to related economic variables in such a way as to satisfy the following framework for the national economy:

$$\dot{V}(t) = dV(t)/dt = (1/k)I(t)$$
$$V(t) = S(t) + C(t)$$
$$S(t) \leq \overline{S}(t) = \overline{S}(0) + \alpha'(V(t) - V(0))$$
$$M(t) \geq \overline{M}(t) = \overline{M}(0) + \mu'(V(t) - V(0))$$
$$E(t) = E(0)e^{\varepsilon t}$$
$$F(t) = I(t) - S(t) = M(t) - E(t).$$

Note that this framework corresponds to Phases II and III (the case of ineffective skill limit) in the analysis of Chenery and Strout. The reason I omitted equation 8 or 8′ of the previous section is that I believe the dominant gap should be determined in the process of maximizing social welfare.[12]

It is now clear that the optimization procedure can be reduced to the following condensed form (omitting the time argument t):

$$\text{Maximize} \int_0^T (C - \gamma F)e^{-it}dt + \eta V(T)$$

with respect to state variable (V) & control variables (C, S, M, I, F) subject to $C = V - S$, $I = S + M - E$, $F = M - E$,

11. See Chenery and MacEwan, "Optimal Patterns of Growth and Aid," p. 155.
12. For reference purposes, the actual parameter values for the Pakistani economy are cited here:

$$i = \cdot08 \qquad \eta = 3\cdot4 \qquad \gamma = 2\cdot0$$
$$k = 3\cdot0 \qquad \alpha' = \cdot24 \qquad \mu' = \cdot10 \qquad \varepsilon = \cdot07$$

$$S \leqslant \alpha + \alpha'V \ (\alpha = S(0) - \alpha'V(0)),$$
$$M \geqslant \mu + \mu'V(\mu = \overline{M}(0) - \mu'V(0)), \text{ and } \dot{V} = (1/k)I.$$

Then the corresponding Lagrangean function becomes

$$L = (C - \gamma F)e^{-it} + p\cdot(1/k)I - q(C - V + S)$$
$$- q_1(I - S - M + E) - q_2(F - M + E)$$
$$- u(S - \alpha - \alpha'V) + v(M - \mu - \mu'V)$$

and the Lagrange multipliers $(q, q_1, q_2, u$ and $v)$ and the auxiliary variable (p) must satisfy

(1) $e^{-it} - q = 0$
(2) $-q + q_1 - u = 0$
(3) $q_1 + q_2 + v = 0$
(4) $-q_1 + p/k = 0$
(5) $-q_2 - \gamma e^{-it} = 0$
(6) $u \geqslant 0$ and $u(S - \alpha - \alpha'V) = 0$
(7) $v \geqslant 0$ and $v(M - \mu - \mu'V) = 0$
(8) $\dot{p} = -q - u\alpha' + v\mu'$
(9) $p(T) = \eta$ (transversality condition).

Note that the conditions mentioned are not only necessary but also sufficient, since the Hamiltonian $(= (C - \gamma F)e^{-it} + p\cdot(1/k)I)$ maximized under the given V, p and t is a linear (that is, concave) function of V for given p and t.[13]

From equations (1) $\sim$ (5) we get

(10) $q = e^{-it}$, $q_1 = p/k$ and $q_2 = -\gamma e^{-it}$

and therefore

(11) $u = p/k - e^{-it}$ and $v = -p/k + \gamma e^{-it}$

which, from equations (6) and (7), lead to

(12) $ke^{-it} \leqslant p \leqslant \gamma k e^{-it}$

where $\gamma \geqslant 1$ is assumed.[14] In other words, the time path of p must lie within the range set by the two bounds with a common rate of decrease $(-i)$. When p coincides with the upper bound (that is, $u > 0$ and $v = 0$) somewhere within the planning period, the savings constraint is effective

13.   See K. J. Arrow and M. Kurz, *Public Investment, the Rate of Return, and Optimal Fiscal Policy* (Baltimore, 1970), chapter 2.
14.   When $\gamma < 1$, the optimal solution does not exist.

$(S = \overline{S}$ and $M \geqslant \overline{M})$ and the *IS* gap becomes dominant. On the other hand, when p coincides with the lower bound (that is, $u = 0$ and $v > 0$) somewhere within the planning horizon, the import constraint is effective $(M = \overline{M}$ and $S \leqslant \overline{S})$ and the *ME* gap becomes dominant. Though the above two cases correspond to Phases II and III in the Chenery-Strout model, they are in general not optimal. Namely, in the case of $u > 0$ and $v = 0$ for some interval of t, there holds

(13) $\quad p = \gamma k e^{-it}$

which is not consistent with equation (8), that is,

(14) $\quad \dot{p} = -e^{-it} - \alpha'(p/k - e^{-it})$

unless

(15) $\quad 1 + \alpha'(\gamma - 1) = i\gamma k.$

On the other hand, in the case of $u = 0$ and $v > 0$ for some interval of t, there holds

(16) $\quad p = k e^{-it}$

which is not consistent with equation (8), that is,

(17) $\quad \dot{p} = -e^{-it} + \mu'(-p/k + \gamma e^{-it})$

unless

(18) $\quad 1 - \mu'(\gamma - 1) = ik.$

The possibility that condition (15) or (18) will be satisfied, however, is very small, therefore the time path on which one of the two gaps becomes dominant somewhere before the terminal year of the plan cannot be said to be optimal.

Therefore, if the optimal solution exists, it must be in a case where the two gaps become identical (that is, $u > 0$ and $v > 0$) throughout the planning period. In fact, the optimal solution exists in this case though η must take a value within an appropriate range limited by the values of other parameters in the economic system. In other words, when u and v are both positive, the strict inequalities hold in equation (12), and the time path of p is determined by equation (8), that is,

$$
\begin{aligned}
(19) \quad \dot{p} &= -e^{-it} - \alpha'(p/k - e^{-it}) + \mu'(-p/k + \gamma e^{-it}) \\
&= -\lambda p - (1 - \alpha' - \gamma\mu')e^{-it} \text{ where } \lambda = (\alpha' + \mu')/k.
\end{aligned}
$$

Then, provided that $\lambda \neq i$,[15] the differential equation (19) can be solved as

$$(20) \quad p(t) = (p(0) - \overline{p})e^{-t} + \overline{p}e^{-it}$$
$$\text{where } \overline{p} = (1 - \alpha' - \gamma\mu')/(i - \lambda).$$

Here I note the following three facts. First, $\overline{p}$ must satisfy the transversality condition (9), that is, $p(T) = \eta$. Second, the time path of pe^{-it} has the same rate of decrease as γke^{-it} (the upper bound of p) and ke^{-it} (the lower bound of p). Third, the difference between $p(t)$ and $\overline{p}e^{-it}$ decreases at a constant rate, that is, $(p(0) - \overline{p})e^{-\lambda t}$ from (20), while the differences between the two bounds of p and $\overline{p}e^{-it}$ also decrease at a different constant rate, that is, $(\gamma k - \overline{p})e^{-it}$ and $(k - \overline{p})e^{-it}$. From these facts one can draw the following six figures of Figure 1 and understand that the time path of p satisfying the necessary conditions for optimization exists provided that η takes a value within the range R. Note that R is dependent on the values of parameters i, γ, k, α', μ', and T. Corresponding to this time path of p, one can derive the time paths of other variables which satisfy the necessary conditions. Since the necessary conditions are also sufficient, the time paths thus obtained are optimal. In the case of the seven variables ($V, C, S, I, M, E,$ and F) which originally appeared in our maximization problem,[16] the optimal time paths can be obtained by solving the seven constraints of the Chenery-Strout framework, all of which hold with strict equalities. The optimal solution for V, for example, is given by

$$(21) \quad V(t) = \frac{1}{k\lambda} \left(I(0) - \frac{E(0)}{\lambda - \varepsilon} \right) e^{\lambda t} + \frac{E(0)}{k(\lambda - \varepsilon)} e^{\varepsilon t}$$
$$+ \left(V(0) - \frac{\overline{S}(0) + \overline{M}(0)}{\alpha' + \mu'} \right)$$

where $\lambda \neq \varepsilon$ is assumed. Corresponding to this value of V, the optimal solution for F is obtained by either the IS gap ($I - \overline{S}$) or ME gap ($\overline{M} - E$), both of which give identical results. The time path of V is chosen to make the two gaps identical.

There are two exceptions to this result of two identical gaps. Namely, when either condition (15) or (18) is satisfied by chance, it is possible that the dominant gap may appear somewhere along the time

15. When $\lambda = i$, the differential equation (19) can be solved as
$$p(t) = p(0)e^{-it} - (1 - \alpha' - \gamma\mu')te^{-it}.$$
In this case the conditions for the existence of the optimal solution become a little more complicated than the preceding.

16. Note that $E = E_0 e^{\varepsilon t}$.

Fig. 1.1. $(i > \lambda, \bar{p} > \gamma k)$
$R = [ke^{-i\tau}, \bar{p}e^{-i\tau} - (\bar{p} - \gamma k)e^{-\lambda\tau}]$
where $(\bar{p} - \gamma k)e^{-\lambda\tau} \leqslant (\bar{p} - k)e^{-i\tau}$

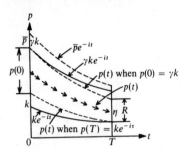

Fig. 1.4. $(i < \lambda, \bar{p} > \gamma k)$
$R = [\bar{p}e^{-i\tau} - (\bar{p} - k)e^{-\lambda\tau}, \gamma k e^{-i\tau}]$
where $(\bar{p} - \gamma k)e^{-i\tau} \leqslant (\bar{p} - k)e^{-\lambda\tau}$

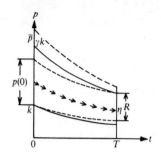

Fig. 1.2. $(i > \lambda, k \leqslant \bar{p} \leqslant \gamma k)$
$R = [ke^{-i\tau}, \gamma k e^{-i\tau}]$

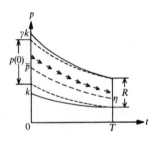

Fig. 1.5. $(i < \lambda, k \leqslant \bar{p} \leqslant \gamma k)$
$R = [ke^{-i\tau}, \gamma k e^{-i\tau}]$

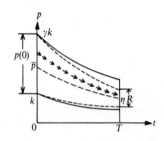

Fig. 1.3. $(i > \lambda, \bar{p} < k)$
$R = [(k - \bar{p})e^{-\lambda\tau} + \bar{p}e^{-i\tau}, \gamma k e^{-i\tau}]$
where $(k - \bar{p})e^{-\lambda\tau} \leqslant (\gamma k - \bar{p})e^{-i\tau}$

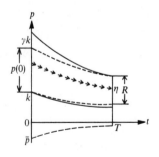

Fig. 1.6. $(i < \lambda, \bar{p} < k)$
$R = [ke^{-i\tau}, (\gamma k - \bar{p})e^{-\lambda\tau} + \bar{p}e^{-i\tau}]$
where $(k - \bar{p})e^{-i\tau} \leqslant (\gamma k - \bar{p})e^{-\lambda\tau}$

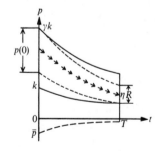

Figure 1.   *Existence of the Solution.*

path of the optimal solution. Several (not all) possible cases are depicted in the figures below, from which we can see the fact that at first $(0 \leqslant t \leqslant \tau)$ one of the two gaps emerges as dominant and then $(\tau \leqslant t \leqslant T)$ the two gaps become identical.

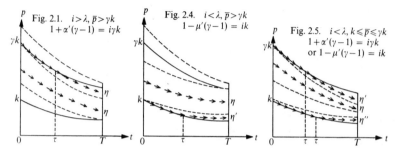

Figure 2.   *Existence of the Solution (Special Cases)*

SUMMARY AND NUMERICAL EXAMPLES

I have tried to clarify the welfare implications of the Chenery-Strout model by using a simple welfare function of the Chenery-MacEwan type. The main result derived from this welfare analysis can be summarized in this way. If the optimal solution exists under the Chenery-Strout framework, it exists in cases where the two gaps are made equal throughout the planning period (except for the two very special cases). The strategy by which the two gaps are always made equal is called the one-gap approach. The result leads to the conclusion that it is more desirable from the welfare point of view to determine the required amount of foreign aid by the one-gap approach rather than the two-gap approach. Two-gap analysis of foreign aid is, so to speak, a one-way (partial) approach in the sense that the causal relations are always one way. In the two-gap approach, the minimum required or maximum potential amounts of investment, savings, imports, and possibly exports are functions of output, and therefore the target growth or growth rate of output determines the *IS* and *ME* gaps in the minimum consistent sense. The converse is, however, out of the question, and there are no repercussions from the two gaps upon the output growth. On the other hand, the one-gap analysis of foreign aid is, so to speak, a two-way (simultaneous) approach in the sense that the causal relations are not one way but permit repercussions. In the one-gap approach, the growth of output determines the minimum consistent *IS* and *ME* gaps and at the same time the equalized gaps determine the level of output growth. The planners can no longer control the output growth rate which becomes merely an outcome of their decisions on policy instruments like public investment, the taxation system, etc. In this sense, the one-gap approach is quite similar to the econometric forecasting model with a simultaneous equations system, especially when the behavioral and technological equations which lead to the minimum consistent gaps are included in the model. The analysis here has provided an example in favor of the one-gap approach with the implications mentioned earlier from the welfare point of view.[17]

TABLE 2
Parameters and Initial Values.*

	South Vietnam	Thailand	Indonesia	The Philippines
k	4.59	3.61	3.50	3.55
α'	.391	.345	.357	.313
μ'	.385	.188	.378	414
ε	.081	.076	.038	.078
sample periods $(1960 \sim t_0)$	$1960 \sim 69$	$1960 \sim 72$	$1960 \sim 70$	$1960 \sim 70$
V_{t_0}	107.6	133.97	548.4	18.642
I_{t_0}	17.2	34.24	63.2	3.308
S_{t_0}	-28.3	29.67	60.2	2.242
M_{t_0}	53.8	31.73	85.3	3.609
E_{t_0}	8.3	27.16	82.3	2.543
unit	U.S. billion piastres	U.S. billion bahts	U.S. billion rupiahs	U.S. billion pesos
	(1960 prices)	(1962 prices)	(1960 prices)	(1955 prices)

*Thai data are derived from Asanuma (1974, pp. 79–81) either directly, or indirectly by processing. Data for the other three countries are derived from the UN *Yearbook of National Accounts Statistics* (1970, 1971). I converted the 1970 Philippine data in the Yearbook to 1955 prices. V is GDP rather than GNP data.

I will next illustrate both the one-gap and two-gap approaches by providing some numerical examples for four Southeast Asian countries (South Vietnam, Thailand, Indonesia, and the Philippines) where real series are available on expenditure in national income statistics. The period of analysis (or the forecasting period) to be dealt with here is from the final year (t_0) of the sample period $(1960 \sim t_0)$ to 1985.

17. B. Balassa writes, "It is often not realized that the two approaches (i.e., the trade gap and the capital-requirements approaches) are complementary rather than competitive and under proper definitions, they should give identical results" ("The Capital Needs of the Developing Countries," *Kyklos* 17 (1964): 197–204). This may be interpreted as support for the one-gap approach.

Table 2 shows the data on parameters and initial values required for the present purposes, all of which were derived from the UN *Yearbook of National Accounts Statistics*[18] and S. Asanuma[19] either directly or indirectly. The marginal capital coefficient (k) was estimated here simply by the formula $k = \Sigma I_t / (V_{t_0} - V_{1960})$, though its estimation, in general, should be made very carefully.[20] The Thai k is the estimate of Asanuma (1974). The Indonesian k, however, showed a very low estimated value $(k = 2{\cdot}45)$ when the formula above was applied, and so an arbitrary value of $k = 3{\cdot}50$, which is near to the Thai and Philippine k's, was chosen. It is indispensable for gap analysis to estimate potential savings function $(\overline{S_t} = \overline{S_0} + \alpha'(V_t - V_0))$ and minimum required imports function $(\overline{M_t} = \overline{M_0} + \mu'(V_t - V_0))$. However, the ordinary least squares estimates are not always appropriate to the concept of "potential" or "minimum required." In this article, the marginal coefficient of potential savings (α') was estimated by averaging the largest five of the year-by-year actual values, excluding extraordinary ones.[21] In the same manner, the marginal coefficient of minimum required imports (μ') was estimated by averaging the smallest five of the year-by-year actual values, excluding extraordinary ones.[22] Their initial values $(\overline{S_0}$ and $\overline{M_0})$ were replaced by the initial values of the forecasting period (that is, the actual figures in the final year of the sample period). Furthermore, exports in the forecasting period were assumed to grow at the same average rate (ε) as in the sample period.[23]

In Figure 3, our simulation results based on the data for parameters and initial values in Table 2 are depicted for each country in the forecasting period $((t_0 + 1) \sim 1985)$. The solid line represents the results derived from the one-gap approach, while the dotted line and the solid-dotted line represent the results derived from the two-gap approach with the target growth rates of 5 percent and 10 percent respectively. Looking at the figures for the two-gap approach, we can reconfirm the general conclusions of the Chenery-Strout analysis for the three countries other than Thailand. That is to say, along the growth path with constant target rate, the phase with dominant *IS* gap emerges first followed by the phase with dominant *ME* gap. Furthermore, the higher the target

18. 1970 and 1971 issues (New York, 1972 and 1973).
19. *Kokusai Kaihatsu Enjo* [International development aid] (Tokyo, 1974).
20. See, for example, Vanek, *Estimating Foreign Resource Needs for Economic Development*, chapter 7.
21. The case $\alpha' < 0$ or $\alpha' > 1$ was regarded as extraordinary.
22. The case of $\mu' < 0$ was regarded as extraordinary.
23. The assumed values for S_0 and ε in the case of the Republic of Vietnam may not be appropriate, because S_0 is negative and the actual ε for 1965–1969 is 7.9 percent.

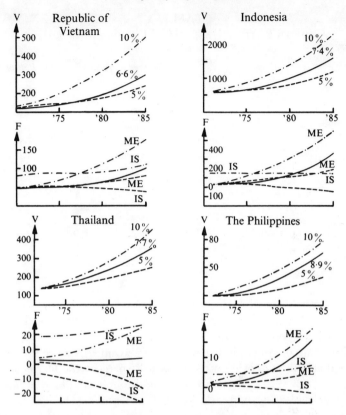

Figure 3. *Simulation Results (one-gap and two-gap approaches)*

rate of growth is, the longer the phase with dominant *IS* gap. This latter result can be restated as follows: when the target rate of growth is set at a relatively higher level, the lack of savings to finance the investment required to attain this target becomes more restrictive compared with the lack of foreign exchange to finance the imports required for this target growth. However, as far as these three countries are concerned, we can expect from the figures that, in the case of a 5 percent target rate, the state of foreign exchange bottlenecks (the phase of dominant *ME* gap) will continue approximately from the beginning of the forecasting period.[24] The Thai economy is quite interesting in that dominant gaps

24. The Indonesian results must be modified to some extent when one allows for the effects of the foreign exchange increases due to the recent rise in oil prices (when, for example, one assumes a higher value for ε).

TABLE 3
GROWTH RATE OF V AND $\Delta F/\Delta V$ (ONE-GAP APPROACH)

		South Vietnam	Thailand	Indonesia	The Philippines
Average growth rate of V	1960–65*	5.3	7.3	1.7	4.8
	1965–t_0*	−0.1	7.8	5.1	4.8
	t_0 −75	4.4	7.2	4.0	6.0
	1975–80	6.7	7.6	7.0	8.8
	1980–85	9.1	8.1	11.2	12.1
	t_0 −85	6.6	7.7	7.4	8.9
Average $\Delta F/\Delta V$	$(t_0 + 1)$−75	.229	−.026	.244	.232
	1975–80	.264	−.017	.302	.282
	1980–85	.294	−.002	.340	.327
	$(t_0 + 1)$−85	.262	−.012	.299	.284

*Actual figures.

respond very sensitively to changes in target growth rate. In other words, the *IS* gap is always dominant when the assigned growth rate is as high as 10 percent, while the *ME* gap is always dominant when the assigned rate of growth is as low (?) as 5 percent.[25] A more important fact is that in the case of low target growth of 5 percent, the Thai economy will pass in a very short period of time through the phase of foreign exchange shortages and reach the phase of foreign exchange surpluses to be used for capital exports (the degree of excess savings is of course far stronger). Target growth of 7 to 8 percent is the critical rate at which the Thai economy is determined to be capital-exporting or capital-importing, though this is omitted from Figure 3.

The Thai results are specific also from the point of view of the one-gap approach. The Thai economy can attain the growth path with a growth rate of about 7.7 percent (averaged for 1973–1985) by taking the strategy by which the two gaps are always made equal. In this case, furthermore, the required amount of foreign aid declines, not only relative to GNP but also absolutely (though in terms of real values). From these facts, the Thai economy seems to be an exceptional case where rapid growth can be attained without strong necessity for foreign aid or foreign capital inflow. Table 3 summarizes the results of the one-gap approach for all four countries in terms of the average growth rate

25.   Phase transition occurs at the target growth rate of 6 to 9 percent, though this is not depicted in the figure.

of GNP and the average marginal coefficient of required foreign aid to GNP. From this table we can see that GNP growth guaranteed by the one-gap approach has a tendency to accelerate trends. This GNP growth, in general, seems feasible and is approximately in line with actual performance in the 1960s. Furthermore, as the data for $\Delta F/\Delta V$ clearly show, the marginal efficiency of foreign aid to GNP gradually declines and, as a result, the ratio of foreign aid to GNP gradually goes up (except for the Thai case). Leaving aside the question of whether Indonesia and the Philippines in the 1980s can realize GNP growth at a rate of more than 10 percent, we can conclude by saying that, if the four countries in question attempt through various policy instruments to encourage domestic savings to the maximum potential level and to restrain imports to the minimum required, it will be possible in the near future (in the 1970s), to attain "automatically," GNP growth rate of 4 to 7 percent in the Republic of Vietnam, 7 to 8 percent in Thailand, 4 to 7 percent in Indonesia and 6 to 9 percent in the Philippines.[26] And these growth rates will be accompanied by a rapidly decreasing ratio of foreign aid to GNP in the case of Thailand, and by gradually increasing ratios in the other three countries. This is what the one-gap approach suggests. The results, of course, depend on the assigned parameter and initial values.[27] But the basic pattern seems not to be greatly influenced if these assigned values are changed to some extent.

26. The meaning of "automatically" can be explained as follows in terms of the model's framework: if $\overline{S} = S$ and $\overline{M} = M$, then $I - \overline{S} = \overline{M} - E$ holds by definition, so that the growth of V is determined in such a way as to equalize "automatically" the two gaps in the minimum consistent sense.

27. Changes in parameter values affect the growth rate of GNP. It is possible to attain the target average rate of growth by changing paramenter values, provided that the parameter values can vary within a certain range specified by the initial values of the system. This is the one-gap approach suggested by Fukuchi in "The One Gap Approach versus the Two Gap Approach." See also note 4, herein.

17

The Impact of the "Oil Crisis" on Southeast Asia

YASUKICHI YASUBA

CHANGES IN PRICES

The "Oil Crisis" had a different impact on the various countries of Southeast Asia.[1] Table 1 shows the balance of the supply and demand of commercial energy in five of these countries. For Indonesia, one of the major oil-exporting countries, the incident was a boon rather than a crisis, though the net gain per capita was not as large as in other major oil exporting countries.[2] Malaysia was affected little since it was, roughly speaking, self-sufficient in oil. Of the three major importers, Singapore, Thailand, and the Philippines, Singapore's position was exceptional in that it exported the bulk of its oil products to foreign countries and ocean-going ships. Although Singapore might have escaped shortages by cutting its exports by a small margin, this was in fact difficult since, as one Singapore newspaper put it, "Singapore [was] a link in a worldwide oil network," and had to "share the effects of common shortages."[3]

Thailand and the Philippines were much more dependent on foreign oil supplies and, therefore, had reason for concern about the shortage. People did not panic as in industrialized countries, but economists were worried. The Bangkok Bank's *Monthly Review* warned that "Thailand's position in the present world energy crisis is . . .

Note: This paper was published (in Japanese) in *South East Asian Studies*, Vol. 14, No. 4.

1. Owing to the scarcity of data, the impact on only five ASEAN Countries will be analyzed in this study.
2. Increase in per capita income due to the rise in oil prices between 1972 and 1974 was about U.S.$20 in 1972 prices. Indonesia's Biro Pusat Statistik, *Monthly Statistical Bulletin*, May 1976, pp. 105–106.
3. *The Straits Times*, December 14, 1973.

TABLE 1
SUPPLY AND DEMAND OF COMMERCIAL ENERGY, 1972 AND 1974

(Coal equivalent in thousands of metric tons)

Country	Year	Production	Imports	Exports	Bunkers	Consumption
Indonesia	1972	84,861	961	69,219	338	19,362
	1974	107,919	481	84,622	320	20,327
Malaysia	1972	6,657	8,875	15,897	202	5,799
	1974	5,799	8,026	6,310	214	6,440
Singapore	1972	—	39,422	24,297	10,391	4,434
	1974	—	40,127	21,325	13,055	4,572
Thailand	1972	346	11,922	635	124	11,947
	1974	476	11,994	249	91	12,325
Philippines	1972	315	13,631	365	782	12,858
	1974	566	13,357	156	260	12,790

Source: U. N., *World Energy Supplies 1950–1974*, pp. 84–91.

critical," and urged the government to "impose austere measures as soon as possible to conserve the use of oil."[4] The Philippines, whose dependence on imported oil was equally large, had examined carefully the future outlook for oil supplies, and in September 1973, more than one month before the "Oil Crisis," adopted a National Energy Plan and Policies to reduce the country's dependence on oil for energy needs from 93 percent to 76 percent by 1985.[5] As a result, when the oil crisis came, the Philippines was relatively well-prepared to absorb the shock; it was even ready to impose formal rationing on gasoline.

Thus, Singapore, Thailand, and the Philippines had to explore the possibility of increasing alternative energy supplies and of economizing on oil consumption. However, except for the agreements with China,[6] none of the short-term measures to increase supplies were very successful.[7] For example, an effort by the Thai government to make a barter agreement (involving cement and sugar) with Middle-Eastern countries did not materialize. The decision of the Philippine government to nationalize an American oil company (ESSO) to avoid the OAPEC

4. *Bangkok Bank Monthly Review*, January, 1974.
5. *National Energy Plan and Policies*. Appendix to *Four Year Development Plan*, FY 1974–1977.
6. Thailand and the Philippines concluded an agreement to import oil from China.
7. Much of the description in this and the fourth section is based on information gathered during a survey trip in spring, 1975. I am grateful to officials who provided information. I am also indebted to JETRO, which financed the trip, and to local JETRO officials who were helpful in many ways.

TABLE 2
Average Retail Prices of Petroleum Products and Their Percentage Changes, July 1973–July 1974
(per liter)*

	July 1973 (U.S. cents)	July 1974 (U.S. cents)	Percentage change
Gasoline (regular)			
Developed countries	22.0	30.0	36.6
Major oil-producing countries†	6.4	6.9	8.1
Nonoil developing countries	18.2	28.4	55.9
Kerosene			
Developed countries	11.1	15.9	43.2
Major oil-producing countries†	3.9	4.0	1.7
Nonoil developing countries	9.4	14.4	53.0
Automobile diesel oil			
Developed countries	17.1	21.6	26.4
Major oil-producing countries†	4.7	4.9	3.3
Nonoil developing countries	11.4	16.8	47.5

*Prices originally presented in cents per gallon were converted into cents per liter to facilitate comparison with figures presented elsewhere.
†Bolivia, Colombia, Ecuador, Indonesia, Nigeria, Saudi Arabia, and Venezuela.
Source: Kathrine W. Saito, "Petroleum Taxes: How High and Why?" *Finance and Development* (December, 1975): 19.

embarto against the United States backfired, because the new national company (Petrophil) was discriminated against by the major oil companies.

Campaigns for economy in use of energy were more successful. Restrictions on outdoor lighting, curtailing operating hours of "non-essential" businesses, and formal and informal rationing were practiced for some time in late 1973 and early 1974 leading to some reduction in per capita energy consumption in Thailand and the Philippines. Yet, ultimately, price increases were necessary.

According to the data collected by Kathrine W. Saito from sixty-four countries, there were certain patterns in the prices of petroleum products in different types of country. Her data, presented in Table 2, do not take into account changes after July 1974, but the general trend is clear. Domestic prices in oil producing (developing) countries were markedly lower than in other countries, and the rate of increase after the "Oil Crisis" was very small. The small rate of increase in the price of kerosene and diesel oil is particularly noteworthy. Precrisis prices in nonoil developing countries, while much higher than in oil-producing countries, were considerably lower than in developed countries.

TABLE 3

RETAIL PRICES OF SELECTED PETROLEUM PRODUCTS, 1973 AND 1975
(PER LITER)

	1973 before the "Oil Crisis" (U.S. cents)	1975 Spring (U.S. cents)	Percentage change
Gasoline (regular)			
Indonesia	9.9	11.1	12.1
Malaysia	18.6	26.2	40.5
Singapore	17.2	27.4	59.3
Thailand	10.3	16.8	63.1
Philippines	4.9	15.4	214.3
Kerosene			
Indonesia	2.8	3.1	10.7
Malaysia	6.3	7.2	11.4
Singapore	7.0	15.6	122.9
Thailand	7.1	11.8	66.2
Philippines	5.0	11.9	138.0
Diesel oil			
Indonesia	2.2	3.1	40.9
Malaysia*	7.2	8.8	22.2
Singapore	6.2	9.5	53.2
Thailand	5.2	11.4	119.2
Philippines	5.5	12.3	123.6

*Gas oil

Source: Indonesia, JETRO, Jakarta Office; Malaysia, "The Production and Consumption of Oil in Malaysia," paper presented to the Intergovernmental meeting on the Impact of the Current Energy Crisis on the Economy of the ECAFE Region, February 1974, and data provided by the Japanese Embassy; Singapore, Shell Singapore and Mobil Oil Singapore; Thailand, *Investor*, (January, 1975): 22; the Philippines, Oil Industry Commission and Mobil Oil Philippines.

However, the rate of increase after the "Crisis" was higher for developing countries than for developed countries, with the result that price differentials narrowed considerably.

The levels of and changes in the dollar price of petroleum products in Southeast Asia were largely consistent with the general pattern just described. As shown in Table 3, the precrisis price in Indonesia was very low, and the subsequent price hike was limited, with the result that energy prices in Indonesia in 1975 were much lower than in the other countries. In Malaysia, the precrisis price was not particularly low, but the country was in a position to restrict the rise in price of kerosene and diesel oil. In other countries, the rate of increase exceeded 50 percent. In the Philippines, which had maintained very low energy

TABLE 4

THE RATE OF INCREASE IN ENERGY PRICES AND IN CONSUMER PRICES
(THIRD QUARTER 1973–SECOND QUARTER 1975, IN PERCENT)

Country	Energy prices	Consumer prices
Indonesia	23.1	57.6
Malaysia	17.6	19.4
Singapore	69.8	19.6
Thailand	84.1	20.7
Philippines	161.3	37.8

Note: A simple average of the rate of increases for regular gasoline, kerosene, and diesel oil.
Source: Energy prices, as in Table 1; Consumer prices, *International Financial Statistics*.

prices, the rate of increase ranged from 123.6 to 214.3 percent. In Singapore, Thailand, and the Philippines, the rates of increase were generally substantial, but the postcrisis prices were still lower than in developed countries.

Another meaningful indicator of the magnitude of change is the relative price of energy. Table 4 shows the rate of increase in average price of three petroleum products in local currencies, and the rate of increase of consumer prices between the third quarter of 1973 and the second quarter of 1975. The relative price of energy declined in Malaysia and, in particular, in Indonesia, whereas it rose considerably in the other countries, particularly in the Philippines.

The decline in the relative price of energy in Indonesia and Malaysia was difficult to defend except on sociopolitical grounds, but it was probably less harmful to the economy than the sharp rises in relative prices that took place in some developed countries.[8] The relative price of energy rose in other countries, particularly in the Philippines and Thailand, which presumably explains a considerable part of the savings in commercial energy consumption in these two countries.[9] However, it should be remembered that, despite these rises,

8. Provided that a rise in the relative price of crude oil is permanent, the relative prices of petroleum products will have to rise significantly, in the long run, to reflect opportunity costs. In the short run, however, the application of the full cost principle to the determination of the prices of petroleum products would not be desirable, since prices are supposed to reflect marginal variable costs, which should be much lower than full costs inclusive of interest and depreciation changes on "sunk" capital costs.

9. In most developing countries, the consumption of energy continued to increase in 1973 and 1974. In Thailand, however, per capita consumption of commercial energy was reduced from 310 kilograms (coal equivalent) in 1972 to 300 kilograms

TABLE 5
RATE OF CHANGES IN CONSUMER PRICES, 1972–1975
(IN PERCENT)

Country	1972	1973	1974	1975
Indonesia	6.7	31.0	41.1	19.1
Malaysia	3.2	10.6	17.5	4.6
Singapore	2.6	25.4	23.0	2.6
Thailand	4.0	11.7	23.3	4.3
Philippines	10.3	11.0	34.5	8.4

Source: *International Financial Statistics.*

the postcrisis dollar prices of petroleum products in these countries were lower than in developed countries.

The direct effect of the rise in the price of oil must have been limited. An estimate by Romeo Bautista showed that a 146 percent rise in fuel costs from September 1973 to September 1974 would have resulted in a 9.1 percent rise in consumer prices according to the 1965 input-output table.[10] Although he suspects that the actual impact may have been greater due to changes in the industrial structure since 1965, it is unlikely that the rise in oil prices would account for the greater part of inflation, considering the limited impact on such energy-intensive economies as Japan.[11]

Much of the two-digit inflation in 1973 and in 1974 (see Table 5) has to be explained by other factors. As will be seen later, the terms of trade, compared with those in 1972, were favorable to all the countries listed, even in 1974, because of the commodity boom in 1973 and the first part of 1974. Hence, it may be argued that these countries could have avoided such inflation by adjusting their exchange rates. In fact Malaysia and Singapore revalued their currencies upward, but the adjustment was small. In the other countries, domestic inflationary pressure was stronger and prices rose faster.

Inflation became such an important factor that all five countries

in 1974. In the Philippines per capita consumption declined from 329 kilograms to 309 kilograms in these two years. (United Nations, *World Energy Supplies, 1950–1974*, St/ESA/STAT/SER. J/19, 1976, pp. 2, 89, 91.)

10. Romeo M. Bautista, "Perspective on the Recent Philippine Inflation," *Philippine Economic Journal* 13, no. 3, Third trimester, 1974, pp. 218–219.

11. A fourfold increase in the price of imported crude oil would raise average consumers' price by only 15 percent. Hideo Nakanishi, "Genyu Kakaku Hendo to Sangyo Renkan" [Changes in the price of crude oil and interindustry relations] in Takao Kaneko, ed., *Sangyo Renkan Bunseki*, (Yuhikaku, Tokyo, 1976).

TABLE 6
RATE OF GROWTH OF REAL GDP, 1972–1975
(IN PERCENT)

Area/Country	1972	1973	1974	1975
Developed market[b] economies	5.6	5.9	0.3	−1.7*
Developing economies[b]	5.5	6.8	5.2	4.4*
Indonesia	8.3	11.3	7.4	8.0[a]
Malaysia	5.8	13.3	7.7	0.5
Singapore	13.4	11.4	6.2	4.2
Thailand	4.2	10.5	3.2	6.4
Philippines	4.8	9.2	5.0	5.7

*: Provisional
Source: *Key Indicators of Developing Member Countries of ADB*, April 1966, p. 8
[a] *ADB, Annual Report, 1975* p. 46.
[b] United Nations, *World Economic Survey, 1975, Summary of the Data Relating to Performance under the International Development Strategy.* (E/5827) 1976, p. 7.

had to adopt antiinflation measures. By 1975, a fall in the rate of inflation was apparent. Except for Indonesia where inflationary pressure was still strong, all the countries kept the rate of inflation below 10 percent. This performance compares favorably with most industrialized countries.

OUTPUT AND THE BALANCE OF PAYMENTS

Table 6 shows the rate of growth of real output (GDP) for two broad regions of the world and the five countries of Southeast Asia. Except for Thailand (in 1974), which suffered sluggish agricultural growth and urban social unrest, and Malaysia (in 1975), which imposed production controls on some major exports, the annual growth rate in Southeast Asia exceeded 4 percent despite the oil crisis. Performance was in line with that in other developing countries and in sharp contrast with the zero or negative growth in developed countries.

How was such growth possible? The relatively low energy prices mentioned in the previous section may have been a contributory factor. The smaller share in Gross Domestic Product of energy-intensive industries and the less monopolistic industrial structure were other factors possibly explaining the continuation of growth.

The effect on output, however, was not the sole impact of the oil crisis. Higher prices had to be paid for imported oil, and this was an important aspect of the problem for Thailand, the Philippines, and, to a lesser extent, for Singapore. One form in which this burden revealed itself was the deficit in the balance of trade.

TABLE 7
OIL IMPORTS AND THEIR IMPLICATIONS, 1973–1975

	Thailand	Philippines	Singapore
Oil imports			
(million of U.S. dollars)			
1973	228.6	187.6	104.6*
1974	694.2	653.4	535.8*
1975	715.3	752.3	552.2*
Total imports			
(millions of U.S. dollars)			
1973	2049	1773	4592
1974	3143	3468	6909
1975	3075	3883	6704
Oil imports			
as a proportion of total imports (in percent)			
1973	11.2	10.6	2.2
1974	22.1	18.8	7.8
1975	23.3	19.4	8.2
Increase in oil imports			
as a proportion of imports (in percent)			
1974	14.8	13.4	6.2
1975	0.7	2.5	0.3

*Net imports of petroleum and petroleum products. Total imports were 660, 2007, and 1981 million dollars, respectively, for 1973, 1974, and 1975.
Source: Net oil imports: Thailand and the Philippines, *Key Indicators of Developing Member Countries of ADB*, April 1976, p. 26; Singapore, Department of Statistics (Singapore), *Monthly Digest of Statistics.* June 1976, pp. 35–37; total imports and exchange rates: *International Financial Statistics.*

Table 7 shows the magnitude of this burden. For Singapore net imports rather than gross imports are shown, since the bulk of petroleum products was exported. Oil imports (net) as a percentage of total imports in Singapore increased from 2.1 percent in 1973, to 6.1 percent in 1974, and 7.1 percent in 1975. The increase in oil import costs in 1974 was not more than 4.9 percent of total imports. In terms of the strain on the balance of payments, the impact on Thailand and the Philippines was considerably greater. Oil imports as a percentage of total imports increased from 11–12 percent in 1973 to 21–22 percent in 1974 and 1975, in both countries. The increase in oil import costs in 1974 amounted to 14.8 percent of the total imports.

Although the figures for Thailand and the Philippines were large, their implication should not be overemphasized. First, these ratios were smaller than in such nonoil developed countries as Japan, where the share of the value of oil imports increased from 17.6 to 34.1 percent

TABLE 8

BALANCE IN CURRENT ACCOUNT, 1972–1975

(IN MILLIONS OF U.S. DOLLARS)

Country	1972	1973	1974	1975
Indonesia	− 370	− 738	91	—
Malaysia	− 248	105	− 273	− 186
Singapore	− 530	− 606	− 1121	− 749
Thailand	− 72	− 129	− 64	− 441
Philippines	7	474	− 207	− 922

Source: *International Financial Statistics.*

between 1973 and 1974, and the increase in oil import costs in 1974 was 23.2 percent of the total value of imports. Second, the prices of these countries' exports rose in 1974, reducing the net burden. This point will be taken up later, when changes in the terms of trade are evaluated.

The last point was particularly relevant to Thailand, which managed to decrease its current account deficit in 1974 (see Table 8). However, all but oil-rich Indonesia ran current account deficits in 1974. The situation deteriorated for Thailand and the Philippines in 1975, which suggests that factors other than oil price increases may have been more important.

Furthermore, finance was available in one form or another. As Holsen and Waelbroeck have pointed out,[12] such middle-income countries as Singapore, Malaysia, Thailand, and the Philippines were by this time accepted in international financial markets as borrowers of good credit standing. Malaysia and the Philippines borrowed $565 million and $1113 million, respectively, in 1974–1975 from the Euro-market.[13] Other countries did not borrow from the Euro-market on such a large scale, but it is apparent from Table 9 that borrowing from private sources provided most of the funds needed to finance the current account deficits. All four countries listed in Table 9 showed a large surplus in the overall balance of payments in 1974. In 1975, while Thailand and the Philippines recorded small deficits, Malaysia and Singapore continued to increase their reserves.

The method of financing differed from country to country. Malaysia relied mainly on direct investment (and government capital in 1975), while Singapore relied on direct investment and short-term

12. *Key Indicators of Developing Member Countries of ADB,* April 1976, p. 32.
13. John A. Holsen and Joan L. Waelbroeck, "Less Developed Countries and the International Monetary Mechanism," *American Economic Review* 66, no. 2 (May 1976).

TABLE 9
FINANCING OF DEFICITS, 1974 AND 1975,
(IN MILLIONS OF U.S. DOLLARS)

	Malaysia	Singapore	Thailand	Philippines
1974				
a. Government capital	88	1	4	90
b. Direct investment	374	572	188	4
c. Private long-term capital	6	76	188	133
d. Private short-term capital, errors and omissions	1	766	161	605
e. Total	469	1415	541	831
f. Current account deficit	273	1121	64	207
g. Overall surplus e–f	196	294	477	624
1975				
a. Government capital	341	1	−7	232
b. Direct investment	229	602	86	97
c. Private long-term capital	−11	47	177	487
d. Private short-term capital, errors and omissions	−311	509	173	89
e. Total	248	1159	429	905
f. Current account deficit	186	749	441	922
g. Overall surplus e–f	62	410	−12	17

Source: *International Financial Statistics.*

capital. Singapore's dependence on short-term capital reflects its growth as Asia's money market. Thailand and the Philippines relied on different sources of capital in different years. Yet, some form of private financing always played a predominant role.

The picture for Indonesia in 1975 is not yet entirely clear. Its balance of trade shrank from a surplus of $3584 million in 1974 to $1456 million in 1975.[14] Since the surplus in 1975 was still considerable, it may be expected that the country should not be facing any serious problems. But the head of the national oil company (PERTAMINA) had to resign because of the company's financial difficulties, and the country had to borrow a huge sum of money abroad. Publicized Euro-currency credits alone amounted to $1537 million,[15] and, in addition, $95 million was drawn from the International Monetary Fund.[16]

---

14. *International Financial Statistics.*
15. *Key Indicators of Developing Member Countries of ADB*, April, 1976, p. 32.
16. Figures shown in terms of SDR in *International Financial Statistics* were converted to U.S. dollars.

TABLE 10
INDICES OF REAL VALUE OF EXPORTS, 1972–1975 (1972 = 100)

Area/Region	1972	1973	1974	1975
Developed market economies	100	112	120	115*
Developing market economics	100	111	115	99*
Indonesia	100	125	132	125†
Malaysia	100	103	104	112
Singapore	100	122	134	123
Thailand	100	95	101	111
Philippines	100	116	89	106
Five countries combined	100	115	116	118

*Provisional.
†The 1975 export price used for deflation was extrapolated from 1974, using value and quantity data for petroleum and petroleum products, rubber, coffee, palm oil, pepper, tin ore, tea, and lumber, obtained from Indonesia's Biro Pusat Statistik, *Monthly Statistical Bulletin*, May 1976, pp. 103–106.
Source: Five ASEAN countries, *International Financial Statistics*; others, U.N., *Monthly Bulletin of Statistics*.

Furthermore, its gross reserves were reduced from $1480 at the end of 1974 to $587 million at the end of 1975.[17] Apparently, excessive optimism led to financial problems, which are forcing a reappraisal of the country's plans.

TERMS OF TRADE

The five countries' exports did not show such smooth growth as output in general. Nevertheless, compared with other countries, particularly other developing countries, growth was impressive. After fast growth in the commodity boom year of 1973, export growth tended to slow down in 1974 and 1975. Yet, in the worst depression year of 1975, the real value of total exports from the five countries increased by 2 percent in contrast to other areas which recorded a considerable loss. Such growth, in a year when demand was sluggish everywhere, could only mean "immiserizing growth," accompanied by sharply deteriorating terms of trade.

As Table 11 shows, the terms of trade have deteriorated since 1972 for industrial countries and turned in favor of developing countries. However, the benefit mostly accrued to oil-exporting countries, of which Indonesia is the only representative in Southeast Asia. Indonesia's terms of trade improved so much that even after a slight setback in 1975, the

17.   As in note 16.

TABLE 11
TERMS OF TRADE, 1972–1975 (1972 = 100)

	1972	1973	1974	1975
Broad regions of the world				
Industrial countries*	100	97	85	87
Less-developed areas*	100	110	152	149
Petroleum exporters†	100	112	137	128
Others†	100	110	106	99
Southeast Asian countries				
Indonesia††	100	113	166	164
Malaysia	100	123	122	96
Singapore§	100	106	105	102
Thailand	100	139	119	108
Philippines	100	127	137	92

*As defined by IMF.
†As defined by U.N. Petroleum exporters include: Algeria, Bahrain, Brunei, Ecuador, Gabon, Indonesia, Iran, Iraq, Kuwait, Libyan Arab Republic, Nigeria, Oman, Qatar, Saudi Arabia, Trinidad and Tobago, Venezuela and United Arab Emirates.
††Indonesian export price as in Table 10. The import price index is constructed from the value and quantity data for rice, fertilizer, iron and steel bars, iron and steel pipes, cement, and cloves and clove stalks (Indonesia's Biro Pusat Statistik, *Monthly Statistical Bulletin*, May 1976, pp. 116–117) and import prices for Less Developed Areas in *International Financial Statistics*.
Source: IMF, *International Financial Statistics*
†U.N., *World Economic Survey 1975, Summary of the Data Relating to Performance under the International Development Strategy*, May 1976, E; 5827, pp. 10–11.
§Singapore, Department of Statistics *Yearbook of Statistics, 1974/1975*, p. 111; *Monthly Digest of Statistics*, June 1976, p. 47.

index was more than 60 percent higher than in 1972. Other countries in the region also experienced an improvement in the terms of trade up to 1974, but a sharp deterioration in 1975 nullified all or most of the gains.

One way to evaluate changes in the terms of trade is to estimate changes in import capacity, or the real value of imports that can be purchased with exports. As Table 12 shows, Indonesia's import capacity more than doubled between 1972 and 1975.[18] The increase for other

18. Indonesia actually gained more than the figure suggests because of a change in agreements. Of the three systems of oil production, contracts of work, production-sharing contracts (P/S contracts), and direct management by PERTAMINA, the former two were changed in such a way that Indonesia's share of income would increase. Whereas 60 percent of the profit and 65 percent of production exclusive of development costs had formerly been taken respectively under the contract of work and under P/S contracts, after January 1, 1974, 85 percent of the price

(*Continued on p. 350*)

TABLE 12

INDICES OF IMPORT CAPACITY IN CONSTANT PRICES,
1972–1975 (1972 = 100)

Country	1972	1973	1974	1975
Indonesia	100	141	219	205
Malaysia	100	127	126	104
Singapore	100	129	140	125
Thailand	100	132	120	119
Philippines	100	147	121	97

Note: Import capacity is the product of the real value of exports and the terms of trade.
Source: Tables 10 and 11.

countries was much smaller, ranging from minus three percent for Thailand to 25 percent for Singapore. It may be noted that all countries made some gains until 1974, a post "Oil Crisis" year, after which they met severe setbacks.

Another way of evaluating changes in the terms of trade is to estimate the resulting loss of income as a proportion of GDP. Since we customarily assess the magnitude of economic variables in relation to income, this is probably a better way of evaluating the effects. Table 13 shows the overall change (A), the change when the effect of imported oil is removed (B), and the effect of the rise in the price of imported oil (C). Indonesia and Singapore are excluded from the calculation for (B) and (C), since both countries were major exporters of petroleum and petroleum products. Malaysia is also excluded, because the nearly equal volumes of exports and imports of petroleum and petroleum products tend to offset each other.

(*Continued from p. 349*)

over $5 (over $5.83, since October of 1974) per barrel was to be taken by the Indonesian Government as excess profit tax. So by P/S contracts, in which development costs were 40 percent, Indonesian income increased from $1.44 a barrel for the precrisis price of $3.70, to $8.30, for the postcrisis price of $12.60 dollar a barrel. (Ng Shui Meng, *The Oil System in Southeast Asia*, Institute of Southeast Asian Studies (Singapore, 1974), pp. 24–25, and information offered by JETRO Jakarta.)

According to recent reports (*Nihon Keizai Shinbun*, August 9; *Asahi Shinbun*, August 10, 1976), Indonesia's share in P/S contracts was changed, effective as of January 1976, from 60 percent to 85 percent. Furthermore, allowances for development costs were to be reduced for earlier years and spread over a longer period. Contracts of work had also been renegotiated so that Indonesian income would increase by $1 per barrel. In all it is expected that the Indonesian government would gain additional revenue of $620 million per year.

TABLE 13
Changes in Income Resulting from a Change in the Terms of Trade as a Proportion of GDP,* 1973–1975
(in percent)

	1973	1974	1975
A. Total change			
Indonesia	2.6	15.7	−0.3
Malaysia	10.3	−0.6	−9.5
Singapore	5.4	−0.9	−2.8
Thailand	5.9	−2.7	−1.9
Philippines	4.6	1.4	−4.8
B. Change when the effect of the rise in the price of imported oil is removed†			
Thailand	6.3	−1.0	−1.5
Philippines	5.2	3.6	−4.7
C. Effect of the rise in the relative price of imported oil (difference between A and B)			
Thailand	−0.4	−1.7	−0.4
Philippines	−0.6	−2.2	−0.1

* Defined as the product of the change in the terms of trade and the proportion of exports to Gross Domestic Product. The latter term for Indonesia in 1975 was assumed to be the same as in 1974.

† First, the adjusted import price index (P^1), which excludes the effect of the rise in the price of imported oil (p_0), was computed as follows:

$$P^1 = \frac{P - \bar{w}_0 \frac{p_0}{\bar{p}_0}}{100 - \bar{w}_0}$$

where P, $\bar{w}_0$ and $\bar{p}_0$ were respectively the original import price index, weight (proportion of total imports) for oil in the base year, and the price of oil in the base year. The unit value of petroleum and petroleum products exported from Indonesia was used as the price of oil. Then the terms of trade and changes in income resulting from its changes were computed.

Source: Data on oil imports, *Statistical Yearbook for Asia and the Pacific, 1973*, and *Key Indicators for Developing Member Countries of ADB*, April 1976, p. 26. Price of oil, Indonesia's Biro Pusat Statistik. *Monthly Statistical Bulletin*, May 1976, pp. 105–6. Other data, Table 10 and *International Financial Statistics*.

Section A of the table reveals extremely wide fluctuations which are not observed in industrialized countries. The impact of changes in the price of oil was significant (15.7 percent of GDP) for Indonesia in 1974, but with that single exception, the direct impact of the oil crisis was minor, as illustrated by the maximum differences of 1.7 and 2.2 percent, respectively, for Thailand and the Philippines in 1974 (section C). Even for these two countries the impact of other changes (section B) was generally much larger. Large gains in 1973 and losses in 1975, in many countries, suggest that the influence of general economic conditions in developed countries was much more important.

This is to be expected. As Table 14 shows, Southeast Asian countries depended very heavily on exports to industrial countries, particularly Japan and the United States. The proportion of the five Southeast Asian countries' exports going to industrial countries was more than 60 percent. For Indonesia and the Philippines, the proportion was of the order of 70 to 90 percent (not shown in the table). If the Malaysian export figures are adjusted to take into account exports to Singapore which are reexported, the dependence of Malaysia on exports to industrialized countries may be nearly as large. Thus, it was only natural that the terms of trade (Table 11) and, to a lesser extent, the quantum of exports (Table 10) changed according to the rise and fall of the quantum of imports of industrial countries (Table 14, section C). The sharp fall in such imports in 1975, particularly for Japan and the U. S., should be noted. It appears that the major impact of the "Oil Crisis" on the countries of Southeast Asia came indirectly through the induced recession in industrialized countries.[19]

OCEAN TRANSPORTATION COSTS

Enthusiasm for developing alternative sources of energy supplies seems to have dissipated as it became clear that oil would be forthcoming, albeit at higher prices. Even so, industrial structure will have to change accordingly; if the higher relative price of oil is here to stay, a shift toward a less energy-consuming type of economy will have to be achieved in the long run.

One factor yet to reveal its full impact is the rise in transportation costs. The rise in the price of crude oil induced a fourfold increase in the price of bunker fuel oil. Yet, due to the world recession, tramp shipping rates have gone down. Liner freight rates have shown an upward movement, presumably reflecting increased costs. (See the figure for the movements of tramp and liner freight rates.)

A rough calculation for typical (efficient) ships shows that on-the-sea fuel costs increased from \$1.95 to \$7.44 per ton of cargo for a round-trip between Japan and Brazil (12,000 miles each way).[20] For a round-

19. The effect of declining demand from Japan has been analyzed, commodity by commodity, in Hikoji Katano, "Japanese Economy and Primary Imports from Countries in Southeast Asia," (in Japanese), *Ajia Keizai* 16, no. 11, (November, 1975).

20. Data for this and further calculations are by courtesey of Osaka Shosen Mitsui Sempaku, K.K. Costs for wood-chip carriers were based on data for a 28,210-ton (D/W) boat with a cruising speed of 14.3 knots, consuming 105 tons of bunker fuel oil per day. Costs for ore-tankers were based on data for three ships ranging from 64,131 to 160,533 tons with cruising speeds of 15.2–15.7 knots, consuming 38–105 tons of oil per day. Finally, costs for traditional liners were based on data

TABLE 14
LEVEL AND STRUCTURE OF EXPORTS FOR SOUTHEAST ASIAN COUNTRIES,
AND QUANTUM OF IMPORTS FOR REGIONS OF THE WORLD 1972–1975

	1972	1973	1974	1975
A. Level (in millions of U.S. dollars)				
Total exports to:	7,833	13,308	22,615	20,815
Industrial countries	4,687	8,211	14,243	12,744
U. S.	1,411	2,256	4,367	4,219
Japan	1,919	3,628	6,906	5,459
Oil-exporting countries	125	230	553	538
Other less-developed countries	2,496	3,887	6,322	6,306
B. Structure (in percent)				
Total exports to:	100.0	100.0	100.0	100.0
Industrial countries	59.3	61.7	63.0	61.2
U. S.	18.0	17.0	19.3	20.3
Japan	24.5	27.3	30.5	26.2
Oil-exporting countries	1.6	1.7	2.4	2.6
Other less-developed countries	31.9	29.2	28.0	30.3
C. Quantum of imports (1972 = 100)				
World	100	113	113	111
Industrial countries	100	112	111	102
U. S.	100	102	104	92
Japan	100	127	124	107
Oil-exporting countries	100	116	135	204
Other less-developed countries	100	111	123	124

Sources: A and B, *Direction of Trade, Annual 1969–75*; C, *International Financial Statistics*.

trip between Japan and Indonesia (3,000 miles each way), the increase in fuel costs would be from $0.48 to $1.86 per ton. In view of the CIF price for imported pulpwood of $27 dollars per measure ton in 1975,[21] the difference in the increase in fuel costs between Brazilian destinations ($5.49) and Indonesian destinations ($1.38) may prove to be significant. Ore tankers are more efficient, but on long hauls fuel costs ($3.68 per ton for a trip between Japan and Brazil) may still have some effect since the price of ore is cheaper, the CIF price of iron ore in 1975 being $16.[22]

for 7 ships ranging from 10,864 to 19,795 tons with speeds of 14.2 to 20.4 knots, consuming 18–63 tons of oil per day. For specialty ships a load factor of 90 percent was assumed only on one trip (ballast on the return journey). For liners, a 60 percent load factor was assumed each way. A bunker fuel price of $21 per ton before the oil crisis and $80 in 1976 was assumed.

21. This figure was computed for "pulpwood broad leaved" from Ministry of Finance, *Japan Exports and Imports*, Commodity by Country, Dec., 1975, p. 59.

22. *Japan Exports and Imports*, p. 72.

Southeast Asia, which is close to Japan, may benefit as a supplier of raw materials, relative to such distant regions as the east coasts of North and South America. However, most Southeast Asian ports are not serviced by efficient specialty ships but by liners, for which fuel costs are higher per ton-mile. If a load factor of 60 percent is assumed for both journeys, the average fuel costs per ton of cargo between Japan and Indonesia would be $0.73 before the oil crisis, and $2.80 in 1976 for most advanced noncontainerized liners. If less efficient ships are used, which is the case with a number of routes in Southeast Asia, the increases in fuel costs will be greater.

Under these circumstances, improvements in port facilities and other infrastructure may pose urgent problems for many Southeast Asian countries. In a country such as Thailand, where the sole major port is handicapped by its inaccessibility to even regular-sized liners (14,000 tons),[23] relocation of industrial and commercial centers may have to be considered.

If transportation costs prove to be an important factor, international relocation of industries will have to be made. Such industries as metal smelting, pulp manufacturing, and cattle raising will be most seriously affected. Environmental problems in some of the present centers may further accelerate relocation in the case of metal smelting and pulp manufacturing industries.

SUMMARY

In Southeast Asia, direct effects of the "Oil Crisis", such as inflation, disturbance of production, balance of payment crises, and loss of income from deterioration in the terms of trade, while undoubtedly real, have proved to be surmountable, even in more seriously affected countries such as Thailand and the Philippines. The single most important impact was indirect, coming from a decline in demand from recession-ridden industrialized countries. Thus, continued recovery of the economies of these countries is vitally important for the economies of southeast Asia.

Changes in industrial structure and in the pattern of international division of labor will continue into the future. One factor neglected in this development is the long-term relative rise of ocean transportation

23.   At present, only 7,000–8,000 ton ships have access to Bangkok, with the result that Thailand is handicapped in transportation costs in comparison with other countries. This may be one factor in the unusual increase between 1970 and 1975 in the Japan/Thailand Conference rate (a 102 to 235 percent increase) compared with other conference rates (at most an 85 percent increase). See *Journal of Japan Shipper's Council*, April, 1975, pp. 34–35.

FREIGHT INDICES FOR LINERS AND TANKERS, 1972–1976

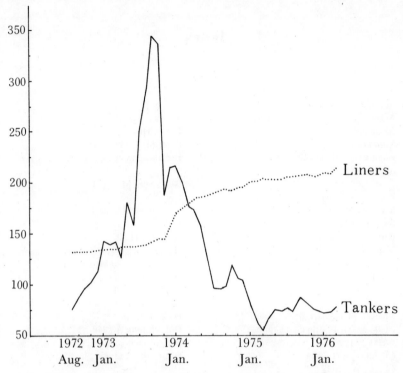

Note: Indices of the Bremen Institute of Shipping Economics; tankers include grain tankers.

Source: Osaka Shosen Mitsui Sempaku, *Kaiun Chosa Geppo*, no. 287, July, 1976, p. 30.

costs due to the rise in the price of oil. A further study of the effects of changes in ocean transportation costs would be particularly relevant for Southeast Asia, which is likely to be very much affected by such changes.

Index

NAMES

SUBJECTS